SECOND
EDITION

2Million
CHILDREN

SECOND
EDITION

2Million
CHILDREN

SUCCESS
FOR ALL

Robert E. Slavin • Nancy A. Madden
Bette Chambers • Barbara Haxby

CORWIN PRESS
A SAGE Company

For information:

Corwin Press
A SAGE Company
2455 Teller Road
Thousand Oaks, California 91320
www.corwinpress.com

SAGE Ltd.
1 Oliver's Yard
55 City Road
London, EC1Y 1SP
United Kingdom

SAGE India Pvt. Ltd.
B 1/I 1 Mohan Cooperative Industrial Area
Mathura Road, New Delhi
India 110 044

SAGE Asia-Pacific Pte. Ltd.
33 Pekin Street #02-01
Far East Square
Singapore 048763

Printed in the United States of America.

Library of Congress Cataloging-in-Publication Data

2 million children: Success for all/Robert E. Slavin . . . [et al.].—2nd ed.
    p. cm.
Includes bibliographical references and index.
ISBN 978-1-4129-5307-8 (cloth)
ISBN 978-1-4129-5308-5 (pbk.)
    1. Success for All (Program) 2. School improvement programs—United States. 3. Children with social disabilities—Education (Elementary)—United States. 4. Academic achievement—United States. I. Slavin, Robert E. II. One million children. III. Title: Two million children: Success for All.

LB2822.82.O54 2009
372—dc22   2008036425

This book is printed on acid-free paper.

08   09   10   11   12   10 9 8 7 6 5 4 3 2 1

Acquisitions Editor:	Arnis Burvikovs
Associate Editor:	Desirée A. Bartlett
Production Editor:	Cassandra Margaret Seibel
Copy Editor:	Gretchen Treadwell
Typesetter:	C&M Digitals (P) Ltd.
Proofreaders:	Jenifer Kooiman, Annette Pagliaro-Sweeney
Indexer:	Jean Casalegno
Cover Designer:	Lisa Riley

Contents

Preface

Every child can learn. Every school can ensure the success of every child. Statements to this effect appear in No Child Left Behind and other legislation, in all sorts of goals statements, commission reports, and school district policies. They are posted in school buildings and appear as mottos on school stationery. But does our education system behave as if they are true? If we truly believed that every child could learn under the proper circumstances, we would be relentless in the search of those circumstances. We would begin by providing comprehensive early childhood programs to ensure that children start school ready to succeed. We would use well-validated instructional methods and materials known to be capable of ensuring the success of nearly all children if used with intelligence, flexibility, and fidelity. We would involve teachers in constant, collaborative professional development activities to continually improve their abilities to reach every child. We would frequently assess children's performance to be sure that all students are on a path that leads to success, and we would respond immediately if children were not making adequate progress. If children were falling behind despite excellent instruction, we would try different instructional approaches and, if necessary, we would provide them with tutors or other intensive assistance. We would involve parents in support of their children's school success, we would check to see whether vision, hearing, health, nutrition, or other nonacademic problems were holding children back, and then we would find a solution to those problems. If we truly believed that all children could learn, we would rarely if ever assign children to special education or long-term remedial programs that in effect lower our expectations for them. If we truly believed that all schools could ensure the success of all children, then the failure of even a single child would be cause for great alarm, and for immediate, forceful intervention.

Success for All is a comprehensive restructuring program for elementary schools designed to make the idea that "all children can learn" a practical, daily organizing principle for schools, especially those serving many children placed at risk. Success for All, first implemented in 1987, was created to show how schools could ensure that virtually all children can read and write. Today the program is used in about 1,200 schools across the U.S. and in England, and has served more than two million children. This book describes the program in detail, presents the extensive research evaluating it, and discusses the implications of this research for policy and practice.

HOW SUCCESS FOR ALL TRANSFORMS SCHOOLS

Success for All puts into daily practice strategies known from research to enhance students' achievement. This includes the following:

- Schoolwide systems to support rapid school improvement including leadership strategies to create a sense of urgency, use of cooperative learning schoolwide to engage students in instruction, use of data to drive instruction and improvement, and a classroom management and conflict resolution curriculum to create a positive school climate.

- Integration of instructional processes with curriculum objectives in literacy supported by daily lesson guides and materials.
  - o Preschool and kindergarten programs that focus on building language, self-concept, and early literacy skills.
  - o A beginning reading approach that uses phonetic minibooks, partner reading, brief video, and fast-paced instruction to help children develop phonemic awareness, phonics, comprehension, vocabulary and fluency, as well as a love of reading and confidence as readers.
  - o An upper-elementary reading approach that emphasizes cooperative learning, teaching of metacognitive skills, fluency, comprehension in many genres, writing, and vocabulary. A rapid pace of instruction, video, and variety build motivation and excitement in learning.
- Constant assessment of children's progress and regrouping across grades and classes to ensure that all children are challenged.
- One-to-one tutoring for children, especially first graders, who are struggling in learning to read.
- A Solutions Team that works on nonacademic issues to help ensure that all children are ready to learn. This includes increasing parent involvement, addressing attendance and behavior issues, ensuring that children have vision and hearing screening, addressing health and social issues, and reaching out to community members to support children's learning and well-being.
- Extensive professional development for teachers, administrators, and others in the school, including a full-time facilitator who works to ensure high-quality implementation of all program elements. Detailed initial training and ongoing coaching from the Success for All Foundation staff are provided to all Success for All schools.

Success for All has been extensively evaluated in more than fifty experimental studies carried out by researchers throughout the world. This includes a three-year national randomized evaluation and a follow-up study that showed continuing impacts of the program at the entry to high school.

NEW IN THIS EDITION

This book is an update of *One Million Children: Success for All* by Robert Slavin and Nancy Madden, published in 2001. The current addition adds substantially to the first, because the program has advanced considerably since the earlier edition was written. In addition to updates in all of the curriculum areas, it adds new material on middle school, embedded multimedia, the new Solutions Teams (which replace the former family support teams), new approaches to leadership development, computerized data management, and more. The new edition presents the research completed since 2000, including the national randomized evaluation and the longitudinal follow-up. It also presents research on new elements of Success for All. Finally, the book discusses the current policy context and policy impact of Success for All.

Acknowledgments

The development, dissemination, and evaluation of Success for All, begun in 1986, is a product of the dedicated efforts of hundreds of educators, developers, trainers, and researchers throughout the United States and other countries. Research and development of Success for All has been funded by the Institute of Education Sciences and the Office of Elementary and Secondary Education, U.S. Department of Education (Grants No. OERI-R-117-R90002, OERI-R-117-D40005, R306S000009, R305J03013804, R305M050086, U215K050117, S332B050004, and R305B070324), and by the Carnegie Corporation of New York, the Pew Charitable Trusts, the Abell Foundation, the France and Merrick Foundations, New American Schools, the Sandler Family Foundation, the New Schools Venture Fund, the MacArthur Foundation, the Ford Foundation, the Rockefeller Foundation, the W. T. Grant Foundation, the Wachovia Foundation, the Goldman Sachs Foundation, the Stupski Family Foundation, and the MRM Foundation. Development, research, and dissemination in Britain has been funded by the Fischer Family Trust, and ongoing research is supported by the Bowland Charitable Trust.

The development and dissemination of Success for All has involved too many talented and dedicated individuals to name here. As of 2008, GwenCarol Holmes is the Chief Operating Officer. Key developers of instructional processes, student and teacher materials, professional development and coaching procedures, and assessment and monitoring tools include Terri Morrison, Cecelia Daniels, Kathy Simons, GwenCarol Holmes, Mark Rolewski, Jane Harbert, John Batchelor, Judith Ramsey, Jennifer Austin, Coleen Bennett, Richard Gifford, Kathryn Conway, Victoria Crenson, Jennifer Pinyan, Kris Misage, Sue Magri, Lois Hybl, Jane Strausbaugh, Tonia Hawkins, Claire Krotiuk, Susan Perkins, Deb Branner, James Bravo, Scott Belt, Steve Choi, David Patrick, Gillian Edgehill, Maureen Keck, Michele Melville, Pam Russell, Traci Cottrell, Irene Waclawiw, Kara Schultheis, Laura Rice, and Judith Sorgen Bornia of the Success for All Foundation. In addition to helping define the U.S. model, Judith Wordsworth and Marilyn Jones-Hill of SFA-UK have adapted Success for All with great insight for schools in England.

Over 120 trainers at the Success for All Foundation provide the professional development and support to schools necessary to create increased achievement. The field staff are directed by Vice Presidents for Implementation Liz Judice and Lynsey Seabrook with Area Managers Amanda Nappier, Cathy Pascone, Connie Fuller, Saundra Pool, Michelle Hartz, Dennis Lee, Tracy Heitmeier, Nichole Weihrauch, Sue St. Claire, and Christina West. Roger Morin, Chief Financial Officer for the Success for All Foundation since it was incorporated as a nonprofit organization, has managed the financial side of the foundation with support from Lynese Biniek and Gail Boswell.

In addition to the authors of this volume, many other researchers have been involved in research and evaluation of Success for All. These include Anne Chamberlain, Alan Cheung, and many others at the Success for All Foundation; Margarita Calderón, Barbara Wasik, Robert Cooper, Amanda Datnow, and Nancy Karweit currently or formerly at Johns Hopkins University; Geoffrey Borman of the University of Wisconsin; Barbara Livermon of Notre Dame College; Robert Stevens of Penn State University; Steve Ross and Lana Smith of the University of Memphis; John Nunnery of Old Dominion University; Marcie Dianda of the National Education Association; Philip Abrami of Concordia University in Montreal; Yola Center of Macquarie University in Sydney, Australia; David Hopkins and Alma Harris of the University of London; and Rachel Hertz-Lazarowitz and Bruria Schaedel of Haifa University (Israel).

Special thanks go to Susan Davis and Sharon Fox, who managed every aspect of putting the manuscript together, assembling appendices and references, spotting gaps, and keeping track of a million details. This task could not have been done without their thoughtfulness and energy.

PUBLISHER'S ACKNOWLEDGMENTS

Corwin Press gratefully acknowledges the contributions of the following reviewers:

Melanie Donofe, Teacher, Gifted Education
Liberty Elementary School, Weirton, WV

Russell Grammer, Fourth Grade Teacher
Jefferson Elementary School, Cape Girardeau, MO

Patti Hendricks, English and Language Arts Teacher
Sunset Ridge Middle School, Midvale, UT

Sandra Kraynok, Kindergarten Teacher
Rock Cave Elementary School, Rock Cave, WV

Christine Landwehrle, Fifth and Sixth Grade Reading and Language Arts Teacher
Bedminster Township Public School, Randolph, NJ

Tanya Marcinkewicz, Sixth Grade Teacher
Harlan Elementary School, Middletown, DE

Pamela Opel, Science Curriculum Coordinator
Gulfport School District, Biloxi, MS

Cynthia Woods, Kindergarten Teacher
Walker Elementary School, Monticello, KY

About the Authors

Robert E. Slavin is Director of the Center for Research and Reform in Education at Johns Hopkins University, Director of the Institute for Effective Education at the University of York (England), and the cofounder and Chairman of the Success for All Foundation. He received his BA in Psychology from Reed College in 1972, and his PhD in Social Relations in 1975 from Johns Hopkins University. Dr. Slavin has authored or coauthored more than two hundred articles and twenty books, including *Educational Psychology: Theory into Practice* (1986, 1988, 1991, 1994, 1997, 2000, 2003), *Cooperative Learning: Theory, Research, and Practice* (1990, 1995), *Show Me the Evidence: Proven and Promising Programs for America's Schools* (1998), *Effective Programs for Latino Students* (2000), and *One Million Children: Success for All* (2001). He received the American Educational Research Association's Raymond B. Cattell Early Career Award for Programmatic Research in 1986, the Palmer O. Johnson Award for the best article in an American Educational Research Association (AERA) journal in 1988 and 2008, the Charles A. Dana Award in 1994, the James Bryant Conant Award from the Education Commission of the States in 1998, the Outstanding Leadership in Education Award from the Horace Mann League in 1999, and the Distinguished Services Award from the Council of Chief State School Officers in 2000.

Nancy A. Madden is President and cofounder of the Success for All Foundation, a professor at the University of York (England), and a professor in the Center for Research and Reform in Education at John Hopkins University. She received her BA in Psychology from Reed College in 1973, and her PhD in Clinical Psychology from American University in 1980. From 1980 to 1998, she was a research scientist at the Center for Research on the Education of Students Placed at Risk at Johns Hopkins University, where she directed the development of the reading, writing, language arts, and mathematics elements of Success for All. An expert in literacy and instruction, Dr. Madden is the author or coauthor of many articles and books on cooperative learning, mainstreaming, Title I, and students at risk, including *Effective Programs for Students at Risk* (1989) and *One Million Children: Success for All* (2001).

Bette Chambers is currently a professor in the Institute for Effective Education at the University of York in England and at the Center for Research and Reform in Education at Johns Hopkins University, where she conducts research in early childhood education and early literacy. She also directs the development and dissemination of the early childhood education and technology-embedded programs at the Success for All Foundation in Baltimore, Maryland. Dr. Chambers received her BA in Early Childhood Education from Concordia University in 1982, and her PhD in Educational Psychology in 1990 from McGill University. She has authored and coauthored numerous articles, books, and practical guides on cooperative learning, technology infusion in literacy, and early childhood education.

Barbara Haxby has served as Vice President of Professional Development at the Success for All Foundation since 1998 and is responsible for managing all aspects of professional development for one hundred trainers and also oversees professional development for 1,100 schools in the U.S. Her activities focus on managing and improving the quality and efficiency of all aspects of the delivery of training and professional support services for schools. In addition, Ms. Haxby has worked closely with the Center for Data Driven Reform in Education at Johns Hopkins University to develop ongoing leadership and data analysis training and professional development for school districts. From 1989 to 1998, Ms. Haxby was employed at the Center for the Social Organization of Schools at Johns Hopkins University. During 1997–1998, she was Director of Implementation, where her responsibilities were similar to those described above. As a Senior Family Support Specialist at the Center during 1989–1997, Ms. Haxby developed, implemented, and consulted on family support activities for schools involved in the Success for All program.

1

Two Million Children

Success for All

Despite the constant public outcry about the crisis in American education, every community has one or more outstanding and often widely recognized public schools. Some of these appear to succeed because they serve children of wealthy, well-educated parents, or because they are magnet schools that attract motivated or high-achieving students. However, there are also schools that serve disadvantaged and minority children in inner city or rural locations and, year after year, produce outstanding achievement outcomes. Such schools play a crucial role in reminding us that the problems of our school system have little to do with the capabilities of children; they provide our best evidence that all children can learn. Yet, the success of these lighthouse schools does not spread very far. Excellence can be demonstrated in many individual schools but rarely in whole districts or communities. There are millions of children who are placed at risk by ineffective responses to such factors as economic disadvantage, limited English proficiency, or learning difficulties. How can we make excellence the norm rather than the exception, especially in schools serving many at-risk children? How can effective practices based on research and the experiences of outstanding schools be effectively implemented every day by hundreds of thousands of teachers?

Success for All is one answer to these questions. Begun in one Baltimore school in 1987, Success for All is used (as of fall 2008) in more than 1,200 schools in forty-seven states, plus schools in Britain, Canada, and Israel. More than two million children have attended Success for All schools. These schools are highly diverse. They are in most of the largest urban districts, but also hundreds of rural districts, inner suburban districts, and Indian reservations. Most are Title I schoolwide projects with many children qualifying for free lunches, but many are in much less impoverished circumstances.

1

Success for All is by far the largest research-based, whole-school reform model ever to exist. It is the first model to demonstrate that techniques shown to be effective in rigorous research can be replicated on a substantial scale with fidelity and continued effectiveness. Both the research and the dissemination of Success for All pose an inescapable challenge to educational policy. If replicable excellence is possible, then how can we accept the abysmal performance of so many children? This is not to say that every school needs to adopt Success for All, but what it does imply is that every school needs to create or adopt some program that is no less effective than Success for All. It is unconscionable to continue using ineffective practices if effective ones are readily available and capable of serving any school that is prepared to dedicate itself to quality implementation.

This book presents the components of Success for All, the research done on the program, and the policy implications of this research for the transformation of America's schools.

SUCCESS FOR ALL: THE PROMISE AND THE PLAN

To understand the concepts behind Success for All, let's start with Ms. Martin's kindergarten class, in an ordinary elementary school. Ms. Martin has some of the brightest, happiest, and most optimistic kids you'll ever meet. Students in her class are glad to be in school, proud of their accomplishments, and certain that they will succeed at whatever the school has to offer. Every one of them is a natural scientist, a storyteller, a creative thinker, a curious seeker of knowledge. Ms. Martin's class could be anywhere, in suburb or ghetto, small town or barrio, it doesn't matter. Kindergartners everywhere are just as bright, enthusiastic, and confident as her kids are.

Only a few years from now, many of these same children will have lost the spark they all started with. Some will have failed a grade. Some will be in special education. Some will be in long-term remediation, such as Title I or other remedial programs. Some will be bored or anxious or unmotivated. Many will see school as a chore rather than a pleasure and will no longer expect to excel. In a very brief span of time, Ms. Martin's children will have defined themselves as successes or failures in school. All too often, only a few will still have a sense of excitement and positive self-expectations about learning. We cannot predict very well which of Ms. Martin's students will succeed and which will fail, but we can predict based on the past that if nothing changes, far too many will fail. This is especially true if Ms. Martin's kindergarten class happens to be located in a high-poverty neighborhood, in which there are typically fewer resources in the school to provide top-quality instruction to every child, fewer forms of rescue if children run into academic difficulties, and fewer supports for learning at home. Preventable failures occur in all schools, but in high-poverty schools failure can be endemic—so widespread that it makes it difficult to treat each child at risk of failure as a person of value in need of emergency assistance to get back on track. Instead, many such schools do their best to provide the greatest benefit to the greatest number of children possible, but have an unfortunately well-founded expectation that a certain percentage of students will fall by the wayside during the elementary years.

Any discussion of school reform should begin with Ms. Martin's kindergartners. The first goal of reform should be to ensure that every child, regardless of home background, home language, or learning style, achieves the success that he or she so confidently expected in kindergarten, that all children maintain their motivation, enthusiasm, and optimism because they are objectively succeeding at the school's tasks. Any reform that does less than this is hollow and self-defeating.

What does it mean to succeed in the early grades? The elementary school's definition of success, and therefore the parents' and children's definition as well, is overwhelmingly success in reading. Very few children who are reading adequately are retained, assigned to special education, or given long-term remedial services. Other subjects are important, of course, but reading and language arts form the core of what school success means in the early grades.

The amount of reading failure in the early grades in schools serving disadvantaged students is shocking. In our studies of Success for All, we found that at the end of first grade about a quarter of students in our disadvantaged control schools could not read and comprehend the following passage:

> "I have a little black dog. He has a pink nose. He has a little tail. He can jump and run." (Durrell & Catterson, 1983)

On the 2005 National Assessment of Educational Progress, only 42 percent of African American fourth graders and 46 percent of Hispanic fourth graders could read at the "basic" level, compared to 76 percent of whites (National Assessment of Educational Progress [NAEP], 2005). What these statistics mean is that despite some improvements over the past twenty years, the reading performance of disadvantaged and minority children is still seriously lacking, and the deficits begin early.

When a child fails to read well in the early grades, he or she begins a downward progression. In first grade, some children begin to notice that they are not reading adequately. They may fail first grade or be assigned to long-term remediation. As they proceed through the elementary grades, many students begin to see that they are failing at their full-time jobs. When this happens, things begin to unravel. A child who has failed to learn to read by the third grade is headed for serious trouble. Failing students begin to have poor motivation and poor self-expectations, which lead to continued poor achievement, in a declining spiral that ultimately leads to despair, delinquency, and dropout.

Remediating learning deficits after they are already well established is extremely difficult. Children who have already failed to learn to read, for example, are now anxious about reading, and doubt their ability to learn it. Their motivation to read may be low. They may ultimately learn to read but it will always be a chore, not a pleasure. Clearly, the time to provide additional help to children who are at risk is early, when children are still motivated and confident and when any learning deficits are relatively small and remediable. The most important goal in educational programming for students at risk of school failure is to try to make certain that we do not squander the greatest resource we have: the enthusiasm and positive self-expectations of young children themselves.

In practical terms, what this perspective implies is that schools, and especially Title I, special education, and other services for at-risk children, must be shifted from an emphasis on remediation to an emphasis on prevention and early intervention. Prevention means providing effective preschool and kindergarten programs so that students will enter first grade ready to succeed, and it means providing regular classroom teachers with effective instructional programs, curricula, and professional development to enable them to ensure that most students are successful the first time they are taught. Early intervention means that supplementary instructional services are provided early in students' schooling and that they are intensive enough to bring students who are at risk quickly to a level at which they can profit from good quality classroom instruction.

Success for All is built around the idea that every child can and must succeed in the early grades, no matter what this takes. The idea behind the program is to use everything we know about effective instruction for students at risk to direct all aspects of school and classroom organization toward the goal of preventing academic deficits from appearing in the first place; recognizing and intensively intervening with any deficits that do appear; and providing students with a rich and full curriculum to enable them to build on their firm foundation in basic skills. The commitment of Success for All is to do whatever it takes to see that every child becomes a skilled, strategic, and enthusiastic reader by the end of the elementary grades and beyond.

Usual practices in elementary schools do not support the principles of prevention and early intervention. Most provide a pretty good kindergarten, a pretty good first grade, and so on. Starting in first grade, a certain number of students begin to fall behind, and over the course of time these students are assigned to remedial programs or to special education, or are simply retained.

Our society's tacit assumption is that those students who fall by the wayside are defective in some way. Perhaps they have learning disabilities, or low IQs, or poor motivation, or parents who are unsupportive of school learning, or other problems. We assume that since most students do succeed with standard pretty good instruction in the early grades, there must be something wrong with those who don't.

Success for All is built around a completely different set of assumptions. The most important assumption is that every child can learn. We mean this not as wishful thinking or just a slogan, but as a practical, attainable reality. In particular, every child without organic retardation can learn to read. Some children need more help than others and may need different approaches than those needed by others, but one way or another every child can become a successful reader.

The first requirement for the success of every child is *prevention*. This means providing excellent preschool and kindergarten programs, improving curriculum, instruction, and classroom management throughout the grades, assessing students frequently to make sure they are making adequate progress, and establishing cooperative relationships with parents so they can support their children's learning at home.

Top-quality curriculum and instruction from age 4 on will ensure the success of most students, but not all of them. The next requirement for the success of *all* students is *intensive early intervention*. This means one-to-one tutoring for primary-grade students having reading problems. It means being able to work with parents and social service agencies to be sure that all students attend school, have medical services or eyeglasses if they need them, have help with behavior problems, and so on.

The most important idea in Success for All is that the school must relentlessly stick with every child until that child is succeeding. If prevention is not enough, the child may need tutoring. If this is not enough, he or she may need help with behavior or attendance or eyeglasses. If this is not enough, he or she may need a modified approach to reading or other subjects. A Success for All school does not merely provide services to children, it constantly assesses the results of the services it provides and keeps varying or adding services until every child is successful.

Origins of Success for All

The development of the Success for All program began in 1986 as a response to a challenge made to our group at Johns Hopkins University by Baltimore's superintendent, Alice Pinderhughes, its school-board president, Robert Embry, and a former Maryland

Secretary of Human Resources, Kalman "Buzzy" Hettleman. They asked us what it would take to ensure the success of *every* child in schools serving large numbers of disadvantaged students.

At the time, we were working on a book called *Effective Programs for Students at Risk* (Slavin, Karweit, & Madden, 1989), so we were very interested in this question. After many discussions, the superintendent asked us to go to the next step, to work with Baltimore's Elementary Division to actually plan a pilot program. We met for months with a planning committee, and finally produced a plan and selected a school to serve as a site. We began in September 1987 in a school in which all students were African American and approximately 83 percent qualified for free lunch.

The first-year results were very positive (see Slavin, Madden, Karweit, Livermon, & Dolan, 1990). In comparison to matched control students, Success for All students had much higher reading scores, and retentions and special education placements were substantially reduced.

In 1988–89, Success for All was expanded in Baltimore to a total of five schools. We also began implementation of Success for All at one of the poorest schools in Philadelphia, in which a majority of the students were Cambodian. This school gave us our first experience in adapting Success for All to meet the needs of limited English proficient students. In 1990–91 we developed a Spanish version of the Success for All beginning reading program, called Lee Conmigo, and began to work in more bilingual schools as well as schools providing English as a Second Language instruction (Cheung & Slavin, 2005; Slavin & Madden, 1999b). In 1992, we received a grant from the New American Schools Development Corporation (NASDC) to add math, science, and social studies to the reading and writing programs of Success for All (Slavin & Madden, 2000), and to help build an organization capable of scaling the program up to serve many more schools.

During the 1990s, Success for All (SFA) grew exponentially, adding from 40 percent to 100 percent to our network of schools each year from 1989 to 2001. As noted earlier, as of fall 2008, SFA is in about 1,200 schools in 400 districts in 47 states throughout the U.S. The districts range from some of the largest in the country, such as Atlanta, Kansas City, New York, Chicago, Los Angeles, and St. Paul, to such middle-sized districts as Alachua County, Florida; Bessemer, Alabama; Long Branch, New Jersey; Lawrence, Massachusetts; and Modesto, California, to tiny rural districts, including schools on several Indian reservations. Success for All reading curricula in Spanish have been developed and researched and are used in bilingual programs throughout the U.S. Almost all Success for All schools are high-poverty Title I schools, and the great majority are schoolwide projects. Otherwise, the schools vary widely.

Theoretical Basis of Success for All

Success for All was designed to put into practice the findings of research on effective practices in elementary school instruction, curriculum, school and classroom organization, assessment, accommodations for struggling students, parent involvement, and professional development. It was designed to anticipate all the ways in which students who are at risk could fail in school and to provide interventions in advance to avoid negative achievement trajectories and increase the chances of positive trajectories. The overall program theory is called multidimensional intervention theory, which holds that making significant differences in the achievement of students who are at risk requires intervening on many fronts.

Multidimensional intervention theory does not, however, mean throwing together disparate elements. Instead, it requires careful assembly of research-proven practices to form a coherent approach. In the area of instructional process, the theory builds on earlier work by Slavin (1987, 1994, 2006), which describes a model of instructional effectiveness called QAIT, for *quality, adaptation, incentive,* and *time.* These are the alterable components derived from Carroll's (1963) model, which combines innate and alterable variables.

Quality refers to presentation of information and skills to help students learn, including curriculum, lesson presentation, and effective use of technology.

Adaptation refers to means of continuously assessing student progress and adapting the level and pace of instruction to the needs of all children.

Incentive refers to strategies to increase students' motivation to learn.

Time refers to both clock time allocated to instruction and effective use of this time.

A key assertion in the QAIT model is that the elements are multiplicatively related to instructional effectiveness (IE), or the ability of a program or teacher to add value to children's learning:

$$IE = f (Q \times A \times I \times T)$$

The multiplicative relationship has two important consequences. First, if any element is zero, instructional effectiveness is zero. Second, efforts to maximize all four QAIT components are likely to have far greater impacts than efforts focused on just one.

Success for All is explicitly built to put the QAIT theory into practice by focusing on multiple dimensions of instructional design simultaneously.

Quality

Success for All impacts quality of instruction on several dimensions. First, it uses reading materials that are colorful, engaging, and well-organized, and in line with the findings of the National Reading Panel (2000). They incorporate use of phonics, meta-cognitive comprehension strategies, fluency strategies, and vocabulary development. The materials include detailed teachers' manuals and daily lessons. At the kindergarten and first grade levels, embedded multimedia is used (animations and puppet skits) to reinforce phonics and vocabulary skills (Chambers, Cheung, Madden, Slavin, & Gifford, 2006, 2007; Chambers et al., in press). Success for All gives teachers effective instructional strategies to maximize active teaching and learning, derived in particular from process-product studies (e.g., Rosenshine & Stevens, 1986). The program uses cooperative learning strategies (Slavin, 1995, in press), which give students opportunities to try out their understandings in a safe environment, to receive immediate feedback, and to "learn by teaching" in describing their current state of knowledge to a peer.

Adaptation

Instructional quality depends on giving students content that is appropriate to their needs, which is in their zone of proximal development (Vygotsky, 1978), but not already learned. The program structure of Success for All is adaptive, as students are regularly given reading assessments, the results of which are used to group and regroup children across classes and across grades for instruction (Guttiérez & Slavin, 1992). For example, a teacher teaching a reading group at an early second grade level might work with a group that includes first, second, and third graders all needing instruction at that level. This allows instructors to focus instruction on a level that is right for all of the students, and to more effectively meet students' needs, remediate specific deficiencies, and challenge students to accelerate their learning. When further adaptation is required for students who are below grade level, especially first graders, the one-to-one tutoring that is part of the Success for All model provides the tailored instruction needed to help them catch up with their peers.

Incentive

High-quality instruction does not matter if students are not motivated to learn. There are several elements built into Success for All to maximize incentives to learn. In cooperative learning, a central feature of SFA, groups can earn recognition only if all team members have learned, so they encourage and help each other to master academic content (Rohrbeck, Ginsburg-Block, Fantuzzo, & Miller, 2003; Slavin, in press). Evidence of progress in reading is also motivating to students, especially if they have had difficulty in the past. Progress based on assessments is explicitly communicated to individual students and parents.

Time

Time is addressed in Success for All in several ways as well. To increase the amount of direct instructional time in reading, students are regrouped across grade and class lines into reading classes at one instructional level. In this structure, each student is involved with the teacher in instruction for the full 90-minute reading block. Because the group is at one level, class lessons are fast-paced and focused, and keep students enthusiastically engaged. Teachers learn routines to improve their classroom management skills and make effective use of time, based on the work of Evertson, Emmer, and Worsham (2000). Further, use of high-interest, motivating strategies (such as cooperative learning) increases time on task, as students exert efforts to help themselves and their teammates achieve individual and team success. The program also extends instructional time for students who need it by providing one-to-one tutoring.

Supporting Instructional Change: Multidimensional Intervention

The QAIT model serves as an organizing concept for the instructional elements of Success for All, but many supports are needed to enable, encourage, and require the use of these powerful instructional processes. Intervention and support must occur in many areas. Success for All is explicitly designed to include essential elements that go beyond the classroom and are described in the multidimensional intervention model summarized in Figure 1.1.

In addition to setting the stage for powerful instruction in the classroom, multidimensional intervention theory requires that these additional elements be fully addressed, including the use of data to keep instruction focused, the development of schoolwide supports to ensure that every student is ready to benefit from instruction, and the availability of strong professional support for all staff.

Figure 1.1   Major Elements of Success for All

Success for All is a schoolwide program for students in Grades pre-K to 6 which organizes resources to attempt to ensure that virtually every student will reach the third grade on time with adequate basic skills and build on this basis throughout the elementary grades, and that no student will be allowed to "fall between the cracks." The main elements of the program are as follows:

A Schoolwide Curriculum. During reading periods, students are regrouped across age lines so that each reading class contains students all at one reading level. Use of tutors as reading teachers during reading time reduces the size of most reading classes to about twenty. The reading program in Grades K–1 emphasizes language and comprehension skills, phonics, sound blending, and use of shared stories that students read to one another in pairs. The shared stories combine teacher-read material with phonetically regular student material to teach decoding and comprehension in the context of meaningful, engaging stories.

In Grades 2–6, students use novels or basals but not workbooks. This program emphasizes cooperative learning and partner reading activities, comprehension strategies such as summarization and clarification built around narrative and expository texts, writing, and direct instruction in reading comprehension skills. At all levels, students are required to read books of their own choice for twenty minutes at home each evening. Cooperative learning programs in writing/language arts are used in Grades 1–6.

Tutors. In Grades 1–3, specially trained certified teachers and paraprofessionals work one-to-one with any students who are failing to keep up with their classmates in reading. Tutorial instruction is closely coordinated with regular classroom instruction. It takes place twenty minutes daily during times other than reading periods.

Preschool and Kindergarten. The comprehensive, theme-based, preschool and kindergarten programs in Success for All cover all domains of learning, with a particular focus on language and literacy.

Quarterly Assessments. Students in Grades 1–6 are assessed every quarter to determine whether they are making adequate progress in reading. This information is used to suggest alternate teaching strategies in the regular classroom, changes in reading group placement, provision of tutoring services, or other means of meeting students' needs.

Solutions Team. A Solutions Team works in each school to help support families in ensuring the success of their children, focusing on parent education, parent involvement, attendance, and student behavior. This team is composed of existing or additional staff such as parent liaisons, social workers, counselors, and vice principals.

Facilitator. A program facilitator works with teachers to help them implement the reading program, manages the quarterly assessments, assists the Solutions Team, makes sure that all staff are communicating with each other, and helps the staff as a whole make certain that every child is making adequate progress.

Data to Drive Instruction

Close monitoring of student progress is a central element of Success for All. Students are informally assessed daily and weekly, and formally assessed on summative measures quarterly. The quarterly assessments and other information are used to guide daily instruction and change class groupings, especially to accelerate students making good progress. Classroom data and quarterly assessments are reviewed by teachers and facilitators to design instructional modifications for struggling students, including assignments to tutoring.

Schoolwide Structures

Success for All schools have Solutions Teams that meet to plan schoolwide strategies for parent involvement, community involvement, classroom management, attendance, and outreach to other agencies to solve health and social problems. Principals and facilitators receive leadership training and support to help them lead a change process, use data effectively, and make effective use of resources. The development of a positive school climate is fostered with the use of Getting Along Together, a program that builds peer cooperative and conflict resolution skills.

Professional Development

Success for All provides a high level of onsite professional development, averaging twenty-six days of trainer time onsite in the first year. Principals, facilitators, and Solutions Team leaders attend a five-day seminar for new SFA school leaders. After a three-day initial training for all teachers, monthly visits from trainers and frequent telephone contacts help maintain program quality. Building facilitators work full time in each school. They visit in teachers' classes and organize large and small meetings to review data, help set goals for students' achievement, and help create individual, class, and schoolwide plans. Annual national conferences supplement onsite professional development by providing opportunities for sharing among leaders from many schools, and by targeting particular issues, sharing updates, and recharging enthusiasm.

Overview of Success for All Components

The elements of Success for All are described in detail in the early chapters of this monograph, but before we get to the particulars it is useful to see the big picture.

Reading Program

Success for All uses a reading curriculum based on research on effective practices in beginning reading (e.g., Adams, 1990; National Reading Panel, 2000) and on development of comprehension strategies (Pressley & Woloshyn, 1995), as well as the use of cooperative learning to increase student engagement and motivation (Slavin, 1995, in press; Stevens, Madden, Slavin, & Farnish, 1987).

Development of oral language and vocabulary as well as a love of reading are the keys to reading success. Reading teachers at every grade level begin the reading time by reading children's literature to students and engaging them in a discussion of the story to enhance their understanding of the story, listening and speaking vocabulary, and knowledge of story structure. In kindergarten and first grade, the program emphasizes development of basic language skills by involving students in listening to, retelling, and dramatizing children's literature. Big books as well as oral and written composing activities allow students to develop concepts of print as they also develop knowledge of story structure. Specific oral language experiences are used to further develop both receptive and expressive language.

KinderCorner

Formal reading instruction begins in kindergarten with Stepping Stones, which emphasizes phonemic awareness, concepts about print, and synthetic phonics. Letters and letter sounds are introduced in an active, engaging set of activities that begins with oral language and moves into written symbols. Individual sounds are integrated into a context of words, sentences, and brief stories. Reading of longer text begins with KinderRoots, using a series of phonetically regular but meaningful and interesting minibooks. KinderRoots emphasizes repeated oral reading to partners as well as to the teacher. The minibooks begin with a set of "shared stories," in which part of a story is written in small type (read by the teacher) and part is written in large type (read by the students). The student portion uses a phonetically controlled vocabulary. Taken together, the teacher and student portions create interesting, worthwhile stories. KinderCorner and KinderRoots are described in Chapter 3.

Reading Roots

Beginning in first grade, students are regrouped for reading based on their instructional reading level. Growth in reading skills proceeds rapidly in first grade with Reading Roots. In Reading Roots, direct instruction in phonics using FastTrack Phonics builds students' mastery of letter/sound correspondences and sound blending. These skills are applied as they are taught in phonetically regular "shared stories" like those in KinderRoots. As students' skills build, the teacher portion diminishes and the student portion lengthens, until students are reading the entire book. This scaffolding allows students to read interesting literature when they only have a few letter sounds. Examples of shared stories appear in Appendices 4.1 and 4.2.

In Reading Roots, instruction is also provided in story structure, specific comprehension skills, metacognitive strategies for self-assessment and self-correction, and integration of reading and writing. Development of oral language and vocabulary continues through thematically related readings and speaking activities requiring every child to use specific language structures and vocabulary.

Spanish bilingual programs use an adaptation of Reading Roots called Lee Conmigo ("Read With Me"). Lee Conmigo uses the same instructional strategies and activities as Reading Roots, but is built around shared stories written in Spanish. Reading Roots is described in further detail in Chapter 4.

Reading Wings

When students reach the second grade reading level, they use a program called Reading Wings (Madden et al., 1996), an adaptation of Cooperative Integrated Reading and Composition (CIRC) (Stevens, Madden, Slavin, & Farnish, 1987). Reading Wings uses cooperative learning activities built around story structure, prediction, summarization, vocabulary building, decoding practice, and story-related writing. Students engage in partner reading and structured discussion of stories or novels, and work toward mastery of the vocabulary and content of the story in teams. Story-related writing is also shared within teams. Cooperative learning both increases students' motivation and engages students in cognitive activities known to contribute to reading comprehension, such as elaboration, summarization, and rephrasing (see Slavin, 1995). Research on CIRC has found it to significantly increase students' reading comprehension and language skills (Stevens et al., 1987).

In addition to these story-related activities, teachers provide direct instruction in reading comprehension skills, and students practice these skills in their teams. Classroom libraries of trade books at students' reading levels are provided for each teacher, and students read books of their choice for homework for twenty minutes each night. Home readings are shared in presentations each week during "book club" sessions.

Materials have been developed to support Reading Wings through the sixth grade level. Supportive materials, called Treasure Hunts, have been developed for more than one hundred children's novels and informational trade books and for most current basal series (e.g., Houghton Mifflin, Scott Foresman, Harcourt, Macmillan, Open Court). The upper-elementary Spanish program, Alas para Leer, is built around Spanish-language novels and basal series. Reading Wings is described in further detail in Chapter 5.

The Reading Edge

The same powerful learning strategies built around cooperative learning are used as the basis for The Reading Edge, the reading program developed specifically to meet the needs of adolescent learners. The Reading Edge is designed for sixth, seventh, and eighth graders. Often students enter the middle grades without the reading skills they need to succeed in challenging content area courses. The Reading Edge provides instruction in phonics, fluency, vocabulary, and comprehension at the level needed by the individual student, and accelerates them as quickly as possible to grade level using age-appropriate text and activities. The Reading Edge is described further in Chapter 6.

Regrouping

Students in Grades 1–8 are regrouped for reading. The students are assigned to heterogeneous, age-grouped classes most of the day, but during a regular ninety-minute reading period they are regrouped by reading performance levels into reading classes of students all at the same level. For example, a reading class taught at the 2–1 level might contain first, second, and third grade students all reading at the same level. The reading classes are smaller than homerooms because tutors and other certified staff (such as librarians or art teachers) teach reading during this common reading period.

Regrouping allows teachers to teach the whole reading class without having to break the class into reading groups. This greatly reduces the time spent in seatwork and increases direct instruction time, eliminating workbooks and other follow-up activities which are needed in classes that have multiple reading groups. The regrouping is a form of the Joplin Plan, which has been found to significantly increase reading achievement in the elementary grades (Slavin, 1987).

Quarterly Reading Assessments

At nine-week intervals, reading teachers assess student progress through the reading program. Assessments include summaries of weekly comprehension and vocabulary assessments, periodic fluency checks, observations of strategy use, and a formal test that gives an estimate of reading level. The formal test may be either a standardized benchmark test, such as the Gates McGinitie or SRI, or it may be a benchmark assessment called 4Sight that is designed to predict scores on state assessments. The results of the assessments are used to examine students' reading-level assignments and organize new reading groups for the next quarter. This regrouping allows students to move to higher reading levels quickly as they gain skill, and enables students who are reading below grade level to catch up. Results are also used to determine who is to receive tutoring, to suggest other adaptations in students' programs if they are not progressing at an acceptable rate, and to identify students who need other types of assistance, such as assistance with behavior, family interventions, or screening for vision and hearing problems. This process is described further in Chapter 4.

Reading Tutors

One of the important elements of the Success for All model is the use of tutors to promote students' success in reading. One-to-one tutoring is the most effective form of instruction known (see Slavin, et al., 1989; Wasik & Slavin, 1993). Some tutors are certified teachers with experience teaching Title I, special education, and/or primary reading. Often, well-qualified paraprofessionals also tutor children with less severe reading problems. Tutors work one-on-one with students who are having difficulties keeping up with their reading groups. The tutoring occurs in twenty-minute sessions during times other than reading or math periods. A computer-assisted tutoring tool, Alphie's Alley, is available. Alphie's Alley provides both a motivating setting for students and strong lesson planning and presentation support for tutors. Tutor and student work together using the computer, which presents the reading and assessment activities. Tutoring can also be provided without the computer.

In general, tutors support students' success in the regular reading curriculum, rather than teaching different objectives. For example, the tutor generally works with a student on the same story and concepts being read and taught in the regular reading class. However, tutors seek to identify learning problems and use different strategies to teach the same skills. They also teach metacognitive skills beyond those taught in the classroom program. Schools may have several teachers serving as tutors depending on school size, need for tutoring, and other factors.

During daily ninety-minute reading periods, certified teacher-tutors serve as additional reading teachers to reduce class size for reading. Reading teachers and tutors use brief forms to communicate about students' specific problems and needs and meet at regular times to coordinate their approaches with individual children.

First graders receive priority for tutoring, on the assumption that the primary function of the tutors is to help all students be successful in reading the first time, before they fail and become remedial readers. Tutoring procedures are described in more detail in Chapter 3.

Preschool and Kindergarten

Most Success for All schools provide a full-day kindergarten for eligible students, and many provide a preschool program as well. The Success for All preschool and kindergarten programs, Curiosity Corner and KinderCorner, focus on providing a balanced and developmentally appropriate learning experience for young children. While both programs are comprehensive programs that cover many developmental domains (personal, interpersonal, cognitive, mathematical, language and literacy, creative, physical, science, and social studies), they emphasize the development and use of language. Both provide a balance of academic readiness and nonacademic music, art, and movement activities in a series of thematic units. Readiness activities include use of language development activities and Story Tree, in which students retell stories read by the teachers (Karweit & Coleman, 1991). Preschool and kindergarten programs are described further in Chapter 4.

Solutions Network

Parents are an essential part of the formula for success in Success for All. A Solutions Network (Haxby, Maluski, & Madden, 2007) works in each school, serving to make families feel comfortable in the school and become active supporters of their child's education as well as providing specific services. The Solutions Network consists of the Title I parent liaison, vice principal (if any), counselor (if any), facilitator, and any other appropriate staff already present in the school or added to the school staff.

The Solutions Network works toward good relations with parents and to increase their involvement in the schools. Solutions Network members may complete "welcome" visits for new families. They organize many attractive programs in the school, such as parenting skills workshops. Most schools use a program called Raising Readers in which parents are given strategies to use in reading with their own children. Solutions Team staff also help introduce a social skills development program called Getting Along Together, which gives students peaceful strategies for resolving interpersonal conflicts and creates a positive climate of cooperation in the school.

The Solutions Network also intervenes to solve problems. For example, they may contact parents whose children are frequently absent to see what resources can be provided to assist the family in getting their child to school. Solutions Network staff, teachers, and parents work together to solve school behavior problems. Also, Solutions Network staff are called on to provide assistance when students seem to be working at less than their full potential because of problems at home. Families of students who are not receiving adequate sleep or nutrition, need glasses, are not attending school regularly, or are exhibiting serious behavior problems may receive assistance.

The Solutions Network is strongly integrated into the academic program of the school. It receives referrals from teachers and tutors regarding children who are not making adequate academic progress, and thereby constitutes an additional stage of intervention for students in need above and beyond that provided by the classroom teacher or tutor. The Solutions Network also encourages and trains parents and other community members to fulfill numerous volunteer roles within the school, ranging from providing a listening ear to emerging readers to helping in the school cafeteria. Solutions Networks and integrated services are described further in Chapter 9.

Program Facilitator

A program facilitator works at each school to oversee (with the principal) the operation of the Success for All model. The facilitator helps plan the Success for All program, helps the principal with scheduling, and visits classes and tutoring sessions frequently to help teachers and tutors with individual problems. He or she works directly with the teachers on implementation of the curriculum, classroom management, and other issues, helps teachers and tutors deal with any behavior problems or other special problems, and coordinates the activities of the Solutions Team with those of the instructional staff. The role of the facilitator is described further in Chapter 2.

Special Education

Every effort is made to deal with students' learning problems within the context of the regular classroom, as supplemented by tutors. Tutors evaluate students' strengths and weaknesses and develop strategies to teach in the most effective way. In some schools, special education teachers work as tutors and reading teachers with students identified as learning disabled as well as other students experiencing learning problems who are at risk for special education placement. One major goal of Success for All is to keep students with learning problems out of special education if at all possible (see Slavin, 1996), and to serve any students who do qualify for special education in a way that builds a strong connection between their regular classroom experience and their additional services. Implications of Success for All for special education are described in Chapter 11.

Teachers and Teacher Training

Support for teachers in Success for All is extensive and ongoing. Every teacher receives teacher's manuals that provide detailed daily lesson plans that integrate the powerful instructional processes built into Success for All with curriculum materials and assessments. Three days of initial training for each teacher at the beginning of the startup year builds a strong understanding of the core research-proven practices as well as the basic procedures. For classroom teachers of Grades 1 and above and for reading tutors, training sessions focus on implementation of the reading program (either Reading Roots or Reading Wings), and their detailed teachers' manuals cover general teaching strategies as well as specific lessons. Preschool (Curiosity Corner) and kindergarten (KinderCorner) teachers and aides are trained in strategies appropriate to their students' preschool and kindergarten models. Tutors later receive two additional days of training on tutoring strategies and reading assessment.

Change at the instructional level requires ongoing support. Success for All Foundation staff members spend twelve to fifteen days onsite during a startup year, making classroom observations, answering questions, holding small group and individual discussions, reviewing data, and assisting with setting goals for continuous improvement in student achievement and implementation quality. In addition, additional inservice presentations are provided by the facilitators and other project staff on such topics as classroom management, instructional pace, and cooperative learning. Facilitators also organize many informal sessions to allow teachers to share problems and problem solutions, suggest changes, and discuss individual children. The staff development model used in Success for All emphasizes relatively brief initial training with extensive classroom follow-up, coaching, and group discussion. Training and monitoring procedures are described further in Chapter 2.

Relentlessness

While the particular elements of Success for All may vary from school to school, there is one feature we try to make consistent in all: a relentless focus on the success of every child. It would be entirely possible to have tutoring, curriculum change, family support, and other services, yet still not ensure the success of at-risk children. Success does not come from piling on additional services, but from coordinating human resources around a well-defined goal, constantly assessing progress toward that goal, and never giving up until success is achieved.

None of the elements of Success for All is completely new or unique. All are based on well-established principles of learning and rigorous instructional research. What is most distinctive about these elements is their schoolwide, coordinated, and proactive plan for translating positive expectations into concrete success for all children. Every child can complete elementary school a confident, strategic, and joyful learner and can maintain the enthusiasm and positive self-expectations they had when they first came to school. The purpose of Success for All is to see that this vision can become a practical reality in every school.

2

Establishing a Structure to Support Success

The implementation of Success for All requires substantial change in school organization and practices. It affects curriculum, instruction, assessment, early childhood programs, Title I, special education, promotion/retention policies, parent involvement, relations with health and social service agencies, and internal school governance. It requires the active participation of every member of the staff. It requires dramatic changes in daily teaching methods for teachers who may have decades of experience doing something else, and also for those who are new to teaching. It requires a change in beliefs about the school's ability and responsibility to ensure the success of every child, no matter what.

How does all this change come about? How does Success for All enter a school, solicit the enthusiastic participation of school staffs, train staff in program procedures, monitor and improve implementation over time, assess progress toward desired goals, and maintain coordination among the many pieces of the program? These are extremely important questions that we have had to address as we "scale up" Success for All from a pilot program to become a replicable, reliably effective model for school change. This chapter discusses our practices and experiences with implementation of change in a wide variety of schools.

ESTABLISHING SUCCESS FOR ALL IN NEW SITES

As noted in Chapter 1, there are 1,200 schools in 400 districts in 47 states implementing Success for All in collaboration with the Success for All Foundation. The majority of U.S. schools are urban or rural Title I schools serving very disadvantaged African American or Latino populations, but many have white majorities, some serve less disadvantaged populations, and some do not even qualify for Title I. Many students in Success for All have limited English proficiency. About 100 of the schools are charter schools, but most are not. Schools and districts involved in Success for All have usually sought us out, after reading or hearing about the program or visiting schools already implementing it.

Our procedures for negotiating with districts vary according to the district's characteristics and needs, but there are several procedures we insist on. One is the clear support of the district's administration. This involves a number of financial conditions (see Chapter 9) as well as a commitment to allow the Success for All schools to deviate from district policies (if necessary) on such matters as curriculum, Title I, special education, and promotion/retention. We require that schools submit an application that commits them to provide the support necessary for successful implementation.

Another requirement is a process by which principals are given a free choice to participate or not, and then in schools with strongly committed principals, teachers must have an opportunity to vote (by secret ballot) on whether or not to participate. In most districts, we require that at least 80 percent of teachers buy in. In practice, most votes are more like 90–95 percent positive, but we insist on the exercise because we think it is essential that the teachers know, later, that they had a free choice, and that any individual disgruntled teachers know that their colleagues were overwhelmingly in favor of the program. Most often, project staff make a presentation to the interested schools (who have already done some investigation about Success for All) in the winter or spring before the program is to begin, and then give the staffs a week or more to discuss, debate, read, and (if possible) send a delegation to visit existing schools. We do everything we can to see that teachers are fully informed, have all of their questions answered, and are not pressured into voting for the program.

At the end of the school selection process, we typically have schools with principals and staffs that have freely chosen to participate, in districts in which the central administration is unambiguously supportive. We have learned that this buy-in process is essential. When rough times come (and they always do), everyone involved in an innovation needs to remember that they chose the path they are on.

PROFESSIONAL DEVELOPMENT

The philosophy of professional development behind Success for All is that while initial training is important, real change in teachers' practices takes place in the classroom, not the workshop. We consider professional development to be a process that never ends. Teachers in Success for All schools are constantly refining their instructional methods, learning new strategies, discussing their methods with other teachers, visiting each other's classes, and using assessments of student progress to guide changes in their teaching methods.

Initial training for a staff new to Success for All is ordinarily provided in July or August for a September start-up. This training is typically scheduled for three days. Beyond an orientation to the program and some team building among the school staff members, the main focus of initial training is on the changes in curriculum and instruction teachers will be making right away, as soon as school starts. Almost all elementary schools start with KinderCorner, Reading Roots for first grade, and Reading Wings for teachers of students reading at the second grade level or above. Tutors (who also teach a reading class if they are certified teachers) also participate in the Reading Roots training. They later receive their own two days of training on strategies for assessment and tutoring of students who are at risk.

Along the way, training sessions are held on such topics as classroom management, cooperative learning, bilingual issues, family support, pacing, assessment, special education, and other topics, and to refine and extend topics presented earlier.

The training makes extensive use of simulations and demonstrations. For example, in learning how to use cooperative teams in Reading Wings, teachers work in teams themselves. In Reading Roots, the teachers pretend to be teachers and students in the classroom. In addition, video tapes depicting each of the program elements are shown to the teachers. Teachers always discuss the theories behind what they are learning, but the main emphasis is on giving them active, hands-on, pragmatic experience with strategies that will work.

After initial training, the main responsibility for staff development passes to the school-based facilitator, and the role of Success for All Foundation staff focuses more on enhancing the facilitator's and principal's skills than on direct teacher training. The facilitator's function in Success for All and the role of Success for All Foundation staff in maintaining quality implementations are described in the following sections.

THE FACILITATOR

The first and most important decision a school makes after it has been designated as a Success for All school is to select a facilitator. The facilitator is the linchpin of the entire program; the effectiveness of the program depends to a substantial degree on his or her skills as a change agent. Facilitators are typically very experienced teachers, usually with backgrounds in reading, early childhood, or Title I. A good facilitator is one who has the respect of his or her colleagues, enormous energy and interpersonal skills, and a deeply felt certainty that every child can learn. Most Success for All schools have full-time facilitators, but a few (in very small schools) have half-time facilitators who do some tutoring in the afternoon.

A five-day training session for new school facilitators and principals is held in a few locations each spring and summer. We strongly encourage new facilitators to spend as much time as possible visiting experienced schools and shadowing their facilitators, so that they can learn firsthand what facilitators do.

Defining the precise place of the facilitator within the school's organizational structure is a delicate process. The facilitator must be seen as a friend and supporter to the teachers, and therefore should not have a formal or informal role in teacher evaluation. Teachers should always be glad to see the facilitator in their classroom and should feel free to share problems as well as successes. The facilitator must resist principals' natural temptations to put them in a role like that of a vice principal. Facilitators need to be observing classes and organizing meetings of key staff, not collecting lunch money or monitoring the playground. They need to spend their time working as change agents, not facilitating the school's routine day-to-day operations.

The overarching responsibility of every facilitator is to ensure that the program achieves its goals—that it delivers *success*, not just services. This means that the facilitator is constantly checking on the operation of the program and its outcomes. Is every teacher proficient in implementing the curriculum? Is every teacher moving rapidly enough to bring all students to grade level? Is every teacher using effective classroom management techniques? Are the tutors supporting students' success in the regular classroom? Is the Solutions Team succeeding in reaching out to parents, and are they on top of any recurring attendance problems? Most importantly, is every child on a path to success, and if

Exploring Options for Children Having Difficulties

A key goal of the Success for All program is to keep students with learning problems out of special education and to keep them from being retained in the same grade for a second year. However, this does not simply mean throwing problems back on the teachers or "socially promoting" failing students. Instead, a Success for All school tries every strategy possible to meet students' needs so they can keep up with their agemates.

The facilitator leads the effort to intervene before a student is assigned to special education. Teacher referrals go to the facilitator before they go to a child study team. The facilitator then meets with the teacher and others to try to understand what the child's problem is and how it can be solved without involving the special education system. For example, if a child is exhibiting serious behavior problems, the facilitator, teachers, and Solutions Team may design a home-based reinforcement program. A child having a problem with one teacher may be transferred to another. The same approach is taken with children in danger of being retained.

A DAY IN THE LIFE OF A SUCCESS FOR ALL FACILITATOR*

It is 7:45 a.m. on an October Monday at Brighton-Early Elementary School, a Success for All school in its second year of implementation. Most of the school is still dark and deserted, but in the library there is a spirited discussion going on. The Reading Roots teachers and tutors are having a component team meeting to discuss problems they are having. Quietly managing the meeting is Alice Lyle, the Success for All facilitator.

Various teachers bring up problems of pacing and classroom management, and discuss individual children who are having particular problems. Ms. Lyle tries to get the teachers and tutors themselves to suggest solutions to their own and each others' problems. She volunteers to cover one teacher's class later in the week so the teacher can observe a colleague who has worked out an effective way to get students organized for partner reading, and sets up a time to coteach a demonstration lesson with a new teacher who is having trouble with modeling reading strategies during listening comprehension lessons. She encourages the tutors to discuss the strategies they are using successfully with children, and the classroom teachers think of ways they can support those strategies in reading class. At 8:15, the meeting ends and teachers go to their classrooms to prepare for the students' arrival.

The building principal, Mr. Walker, is supervising the free breakfast program in the cafeteria. Ms. Lyle joins him there to catch up with him "on the fly" on several issues, including those she discussed with the first grade team. During the brief homeroom and announcement period, Ms. Lyle brings boxes of softcover trade books to two of the third grade teachers who have requested them for their home reading program.

At 8:45, reading period begins. To the sounds of "Reading Jogs Your Mind" played over the loudspeaker, children change classes for reading. Ms. Lyle is pleased to see that the changing of classes is going very smoothly, and she smiles and gives a "thumbs up" sign to several teachers who are monitoring the process in the hall.

---

*This vignette is a composite of the experiences of several facilitators in several Success for All schools. It is primarily the work of Alta Shaw and Lynne Mainzer, both of whom have been building facilitators and Success for All trainers. All names, including that of the school, are fictitious.

When the children are settled, Ms. Lyle starts her "Monday stroll" through the building. She visits all the classes briefly, just long enough to see what lesson each teacher is on and to get a flavor of what is happening. She keeps notes on a clipboard, identifying issues to bring up with teachers later on. After the "stroll," Ms. Lyle spends time with two fourth grade teachers who are using Reading Wings for the first time this year. During her class visits, Ms. Lyle listens to children read, models how to monitor partner reading, praises students who are working well in their cooperative groups, models preventative classroom management strategies by moving close to a pair of students who are giggling with each other, and signals to the teacher that she likes what she's seeing.

In her "Monday stroll" and other brief classroom visits, Ms. Lyle is identifying teachers who need more intensive help. Later in the week, she will meet with these teachers, discuss any problems, and collaboratively work out a plan. The plan could include having Ms. Lyle teach a demonstration lesson, covering a class so the teacher could observe another teacher, or a series of observation sessions followed by feedback and additional observations.

At 10:15, the reading lesson ends and students return to their homerooms. Ms. Lyle checks in with a preschool teacher who had asked for help with her STaR program, and then looks in briefly on two kindergarten classes that are doing thematic units on African American history. At 10:45, Ms. Lyle visits a tutor who is experiencing a great deal of trouble with one child. In the observation she notices that the child is squinting at the page. After he leaves, she suggests to the tutor that the child may need glasses, and she makes a note to mention this to the Solutions Team.

At 11:00, the Solutions Network meets. It is attended by the principal, the school's social worker, the parent liaison, and a second grade teacher, as well as Ms. Lyle. The teacher is there to discuss a problem she is having with two children. One has inconsistent attendance, frequently coming to school late or not at all. Another is constantly getting into fights. The team first discusses the truant child. After trying out several ideas, they decide to have the social worker meet with the child's mother and to arrange to call her at 9:00 each day the child is absent. In addition, they propose to ask a neighbor who walks her child to school every day to stop by and pick up the child each morning. The teacher suggests a behavior contract system for the child who gets into fights focusing on rewarding the child with a point for each activity completed during team activities. The parent liaison agrees to meet with the child's parents and to set up a system in which the teacher will send home a note each day the child gets five points. The parents will be given ideas for fun things to do with the child when he brings home a "good day" note.

After the teacher returns to her class, Ms. Lyle brings up the child who seems to need glasses, and the group discusses how to get vision screening for all children and how to get glasses from the local Lions Club for those who cannot afford them. They also discuss upcoming "parent evenings," additional ways to involve parents in the school, and other topics.

It is now 11:45—lunchtime. As usual, it's a working lunch for Ms. Lyle. Today she meets with the school's special education resource teacher to plan a workshop on strategies teachers can use in the classroom to help students with learning disabilities. The special education teacher teaches a reading class composed of students with and without Individual Education Plans (IEPs) and she tutors identified special education students in the afternoon. However, much of her job is preventing students from being referred to special education by helping classroom teachers and tutors meet students' needs. Ms. Lyle and the special education teacher discuss several children who are having serious learning problems and brainstorm strategies to adapt to their needs without entering the formal special education referral system.

After lunch, Ms. Lyle videotapes two tutoring sessions. The videos will be sent to the school's lead Success for All Foundation (SFAF) trainer for feedback and suggestions, and used in telephone conferences with SFAF staff to help Ms. Lyle build her own skills in noticing and responding to effective and ineffective tutoring strategies. Afterward, she meets with a third grade teacher to plan an observation the next day. She drops in on a "Read-In" going on for first graders, where parent volunteers and some students from the middle school across the street are listening to first graders read. At 1:45, she meets a student who is new to the school and gives him an informal reading inventory to place him in a reading group. She then briefly visits all of the fourth grades, which are beginning to use MathWings.

Immediately after school, Ms. Lyle has a brief meeting with the fifth grade teachers to discuss their writing program. They are having their students prepare class "mystery books" to be read to the school at a winter assembly. They discuss some problems they are having with the peer editing process, and Ms. Lyle promises to visit their classes to see if she can make some suggestions.

At 3:30, Ms. Lyle has a cup of coffee with the principal, Mr. Walker, who has had an equally exhausting day. She tells him all the good things she's seen that day, and discusses vision screening, an upcoming workshop on classroom management, and some issues around special education and Title I. At last, Ms. Lyle goes home, where she will spend part of the evening going over the results of the first quarterly reading assessments to identify children who need to be in a different reading group, need tutoring, or are not making adequate progress.

Is every facilitator's day as full as this one? Most facilitators would say that Ms. Lyle's day is, if anything, an easy one, since there were no crises in it. What our experience with facilitators tells us is how much it takes to bring about systemic change throughout high-poverty elementary schools. Nothing less than the extraordinary efforts of talented facilitators whose entire job is to bring about change will ensure the full implementation of a program as comprehensive as Success for All.

MAINTAINING PROGRAM INTEGRITY: THE SUCCESS FOR ALL FOUNDATION ROLE

Trainers from the Success for All Foundation, located throughout the U.S. and in England, are responsible for the initial and ongoing training provided to new Success for All schools. Two trainers visit new schools for about six days in the first implementation year and two to four days in later years to conduct additional training and to monitor implementation.

After the initial training, our efforts in new Success for All schools focus on enhancing the skills of the school-based facilitators to manage the program on their own. For example, in visits to the schools, our trainers spend time in classes and tutoring sessions with the school-based facilitators. The main purpose of these visits is to help the school-based facilitators see what our trainers see. They share observations and insights to come to a common understanding of what portions of each teacher's lessons are good, what portions are in need of improvement, and what strategies the school-based facilitators might try to improve the teachers' skills.

These visits are supplemented by frequent telephone contacts between our staff and the school-based facilitators. In addition, we sometimes use speakerphones at the schools to enable our facilitators to have "meetings" with several school staff members, and we are beginning to have school-based facilitators videotape teachers' lessons and send them to us so that our staff can offer feedback and suggestions. In addition, school-based facilitators send us monthly reports to keep our staff informed of the program's progress and problems.

Maintaining the integrity of the program while allowing it to meet the different needs of different schools and communities is a constant, dynamic process. Part of this process takes place in the early negotiations, when our staff works with district and building administrators to adapt the model to district resources, needs, and interests. When the program is under way, there are frequent questions about adaptations and alterations to meet the needs of specific groups of children or local circumstances.

In addition to training and supporting implementation of Success for All, our staff has several other roles. We are continually working to develop and improve our curriculum materials, teachers' manuals, and training materials and procedures. Our research and development staff leads the development activities, but some of our trainers have one or more area of curricular expertise in which they do some development.

We are very conscious of the problems of "scaling up" a program from pilot to national dissemination without watering down the program or losing the features that made it effective in its early sites. We try at every stage to maintain the quality and integrity of the model by building on our strengths and insisting on systems that ensure top-quality implementation at every participating school without being so rigid or prescriptive that the program cannot adapt to meet local needs (see Slavin & Madden, 2007).

Goal-Focused Implementation Process

In working with schools, Success for All Foundation trainers apply the Goal-Focused Implementation Process. This is a system for helping schools organize and understand student achievement data and other indicators of success, to identify areas of strength and weakness, and to create plans for addressing the most critical gaps. The idea is to focus school staffs on outcomes, not just on following rules. The Goal-Focused Implementation Process is led by the principal, facilitator, and SFAF trainer, working with all school staff. There are nine steps in the Goal-Focused Implementation Process, as follows:

1. *Determine School Goals.* The school staff sets achievement goals aligned with state and district standards, taking into account requirements for meeting adequate yearly progress (AYP) targets.

2. *Analyze State Achievement Data.* School staffs review the most recent data from the state tests, in addition to previous years' data, to identify strengths and weaknesses by subtest, grade, subgroup, and other categories. Participation rates as well as percent passing are considered. School staffs examine trends over time and begin to identify patterns that might suggest causes and solutions.

3. *Analyze Program Achievement Data.* Success for All staff routinely obtain achievement data on quarterly benchmark assessments, as well as other data at various grade levels. While state achievement data typically cover Grades 3–8, school data go down to preschool and kindergarten. School staffs organize these data and examine them to identify strengths and weaknesses, and they compare them with state data and AYP indicators. Using both sets of data, they identify individual

students in need of additional assistance as well as broader areas in which solutions are needed.

4. *Prioritize and Verify Strengths and Areas of Concern.* The data reviews typically identify too many areas of concern to address effectively all at once. School staffs review their data and goals to prioritize those areas of concern that are both most important and most likely to be changeable.

5. *Identify Targets.* School staffs identify student outcome targets that would indicate that the school is on track toward meeting its goals. These targets should be focused on student outcomes, measurable, appropriate, realistic, timely, and specific. For example, targets may include increasing the proportion of students meeting adequate fluency levels by 20 percentage points, or increasing attendance to 95 percent.

6. *Determine Root Causes of Problems.* School staffs discuss goals, data, and their experiences to suggest root causes for areas of concern.

7. *Determine Interventions.* Based on goals, priorities, and suspected root cases, school staffs propose interventions most likely to solve their high-priority problems.

8. *Design Quarterly Achievement Plans.* School staffs create a plan to implement and evaluate one or more interventions designed to solve high-priority problems. The plans include targets, assignment of responsibilities, and a layout of the process for making and then evaluating any changes made.

9. *Determine Results and Future Actions.* The results of each quarter's achievement plans are reviewed to see what seems to be working and what does not. In light of the results, school staffs either determine that solutions are working or should be given more time, or they propose changes or new directions. Finally, school staffs settle on a set of future directions that lead into a new cycle of review, planning, and implementation.

The Goal-Focused Implementation Process has transformed the Success for All program, helping SFA schools to use the tools provided by SFA in an intelligent, flexible way to solve their problems. It has moved SFA from a focus on scripts and procedures to a focus on outcomes, and the result has been greatly enhanced outcomes on the measures that schools care about most, especially state test scores and AYP.

Achievement Snapshots

One tool in the Goal-Focused Implementation Process is a School Achievement Snapshot, used to summarize a broad range of data relating both to student outcomes and implementation quality. The Snapshot is filled out each quarter. The data on it provide a quick and immediately interpretable indicator of where the school is and where it is going, and critical information in planning within the school as well as interactions with SFAF trainers. A Snapshot is shown in Appendix 2.1 on pages 26–31.

Networking

Building a national network of Success for All schools is one of the most important things we're trying to do at the Success for All Foundation. An isolated school out on the frontier of innovation can sometimes hang on for a few years, but systemic and lasting change is far more likely when schools work together as part of a network in which school staff share a common vision and a common language, share ideas and technical assistance, and create an emotional connection and support system. This is the main reason we have annual conferences for experienced and new sites. At the annual conferences, we provide valuable information on new developments and new ideas (most of which we have gotten directly from the schools we work with). We are also trying to build connections between the experienced schools, so that they can share ideas on issues of common interest and build significant relationships with other schools pursuing similar objectives, and we are also trying to create an esprit de corps—a pride in what we are all trying to do together, an understanding and acceptance of the struggle needed to achieve the goal of success for every child.

In addition to national conferences, there are many other things we do to build an effective support network. In our conversations with schools, we are constantly putting schools in touch with other schools to help them with specific issues, such as bilingual education, year-round schedules, use of Title I funds in nonschoolwide circumstances, use of special education funds to support tutoring, and so on.

One of the most common activities of local support networks for Success for All is regular meetings among key staff. Most often it is facilitators or facilitators and principals together who meet about once a month to discuss common problems and explore ways to help each other. Sometimes principals or family support teams meet separately from time to time to discuss issues of particular concern to them.

Appendix 2.1   Success for All Foundation School Achievement Snapshot K–6

School		District:	
Subject:		SFA Point Trainer:	
Grades:			
Programs:			

AYP Status

Target Area	2003/2004	2004/2005	2005/2006	2006/2007	2007/2008
Reading					
Math					
Language Arts					
Writing					
Additional Indicators					
Participation					
Overall					

Test Prediction Summary—Predicted % Meeting Goal

Grade	Goal	% Needed	Baseline GP Predictor	1st GP Predictor	2nd GP Predictor	3rd GP Predictor	4th GP Predictor
Grade 3							
Grade 4							
Grade 5							
Grade 6							

% at Grade Level or Above using Multiple Measures

Grade	B	1st	2nd	3rd	4th
Kindergarten					
Grade 1					
Grade 2					
Grade 3					
Grade 4					
Grade 5					
Grade 6					
Schoolwide Average					
National Schoolwide Average					

Overview

Attendance/Referrals	Focus	B	1st	2nd	3rd	4th
Attendance						
# Disciplinary Referrals						
% of Read and Respond forms returned complete each week						

Achievement Growth	Focus	B	1st	2nd	3rd	4th
# Fluent below grade level (2–8)						
# Students below grade level						
# Fluent at or above grade level (2–8)						
# Students at or above grade level						
Clarifying average for levels 2–8 (40 points possible)						
Questioning—Narrative average for levels 2–8 (28 points possible)						
Questioning—Expository average for levels 2–8 (28 points possible)						
Predicting—Narrative average for levels 2–8 (28 points possible)						
Predicting—Expository average for levels 2–8 (26 points possible)						
Summarization—Narrative average for levels 2–8 (48 points possible)						
Summarization—Expository average for levels 2–8 (44 points possible)						
# Students in grades 3–8 in Reading Roots (mastery)						

Schoolwide Structures

	Focus	B	1st	2nd	3rd	4th
All leaders and staff have received essential training.						
Materials necessary for program implementation are complete.						
GAT structures are in place (Class Council Meetings, Peace Paths, Think It Through sheets).						
Facilitator is a full-time position.						
Classes in Roots or at Levels 1–3 in Reading Edge do not exceed 20 students.						
90-minute (elementary) uninterrupted reading block.						

Assessment	Focus	B	1st	2nd	3rd	4th
Accurate, quarterly Grade Summary Form is maintained.						
Quarterly assessment is implemented with consistent measures.						
Quarterly Assessment Summary is completed by each teacher.						

Aggressive Placement	Focus	B	1st	2nd	3rd	4th
Quarterly cross-grade regrouping is used in all grades except Pre-K and kindergarten.						
Multiple measures are used to determine placement.						
Placement is aggressive—students are placed at the highest level at which they can be successful.						

Tutoring	Focus	B	1st	2nd	3rd	4th
Tutoring slots are available for 20% of 2nd grade and 10% of 3rd grade students.						
Tutoring slots are available for 30% of 1st grade students.						
There is at least one certified teacher-tutor as coach/tutor.						
Tutoring is one-to-one, every day for each tutored student.						

Solutions Network	Focus	B	1st	2nd	3rd	4th
Solutions Network Coordinator duties are fulfilled.						
Intervention team meeting occurs weekly.						
Solution Network planning meeting occurs quarterly.						
Measurable targets are set for selected Solutions subcomponents.						

Data-Driven Continuous Improvement	Focus	B	1st	2nd	3rd	4th
School leaders conduct quarterly data review meetings.						
School leaders know the % of students at grade level.						
Component team meetings are held at least twice a month.						
KinderCorner						
Teachers set measurable intervention targets based on classroom data, are charting progress, and are working collaboratively to meet their targets. (Use P-M-S-L rating. Optional in year 1.)						
Reading Roots 3rd Edition						
Teachers set measurable intervention targets based on classroom data, are charting progress, and are working collaboratively to meet their targets. (Use P-M-S-L rating. Optional in year 1.)						
Reading Wings—Traditional						
Teachers set measurable intervention targets based on classroom data, are charting progress, and are working collaboratively to meet their targets. (Use P-M-S-L rating. Optional in year 1.)						

Implementation Visit Participation	Focus	B	1st	2nd	3rd	4th
Principal and facilitator participate in walk-through.						
Principal participates in debriefing discussion and achievement planning.						
Teachers participate in discussion of implementation quality, student progress, and achievement planning.						
School leaders are prepared with self-assessment Snapshot totals and participate in pre-walk-through discussion.						

Instructional Process*

KinderCorner						
Teachers use lesson structure and objectives at least at a routine level.						
Teacher instruction is appropriately paced and includes modeling and guided practice that is responsive to students' understanding of the objective.						
Teachers use Think-Pair-Share, whole group response, Numbered Heads, or similar tools that require verbal student responses and check student understanding, frequently and effectively during teacher presentation.						
Teachers provide time for partner, team talk and lab activities to allow mastery of learning objectives by all students.						
Teachers facilitate partner and team discussion and student interaction by circulating, questioning, redirecting, and challenging students to increase the depth of discussion and ensure individual progress.						
Reading Roots						
Teachers use lesson structure and objectives at least at a routine level.						
Teacher instruction is appropriately paced and includes modeling and guided practice that is responsive to students' understanding of the objective.						
Teachers use Think-Pair-Share, whole group response, Numbered Heads, or similar tools that require verbal student responses and check student understanding, frequently and effectively during teacher presentation.						
Teachers provide time for partner and team talk to allow mastery of learning objectives by all students.						
Teachers facilitate partner and team discussion by circulating, questioning, redirecting, and challenging students to increase the depth of discussion and ensure individual progress.						
Read and Respond forms are collected each week and return is celebrated.						
Reading Wings—Traditional						
Teachers use lesson structure and objectives at least at a routine level.						
Teacher instruction is appropriately paced and includes modeling and guided practice that is responsive to students' understanding of the objective.						
Teachers use Think-Pair-Share, whole group response, Numbered Heads (or similar tools that require every student to respond) frequently and effectively during teacher presentation.						

Reading Wings—Traditional						
Teachers provide time for partner and team talk to allow mastery of learning objectives by all students.						
Teachers facilitate partner and team discussion by circulating, questioning, redirecting, and challenging students to increase the depth of discussion and ensure individual progress.						
Following team talk, teachers conduct a class discussion in which students are selected randomly to respond to questions for the team (i.e., Numbered Heads, Equity Sticks). Teachers note team's responsibility for preparation.						
During class discussion, teachers effectively summarize and address misconceptions or inaccuracies and extend thinking through thoughtful use of questioning.						
During class discussions, teachers ask students to share both successful and unsuccessful use of clarification, as well as questioning, prediction, and summarization strategies.						
Teachers use team scores that include academic achievement points in every instructional cycle, and celebrate team success in every cycle.						
Teachers help students set goals for improvement using their team score sheets or learning guides, and students receive points for meeting goals.						
Read and Respond forms are collected each week and return is celebrated.						

Student Engagement*

KinderCorner	*Focus*	*B*	*1st*	*2nd*	*3rd*	*4th*
Students are familiar with routines.						
Students speak in full, elaborate sentences in responding to teacher questions.						
Student talk equals or exceeds teacher talk. (Each student should be engaged in partner/team discussion as a speaker or active listener during half of class time.)						
Students are engaged during team/partner practice and labs. If needed, strategies such as talking chips or role cards are in use.						
Reading Roots						
Students are familiar with routines.						
Students speak in full, elaborate sentences in responding to teacher questions.						
Student talk equals or exceeds teacher talk. (Each student should be engaged in partner/team discussion as a speaker or active listener during half of class time.)						

KinderCorner	Focus	B	1st	2nd	3rd	4th
Students are engaged during team/partner practice. If needed, strategies such as talking chips or role cards are in use.						
Partners assist each other effectively with difficult words and use retell everyday during partner reading.						
Students know their reading level and can articulate what they need to do to increase their reading achievement.						
Reading Wings—Traditional						
Students are familiar with routines.						
Students speak in full, elaborate sentences in responding to teacher questions.						
Student talk equals or exceeds teacher talk. (Each student should be engaged in partner/team discussion as a speaker or active listener during half of class time.)						
Students are engaged during team/partner practice. If needed, strategies such as talking chips or role cards are in use.						
Partners assist each other effectively with difficult words and use retell everyday during partner reading.						
Teams are engaged in highly challenging discussion, in which students are explaining/and offering evidence from the text to support their answers.						
Students value team scores and work to ensure that every student masters the objectives.						
Students assist each other using Strategy Cards during reading and discussion.						
Students know their reading level and can articulate what they need to do to increase their reading achievement.						

* Verified by observation or artifacts such as team score sheets, facilitator observation records, videos, audio records, transcripts of instruction, or teacher records of student responses. Leave blank if documentation is not yet available.

P = Power Schoolwide—Objective verified for 95 percent of teachers.

M = Mastery—Objective verified for 80 percent of teachers.

S = Significant Use—Objective verified for 40 percent of teachers.

L = Learning—Staff members are working toward verification of this objective.

3

Early Childhood

Curiosity Corner and KinderCorner

When you walk into Laura Gardner's preschool class, you might have a hard time finding her. She might be on the floor helping children build a bakery with blocks, in the dramatic play center buying a loaf of bread from the "bakers," observing a child measure the flour for the tortillas they are making for snack, or cuddled up in the library corner with a couple of children on her lap reading *Bread Bread Bread* by Ann Morris (1989). There is a buzz in the air as the children explore their rich environment, discovering the different forms bread takes, investigating where it comes from, grinding grain to make flour, graphing their bread-type preferences, and tasting their creations. Curiosity Corner, the SFA preschool program that Laura is implementing, and KinderCorner, the SFA kindergarten program, foster children's development in all domains and support the children's families, teachers, and communities.

Success for All emphasizes *prevention,* doing everything possible to ensure that students succeed in school the first time they are taught so that they will never need remediation. Prevention takes many forms in Success for All, including providing high-quality curriculum and instruction and involving parents in their children's education. Some of the most important program elements directed at preventing learning problems are those provided before students enter first grade, in prekindergarten and kindergarten.

Because disadvantaged students often enter kindergarten well behind middle-class children in their oral language development, it is critical that they participate in preschool and kindergarten experiences that will help them develop the kind of oral language skills necessary for success in school (Barnett, Tarr, & Frede, 1999). Mounting evidence indicates that for preschool to have a lasting impact on achievement, programs must focus on oral language, emergent literacy, and social development (Schweinhart, Barnes, Weikart, Barnett, & Epstein, 1993). Success for All, then, emphasizes the importance of children attending quality prekindergarten and kindergarten programs. Research demonstrates that for disadvantaged students, prekindergarten experience reduces the chances of being retained or assigned to special education (Ramey & Ramey, 1998). There is some evidence, too, of long-term effects of high-quality preschool experiences on high-school completion, increased employment rates, and other outcomes (see Reynolds & Temple, 1998; Schweinhart et al., 1993). In a recent multisite randomized study of fourteen preschool curricula conducted by the Institute of Education Sciences, Curiosity Corner was one of only three programs to have a positive impact on kindergartners' language and literacy. Curiosity Corner children achieved significantly better on end-of-kindergarten reading than those in control classes. Full-day kindergarten has been found to also be advantageous, showing consistent increases in end-of-kindergarten achievement more than half-day programs (Karweit, 1994).

The philosophy of Success for All is to build success one year at a time. Our prekindergarten and full-day kindergarten programs stand on their own, but are also designed to better prepare students to profit from a high-quality first grade experience. Curiosity Corner and KinderCorner provide experiential, child-centered curricula designed to ensure that all students enter first grade with the self-confidence, positive attitudes toward school, and orientation to reading they will need to succeed in the elementary grades. Also, these programs emphasize involving parents in their children's early learning experiences and creating a strong home-school connection.

Curiosity Corner and KinderCorner are based on:

- the Success for All Foundation's experience in developing educational programs, particularly Reading Roots and Math Wings
- research on child development and early childhood education
- the joint International Reading Association and the National Association for the Education of Young Children guidelines
- the National Council of Teachers of Mathematics (NCTM, 2000) standards
- the federal No Child Left Behind legislation and Reading First requirements
- state curriculum standards

TEACHING STRATEGIES

This section describes the routines, strategies, and approaches that help teachers implement Curiosity Corner and KinderCorner easily and effectively. The goal of these strategies is to make the most productive use of children's time in school, minimize the time that students spend waiting or being engaged in unproductive activity, and enhance classroom management.

The Classroom Environment

The environment in the class has a dramatic effect upon the children's comfort level and behavior. A warm, well-organized classroom leads children to behave in a friendly, relaxed manner. Curiosity Corner and KinderCorner guide teachers to establish bright, safe, comfortable environments that foster learning by dividing the classroom into small, clearly defined learning centers, called Learning Labs. Materials are well organized and accessible to the children, with children sharing the responsibility for helping keep the classroom neat. Children's work is displayed and changed frequently.

Learning Routines

At the beginning of the year, teachers teach the children consistent, predictable classroom routines that are used throughout SFA programs to give them a sense of security, make efficient use of time, and improve classroom management.

Sign-In

Each day children "sign in," writing their names in any way that they are able on a sign-in sheet. They then check the Arrival Activities Poster to find out what routine tasks they need to do (e.g., hang up their coats) and find something productive to do right away.

Zero Noise Signal

On the very first day, teachers begin teaching the children management signals. If children know what they are supposed to be doing, classrooms are comfortable, orderly places. Throughout SFA, to get the students' attention, teachers use the Zero Noise Signal, holding their hand up and looking around the room without speaking. The children learn that when they see the teacher do this, they should stop what they are doing, raise their own hand, and look at and listen to the teacher. Children learn this signal very easily. The advantage of the Zero Noise Signal is that the teacher can be anywhere in the room, or outside the room, and use this signal. Children who are not facing the teacher at that moment see the other children raise their hands and listen. It is a respectful way to quickly get everyone's attention.

Choral Response

Children learn a great deal by imitating adults and peers. There are a number of choral response routines that are embedded in most SFA programs that teach children to respond in unison. When the teacher asks a simple question, he or she prompts the children to respond in unison and then sees roughly how many of the children had the correct response. This is an easy way for the teacher to find out whether students are grasping the skills being taught. "Jump Right In" is a choral response auditory cloze strategy that teachers use frequently, particularly during Rhyme Time, when they are teaching songs or rhymes to the class. The teacher will recite a rhyme and then pause when the children are expected to supply a rhyming word, to "jump right in" with the missing word. "My Turn, Your Turn" is another variation of choral response. When teaching a rhyme or a phonics skill, the teacher uses hand signals while saying a word or reciting a line, and then gestures toward the class, indicating that it is their turn to repeat the word or line.

Classroom Jobs

Children thrive on responsibility. It makes them feel as if they are important, contributing members of the classroom community. In Curiosity Corner and KinderCorner classes, children have weekly jobs. Each class has a jobs chart so that children can check to remind themselves what their jobs are.

Transitions

Much time is often wasted in schools with teachers waiting for children to line up and transition from one area to another. SFA teachers try to keep transitions as brief as possible and use the time doing them as productively as possible.

To increase efficiency, signals are established to indicate transitions in the schedule. For example, a class sings the same song to indicate when the children should gather together for a particular activity. For instance, when it is time for Rhyme Time the teacher begins to chant "Penny Nickel Dime," the introductory rhyme. The children join in, and make their way to the area where they conduct Rhyme Time. Naturally, there are unavoidable occasions when children are required to wait. These transition times can also serve as a learning time. If children must line up to move from one room to another, teachers make productive use of the time by having children count, sing, observe, compare, do auditory blending, play word games, and move in interesting ways.

Cheers

Very simple techniques for recognizing achievement can go a long way toward helping children feel appreciated. One way to do this is to teach children simple cheers, done as a class, when an individual, a small group, or the whole group does something that deserves recognition. For example, children learn to do a "firecracker cheer" and a "round of applause."

Resolving Conflicts

Teachers want their classrooms to be peaceful places. The first few theme guides in Curiosity Corner and KinderCorner provide guidance for establishing a positive classroom community where individuals are respected. To achieve a warm classroom community, it is necessary to help the children and families learn to resolve their own conflicts and problems by learning and using conflict resolution skills. If teachers jump in and offer solutions to children's problems, they may inadvertently communicate to the children that they are incapable of finding their own solutions. KinderCorner uses some of the strategies found in Getting Along Together, which is contained in the program for the elementary grades. However, in KinderCorner, Getting Along Together is a year-long process, infused throughout the curriculum.

Children are taught to work things out themselves when conflicts arise. Teachers only intervene when a child is in tears or in danger of being hurt or bullied.

Class Meetings

In Unit 3 of KinderCorner, Those Nearest and Dearest, the process of class meetings is introduced. These meetings provide teachers and children with an opportunity to deal with general interpersonal or management issues that anyone in the class wants to raise. It is not a time to try to correct one individual child's misbehavior but rather a time to deal with general problems that arise on the playground or in the classroom. The teacher and children come to consensus about what acceptable solutions they will adopt. There are suggestions in the theme guides for typical issues, often based on issues raised in Story Tree books.

Thematic Units

The SFA early childhood programs are based on science and social studies thematic units that form a basis of general knowledge that children need to succeed in primary school and in life. Most of the activities are related to the theme so that the children do not have to refocus on many different concepts throughout the day, and are presented with a cohesive set of experiences. Thematic learning provides multiple repetitions of vocabulary focused around a topic, making learning that vocabulary easier and more meaningful.

Both Curiosity Corner and KinderCorner have global monthly themes, each of which is divided into smaller units. There are thirty-eight week-long units for each of the three- and four-year-old programs in Curiosity Corner and sixteen two-week units in KinderCorner. The themes are similar in each program, flowing logically throughout the year (see list of themes in Appendix 3.1 on page 52). Many of the themes are determined by the season (e.g., Fall into Fall), or time of school year (e.g., Welcome to School).

Curiosity Corner and KinderCorner are developed as spiral curricula. Children are introduced to a concept or skill initially in the three-year-old Curiosity Corner program and engage in related concrete activities. Children are not expected to master all of the concepts the first time they are exposed to them. They usually revisit the concept or skill later in the unit, in future units, in the four-year-old Curiosity Corner program, and again in KinderCorner. They build their knowledge and expertise through repeated exposure to the concept or practice using the skill. Because children function at different levels in the different domains, the SFA early childhood programs provide activities at a variety of levels to meet the needs of all the children in the class.

Cooperative Learning

Like all SFA programs, the early childhood programs make extensive use of cooperative learning. The cooperative learning in the early childhood programs is adapted to accommodate young children's more limited interpersonal skills and attention spans. The activities are short, use partners, and have simple structures. For example, in Curiosity Corner children might "Buddy Buzz" about their favorite fruit. In KinderCorner, students "Think-Pair-Share" with their partners as they think of words that begin with a certain sound, as they predict the next event in a story, and as they orally read Shared Stories. Simple peer practice routines are used throughout the lessons as a means of reinforcing and building mastery of basic reading skills. These activities increase the amount of time that each child can be actively engaged with text rather than passively listening as other children read.

OBJECTIVES

The principles of developmentally appropriate practice are interwoven through the concrete, age-appropriate activities that target nine developmental domains that cover the development of the whole child:

- Emotional/Personal
- Language/Literacy
- Mathematical
- Interpersonal
- Cognitive
- Science
- Social Studies
- Creative
- Physical

Emotional/Personal

Young children need to learn to trust others, to gain autonomy, and to take initiative. Only when children's basic needs for food, shelter, safety, love, and belonging are met can they focus their attention on working toward meeting the higher-level needs of achievement and creativity. To help children get started on the right foot, each day begins with a warm welcome for all children, helping them feel that they belong to a caring community. They know that the day will offer opportunities to ask questions, explore new and interesting materials, and share exciting literature.

The structure and routine gives children a sense of security, and offers a predictable schedule so that children know what will happen next during their day. A balance between child-initiated and teacher-directed activities gives children opportunities for self-directed play, which helps them become self-regulated learners.

Using an SFA early childhood program, the teacher creates a safe, secure environment, provides structure and routine in the daily schedule, and offers a balance of teacher-directed and child-selected, problem-based, open-ended activities.

Language/Literacy

Research has found that by the time children from economically disadvantaged environments enter kindergarten, they score on average eighteen months behind more advantaged children in their oral language abilities (Barnett, Tarr, & Frede, 1999). The SFA early childhood programs provide children with a wide array of literacy-enhancing experiences to promote their language and literacy development. They participate in listening, speaking, reading, and writing activities throughout their entire day.

Listening

The ability to listen is promoted by making the opportunities for listening purposeful. The children listen to each other as they share ideas in the cooperative learning activities. Their listening comprehension is enhanced by participating in the interactive story reading and retelling. Throughout the day, children are taught to actively listen and paraphrase what others have said to them.

Speaking

Children's speaking abilities are enhanced by providing meaningful reasons for communicating. Throughout the day, they are provided with many opportunities to build their vocabulary, to express themselves verbally, and to learn to speak clearly enough in complete sentences to be understood by others. Increasing children's oral language skills provides a solid foundation for their future reading ability (Huffman, Mehlinger, & Kerivan, 2000), and is of particular value to English language learners (August & Shanahan, 2006).

Reading

In both Curiosity Corner and KinderCorner, children are exposed to a wide array of literacy-enhancing experiences throughout their entire day—experiences that foster phonemic awareness, letter-sound correspondence, concepts of print, and literacy comprehension. Additionally, in KinderCorner children are engaged in reading phonetically regular stories with teacher and peer support to put them on the road to literacy.

During the Rhyme Time component in Curiosity Corner and KinderCorner, the focus is on phonemic awareness with students learning that words are made up of separate sounds. Through rhyme and alliteration, children learn songs, fingerplays, rhymes, and games related to the thematic concepts. The games teach children skills such as identifying initial and final phonemes in simple words, breaking words into syllables. During Stepping Stones (in KinderCorner), children learn auditory blending and auditory segmenting.

In KinderCorner, Stepping Stones introduces phonemic awareness, letter-sound correspondence, and basic decoding skills in a fast-paced, lively way. Children learn letter-sound correspondence quickly and soon begin blending the sounds to read simple words. Then they practice reading simple phonetically regular sentences, with a few simple sight words. Finally, they are introduced to the KinderRoots Shared Stories, brief phonetically regular books with text in a small font that the teacher reads to make the story interesting and simple, and larger, decodable text that the children read. Working with a partner, children practice story words, sentences, and comprehension questions on the inside covers of the books. KinderCorner students take these books home to read to family members, giving them lots of reading practice and pride in their reading.

Engaging video vignettes (Reading Reels) are embedded in the reading lessons to support the development of children's letter-sound correspondence, word level blending, and acquisition of vocabulary in the KinderRoots stories. More detail about beginning reading instruction, Reading Reels, and the research behind this embedded multimedia is provided in Chapter 4 on Reading Roots.

The early childhood programs promote children's reading and narrative development by engaging them with interactive experiences around authentic children's literature. When Laura Gardner reads a story to her class, the children are mesmerized. She rarely has children acting out or gazing off at other things around the room. She makes the story the children's own by enthusiastically introducing the story, author, and illustrator, having the children make predictions, encouraging them to express their ideas, and having them critique and retell the story in a variety of ways.

SFA early childhood programs also include many expository books to support children's learning of letters, counting, and thematic concepts.

Children are exposed to many types of activities that promote their writing abilities from the earliest Curiosity Corner lesson. At the beginning of the day, in Learning Labs, and in KinderCorner during Write Away, children write about topics of interest to them, inspired by meaningful contexts for their writing. They sign in when they arrive at school, write in journals, construct signs, write letters, invitations, thank-you notes, recipes, instructions, stories, poems, lists, and thoughts. They are immersed in print and the teacher models writing for them daily. At first, "writing" may just be a mark on paper. Later, squiggles, then letter shapes, then recognizable words emerge. In KinderCorner, children also engage in writing activities related to the Shared Stories from the phonics component.

Mathematics

The SFA early childhood mathematics curricula are based on the National Council of Teachers of Mathematics (NCTM, 2000) standards. Mathematics activities, infused throughout the day, include reciting counting rhymes, graphing favorite ways to eat apples, sorting attribute blocks, estimating the number of buttons in the Estimation Jar, and matching patterns on mittens. The Math/Manipulatives and Blocks Labs are especially rich environments for experimenting with mathematical concepts.

It is through the distributed practice of these skills that children begin to internalize them. The programs show teachers how to model and think out loud when solving problems so their students will learn that there are different ways to solve them. Children have many opportunities to see how math works in their everyday lives, focusing on finding patterns, classifying, and counting. For example, when children are lining up their boots, the teacher points out the pattern that the boots make, counts how many there are of each color or style, and uses the word "pair."

In KinderCorner, there are also two times during the day when the specific focus is on mathematical concepts. The first is 15-Minute Math, which centers around the calendar and routines associated with it, along with other basic skills practice. The second is Math Mysteries, in which basic mathematical concepts are introduced in a brief, structured activity with concrete, manipulative objects. These activities are also related to the theme so that they have a meaningful context for the children. The categories of skills that are practiced in the math components are application, computation, fractions, geometry, measurement, money, numeration, problem solving, statistics/probability, and time.

Interpersonal

In KinderCorner and Curiosity Corner, children spend a great deal of time interacting with one another. In the partner and small-group activities, children share, take turns, negotiate, and collaborate in their play. In most early childhood classes children have opportunities to play together. What often happens is that the children who are more socially adept take advantage of those opportunities and those who are less adept play alone or engage in parallel play. In SFA early childhood classes, many activities are structured to require cooperation, ensuring that all children enhance their interpersonal skills.

By engaging in peer interaction, young children learn to take another's perspective and become more prosocial in their behavior (Chambers, 1993). As children are exposed to others' points of view, they come to see that there are different ways of seeing things, approaching problems, and interacting with people. In Curiosity Corner and KinderCorner, children come to see teachers and peers as resources for solving interpersonal problems. They develop their abilities to resolve conflicts with peers using negotiation and discussion.

Cognitive

At the end of the class period, the children gather to review what they have learned that day or week. Through active engagement with not only thematic concepts but other knowledge and skills, children process their newfound knowledge. For example, Laura Gardner asks her class to recall the types of bread they ate, to recall where some of the breads came from, to recall the ingredients of the bread they made, and to evaluate which ones they liked the best. She does this by creating with the children a graph of their favorite types of bread.

Problem-Based Learning

Children are introduced to many concepts through problems that the children can solve by exploration, experimentation, observation, and discussion. The children's curiosity is aroused by asking them what they already know about a thematic object and asking them what they might like to find out about it. Through each component, they discover the answers to their questions. For example in the KinderCorner unit Those Nearest and Dearest, children solve all sorts of problems that are presented:

Science Problems—What materials are attracted to magnets?

Mechanical Problems—How do we get sand to stick together?

Mathematical Problems—What should I put in my "Just One" booklet?

Social Problems—How can we cooperate to make necklaces?

Language Problems—What words rhyme with "friend"?

Literacy Problems—What sound is at the beginning of the word "family"?

Emotional Problems—If you were the Little Red Hen, would you share with the other animals?

Time Management Problems—What shall we do to finish the friends mural before cleanup time?

Health Problems—What things should friends share?

Resource Problems—Where will we get playdough to make our muffins?

Throughout the themes, the children work on projects that extend over time. The projects range from group activities, where all children participate in making one product such as a group mural, to more individual projects such as making their own books. These projects provide ideal opportunities to build on children's emerging understandings of concepts.

Metacognition

Metacognitive skills are emphasized in the reading instruction in KinderCorner to help children think about the process of reading, to predict what is going to happen in a story, to assess their own comprehension, and to use effective strategies to find meaning when they experience difficulties.

In order to become self-regulated learners, children need some time when they have opportunities to decide what they will do and where they will do it. The Learning Labs component offers opportunities for children to learn through active engagement in a playful manner, in activities that they choose for themselves.

Science and Social Studies

The SFA early childhood programs begin by exploring concepts that are in the children's environment. These include families, friends, and common foods. As the year progresses, children explore concepts that are a bit removed from their immediate experiences, such as mapping their neighborhood and exploring new art techniques. Many of the units are based on social studies themes, such as heritage, community helpers, and communication. As children learn about their own and other cultures, they learn to appreciate the diversity in our society. The importance of community is stressed in most of our units so that children feel that they belong and are valued members of their class, school, and neighborhood.

Many of the Curiosity Corner and KinderCorner themes are based on scientific concepts such as animals, seasons, nutrition, transportation, and growth. Through active engagement with concrete materials, children learn information and construct concepts more vividly than by merely hearing about them or seeing them.

Children have the opportunity to explore scientific concepts with equipment such as magnets, scales, and magnifying lenses. They conduct simple experiments to discover concepts. For example, they slide and roll objects down an inclined plane to observe the characteristics of objects that roll. They observe and record what happens when plants are grown under various conditions. They observe the effects of natural phenomena with wind blowing streamers and pinwheels. They use their senses to discriminate differences in materials, scents, textures, and sounds.

Creative

Curiosity Corner and KinderCorner offer many opportunities for children to expand their creative abilities in the areas of visual arts, music, movement, and drama. Through theme-related activities, children observe works of art, explore materials, and experiment with various techniques. Children gain skill in using art materials such as paint, glue, and clay.

Children explore music through listening, singing songs, and dancing. They experiment with various musical instruments and create their own interpretations.

Creative drama is a vehicle for much learning, both through unstructured sociodramatic play in the Dramatic Play Lab and other labs and through guided dramatization in activities such as acting out stories or situations.

Physical

Children need daily opportunities to engage in gross motor play. They need to practice their locomotor, balance, and manipulation skills. In Outside/Gross Motor Play activities children move in different ways; balance both in place and when moving; and manipulate balls, bean bags, hoops, etc. Cooperative games and other guided activities related to the theme are used throughout the year.

Children also need ample opportunities to practice their fine motor skills. Activities such as cutting, folding, ripping, drawing, painting, writing, and gluing help develop children's fine muscles.

FAMILY INVOLVEMENT

Each day children have an activity to do at home that connects to what they are learning in class. For example, in the Bread and Butter unit, Laura asks the children to find out if they have anything at home that has flour in it. The next day she asks the children if they found anything at home that had flour in it and talks about this with the children. This helps children see the relevance to their lives of what they are learning at school.

The *Home Link Page* newsletters go home to the children's families to let them know what children will be learning in the next unit and how they can support their child's learning. These newsletters include titles of books family members might like to read to the children, a poem to recite together, and sometimes a request for someone to come to school to help out during a particular activity or contribute a special material.

Each class has a lending library, whose goal is to teach families how important reading to children is and to help families promote their children's literacy. The children borrow the books, which come in bags with ideas for their parents on how to read the book to their child and on how to extend their child's learning. For example, there might be a book bag with *The Very Hungry Caterpillar* by Eric Carle (1994) in it and a Story Sharing Sheet for parents, which would give them ideas for how to introduce the book, what questions to ask while reading the book, and suggestions for parents to have their children identify the fruit from the story that they see in the market when they go shopping.

Both Curiosity Corner and KinderCorner are based on the principles and practices outlined above but they are implemented somewhat differently and have different schedules based on young children's different developmental levels. The KinderCorner two-week thematic units are extensions of the Curiosity Corner themes that allow for in-depth investigation of topics. Most of the KinderCorner daily components are similar to those of Curiosity Corner, with activities provided at an appropriate level for kindergarten children.

PROGRAM COMPONENTS

The following section describes daily the components of both Curiosity Corner and KinderCorner and how they are implemented. Many of the components are implemented the same way but have different names and, of course, more advanced concepts are taught in KinderCorner. The parallel components are described together, with the Curiosity Corner component title listed first, followed by the KinderCorner component title. Then, the specific reading, writing, and math components of KinderCorner are described afterward.

The time allotted for each component varies, depending on the length of the school day, the age of the children, and how the instruction is structured. Curiosity Corner is implemented in a wide variety of early childhood settings, from half-day preschool classes in elementary schools to whole-day programs in child-care centers. Two sample schedules are provided below, a sample half-day for Curiosity Corner in Figure 3.1 and a sample whole-day schedule for KinderCorner in Figure 3.2. A sample day from the Boxes and Balls theme guide of Curiosity Corner appears in Appendix 3.2 on page 53 and a sample day from the KinderCorner Unit 3, Those Nearest and Dearest, appears in Appendix 3.3 on pages 54–74.

Daily Components

Greetings & Readings/Greetings, Readings, & Writings

Each day during Greetings & Readings and Greetings, Readings, & Writings, the teacher and assistant welcome the children and whoever brings them to school with a smile and make a positive connection between the child's home and school by asking, for example, how the children had slept the night before and how they are feeling. Success in school and in life means feeling capable and good about oneself. Children experience their Curiosity Corner classroom as a safe, comfortable, supportive place where they feel they belong and can achieve, where they feel confident enough to take risks and try out new activities.

Figure 3.1 Sample Half-Day Schedule for Curiosity Corner

Component	Minutes
Greetings & Readings	15–20 minutes
Clues & Questions	10–15 minutes
Rhyme Time	5–10 minutes
Learning Labs	45–50 minutes
Story Tree	10–20 minutes
Outside/Gross Motor Play	15–25 minutes
Snack Time	5–15 minutes
Question/Reflection	5–15 minutes
Departure	5–10 minutes
Total	115–180 minutes = 1.9–3 hours

Figure 3.2 Sample Whole-Day Schedule for KinderCorner

Component	Minutes
Greetings, Readings, & Writings	15
Let's Get Together	15
Rhyme Time	10
Story Tree	20
Learning Labs	40
15-Minute Math	15
Snack/Outside/Gross Motor Play	20
Stepping Stones	25
Eat & Run	40
Math Mysteries	20
Let's Daydream	25
Write Away	20
Specials	45
Let's Think About It	10
Home Link/Departure	10
Total	330 minutes = 5.5 hours

Children's language and social abilities are enhanced through informal conversation with the educators. During Greetings & Readings and Greetings, Readings & Writings, children ease into the day by snuggling up with an adult, looking at a book, or playing with puzzles or playdough.

Children's language and social abilities are enhanced through informal conversation with their peers and adults. Not only is language development supported through the greeting conversation, but attendance-taking promotes learning too. The children write their names on a sign-in sheet beside their printed name and write in their journals. Teachers keep samples of these sign-in sheets and journals as data that show how children's writing ability emerges over time. Especially in KinderCorner, the teacher meets with individual children to plan what Learning Labs they will work in that day.

At the end of Greetings & Readings, the class gathers for a short whole-group time and children share information and ideas through the Daily Message, which models reading and writing and serves as an advance organizer for the thematic concepts to be explored that day.

Clues & Questions/Let's Get Together

Clues & Questions and Let's Get Together introduce the children to the concepts that will be focused on that day. The teacher uses Curiosity Cat in Curiosity Corner or KinderRoo in KinderCorner—the puppet mascots—to stimulate the children's curiosity about an aspect of the theme by giving them clues and having them predict what a hidden object is. The teacher encourages the children to ask questions about the object or concept. This component focuses on enhancing children's oral language and cognitive development and their acquisition of thematic concepts. Sometimes the class creates a KWL chart, recording what the children already *know* about the topic, what they *want* to learn about it, and then later, what they have *learned* about it.

Also in KinderCorner, each Friday there is a class meeting, in which the teacher facilitates a class discussion around an interpersonal issue that might be interfering with the smooth functioning of the class.

Rhyme Time

The goal of Rhyme Time is to build the children's phonemic awareness, teaching them to identify initial, final, and medial sounds in words and to auditorally blend and segment words. This is accomplished through rhymes, songs, and sound games that promote phonemic awareness. For example children might play a version of "I Spy," in which children say, "I spy something that starts with /b/." Say-It-Fast and Break-It-Down are fast-paced activities that enhance children's auditory blending and segmenting abilities. Children learn many rhymes that also teach them vocabulary from the current theme.

Learning Labs

Learning Labs are engaging discovery or problem solving–based learning centers where children explore and experiment with concrete objects related to the theme under study. Teachers typically set up between seven and ten Learning Labs, depending on the space available and the number of children in the class. These labs include: the Literacy Lab, Library, Science Lab, Listening/Media Lab, Writing Lab, Blocks Lab, Water Lab, Sand Lab, Math/Manipulatives Lab, Dramatic Play, Art Lab, often a Computer Lab, and occasionally a Cooking Lab. Most of the activities at these labs are tasks that the children can do independently.

The Learning Labs engage children like little scientists, where they make hypotheses, observe, experiment, collect and record data, make discoveries, and solve problems. One difference between Learning Labs and learning centers found in many early childhood programs is the degree of support that teachers receive in fostering the learning that takes place in the centers. Each theme guide provides specific suggestions for how teachers can facilitate children's learning at each Lab. The Learning Lab time also provides opportunities for teachers to observe, assess, reinforce, and personalize their students' learning.

Children choose which Labs to work in, engaging in self-regulated learning, increasing their independence, and taking responsibility for their own learning. They may complete the contracts that are set at the beginning of the unit to ensure that over the unit they complete the essential activities in the most critical Labs.

Language and literacy are promoted in each of the Labs, with reading and writing materials provided. For example, in the Blocks Lab, road signs and materials for making additional signs are incorporated into the road building. Cookbooks and shopping lists are an important part of the Dramatic Play Lab. In the Science Lab, children record their observations. In the Writing Lab, an assortment of writing materials awaits the children's creative ideas.

For each Lab, the theme guides provide suggestions for teachers to facilitate children's learning and to model elaborated language, speaking in complete, rich sentences. Teachers are reminded to describe thoroughly what they are seeing and doing when they interact with the children in the Labs. Teachers ask children open-ended questions and encourage them to speak in complete sentences as well.

Learning Lab time also provides opportunities for the teacher to observe, assess, reinforce, and personalize the students' learning. Teachers conduct Structured Oral Language Observations and other informal assessments during Lab time.

Several times a week, for a short period of time during the Learning Lab time, the teacher takes a small group of children and engages them in a focused lesson related to the theme. The Small Group Lab activities are brief lessons, often on targeted literacy skills that assessments and teacher's observations have shown need reinforcement. Often the lessons begin with an introduction to a cooperative activity in which pairs or small groups of children work together to achieve a common goal.

Story Tree

Story Tree is an interactive story reading component designed to promote children's listening comprehension through engagement with authentic children's literature. One of the most important goals is to build children's expressive and receptive language skills. During the Before Reading segment, the teacher enthusiastically previews the story, introduces the author and the illustrator, and engages the children in predicting what will happen in the story. The While Reading segment contains suggested questions and "Think Aloud" dialogue that models for the teacher how to enhance children's understanding of the text and promotes higher-level thinking skills.

After finishing reading the story, the children recall events from the story, ask and answer a variety of questions, and often retell the story in a variety of ways. The programs provide many opportunities for children to critique the stories, and to compare stories and the work of different authors. Teachers encourage children to see the relationship between the stories they have read and their own lives. They frequently reread stories later in the unit and/or in later units to promote children's oral language and literacy development.

With four-year-old classes, teachers implement an alphabet awareness program designed to assist children in recognizing letter names and sounds through active engagement with their environments. This program shows children how letters work in and around their everyday lives. Teachers play a DVD with the *Animated Alphabet*, thirty-second animations that provide memorable images to help children remember the letter sounds.

Outside/Gross Motor Play

In order to improve their skill and fitness, and to feel successful and develop positive attitudes toward an active lifestyle, Curiosity Corner and KinderCorner offer ample opportunities for children to engage in physical activities: locomotor activities, such as running and jumping; balance activities, such as standing on one foot and walking on taped lines on the floor; and manipulative activities, such as throwing and catching bean bags, balloons, and balls.

Through this gross motor play, children also develop their interpersonal skills through the sharing, turn taking, and negotiating that is involved in the many cooperative activities. Children's cognitive abilities are fostered through learning about thematic concepts that many of the activities reinforce.

Snack Time

Snack Time also offers opportunities to foster children's interpersonal development by modeling and reinforcing the use of polite social conventions when the adults sit with the children while they learn about nutrition and hygiene.

Children learn thematic concepts even during snack time. For example, during the Bread and Butter unit in Curiosity Corner, children eat the biscuits, tortillas, or pretzels, and the butter that they made in the Cooking Lab. Language skills are fostered through the conversations between the children and between the children and the adults. Children are encouraged to pour their own water, milk, or juice and to serve themselves as much as possible, fostering their independence.

Question/Reflection/Let's Think About It

At the end of the class period, the children gather to review what they have learned that day or week. Through active engagement with thematic concepts and other knowledge and skills, children process their newfound knowledge. For example, in the Bread and Butter unit, the children recall the types of bread they ate, where some of the breads came from, and the ingredients of the bread they made, and make a chart recording which ones they liked the best.

Home Links

Each day the teacher gives the children a Home Link activity, something to do that connects to what they are learning in class. For example in Here We Go!, the transportation unit, the activity might be counting the wheels of vehicles they see on their way home. In KinderCorner, children read at home every night, taking home KinderRoots Stories and books from the lending library. They often take home Math Home Link sheets to complete, as well.

At the end of each unit, the children take home copies of the *Home Link Page* to let their families know what they will be learning in the next unit and how they can support their child's learning. It includes:

- titles of some books family members might like to read to their children
- a rhyme to recite together
- activities children can do at home to reinforce thematic concepts
- a request for someone to come to school to help out during a particular activity
- a request to contribute a special material

Children then gather their things, dress for home, and borrow books from the lending library to take home to read.

KinderCorner Reading, Writing, and Math Components

This section describes the explicit reading, writing, and mathematics components that are found in KinderCorner. A sample day from the KinderCorner Those Nearest and Dearest theme guide can be found in Appendix 3.3 on pages 54–74.

Stepping Stones

The abilities that people need in order to read include oral language, concepts of print, phonemic awareness, decoding, and comprehension skills. Throughout the day, KinderCorner addresses all of these and the Stepping Stones component focuses on them explicitly. In the first half of the year, Stepping Stones focuses primarily on developing phonemic awareness and teaching the sounds associated with letter shapes and concepts. In the second half of kindergarten, children are introduced to engaging, phonetically regular stories. (The processes in Stepping Stones are very similar to the FastTrack Phonics lessons described in Chapter 4, with adaptations to make them developmentally appropriate for kindergarteners). See Appendix 3.4 on pages 75–78 for a sample Stepping Stones Lesson.

After the basic letter sounds have been learned in Units 1 through 6, the letter names are explicitly taught in Unit 7. Many children will begin kindergarten already knowing some of their letter names. For those who do not, it can be confusing trying to learn both the names and sounds at the same time. For example, the name for "c" does not sound like the sound /c/ in the word "cat" and may mislead children to try to read it as "sat." Knowledge of the letter sounds is what is needed to begin decoding, so KinderCorner begins by focusing only on the letter sounds.

Concepts of Print. One of the goals of the Stepping Stones component is to have children gain an awareness of books and concepts of print. This awareness is also targeted through the Story Tree and other thematic books that are read during Spotlight On . . . and other components during the day. However, these concepts are explicitly taught using the SFA Big Books and other enlarged texts during the Stepping Stones component on Day 1 and Day 6 in each unit. In addition to thematic concepts and vocabulary, some of the concepts of print that children learn through exposure to all of these texts are that:

- Books have titles, authors, illustrators, pages, words, spaces, and sentences.
- Print is read from left to right and top to bottom.
- Words, not pictures, are read, though pictures support the text.
- Words are made of different letter combinations.
- One-to-one correspondence exists between words written and words read.
- Punctuation tells the reader when to pause and change the reading tone.

After children learn and practice most of the letter sounds, basic blending and segmenting, and read some simple sentences with a few sight words, KinderRoots Stories are introduced. These have simple decodable texts that will help children practice these skills. Of course, children have lots of contextual practice throughout the day, with SFA Big Books and other enlarged texts, Spotlight On . . . , Daily Message, environmental print, Story Tree books, and other meaningful texts so that decoding has meaning and is not an exercise in isolation.

KINDERROOTS OVERVIEW

Beginning in Unit 8, KinderRoots lessons are introduced in the Stepping Stones component to continue with the reading instruction begun in Units 1 to 7, introducing "shared" stories that include connected, mostly decodable text.

KinderRoots' thirty-minute, four-day lessons center around simple, short stories (like those in Reading Roots). These contain small font text that the teacher alone reads, and larger font, phonetically regular text that the students read. The goal of each lesson is to enable children to use sound blending, pictures, and context strategies to successfully read the story that is the focus of the lesson. Each lesson begins with a quick review of letter sounds using familiar Stepping Stones routines and then proceeds to review decoding strategies as the new phonetically regular words from the story are included. The children read the story, either as a group or in pairs, depending on the day and the children's abilities. (See the description of Reading Roots in Chapter 4 for more detail on lesson routines.)

KinderRoots Shared Stories

The teacher sections of the KinderRoots books provide a context for the story and include predictive questions and suggestions for explaining vocabulary that children with limited English skills might have difficulty understanding. This "scaffolding" permits children to read meaningful and worthwhile stories, even when they know just a few sounds. As they learn systematic strategies for finding the meaning of words, sentences, and stories, children take increasing responsibility for their reading. See Appendix 4.1 on pages 131–151 for an example of a "shared" story from a Reading Roots Lesson.

Each of the nineteen KinderRoots Stories focuses on a particular sound that the children have been taught before in Stepping Stones. Inside the front cover of each book are the new words and some sentences from the story that the children practice reading. Inside the back cover are comprehension questions about the story. KinderRoots Stories allow children to read engaging and interesting stories even if they only know a few letter sounds. The first KinderRoots story, *The Wet Dog,* begins with text that uses very few sounds and only a couple of sight words. Each story adds a focal sound and contains numerous words that contain that sound.

Student response to this beginning reading instruction will be varied. Some children who have caught onto the decoding process in the beginning Stepping Stones lessons will be able to sail through the stories. Others who might not have picked up these skills in beginning phonics instruction may catch on to the letter-sound correspondence, sound blending, and other strategies as they are presented again in the stories. And others will enjoy the activities and stories, but will not show evidence of mastering the content presented. Whatever strategies the children use to read the stories, their attempts are encouraged and celebrated. All kindergarten students are exposed to the lessons and have a positive experience with initial reading whether they master it at this point or not. Children who need another opportunity at the beginning of first grade will start at the beginning of Reading Roots at that time. Children who have gained mastery of the strategies during kindergarten will start at more advanced levels of Reading Roots.

KinderRoots Schedule

The following KinderRoots Schedule is an example of the structure of the KinderRoots lessons. Not all activities are present in each lesson. For a sample KinderRoots lesson see Appendix 3.5 on pages 79–90.

Figure 3.3   Sample KinderRoots Schedule

Day 1 & 6	Day 2 & 7	Day 3 & 8	Day 4 & 9	Day 5 & 10
Concepts of Print using enlarged texts	Wall Frieze Review—1	Alphabet Chant—1	Wall Frieze Review—1	Alphabet Chant—1
	Partner Reading of any familiar story—5			
	Letter and Word Activities			
	Read Sounds—2 Stretch and Read—3 Say-Spell-Say (Red Words)—2 Introduce Readles—1	Say-It-Fast—2 Read Sounds—2 Stretch and Read—3 Quick Erase—3	Break-It-Down—2 Read Sounds—1 Stretch and Read—2 Word Wall Review (Red Words)—1 Writing Sounds & Stretch and Spell—4	Read Sounds—1 Stretch and Read—2 Word Wall Review (Red Words)—1
	Story Activities			
	Introduction to new story—Vocabulary, Background and Predictive Questions—2	Story Review—3		
	Guided Group Reading—6	Partner Reading—7	Partner Reading—7	Guided Group Rereading—6
	Story Discussion-3		Shared Treasure—3	Story-Related Writing—10
	Celebration			
		2 children read—4	2 children read—4	2 children read their writing—4
	Homework			
	Look for words with focal sound & take previous story home.	Read previous stories and look for words with the focal sound.	Read previous stories.	Take Story-Related Writing home.

NOTE: The number after the activity refers to the approximate number of minutes the activity should take.

Let's Daydream

In a full-day program, children need time to rest and recuperate partway through the day, so that they can function effectively for the rest of the day. By reading them some descriptive poetry or prose, teachers can encourage them to rest and let their imaginations take them to wonderful places and restore their energy. The theme guides include suggestions for readings, mostly from the poetry books provided with the program, and many connected to the theme. These readings provide motivation and ideas for the creative writing time that follows the rest time.

Write Away

After Let's Daydream children get up and write about anything that they desire. They might be inspired to write about the topic of the reading from Let's Daydream. They might write about the theme or something else that they have been learning. They might also write about a current issue in their lives.

Children's writing may range from scribbling to conventional spelling. Teachers accept their efforts whether they draw pictures to communicate their ideas or write letters that approximate spelling. Teachers think aloud as they model different levels of writing for their students. In order to motivate children to write and to see themselves as writers, it is important to encourage their attempts.

15-Minute Math

There are two times during the day when the specific focus is on mathematical concepts. The first is 15-Minute Math, which centers around the calendar and routines associated with it, along with other basic skills practice. The details of 15-Minute Math are outlined in the *15-Minute Math Manual* and in each theme guide these activities are related to the theme.

The categories of skills that are practiced in 15-Minute Math are: application, computation, fractions, geometry, measurement, money, numerations, problem solving, statistics/probability, and time.

The particular skills are detailed in the *15-Minute Math Manual* on pages 65–66.

Math Mysteries

Math Mysteries is the other time when basic mathematical concepts are introduced in a brief, structured activity with concrete, manipulative objects. These activities are also related to the theme so that they have a meaningful context for the children. The mathematical content is rich, varied, and relevant to the children. It includes the five content areas of number and operations; patterns, functions, and algebra; geometry and spatial relationships; measurement; and data analysis and probability.

Math Mysteries engage children in the processes of math, which include solving problems, reasoning, thinking, communicating, representing concepts, and making connections. These are active behaviors on the part of the children, as they investigate, apply, integrate, and interact to construct their knowledge. At the beginning of the school year, teachers begin with the most basic concepts to make sure that all children can succeed in their mathematics learning. For example, the teacher asks the children to think about what they learned during the last math lesson. Using Think-Pair-Share, children collaborate with a peer to think of one of the counting rhymes they have learned.

To start, for example, the teacher writes the numeral 1 in the middle of a piece of chart paper. The children Think-Pair-Share about what they know about the number (e.g., my brother is 1 year old; I have 1 sister.). Next, the children look around the room to see if they can see the number 1 and point out where they found the number (e.g., on the calendar, the number line, the Hundreds Chart, the clock).

The teacher leads the children drawing a number 1 in the air, on each other's backs, and on the rug. Next the children are instructed to take one multilink cube out of a tub that is passed around while the class sings "This Old Man" or another number song. When every child has a cube, the teacher asks, "How many cubes do you have?" The children answer, "1." "Show me 1 cube." The children should each hold up 1 cube. When they return their cubes to the tub, each child says how many cubes he or she had. And the teacher ends the lesson by asking the children, "What do we have only one of in the room?"

There are also Math Home Links, activities that provide children with additional practice in math. For example, on the day of the lesson described above, children are asked to find one object at home that they can't share with other people.

Appendix 3.1   Curiosity Corner—KinderCorner Theme List

Global-Theme 7	#	Theme	#	KinderCorner
September—Creating a Classroom Community		Welcome to School		Welcome
		Marvelous Me		Me, Feelings
		Fun With Families		
		Fun With Friends		Friends, Families
		How Do You Feel?		Those Nearest and Dearest
October—Seasons: Fall		Sensational Senses		Body Awareness, Senses
	1.	Fall Into Fall		From Head to Toe
	2.	Apples & Pumpkins	1.	Harvest/Fall
November—Life in Our Community	3.	To Market, To Market		Cornucopia
	4.	Bread and Butter	2.	Nutrition, To Market
	5.	Here We Go!		What's on the Menu?
	6.	Many Thanks		
December—Fun with the Familiar	7.	Art & Artists	3.	Art/Artists, Music
	8.	Making Music		Sing a Song; Paint a Picture . . .
	9.	Celebrate Curiosity	4.	Weather
January—Seasons: Winter	10.	Winter Wonders		Winter Weather Land
	11.	Good Morning, Good Night		
	12.	Boxes & Balls	5.	Opposites,
	13.	Pet Parade		Day and Night, Dark and Light
February—It Takes a Village	14.	Highlighting Heritage	6.	Communication, Transportation
	15.	Ways to Say "I Love You"		Roads and Words Take Us Places
	16.	Where We Live	7.	Safety, Community Helpers
	17.	Something from Nothing		Safe & Sound
March—Healthy Habits	18.	Body Talk		
	19.	Yum! Yum! Nutrition	8.	Creepy Crawlers/Spring
	20.	Stay Safe		
	21.	On My Own Two Feet	9.	Plants, Farm
April—Seasons: Spring	22.	Blowing in the Wind		
	23.	Swing Into Spring	10.	Animals, Pets
	24.	Roots & Shoots		
May—Animals	25.	Farm Animals	11.	Water, Fish
	26.	Zoo Clues		
	27.	Six Legs Or Eight	12.	Ecology/Environment
	28.	Go Fish		
June—Seasons: Summer	29.	Just Add Water		Review
	30.	Splash Into Summer		
	31.	Gather for Games		
	32.	Fun With Favorites		

Ready, set...

Focus

Balls are round;
they are very different
from boxes.

How will children grow today?

- Show increasing skill in cooperative play

- Contribute to group discussions

- Use simple prepositions such as "in front of," "beside," "between"

- Express themselves with increasingly complex oral language

Thinking ☆ about you...

"Remember, the challenge of teaching is not in holding good cards but in playing well those you are dealt."
~ Algozzine, #35

Additional Materials for Day 3

Learning Activities	Materials
Greetings & Readings	• Prewritten Daily Message: "Today is _____. We will put balls inside boxes today."
Clues & Questions	• Soft indoor ball • Box large enough for a ball to fit in, and closed so that a ball can rest on top of it
Rhyme Time	• "Guess What It Is" poster
Library/ Listening	• *A Child's Book of Art* marked at pages 33 and 54
Manipulatives	• Cutout Matching Boxes with varied designs from Day 1 (one set) (Appendix) • Photocopies of Designer Balls, cut separately (one set) (Appendix)
Story Tree	• *Cubes, Cones, Cylinders, & Spheres* • Circle cutout of construction paper or cardboard
Outside/ Gross Motor Play	• Large, somewhat heavy box • Wagon, if available
Snack Time	• Cheese cubes • Crackers • Juice
Question/ Reflection	• Cardboard or wooden box large enough to be used as a lamp table • Object to place on top of box such as a decorative statue, lamp, or clock • Ball

Appendix 3.3   Sample KinderCorner Lesson Plan

 A sample day from Unit 3:
Those Nearest & Dearest

Day 1

Greetings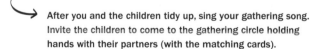
Readings & Writings

▷   As the children sign in, greet them and hand them a Making Matches Card. Make sure that each card you hand out matches that of another child.

   Note: If a child is having difficulty, ask her to describe the picture on her card. Then help her check her classmates' cards; or you say, "Mariella has a picture of a bell. Whose picture card matches hers? Who else has a picture of a bell?"

▷   Talk with the children about their weekend activities.

▷   Be sure to confer with family members or caregivers who bring in children so that they have an opportunity to let you know if there is any change in their children's environment of which you should be aware.

▷   Encourage the children whose cards match to work together on tabletop activities or to read together in the Library Lab. For example, divide the pieces of some puzzles into two piles. Suggest that the children take turns putting a puzzle together again, or have them sort interlocking blocks or other manipulatives into two colors and take turns building an alternating-pattern tower.

▷   Lay out materials in the Writing Lab and invite the children to write in their journals, make cards for their card partners, etc. Creative Writing is a suggested activity—not a required one— each morning.

☑   Note which children participate regularly in singing and chanting activities during transitions and Rhyme Times.

   ↪ **After you and the children tidy up, sing your gathering song. Invite the children to come to the gathering circle holding hands with their partners (with the matching cards).**

Let's Get Together

▷ **Good morning! I hope you all had a nice weekend and are happy to be back with your friends in school. I missed you and I'm glad to see you today. Let's look around and see if any of our friends are absent—or not here—today.** Pause to let the children count those present, check name cards, or employ whatever method you use to check attendance.

Assist the children in recalling the names of absent friends.

It doesn't feel like we're quite complete when our whole class isn't here, does it? We're becoming like a family of people who belong together.

▷ **It's time to assign jobs for the week. We all need to share the work in the classroom because that's what friends do.**

Your partners for your jobs and your Think-Pair-Share partners this week will be the person whose card matched yours this morning.

▷ Assign jobs.

Let's Talk

▷ Recite "I Am Listening."

▷ Hand the Speaking Stone to a volunteer.

Suggested prompts, if necessary:

Perhaps you'd like to…

- **tell something you did this morning with your partner.**

- **tell something about your weekend.**

- **ask me a question or ask your classmates for help with a problem.**

Spotlight On...

▷ Daily Message: **What is a friend?**

▷ Say, **The message on the Daily Message board asks a question.** Point to the question mark. **This mark is called a question mark. You see it at the end of a sentence that is asking something. The question that this sentence is asking is "What is a friend?"**

▷ **I'd like to know how you would answer that question. Think about the question and turn to your partner and tell him or her what you think a friend is. {T-P-S}**

As the children respond, you may wish to write their responses on the chart paper, indicating who is responding (e.g., "A friend is someone you like." ~ Jawon and Mehul). You may wish to simply restate what each pair says and expand their statement into a discussion (e.g., "Ana and Miguel think that friends are people who always like to do the same things. Do you all agree? Do you always want to do what your friend wants to do?").

▷ **To start our morning, I'd like you to practice introducing someone. When we introduce a friend to our other friends, we say, "This is my friend..." and then we say our friend's name. For instance, I would say** (turn to a child next to you, hold her hand, and introduce her to the class), **"This is my friend** (child's name).**" Then you would greet my friend by saying something like, "Hi,** (child's name).**"**

Let's practice introducing our partner friends. Even though we already know one another's names, it's a good idea to practice, in case you're ever introducing a friend to someone who doesn't know your friend. So, let's go around the circle and introduce our partners to the class.

You'll introduce your partner and we'll say "Hi" and then say your friend's name. Then your friend will introduce you and we'll say "Hi" and then say your name.

▷ Go around the circle having the children introduce their partners.

This activity fosters the development of social skills, of speaking in a group, of acknowledging each child as a friend, and of using each other's names. Most children love to hear their names spoken positively by a group.

Rhyme Time ♫

▷ **Let's listen to a rhyme about friends.**

Play the "Friends" poem on the *KinderCorner Stories & Rhymes Units 1–4* CD.

Friends

I like my friends. (point to others)
My friends like me. (point to self)
We are great friends.
It's plain to see. (point to eyes)

We play together
And always share. (put arms around partner)
We help each other (shake hands with partner)
And show we care. (put hands on heart)

▷ **We'll learn and say this rhyme throughout the week as we think about how special it is to have friends.**

Use My Turn, Your Turn and invite the children to practice saying each line of the rhyme, using the hand movements.

Ask the children to stand up next to their partners and form two lines facing each other. If you have an odd number of children, you become one of a pair.

Ask the children to repeat the poem several times using the gestures on the rhyming words.

☑ Observe the children to determine the level of interest in classroom activities.

By now, children who are feeling a positive attitude toward school will be relaxed, attending, and attempting participation in this and most activities offered throughout the day.

"Let's Read Together"
Invite the children to sit next to their T-P-S partners and ask them to do this for every Story Tree time.

Story Tree

 Title: *My Best Friend*
Author/Illustrator: Pat Hutchins

In this charming story, one child proudly tells about the many skills of a best friend. Although the friend is better at so many activities, the narrator is able to comfort the friend who is afraid. They can both teach and learn from each other and provide comfort when it is needed.

How are you using our suggestions for facilitating comprehension during Story Tree? Some teachers, when they <u>pre</u>read the book to themselves before class, attach self-stick notes to the appropriate pages to remind them to ask the specific questions we recommend. Others keep the Theme Guide open beside them to refer to as they read. You might try both methods to see which works better for you or come up with a style of your own that feels more comfortable. It is important that you engage the children appropriately with the text so that they are getting as much as possible from the story on the first reading. We caution you, however, not to <u>over</u>-question during a story so that it loses its flow. We strongly urge you to <u>re</u>read most books to the children at least once—during Story Trees on Days 5 and 10 and/or throughout the week during Let's Daydream; Greetings, Readings, & Writings; Library Lab; and transition times.

Before Reading

▷ **The title of today's story will tell you that it's about what we have been discussing this morning.** Read the title of the story *My Best Friend,* as you point to each word.

▷ **Let's look at the illustration, or picture, on the cover of this book and guess from the title and the picture how these two children feel about each other.** Pause for the children to look and think. **How do you think they feel about each other?** *[replies]* **How do you know? What were your clues?** *[replies; the title said "best friend"; they're reading together; they're smiling; one has an arm around the other; etc.]*

▷ **Tell your partner something you like to do with your friends. {T-P-S}** Restate the children's responses, adding language to form complete, meaningful sentences such as "Isabella likes to play baseball with her friend."

▷ **Let's read this story by Pat Hutchins and find out what these two friends like to do together.**

During Reading

▷ Read up to "My best friend knows how to read. I'm glad she's my best friend" (on pages 17 and 18) before discussing the story.

▷ **How do you think the child next to the lamp feels about all the things the best friend can do?** *[replies]*

▷ **Do you have a friend who can do some things that you can't do?** *[replies]*

▷ **Can you do some things that your friend can't do?** *[replies]*

▷ **Do you think there is anything that the friend next to the lamp might be better at doing than the friend who can read? {T-P-S}**

Maybe the friend next to the lamp is better at bouncing a ball.

▷ Continue reading the story through page 23 ("And I know if I close the window, the curtains won't blow."). Ask, **Why did the friend close the window? {T-P-S}**

RWE: **Yes, the friend closed the window so that the curtains wouldn't move and the best friend wouldn't be afraid.**

▷ Finish the story.

After Reading

▷ **How did the friends help each other?** *[replies]* Restate the children's replies.

▷ **Were the two friends able to do everything in the same way?** *[CR: no]*

▷ **Is it okay to be different from your friends?** *[CR: yes]*

▷ **So, we saw several things in that story:**

- **We saw that friends like each other.**

- **We saw that friends don't have to be the same.**

- **We saw that everyone has trouble with something and everyone is good at something.**

- **We saw that friends help each other and show that they care.**

▷ After writing the title on the story leaf and placing it on the Story Tree say, **Let's stand up and hold hands with our friends again as we say our "Friends" poem together.**

 Through a verbal or physical tour, briefly explain the activities available in each of the labs.

Learning Labs

▷ Introduce the new activities. The children may then select the labs in which they wish to begin.

▷ If you have access to a camera this week, try to catch your children in the act of cooperating, sharing, and caring. Put the photos in a book and ask the children to identify the friendly behaviors and suggest the text for each page.

Note: The labs marked with an asterisk (*) are labs that you expect every child to visit at some time during the week because they will be addressed later.

Art: Friends Art Project*

 When You Tour: Point out the large sheet of butcher paper (that you have hung on a wall or laid on a table or floor) that all the children may decorate with the available materials. Tell the children that they may use these materials and others of their choice throughout the week to create a picture of themselves with their friends in the classroom.

Facilitating Learning: Ask the children to tell you about their friends in the classroom and about the activities they like to do with them. As the children are working on the picture, ask them to tell you about their art. You might ask questions such as: "Tell me about the person you are drawing (painting)." "What are you and your friend doing in this picture?" "How do you feel when you're with your friends?" "How did you make the red construction paper into that shape?"

Blocks: My Turn, Your Turn Tower

 When You Tour: Ask the children to name some things they need to remember when playing with the blocks. Suggest that the children build a tower (no higher than their shoulders) with a partner—or several children—taking turns adding blocks to the tower.

In addition to promoting the social skill of taking turns, this activity and the questioning promote development of <u>language</u> skills in explaining, <u>creative thinking</u> skills in planning an activity, and <u>problem-solving</u> skills.

Facilitating Learning: Modeling the My Turn, Your Turn procedure, ask one of the children to take turns building a tower with you. Ask, **Why do we take turns?** *[replies]* **What would happen if we both tried to add blocks at the same time?** *[replies]* **How could several of you work together to make a large structure?** *[replies]* **What could you talk about with your friends before you build and while you are building, so that you'll each know what to do to make the building?** *[replies]*

Dramatic Play: Sleepover

 When You Tour: Point out the stuffed animals, blankets, and other props in the lab. Remind the children of the book they heard during Story Tree and show the cover. Suggest that they pretend that they are the children in the story *My Best Friend* having a sleepover.

Facilitating Learning: Ask, **Have you ever slept over at a friend's house?** *[replies]* **What did you and your friend do?** *[replies]* **What did the two children in *My Best Friend* do?** *[ran, jumped, ate spaghetti, read]* Role-play the host to promote participation, welcoming the sleepover guest, serving spaghetti, etc., or suggest this role for a third child.

Library: Reading Together

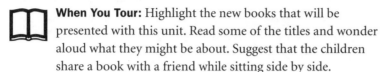

When You Tour: Highlight the new books that will be presented with this unit. Read some of the titles and wonder aloud what they might be about. Suggest that the children share a book with a friend while sitting side by side.

Facilitating Learning: Suggest that the children invite their partners to look at some of the new books and guess what they might be about before they are read to the class. Say, **Look at the cover of the book. Tell me what you see.** *[replies]* **What do you think the book is about?** *[replies]* Encourage the children to look at the books, beginning with the first page of each, and tell each other the stories as they "read" what the pictures depict.

Literacy: Dan the Dazzling Dinosaur

ABC **When You Tour:** Remind the children about Dan the Dinosaur, showing the outline. Say, **If you didn't have a chance last week to make a dull dinosaur become a dazzling dinosaur, you have another chance today.**

Facilitating Learning: Ask the children to trace the shape of the letter /d/ on Dan the Dinosaur. Remind them how to form the shape of /d/: Left around his back, then head to toe—/d/ /d/ /d/. Point to the letter side of the Key Card and ask, while tugging your ear, **What sound?** *[/d/]* Point to the sequins or glitter and say, **Sequins** (or glitter) **remind me of diamonds.**

Ask, **What sound do you hear at the beginning of the word "diamond"?** *[/d/]*

 Note which children can distinguish the beginning sound.

 Note which children can match the letter sounds taught so far with the corresponding letter symbol.

Math/Manipulatives: Puzzle Pairs

 When You Tour: Point out the puzzles and other manipulatives available in the lab. Suggest that the children select a puzzle or other manipulative to work on together with their partners.

Facilitating Learning: Encourage the children to work together to complete puzzles and to use other manipulatives.

<u>Note</u>: If the children do not wish to work with their partners, you may want to help pair children who are skilled with a particular material with children who may need guidance with that material. Another approach would be to have some children select manipulatives and then see who else would like to work with those manipulatives.

Talk with the children about how working together and cooperating can make an activity or project more fun and can help them learn from one another.

You might suggest dividing the pieces of a puzzle between two classmates. Have them take turns putting in the pieces. You might ask, "How is this working?" "What problems might happen when you do it that way?" "How could you fix that problem?"

Media: "Won't You Be My Friend?"

 When You Tour: Help the children find "Be My Friend" on the *Getting to Know Myself* CD so that they can sing along with a group of friends. They may want to continue to dance together to the instrumental "Change," which follows.

Make the *KinderCorner Stories & Rhymes Units 1–4* CD and any book read on the CD and labeled with its respective track number available to the children throughout the unit.

Facilitating Learning: After the children listen to the music, ask them to tell you about what they heard and what they did with their classmates. They might like to use materials in the Art Lab or the Writing Lab to illustrate or write about what they heard and did.

Sand: Sharing Sand

 When You Tour: Point out the sand toys in the sand table. Tell the children that they will share the sand toys while they play here. Challenge them to fill a container by taking turns with their partners adding scoops of sand.

Facilitating Learning: Assist the children in deciding how many will be able to play cooperatively and comfortably at the sand table at the same time. Include them in making a decision about how long each child will be able to stay at the sand table so that many children who want to will be able to have a turn. Ask them how sharing materials, working together, and taking turns helps everyone in the class be friends. Ask, **If you weren't able to have a turn here today, how would you feel?** *[replies]* **What would you do if someone wanted to play at the sand table but there was no room for anyone else?** *[replies]* **If we have two toys in the sand table and four children playing, what could you do so that everyone gets to play with a toy?** *[replies]*

Science: Friends Stick Together

 When You Tour: Point out the magnets and magnetic and nonmagnetic items in the lab. Encourage the children to explore the properties of magnetic and nonmagnetic items.

Facilitating Learning: Ask, **Can you think of a way that magnetic things are like friends?** *[replies]* **Are all magnetic things exactly the same?** *[no]* **Are a paper clip and a staple exactly the same?** *[no]* **Can they both stick to a magnet?** *[replies* (after trying it)*]* **Can they stick to each other without a magnet?** *[replies* (after trying it)*]* **Can they stick to each other when one of them is sticking to the magnet?** *[replies* (after trying it)*]*

Writing: Friendly Notes

 When You Tour: Point out the envelopes and stationery, stickers, etc. Ask, **Has anyone ever written you a letter or given you a card for a special occasion?** *[replies]* **How did it make you feel?** *[replies]* **This is a chance to make a card or write a note or make a picture for a friend at home or at school or for your partner this week. I think we all like to get something from a friend that lets us know that someone is thinking of us.** Invite the children to make written or drawn cards or notes for friends.

Facilitating Learning: Set up "mailboxes" for each child in the classroom so that they can send mail to and receive it from classmates. Check periodically to ensure that every child receives mail periodically, if only from you. Encourage every child to "send" something to his or her partner. Always foster the children's sending "We missed you" cards to classmates who have been absent for more than a day or two.

 Observe which children are following classroom rules and routines.

Tidy-up song

15-Minute Math

Calendar

Repeat the usual calendar activities to engage the children in naming the months of the year and the current month and the days of the week and the current day and date. Then say, **Count the months of the year.** Touch and count, **1, 2, 3, 4, 5, 6, 7, 8, 9, 10, 11, 12. How many months are in a year?** *[12]*

Point to the days of the week on the calendar and ask, **How many days do you think there are in a week?** *[7]* **Let's practice counting again.** Touch and count, **1, 2, 3, 4, 5, 6, 7. There are 7 days in a week.**

Days of the Week

Turn the card to reveal today's date. Place the "Today" card in the pocket holder behind the appropriate date card and say, **Today is** (day of the week), **the** (date) **of** (month)**.**

Transitions from one activity to another as well as school arrival and departure provide excellent opportunities to observe which children are following classroom rules and routines. Some children may need more than one reminder while others may need only a brief reminder to comply.

Days of School Tape

Repeat the usual activities to help the children determine the new number to be written and what the purpose of the activity is. Have them read the numbers and determine how many days they've been in school.

Hundreds Chart

After determining what number to color in and reading the numbers colored in on the chart, point out that when you colored in the number, you completed one row plus __ squares on the Hundreds Chart.

Ten-Frames

Point to the Ten-Frames. Add a dot in the appropriate spot and say, **Now there should be** (number) **dots on the Ten-Frames.** Point to and touch the dots as you count aloud.

<u>Note</u>: If today is a Monday, add 2 dots to the Ten-Frames for Saturday and Sunday <u>before</u> the children arrive.

 Sing some favorite "number" nursery rhymes or songs (e.g., "Sing a Song of Sixpence") or encourage selection of a book from the Library Lab as the children wait for one another to get ready for the next activity.

Snack/Outside/ Gross Motor Play 🍎🥚

▷   For Snack, you might place a whole apple, cut in half and cored, at every other place.

▷   Ask the children, **What could you do to make sure that everyone has half of an apple?** *[share]* Talk with the children about how sharing helps us be friends.

▷   You might ask, "How would you feel if someone gave you half of his or her apple?" "How would you feel if no one gave you half of his or her apple?" "What could you do if there were only one half of an apple and two children?"

▷ For Gross Motor Play some children might like and need unstructured supervised gross motor activities. Others might like to participate in the group activity Today We Met Some Friends.

▷ Begin with one child standing in the center of the circle while the other children walk, skip, etc., around the circle singing "Today We Met Some Friends."

Today We Met Some Friends
(Tune: "The Farmer in the Dell")

Today we met some friends
Today we met some friends
When we came to school today
Today we met some friends

▷ Insert the name of the child in the center of the circle for "Today we" in the song and "he" or "she" for "we" in the third line. For example, "Latasha met some friends/Latasha met some friends/When she came to school today/Latasha met some friends." When the song ends, the children in the circle stop moving and the child in the center calls the name of a friend to come join her in the center.

The song is then repeated, using the second child's name. The process is repeated until everyone is in the center.

Note: Make the last child selected feel special by holding her hand as you circle the group in the center. When she is selected, tell everyone that she is the "key" that "unlocks" the group in the middle and turns them into a handholding circle of friends again.

After the last child's name is sung and all are standing in the center, invite the children to form a circle by joining hands. Then have them walk around singing "Today We Met Some Friends."

↳ Sing, discuss, read, recite, etc.

↳ "Step, Step, Stepping Stones"

Stepping Stones

▷ **This week we're talking about friends. I'd like us to read again a book about some friends who share many different things at school.**

▷ Present the *In Kindergarten* Big Book in an upside-down position. As you point to the title, Think Aloud: **Silly me. The book is upside down. I need to turn the book around so that I can read the words.** Turn the book around and point to the title as you say, **Now we can read it. Please read the title with me.** *[In Kindergarten]*

▷ Turn to the words on the title page and say, **Here is the title of our book again. This page is called the title page. It has the title on it again. Please read the title with me again.** *[In Kindergarten]* **Turn to your partner and tell him or her some of the things that you remember the children doing together in their kindergarten class. {T-P-S}** Acknowledge the children's recall from reading the book in class and at home.

▷ **Do you remember the three words that begin every page of this book?** *[replies]* **Each page begins "In kindergarten we." Do you remember what word is the last word on each page?** *[replies]* **Each page ends with the word "together." We can tell that the kindergarten class we see in this book is like our class because they do things together. They must be friends too. Let's read the book again.**

Remember that we read the words from left to right and from top to bottom. You'll see that that is how my finger moves as I point to the words as you read them.

As the children read the Big Book, model tracking the words with your finger. If some children are still unsure of the text, read along with the class. Pause before the repetitive words "kindergarten" and "together" so that the children can Jump Right In on those words at least. Notice those children who seem uncertain of the text and make a point of reading the story individually with them

The concepts of print addressed here are: where to start reading on the page, left-to-right reading, and one word read equals one word spoken.

during Greetings, Readings, & Writing; Learning Labs; or other opportunities during which they seem receptive to it.

This modeling encourages the children to use context and pictures to make logical guesses about what the unknown words might be.

▷ After reading the entire book, turn to page 4. Say, **When we get to this page we know that every page begins** (point to the words as you read them) **"In kindergarten we" and ends with the word** (point) **"together." But how might you figure out this word** (point to "eat")**?** *[replies]* **This is what I'd do: I'd say to myself, "In kindergarten we do something together" and then I'd look at the picture and say to myself, "What are they doing together? They're eating. So this word must be 'eat.' This page probably says, 'In kindergarten we eat together.'" If that made sense I'd figure that I was probably right.**

▷ Ask, **How do you think the children feel about doing things together?** *[replies]* **What makes you think that?** *[replies; they're smiling, talking, looking happy, etc.]* **When I see the picture of the children smiling, I know that they like working and playing together. When I see you smiling with your friends in school, I know that you like working and playing together too.**

▷ **What things did the children share in school?** *[replies; books, teacher's attention, paper, markers, paint, blocks, slide]* As the children respond, show the corresponding illustrations in the book. Show illustrations, if necessary, to assist their recall.

▷ **You should feel proud of yourselves for reading some of the words in the book *In Kindergarten*. You can read this book again during Learning Labs. I'll keep it in the Library Lab. As we work together this week in our classroom, let's think about all the things that we share in our kindergarten classroom.**

⤷ As the children get ready for the next activity, which should involve gross motor movement and perhaps lunch, recite "Friends" or some nursery rhymes or discuss the children's interests or activities in the Learning Labs today.

⤷ Math chant

Math Mysteries ?

▷ As they get to the area, ask the children to sit beside their partners. Say, **Now show me what you know.**

☑ **Please count to 10 with me. 1, 2, 3, 4, 5, 6, 7, 8, 9, 10.** Ask if any of the children would like to count to 10 on their own and invite them to do so for the class.

▷ Ask the children to think about what they learned the last math time. Invite them to recall with a friend one of the counting rhymes they have learned. **{T-P-S}**

Say, **Yes, we learned different counting rhymes. Singing counting songs and rhymes is a fun way to learn about numbers.**

We're going to learn more about numbers. Write the numeral "1" in the middle of a piece of chart paper. Ask, **What do you know about the number 1?** *[replies; my brother is 1 year old; I have 1 sister, etc.]* Write a list of the children's responses, and then read the entire list.

▷ Invite the children to look around the room to see if they can see the number 1. Select a few children to point out where they found the number 1. *[replies; on the calendar, the number line, the Hundreds Chart, the clock, etc.]*

▷ **What does the number 1 look like?** *[replies]* Say, **Let's draw a number 1 in the air.** Model how to draw the numeral in the air. Remind them to start at the top and draw a line straight down.

Ask the children to practice writing the numeral 1 in the air, on one another's backs, and on the rug.

▷ Explain to the children that you are going to pass a tub of linking cubes around the room. Ask them to take 1 cube out of the tub and place it on the floor in front of them.

While the children may be familiar with the concept of 1 and 2 already, it is crucial that they develop a <u>number sense</u> for the numbers 1 and 2. They will continue to develop their concept of the numbers to 20 throughout the year. They will need to recognize, make a set of, and write the numerals 1 and 2. Number sense directly contributes to numerical problem-solving abilities.

▷   Pass the tub of cubes around so that every child has the opportunity to take 1 cube. While waiting for each child to take a cube, invite all to sing "This Old Man" or another number song. When every child has a cube ask, **How many cubes do you have?** *[1]* **Show me 1 cube.** The children should hold up 1 cube.

Invite the children to come up one at a time and return their cubes to the tub. As they place their cubes in the tub, ask each child how many cubes she had.

▷   After completing the activity, reread the list generated at the beginning of the lesson. Ask, **What do we have only one of in the room?**

↪   Invite the children to get ready for Let's Daydream by calling groups with different family members ("If you have <u>one</u> younger brother, please get your items for rest…If you have <u>one</u> older sister, please get your items…If you…").

Let's Daydream

▷   Introduce today's poem by saying, **I'd like to read you a poem by Langston Hughes. He is writing about caring for someone. We saw in *My Best Friend* that friends care for each other, are careful of each other's feelings, listen to each other, and try to protect each other from things that might hurt them.**

▷   Read the gentle poem "The Dream Keeper" (on page 31 of *The 20th Century Children's Poetry Treasury*) a couple of times, so that the calm imagery in it creates a quiet, caring atmosphere.

↪   Gather as usual after 20 minutes of rest, stories, music, etc.

Write Away

▷ **In your journal today, I suggest that you write something about being a friend. You can draw a picture of you and a friend doing something together. You can make a card for your friend. You can write some sounds that tell how you feel or what you and your friend like to do. You may begin while you are waiting for the date stamp.**

▷ If the children request that you write some phrases for them that they dictate, you should do so as time permits. It is very empowering for children to see that their words are translatable to text and readable by others. You should encourage them to write as many sounds as they know so that they don't rely on you and think that you are the only one who can write in "grown-up" writing.

 As the children acquire more letter-sound associations, elicit from them, using the Key Cards wall frieze or letters in the pocket chart, which letters you should write next. For example, if a child asks you to write "My friend and I sang today," as you sound out the words and write the letters say, "My – mmmy. What is the first sound you hear?" [/m/] "Yes, so the first letter I will write is /m/." Write "m," and then, without comment, write "y." Continue to write words, saying them aloud, stopping at the /a/ sound for "and" and /s/ for "sang" and /d/ for the /d/ sound in "today," eliciting the sounds from the children that they have learned in Stepping Stones. Focus only on sounds that are true to the sound the children have learned to associate with that letter— that is, for example, do not focus on the "a" in "today" but rather on the /a/ in "and." Also, until the children are very comfortable with hearing sounds in the middle of words, as you elicit sounds (letters) for words that you are writing, elicit only the sounds at the beginning of words or the beginning of syllables in words (like /d/ in "today") where the sounds are usually "pure" and more clearly heard.

▷ Remind the children who collected journals last week to show their successors how to collect the journals and where to put them.

  "Let's Think About It" (about friends)

Let's Think About It

*Review the concept that friends are people with whom we
like to play.*

▷ Hold up *My Best Friend*. Ask, **What did we learn in this book
about best friends?** *[replies]* **Are friends exactly the same?**
[CR: no] **No, friends can be different, but they can still enjoy
being together and playing together and caring for and helping
each other.**

▷ **Let's play together! How many classmates do we have in our
class today?** *[replies]* **Okay, we have** (number in the class)
friends. Half of (number in the class) **is ___. Let's stand with our
partners.** Pause. **Now we need** (half the number of children) **to
move to that side of the room. Let's count as each pair moves
to that side until we get to** (half the number). Count (1-2, 3-
4, 5-6, etc.) as you direct pairs to move to one side of the room.
**Now, we have half on that side of the room. The rest of you—the
other half—can move with your partners to the other side of the
room.** Pause as the remaining children move to the other side of
the room.

▷ **Are you ready for a challenge? It might be a little difficult but it
will be a fun way to play with each other. The challenge is this:
You must crawl on your hands and knees with your partners to
the other side of the room—but wait! You and your partner must
always be touching each other while you crawl to the other side
of the room. Do you think you can figure out together how to do
that? You don't have to do it like everyone else. You can figure
out how you and your partner want to do it.**

Note: You might need to stagger the pairs' attempts if you have a
small space.

▷ After the children have accomplished the challenge, point out that there were several ways they figured out how to solve the same problem by working together—holding hands, holding onto the leaders' feet as the follower crawled behind, arms intertwined, touching shoulders as they crawled side by side, etc.

▷ **When friends work and play together, they can be very creative as they share their ideas!**

▷ **Let's say our "Friends" poem before we go home.**

Home Link/ Departure ♥

▷ **When we read *In Kindergarten* today, you noticed that the children in that classroom shared many things together. In our classroom we also share because we don't have one of every thing for everyone.**

▷ **Today when you go home, please think of one thing that you share with other people in your home because you don't have one of that thing for everyone.**

↪ Hugs, goodbye song, or other end-of-the-day custom

Stepping Stones

/p/ — a snipped sound

Review Picture Names

Have the children say the names of *all* the picture mnemonics on the wall as well as the sounds of the attached letters.

Alliterative Phrase

Say the alliterative phrase, **Peek at the proud parrot.** Then ask the children what sound they hear at the beginning of the words. *[/p/]* **What does proud mean?** *[replies]* **When you feel proud you feel pleased with yourself, don't you?** *[yes]* **Sometimes people stick out their chests and smile when they feel proud. Look at parrot's round chest. I think he looks like he is <u>p</u>osing to have his <u>p</u>icture taken.**

Introduce /p/

KinderRoo joins the class with a bag of /p/ pictures, objects, and the "p" Key Card. Display the picture side of the "p" Key Card saying, **Look at the parrot. <u>P</u>arrot.** Emphasize the /p/. **The first sound I hear in "parrot" is /p/. Say /p/.** *[/p/]*

Careful! Not /puh/! We need to get out our imaginary scissors again. As we say /p/ we need to snip off the sound at our lips so that the /uh/ doesn't get out. It's like we are just puffing a little air out of our mouths. Demonstrate.

 Play the Animated Alphabet segment (optional) for the focal sound.

/p/ Names

In the usual manner, have KinderRoo search for children whose names begin with the sound focus /p/.

/p/ Pictures and Objects

Have KinderRoo display the picture cards as the children repeat the pictures' names in the usual manner: pig, pillow, popcorn. Do the same with the names of the common objects, e.g., pencil, paint, and puzzle. Repeat, in a My Turn, Your Turn fashion, the names of the children, objects, and pictures that begin with /p/. Leave the objects and pictures displayed at the Stepping Stones area.

Make the /p/ Sound

Emphasize the sound. Have the children make the /p/ sound and then ask if they used their lips or their tongues to make the sound. *[lips]*

Let's all say /p/. *[/p/]* **Look at your partner. Take turns saying /p/ to each other.** *[/p/]* Notice how each child forms the sound and remodel for those who need help. Remind them, if necessary, to use their imaginary scissors to snip off the /uh/.

Introduce the Shape of /p/

Show the picture side of the Key Card and trace your finger over the letter within the picture starting at the parrot's head as you say, **From head to tail, then right around the parrot—/p/ /p/ /p/.** Repeat the cue a couple of times with the children while following the shape of the letter within the picture.

Turn the card over to the letter side and repeat the cue following the letter shape with your finger. Invite the children to say the cue with you until they seem to have it.

Guide the children in the usual manner to visualize a parrot as they look at the letter.

Write /p/

Write a large "p" on chart paper as you say, **From head to tail, then right around the parrot—/p/ /p/ /p/.**

Show the picture side of the Key Card and ask what picture /p/ looks like. *[a parrot]* Turn back to the letter side and say, **/p/ parrot.** Place the Key Card in the pocket chart with the letter facing outward.

Practice Writing /p/

In the usual manner have the children practice with their finger pencils the formation of /p/, repeating the cue, **From head to tail, then right around the parrot—/p/ /p/ /p/.**

Review It

Point to the letter in the pocket chart and tug on your ear as the children say the sound.

Attach the "Pp" card to its picture on the wall frieze, pointing out the upper- and lowercase letters.

Say-It-Fast

Bring out the Joey puppet. Have Joey whisper in your ear for several seconds. Then say, **As you know, Joey is quite young, and he is learning to say words. He is learning how to say the names of parts of our bodies and would like your help. He wants you to pat the parts of your body that he says so that he can learn the names of those body parts.**

Joey, what parts of our bodies would you like us to show you by patting?

Have Joey say, **/h…e…d/.**

Say, **Can you say that again, please, Joey?** Have Joey repeat, **/h…e…d/.**

You say, **/h…e…d/, /h…e…d/, /h…e…d/.** Think Aloud: **Joey, are you trying to say "head"?** Have Joey nod vigorously.

Note: This is the introduction to auditory blending.

Oh! Girls and boys, Joey is trying to say "head." Pat your head and let Joey know what part of your body is your head. The children respond by patting their heads. **Joey, I will pat your head.** Pat Joey's head. **Now do you know where your /h…e…d/—head—is?** Have Joey nod.

Stretch and Read

Play *The Sound and the Furry* segment (optional) for /p/.

Let's make a word the way we made the word "lid" yesterday.

Place the "p" side of the Key Card in an empty pocket of the pocket chart. Tug on your ear and say, **Sound?** *[/p/]*

Place the "a" side of the Key Card to the right of the "p" but at some distance away. Tug on your ear and say, **Sound?** *[/aaa/]*

Place the "t" side of the Key Card to the right of the "a" but at some distance away. Tug on your ear and say, **Sound?** *[/t/]*

Let's say the sounds as I point. In succession, point to "p," "a," and "t" as you tug on your ear and say the <u>sound</u> of each. **/p...a...t/**

Move the letters closer together and repeat, having the children say the three sounds in closer succession. **/p..a..t/**

Move the letters closer together until they touch. **/p.a.t/** **Blend those three sounds together.** Sweep with your finger left to right under the letters as you say, **Pat.**

That's how to read "pat." Those three sounds (point to the three letters), **/p/ /a/ /t/, make the word "pat."** Pat your head as you point to the word and say, **Pat.**

Play the *Between the Lions* segment (optional) for the focal sound.

Recite nursery rhymes (such as "<u>P</u>eas, <u>P</u>orridge, Hot"; "<u>P</u>eter, <u>P</u>eter, <u>P</u>umpkin-Eater"; and "<u>P</u>olly <u>P</u>ut the Kettle On") as the children wait for their classmates to get ready for the next activity.

Appendix 3.5   Sample KinderRoots Lesson Structure

Lesson Structure

Instructions to effectively implement the activities of the KinderRoots program are discussed below. You have already been doing some of these activities as part of your Stepping Stones instruction. They are described here as a reminder of how they should be implemented, and because some of them have been slightly changed to adapt to your students' continued progress.

Not all of the activities are present in each lesson. Some are introduced in later lessons, and other activities are discontinued. The KinderRoots schedule indicates when each activity is implemented. The specific materials and activities for each lesson are explained in detail in the Theme Guides.

Review and practice are essential elements to acquire proficiency in any skill area. Review segments are spread throughout the KinderRoots lesson and should be seen as important parts of the lesson, since this structured practice is essential for the development of fluency with letters, sounds, and words. The amount or type of review should be based on the individual needs of the children. Too much drill can kill a love of reading, so keep these practice activities short, fast-paced, fun, and nonthreatening. Remember that KinderRoots is an introduction to reading and should be a positive experience.

Begin lessons with either "The Alphabet Chant" or the Wall Frieze Review.

Letter and Word Activities

The children begin each lesson with either a quick review of the Wall Frieze or by doing "The Alphabet Chant" as before.

"The Alphabet Chant" (letter names)
Have the students recite "The Alphabet Chant" with the actions. This will motivate them, give them an opportunity to hear the letter names regularly, and enable them to become familiar with the letters and their order in the alphabet.

Wall Frieze Review (letter sounds)
This is a quick review of all the letter sounds on the wall frieze. Do not say the picture names unless there are still children who do not know them all.

Read Letter Sounds (letter sounds)
This is a very brief review of the letter sounds from a few previous stories and the current story. It provides a quick warm-up practice of

Story vocabulary is introduced during the Word Activities and is reinforced throughout the Story Activities.

previously taught letters. It uses the Key Cards and the letter cues to remind the children of the shape and sounds of the letters and how to write them.

Review the focal sound from the current story last, emphasizing it a bit more, reciting the alliterative phrase, and using the Stepping Stones Picture Cards to review words that begin with this sound. The children repeat the picture names and identify the beginning sound for each one.

Say-It-Fast (auditory blending)

This phonemic-awareness activity prepares the students to use sounds for reading by practicing auditory-sound blending. In this activity, use Joey Talk to say a word one sound at a time and then prompt the students to Say-It-Fast. The objective of this activity is to sharpen auditory awareness while helping the children develop the ability to synthesize the sounds that they hear into meaningful words. When the children are able to connect sounds with familiar words— e.g., /b/-/e/-/d/ with "bed"—they should be able to blend sounds into recognizable words. Say-It-Fast is also great to do during transitions, such as when children are lining up or waiting. You can have them blend simple thematic vocabulary. There are often suggested words to blend in the transition that follows Stepping Stones.

Break-It-Down (auditory segmenting)

After the children practice hearing individual sounds and sound blending, they will do the opposite task of segmenting or breaking simple words into their separate sounds. You say the word and then ask the children to say the word in the segmented language of Joey Talk. The children then break the word down into its separate sounds, the way Joey, the baby kangaroo, would say it. Review the word with the whole group, sound by sound. This activity allows you to monitor whether the children are hearing the separate sounds in words. It also helps the children's efforts with sound spelling during Write Away or any other time they try to write words.

Stretch and Read (decoding Green Words)

Color coding is a technique that has been successfully used to help children learn that some words are decodable and others are not. Very simply, decodable words are labeled Green Words, and non-phonetic words are labeled Red Words. The following verbal cues can then be used:

> "Green means: Go ahead and sound it out."
> "Red means: Stop and ask."

For Green Words, the children learn that saying the sounds for letters in order (left to right) produces real words. This is done in a slow, exaggerated fashion at first, and then, as the children become proficient in letter-sound matching, becomes more of a rapid-drill activity.

Introduce the decodable words from the story by sounding them out. Since the words presented in Stretch and Read are words that the students will use to read the story, the skill presented is immediately applicable in a meaningful reading situation. The Stretch and Read strategy will be familiar to them if they need to use a strategy besides memory and context to unlock a word as they read.

On the second, third, and fourth days of a story, partners will practice stretching and reading the words together, reminding each other of letter sounds and the process of sounding out words. If you have *Reading Reels* for KinderCorner, you can remind the children how to sound out words by showing the *Sound It Out* segments where Alphie the alligator and his wacky friends model blending words with the focal sound.

Children who can read the words easily will be encouraged to go on and read the sentences to each other.

Quick Erase (decoding)

This activity gives the children an opportunity for a fun and fast-paced drill using letters and sounds that they practiced during Stretch and Read. It involves changing one letter of a word at a time to create a new word. "Tad" becomes "mad," "mad" becomes "dad," and so forth. Quick Erase provides a way to explore word patterns and helps children generalize from known words to new words. Its fast pace increases automaticity, and children find it fun.

Stretch and Spell (sound spelling)

This activity teaches sound spelling. Guide the children through the process of hearing, identifying, and writing sounds in words, so that they can spell the decodable words in the stories. Have them write the words in their KinderRoots Writing Books. This is called Stretch and Spell because it reminds the children to stretch the word by identifying the separate sounds and then to spell the word by writing the letters for each sound.

Say-Spell-Say (Red Words)

Some of the common words in the KinderRoots Shared Stories, and other texts that the children will encounter, need to be learned as Red Words (sight words) because they contain sounds that have not yet been taught or are phonetically irregular. A Red Word is simply a sight word that must be recognized visually (without the aid of phonetic cues) "on sight."

You will continue to use Say-Spell-Say as a cue to help the children remember the words. The Red Words that are presented with the Say-Spell-Say process include nouns, pronouns, articles, and prepositions that the children will encounter often in their early reading. The children (1) say the word with you; (2) spell the word, clapping softly along with each letter; and (3) say the word again. The clapping adds a rhythmic and kinesthetic element to the spelling.

In all the KinderRoots stories, there are a few sight words that can be understood from the context of the story. These context words are presented by going back to the story and analyzing the sentences in which they are found. Knowing that there are different kinds of words helps young children to understand that there are different strategies for recognizing words.

Word Wall Review (Red Words)

The Word Wall Review provides a quick review of previously practiced Red Words. This facilitates the integration of these words into long-term memory, thus providing instant recall that will result in smoother reading.

The Word Wall displays Red Words for at least the last two stories read. You may want to keep high-frequency words posted longer, depending on student needs. The students review the words on the Word Wall in order and out of order very rapidly, using whole-group response. Once the children have thoroughly learned a Red Word, remove it from the wall. Review only a few words that the children need to practice at a time.

Readles (rebus pictures)

There are some nonphonetic words in the stories that are not likely to appear in other texts that the children may read at this time. Rather than teach those words now, we replaced them with little rebus pictures called Readles for the children to "read."

As you lead these letter and word activities, it may be clear that the children have mastered the skill even before you have gone through all the activities. If so, skip the remaining steps, and focus on the story activities.

Pacing the steps is important. Most of the word-activity practice steps should be repeated until almost all members of the class have mastered the skill. Assess group mastery by listening closely as the whole group responds to the task. When the group seems to be responding correctly 80 percent of the time, check individuals by asking them to respond one at a time. When about 80 percent of the children can respond correctly, consider that the group has mastered the step.

If the children need more practice with individual sounds or with review of previously learned sounds, it is most productive to spend extra time on rereading the story and working with the word activities, rather than on repeating letter activities. Often, children who have difficulty remembering sounds and letters in isolation can use the meaning contained in words and stories to help them remember the individual sounds and letters. If some children are struggling with particular sounds, select an appropriate Small Group activity for the Literacy Lab to practice those sounds with those children. Also, remember that the children who do not catch on now can begin at Level 1 of Reading Roots when they enter first grade. They can master these concepts at that time.

Story Activities

Use the following activities to present the story:

Introduction to the Current Story. Show the children the Shared Story that you will be beginning on that day. The text in this segment will suggest a way to make a connection between the previous story and this new story. If you have *Reading Reels* you should show the Word Plays at this time to introduce the vocabulary in the new story. Then you will move into the Letter and Word Activities.

Introduction to the New Story. Introduce any vocabulary that may be unfamiliar to your students. There are suggestions in the teacher version of the Shared Story for the use of realia (objects), pantomime, and ways to explain essential vocabulary so that the children will better understand the story when they read it. Invite the children to preview the story by examining the book cover and looking at the pictures.

Background Questions. Ask background questions designed to help the children relate their own experiences to the story. This encourages the children to share, discuss, and build any previous knowledge they might have related to the story. This brings meaning to the story they will read.

Predictive Questions. Model asking predictive questions that are based on the introduction. This helps motivate the children to find out what will happen in the story.

Guided Group Reading. On the first day the story is presented, use Guided Group Reading to assist the students in learning to read the story by themselves. Use the teacher text at the bottom of each page of the teacher version of the Shared Stories. It contains questions and comments to add meaning to the students' text and to keep them focused on understanding what they are reading. Sound out each decodable word with the children to model using the blending process when reading words for the first time. Then read each sentence twice to help the children gain fluency.

Also, review metacognitive strategies during this segment. Use Think Alouds to model using context and other strategies to figure out challenging words. Ask the predictive and comprehension questions. Encourage the children to support their predictions through text-related explanations.

Story Review. Revisit the story on the second day of reading, asking questions to confirm that the children understand the story. Decoding alone is not really reading. One must comprehend what one has read.

Partner Reading. On the second and third days of a story, the children practice reading the story with their partners. Remember to assign one child to be "Peanut Butter" and the other "Jelly" (or some other nondiscriminatory label), so that you don't have to designate who will read first in each partnership every time you do a partner activity.

In Partner Reading, students work cooperatively in their pairs, taking turns reading one page at a time aloud to their partners. The partner supports the reader, giving help if it is needed. The children should practice thinking about what they are reading in this process. You should circulate during Partner Reading to facilitate the partners' collaborative work. Keep the students in partner positions after Partner Reading so that you can direct a discussion with the comprehension questions using Think-Pair-Share.

Particularly during the second Partner Reading, the children should be aiming for accuracy, expression, smoothness, and appropriate speed in their reading.

Partner Reading of a Familiar Story. Once a week, the Stepping Stones lesson begins with a Partner Reading of a familiar story. If the children are progressing well with their reading, this should be the previous story or another story that they have mastered. If they have not caught on to decoding yet, the story should be something that they have memorized or can "read" with the help of the illustrations, perhaps an SFA Big Book. Whatever it is, it should be something that the children will feel successful reading. Beginning the lesson with a successful experience like this gives children confidence when beginning a new story.

Guided Group Rereading. The goal of Guided Group Rereading, conducted on the fourth day of a story, is to assist students in learning to read the story by themselves with expression and fluency. Read only the teacher script if some children do not seem to understand the story. In Guided Group Rereading let the students take the lead in reading, while you read in a quieter voice. Listen for the children's voices to see if they can sound out the words. Read each sentence once. If you hear the children having difficulty with particular words, use Think Alouds to model using context and other strategies to figure out an unknown word.

Successful readers use metacognitive strategies to help them effectively read and comprehend. These strategies are presented within the context of the reading process. We need to teach children why, when, and how to use reading strategies that will help them assess and expand their comprehension of what they read. Word-reading strategies include rereading and thinking, reading on and thinking, looking at the illustrations, and sounding out words.

Partner Words and Sentences and Partner Story Questions. Story words and sentences from the story are located on the inside front cover of the story. Initially, you will Stretch and Read the Green Words as a whole-group activity. After the children become familiar with the process, have them work with their partners. Partners practice and give feedback to each other on their reading. This partner practice increases the opportunities for oral reading and giving and receiving explanations. The children will take turns being the "teacher" who asks the "student" to give the sounds for each of the words.

Proceed in the same manner with the sight words. Then have the children read the sentences with their partners as many times as they need until they can read them smoothly and with expression. The children take turns with their partners reading aloud sentences about the story. These sentences summarize the major points of the story. Encourage the children to have fun reading the sentences with as much expression as they can. The purpose of this activity is to give the students practice in reading and also to help them review what happened in the story.

On the inside back cover of the books there are story comprehension questions. Initially, the responses require just pointing to "yes" or "no" or filling in one word. Questions that require a written response come later. Partners read the questions together and discuss their responses, and then each writes his or her own response.

Some simple behavior-management techniques may be helpful in encouraging cooperation between partners and setting the tone for enjoyable, productive interactions. Teach the children to acknowledge one another for good work or encourage one another for good effort even if the work is not correct. Let them know that there are positive ways to correct incorrect answers. Everyone benefits from a friendly work setting. Be sure to identify cooperative and helpful behavior so that the children will know what they are working toward. Recognize pairs of students who are working well together as you identify helping skills. It will be very important during the initial peer-practice sessions to explicitly teach partner cooperation in addition to reading skills.

Once the children are familiar with the activities and are able to work independently, this portion of the daily schedule will provide time for you to informally assess the children and provide individualized instruction and partial feedback. As the children are practicing, your task is to circulate to look at and listen to their work. Help them to understand the process of partner work and provide any reteaching that is necessary. Teach the children to help their partners by letting them know that they can give an answer when their partners need it. They can then go back at a later time and check to see whether their partners remember.

With all KinderRoots reading activities, adjust what you do to the average level of the students. If most of the children are struggling with decoding the words, spend more time focusing on the word and sentence activities. If they read very slowly, have them read each sentence twice both during Partner Reading sessions and again during the Guided Group Rereading. If most of them can read the words fairly accurately, focus the second Partner Reading on expression and appropriate speed. Ensure that all the children comprehend the text that they are reading.

Story-Related Writing. The students are encouraged to write to reinforce their comprehension and to express their response to stories. Writing activities may vary from completing simple letter- and word-writing activities, which reinforce letter shapes and sounds, to composing specific responses to a story, writing personal experiences related to a story, sharing feelings about characters, and summarizing story events. Sound-based spelling is explicitly taught, and you are encouraged to respond to the meaning of the ideas the children express rather than to errors in spelling or punctuation. Peers assist one another in the writing process as they share their plans and celebrate one another's writing. Each week the children take their KinderRoots Writing Books home to share their writing with their families.

Letter Writing. The children say the sounds that they are writing. They write the letter three times in their KinderRoots Writing Books. Eventually, this enables them to write unfamiliar words by sound spelling—first sounding the words out and then writing the sounds that they hear.

Writing Words With Sound Spelling. Children's writing vocabularies are very limited at this age, while their speaking vocabularies are extensive. This approach to spelling teaches your students that they can write anything they can say by writing down the sounds they hear in a word. They need to feel that their writing is not limited to the words that they know how to spell or form perfectly. Teach them the concept of spelling the words they wish to write by using sound spelling. Talk individual children through the process, as needed, while they are writing, and allow them to get help in sounding out words from other students.

Children's abilities to use sound spelling will vary greatly. Some will be able to hear and write most of the sounds in a word, while others will leave out important sounds. The children write the first letter or other known letters of a word and then draw a line to substitute for the missing letters. Encourage each student to do his or her best. Continue modeling and helping individual children to use the sound-spelling process.

Spend no more than four minutes on sound spelling on the third day of a story. Have the children write some of the Green Words from the KinderRoots story in their KinderRoots Writing Books. Use illustrations from the KinderRoots story to prompt the children to write the words. Have partners take turns sound spelling the words. They write the first letter(s) of the word. Use your discretion in the number of words that you have them write.

Writing Prompts. The Theme Guides include prompts for writing sentences about each story. During the fourth day of a story, write these prompts on the board.

Encourage your students to write as much as they can.

<u>Reading</u>. Have the children read the prompt or question with their partners, and then read it all together.

<u>Planning</u>. Before the children begin to write in response to the prompt, have them talk about their ideas with their partners. Partner planning will allow the children to get their ideas flowing and will stimulate their writing.

<u>Writing</u>. At the beginning stages, the children will vary tremendously in their abilities and confidence in writing. Some will be able to use sound spelling to write several words or even sentences. Others may be able to write only the initial sound of a word. Still others may draw a picture rather than express themselves in written words. It is important to accept and note whatever each child is able to accomplish.

To encourage the children not to interrupt their writing to ask how to spell words, stay away from the idea that there is a "correct" spelling for a word. Many spellings can be understood as indicating a particular word, especially to the author, who will be reading his or her own writing aloud. However, students do not want to be wrong. Let them know that their job at this point is to get their ideas down using the best spelling they can. They may not have the complete spelling at this point, but they will learn that later. Use the terms "sound spelling" and "dictionary spelling" rather than "right and wrong spelling" to further emphasize these points. Monitor and support your students in their writing attempts.

<u>Sharing Writing</u>. The goal is to have the students enjoy the opportunity to share their ideas through writing and to become confident and fluent writers. Some children will need to have more experience with the sounds and letters presented in the lessons before they will be able to form words. The important thing is to celebrate the ideas that the children have expressed in their writing. Do not worry at all about spelling or mechanics. The development of these skills can be addressed later.

As the children share their writing with one another, they will see what others have done. Have them share with their partners first, and then have several students share their writing with the class as a whole. Be sure that you give everyone a chance to share with the class over time. Some children may need to be encouraged more than others to share.

Story Discussion. Depending on the instructional focus of the story, the students are asked to answer questions with you and then with their partners about the story's plot, main characters, setting, theme, and topics. Initially, have the students think about and discuss the story with you. Ask, **What happened in this story?** Have them compare their predictions about the story with what they learned after reading it.

Then, working with their partners, encourage the students to use the book to find specific clues to answer the discussion questions. The answer to the question is less important than the discussion the children participate in to discover the answer. As the partners talk about the questions and possible answers, they will deepen their own thinking and understanding skills, as well as sharpen their expressive language skills. They are asked not only to recall what happened in the story but also to use their higher level thinking skills to make inferences and judgments about what they have read. Invite the children to imagine what they would have done if they had been a specific character. The children are encouraged to go back and reread the story as they proceed through the questions. This will help them practice their reading comprehension and review skills.

Celebration

At the end of the second and third days of a story, celebrate the children's achievements by having two children read parts of a familiar story while the rest of the class provides support and encouragement. These readers should be notified the day before and given time to practice. Children who are not prepared to read something or are too shy to perform in front of the class should not be forced to do so. They can always read to you privately.

This must be a positive experience for the children. Even if children just memorize what they read, they need to feel that their achievement is as valuable as achievements of the children who are decoding more complicated text. Each child will have accomplishments to celebrate.

On the last day of a story, the children celebrate by reading their Story-Related Writing to the class. Again, accept and encourage the children at whatever level they can write. Teach them to make positive comments and to ask probing questions about one another's writing.

Home Link

The students should take KinderRoots Shared Stories and their writing home to read to family members. This provides opportunities to build fluency as well as to celebrate success at home. Send a note to parents explaining how they can encourage their child as he or she reads at home each evening.

Read & Respond. There are new Read & Respond bookmarks for KinderRoots to replace the ones used for the SFA Big Books. Remind the children to do the activities on the Read & Respond bookmarks and have their parents sign them. After four days of reading the story, keep the signed bookmarks in the children's portfolios.

Remember, KinderRoots provides an exposure to reading. If children do not master blending and segmenting, they will have an opportunity again in the Reading Roots program in the first grade.

4

Beginning Reading

Reading Roots

In Success for All, the heart of the instructional program is reading. As stated earlier, in the early grades, success in school is virtually synonymous with success in reading. Very few primary-grade students are retained or assigned to special education solely on the basis of deficits in math performance, for example. A child who *can* read is not guaranteed to be a success in school, but a child who *cannot* is guaranteed to be a failure.

The philosophy that guides the development of the reading curriculum in Success for All emphasizes the need for reading instruction to work for *all* students. We recognize that different children learn to read in different ways, so our approach emphasizes teaching reading many different ways at the same time. For example, each beginning reading lesson has students reading silently and aloud, singing, tracing letters with their fingers, writing, making visual and auditory discriminations, discussing stories, viewing videos, making predictions, using context clues, and engaging in many other activities. Teaching the same concepts and skills in many different ways both provides reinforcement and allows the curriculum to utilize the learning strengths of every child.

GROUPING

Homeroom classes in Success for All are fully heterogeneous. However, in order to have enough instructional time to be able to teach reading in many different ways, students are regrouped for reading across grade lines (beginning in Grade 1) according to reading level, so that all reading classes contain just one level. For example, a reading class working at an early second grade level might contain first, second, and third graders all reading at the same level. During reading time (ninety minutes per day), additional teachers are available to teach reading since certified tutors (and, in some schools, media specialists, and physical education, special education, or ESL teachers) teach a reading class. This means that reading classes are smaller than homeroom classes. Based on regular curriculum-based assessments given quarterly, reading group assignments are constantly reexamined (see below). Students capable of working in a higher-performing group are accelerated, while those who are not performing adequately are given tutoring, family support services, modifications in curriculum or instruction, or other services to help them keep up. Only very rarely would a child repeat a given segment of instruction.

There are many reasons for cross-class and cross-grade grouping for reading in Success for All. First, having all students at one reading level avoids any need for the use of reading groups *within* the class. The problem with within-class reading groups is that when the teacher is working with one group, the other groups are at their desks doing seatwork or other independent tasks of little instructional value. To have a full ninety minutes of active, productive instruction, having only one reading group is essential. Research on cross-grade grouping for reading, often called Joplin Plan, has shown that this method increases student achievement (Slavin, 1987).

In addition, use of cross-class and cross-grade grouping allows the use of tutors and other certified staff as reading teachers. This has many benefits. First, it reduces class size for reading, which has important benefits for achievement in the early grades (Slavin, 1994). Perhaps of equal importance, it gives tutors and other supplementary teachers experience in teaching the reading program, so that they know exactly what their students are experiencing. When a student is struggling with Lesson 17, the tutor knows what Lesson 17 is, because he or she has taught it.

QUARTERLY ASSESSMENTS

A critical feature of reading instruction in Success for All at all grade levels is assessment of student progress every quarter—about every eight or nine weeks. These assessments are closely linked to the curriculum. In the early grades they may include some written and some oral assessments; in the later grades schools use a leveled assessment of reading comprehension to track progress and determine reading group assignment. Quarterly assessments usually include assessments of skills above students' current level of performance to facilitate decisions to accelerate students to a higher reading group.

Quarterly assessments are used for three essential purposes. One is to change students' reading groupings; in particular, to identify students capable of being accelerated. A second is to decide which students are in the greatest need for tutoring and which no longer need tutoring (see Chapter 7). Finally, the quarterly assessments provide an internal check on the progress of every child. They can indicate to school staff that a given student is not making adequate progress, and lead them to try other strategies.

The quarterly assessments are given and scored by reading teachers but are collated and interpreted by the facilitator, who discusses them with the teachers to review the progress of all children and to suggest changes in grouping, tutoring assignments, behavioral interventions, hearing and vision assessment, involvement of parents, or other approaches to ensure progress. The Solutions Network (see Chapter 9) serves as the broker of services as well as a prevention-planning group when needs are identified.

READING APPROACHES

The Success for All reading approach is divided into several levels to address the instructional needs of students at different age and skill levels. In kindergarten, Stepping Stones (see Chapter 3) guides students from the basics of concepts about print and phonemic awareness into learning letter-sound correspondences, basic sound synthesis, a few "sight" words, and reading of simple phonetically regular stories. Beginning reading skills are taught in KinderRoots in kindergarten and in Reading Roots beginning in first grade. (Because students are regrouped across class and age lines beginning in first grade, those who have already mastered the basics start at a higher level. See Chapter 1 for more on regrouping.) Reading Roots continues through what would usually be thought of as the first reader, focusing on the mastery of letter/sound correspondences, and on developing fluency, increasing vocabulary, and introducing students to comprehension monitoring strategies. Reading Roots is usually completed by the end of first grade, yet a small number of students may not finish Reading Roots until the first quarter of second grade. Reading Roots and KinderRoots replace the usual basals and workbooks with a completely different set of materials. Bilingual schools choosing to teach in Spanish use Lee Conmigo, which applies the same instructional strategies and processes as Reading Roots but is built around stories and materials in Spanish.

Starting at the second grade reading level, students go on to Reading Wings, which continues through the fifth or sixth grade. Reading Wings (Madden et al., 2007), described in Chapter 5, uses the district's usual basals, anthologies, and/or trade books, but replaces teacher's guides, workbooks, and other supplementary materials with a student-centered cooperative learning process that focuses on developing comprehension, vocabulary, fluency, and word structure skills. Student use of strategic reading tools, including comprehension monitoring and clarification, prediction, questioning, and summarization is modeled and monitored. Reading Wings involves students in many kinds of active interaction with reading, discussion, and writing. The Reading Wings process, when used with Spanish novels or basals, is called Alas Para Leer.

At the middle grades (Grades 6, 7, and 8) students' reading skills are further developed using The Reading Edge, described in Chapter 6, which is built around a wide range of narrative and expository texts that are engaging to young adolescents. Because many students enter middle school without adequate preparation in reading, The Reading Edge includes instruction at levels ranging from high school down to beginning reading. Students reading below grade level are assigned to groups providing instruction in decoding, fluency, comprehension, and vocabulary at the highest level at which they can succeed, and are accelerated toward grade level rapidly. The Reading Edge is similar to Reading Wings. At all levels, it is built around student-centered cooperative learning that involves students in rich discussions and peer interactions around their reading.

BEGINNING TO READ: READING ROOTS

There is both magic and method in learning to read. Students come to school knowing that learning to read will be their most important task, and see reading as an exciting step in growing up. Taught with effective methods, every child can experience the magic of reading and become a confident, joyful, and strategic reader by the end of first grade.

Reading Roots is designed to ensure that students are off to a successful start in reading. It is based on research that points to the need to have students learn to read in meaningful contexts and, at the same time, to have a systematic presentation of word attack skills (see Adams, 1990; National Reading Panel, 2000). Reading Roots addresses the core elements of reading instruction—phonemic awareness, phonics, fluency, comprehension, and vocabulary—with five lesson strands:

Phonemic Awareness and Phonics

Learning the code that represents sounds in English gives students the power to read new words that they have never seen before. With clear instruction and adequate practice, virtually every student can learn to unlock the code. In Reading Roots, fast-paced systematic phonics lessons provide engaging instruction and lots of peer practice to develop phonemic awareness, knowledge of letter-sound correspondences, skill in blending sounds to make words, and practice using sounds to write words. Brief video vignettes, colorful picture cards, rhythmic chants, and kinesthetic games all combine to provide powerful mnemonics and bring the lessons alive. Lessons progress from basic to advanced, so teachers are able to assess their children and tailor the program to best suit their needs. Also, the many opportunities for partner work and sharing promote cooperative learning and increase student participation.

Reading for Meaning

Beginning in the second semester of kindergarten, students read "Shared Stories," decodable student text built from letter sounds students have been taught and a few sight words. Interest and meaning is added by surrounding student text with brief teacher-read sections that elaborate characters, setting, and events. Thus, the development of meaning is shared between student and teacher texts.

Shared Stories allow students to read complex, engaging, and interesting stories even when they know only a few letter sounds. Students are able to read the decodable "Green Words" from the story by applying "Stretch and Read," the sound blending strategy taught in phonics lessons. They gain reading independence one step at a time, first by reading stories in a teacher-guided situation, then by reading them with a partner, and finally by reading them individually. Students are provided with many opportunities to celebrate their reading success and gain fluency by reading the stories aloud to partners, to the class, and to people at home.

Each page in a Shared Story has both teacher text and student text. The student text uses only letter sounds and words that students have already learned and a few key sight words ("Red Words"). The teacher text presents a context for the story and includes predictive questions that are answered in the student sections. In the earliest stories, the teacher text adds a great deal to the meaning of the stories. Over time, the student text increases and the teacher text diminishes. This scaffolding allows students to read meaningful and worthwhile stories from the very start of their reading instruction.

Fluency

Fluency is addressed one step at a time within the Shared Story lessons. In the beginning, only the accuracy of reading is addressed and tracked for each student. As accuracy increases, the focus shifts to reading smoothly, with attention to periods and commas. Reading with rich expression, like a storyteller, becomes the next goal. Finally, reading rate is tracked and increases are celebrated with continuing attention to the quality of the reading. By the end of first grade, it is expected that students will be reading at a rate of sixty words correct per minute.

Vocabulary and Oral Language

To develop students' concepts about print, listening comprehension skills, and vocabulary, teachers read children's literature thematically connected to the Shared Story daily.

Vocabulary and oral expression are further developed in structured peer practice activities related to the theme of the lesson.

A major principle of Reading Roots is that students need to develop vocabulary and comprehension strategies at a level *above* their current independent reading level to continue the development of their language skills. To develop these skills, teachers read rich children's literature to students and engage them in discussions, retelling of the stories, and writing. The idea is to build listening comprehension skills with material more difficult than that which students could read on their own, because, in the early grades, material children can read independently does not challenge their far more advanced language comprehension skills. As they read literature to students, teachers teach their students to understand new vocabulary; to identify characters, settings, problems, and solutions in narratives; to visualize descriptive elements of stories; to identify sequences of events; to predict story outcomes; and to identify topics and main ideas in expository selections. All of these skills require that students stretch not only their receptive language and vocabulary, but also develop their ability to express their thinking about what they read. At the early stages, students also learn basic concepts about print: that letters and words represent speech and are meant to communicate a message with meaning, that print progresses from left to right, that spoken and written words are made up of sounds, and other critical concepts. At all stages, children gain an experience of the joy of reading.

Writing

Writing opportunities are threaded throughout each lesson, and range from using "sound spelling" to write words in phonics lessons, to writing words and sentences to answer story questions, to writing creatively in response to children's literature. The level of challenge presented in each of these kinds of writing increases as children's skills grow.

In extended writing segments of the Reading Roots lesson called Adventures in Writing, students write about their thoughts and ideas prompted by the shared stories and literature read and discussed in class. Students practice using a variety of emergent-writing strategies that are structured so that they increase in difficulty, but, at the same time, allow them to express their thoughts and ideas from the very beginning of the program. Students celebrate their writing by sharing it with classmates and seeing it displayed in the classroom.

A READING ROOTS LESSON

Effective instruction is like a piece of cloth—it is woven with strands of essential content on the one hand, and powerful instructional process on the other. The fabric does not hold together unless both are right. The Reading Roots lesson is built to teach the critical content described above using research-proven instructional processes that involve a fast-paced, multimodal presentation followed up with rich, varied, and highly engaging opportunities to practice skills to fluency. For some students, mastery of the goals of beginning reading takes a great deal of practice. The Reading Roots lesson is designed to ensure that they get it. The focus on effective instructional processes is probably the feature that most differentiates Reading Roots from other beginning reading programs, as it does not differ in content from most programs currently in use. The instructional processes used in Reading Roots, now in its third edition, were developed and researched over a period of twenty years, and have been proven in randomized experiments to be significantly more effective than traditional classroom instruction for teaching reading (Borman, Hewes, Overman, & Brown, 2003).

One focus of the SFA research is on how best to support teachers in using effective instructional practices. The structure of the Reading Roots lesson reflects the integration of feedback from thousands of teachers and hundreds of teacher trainers and coaches. It is highly structured (sometimes called "scripted") because structure enables teachers to achieve the rapid pace of instruction and interaction that make it effective. (It also reduces the time that teachers need to spend in preparation.) In the hands of an experienced teacher, Reading Roots is dynamic and exciting, and pulls in every child.

A ninety-minute Reading Roots lesson has four major parts—FastTrack Phonics, Shared Stories, Story Telling and Retelling (STaR), and Language Links. The activities in the lesson usually are completed over three to four days of instruction, depending on the time needed by the particular group to master the story.

Specific activities in each part of Reading Roots are discussed below. As students progress through the sequence, some of the activities described may no longer be used, but the basic parts of the lesson remain.

FastTrack Phonics

FastTrack Phonics is a systematic phonics program that enables students to master the following skill areas:

Auditory Segmenting

Auditory Blending

Letter-Sound Correspondences for 44 phonemes and 60 graphemes

Word-Level Blending

Sound Spelling

Auditory Blending and Segmenting

It is important for beginning readers to grasp the concept that all words are made up of separate units of speech (phonemes). When students hear the word "cat," they hear three sounds (/c/, /a/, and /t/), quickly blended together to sound like one unit of speech. When students learn that there are three separate sounds in the word, it logically follows that there are three graphemes needed to represent the sounds. Understanding the concept of the separability of sounds in words gives students the building blocks for understanding how the alphabet works to represent those sounds and how words represent speech. Understanding this concept also minimizes the chances that students will rely on memorization to read words; it encourages them to apply their blending and segmenting skills to read and write words.

In FastTrack Phonics, Alphie the puppet teaches students how to orally blend and segment sounds in an enjoyable and interactive way. Students learn that Alphie speaks a "special language" called "Alphie Talk." Alphie says words slowly, so that each distinct phoneme is heard. Students listen to the separate sounds, then say them quickly together to figure out the word that Alphie is saying. Students also are taught to speak in Alphie's special language. They listen to a word, and then break it down to say each sound. Students work with partners to "guess" Alphie's words and practice Alphie Talk, so that

Figure 4.1   Alphie the Puppet

every student participates and learns together. Students look forward to Alphie's daily visits, which keep them motivated and interested in the lessons.

The concepts of auditory blending and auditory segmenting are introduced using puppet skits presented on video in the lesson. A section of a lesson showing this auditory blending and segmenting activity is shown in Figure 4.1 and Figure 4.2.

Letter-Sound Correspondence

To become fluent readers, students need to establish an automatic connection between letters and sounds. The forty-four phonemes (distinct sounds) in English words are represented by sixty separate graphemes (individual letters or letter groups). Students use their knowledge of these letter-sound correspondences to sound out and read words. The more automatically they link letters to sounds, the easier it is to begin blending sounds into words and reading.

Students are introduced to each new grapheme with a lesson process that helps them first focus on the sound itself, isolating the initial sound after they name familiar pictures and objects. After students have heard the sound of the letter being presented in words, they explore the shape of their mouths while producing the sound. This gives students another cue to help them hear and "see" the separate sounds. As they learn to feel the changes in the shapes of their mouths and watch the teacher's mouth, they more clearly understand the concept that words are made up of groups of sounds. This understanding is crucial for decoding. Later, as they begin to write words, students are able to use the feeling of change between sounds as an important way to recognize separate sounds. The "Making the Sound" activity used to help students make the sounds of "a," "n," and "c" is shown in Figure 4.3.

When students can isolate a sound, they learn the letter shape that represents it with a Key Card, which shows a picture that prompts the sound in the shape of a letter. For example, the letter "a" Key Card shows a red apple in the shape of the letter "a." Students then learn an alliterative phrase that uses the phoneme represented and describes the picture. For "a," students learn the alliterative phrase "Alphie asks for apples."

Figure 4.2   Sample Lessons From Say-It-Fast and Break-It-Down

The Sound and the Furry: Say-It-Fast

Students learn to blend sounds into words.

Say-It-Fast

Video Option: *The Sound and the Furry*—Introduce and play the Say-It-Fast segment. **Today we are going to put sounds together to make a word and Say-It-Fast. This game will help us sound out words when we read. Let's watch Alphie and his friends play Say-It-Fast.**

Teacher Presentation—Another thing you will learn about Alphie is that he can speak in a special language. When Alphie says a word, he says it very slowly so you can hear every sound. With just a little practice, I bet you'll be able to understand every word he says. Alphie is going to say a word now. Listen carefully, and I'll show you how to figure out what he's saying.

Have Alphie say the word "me" by separating the two sounds. It should sound like this: **/m——→m/ /ē——→ē/.** Don't stretch the sounds so that they run together. Each letter sound should be separate, and you should have clear pauses between each sound. Ask Alphie: **Can you say that one more time?** (repeat)

Say: **I can figure out what Alphie is saying by putting those sounds together.** Repeat the word as Alphie did a few times, shortening the length of time that you pause between sounds. **/m——→m/.....**/ē——→ē/, /m——→m/... /ē——→ē/, /m——→m/. /ē——→ē/, /m——→m ē——→ē/, me. That's it! The word Alphie said was "me." Do you think that you can understand Alphie's special language now? Let's try it. Alphie will say a word in Alphie Talk. I want you to tell me the word that he's saying.**

Have Alphie make the sounds in each word. Give students a few seconds to think, then point to the class as a cue. Students will respond with the word using whole group response.

Whole Group Response →

2 Phonemes		3 Phonemes	
/m-y/	*my*	/m-a-d/	*mad*
/a-m/	*am*	/m-a-ke/	*make*
/m-e/	*me*	/m-i-ss/	*miss*

The Sound and the Furry: Break-It-Down

Students learn to segment words into sounds.

Break-It-Down

Video Option: *The Sound and the Furry*—Introduce and play the Break-It-Down segment. **Today we are going to take a word and Break-It-Down. This will help us when we spell words. Let's watch Alphie and his friends use Break-It-Down.**

Teacher Presentation—I can see that you understand Alphie's special language. Now we're going to see if we can <u>speak</u> in Alphie's special language. Remember that when Alphie says a word, you can hear each sound that he says. I'm going to show you how you can hear the different sounds in words that you say.

Place your fingers on your cheeks. **When I put my hands here, I can feel how my mouth changes when I make different sounds. Listen to this word, and watch my mouth. mmmmaaaannn.** Slightly exaggerate the shape of your mouth as you do this. **Did you see my mouth change as I made different sounds? Good. I can also feel the different sounds with my hands. Let's all try it.**

Ask students to place their fingers on their cheeks. **Say "man."** [man] **Now: /m⎯⎯→ma⎯⎯→an⎯⎯→n/.** [responses] **Did you feel your mouth change shape as you made the different sounds? Good. Let's try another one. Say "sad." Now say this: s⎯⎯→sa⎯⎯→ad.** [responses] **Did you feel your mouth change as you made the different sounds? Great! Let's say some more words in Alphie's special language.** Say each word in a normal tone of voice, and ask students to repeat it. Then, separate each sound in the word with the students. Say the entire word one more time. Gradually reduce your support until students can stretch the words by themselves. Students can keep their hands on their cheeks during this exercise so that they can feel the different sounds in the words.

When students feel their mouths changing shape, they know there is another sound. Remind students to use this strategy when needed to help segment words.

Whole Group Response ⎯⎯⎯→

2 Phonemes		3 Phonemes	
my	/m-y/	**moon**	/m-oo-n/
me	/m-e/	**mitt**	/m-i-tt/
moo	/m-oo/	**mat**	/m-a-t/

Say: **You did a great job with Alphie Talk today. Learning to speak like Alphie will help you read and write!**

Figure 4.3 The "Making the Sound" Activity

Making the Sound—Ask students to say /a/. **Today's sound is /a⎯⎯→a/. You have to open your mouth wide to say /a⎯⎯→a/, don't you? /a⎯⎯→a/ is a loud sound. It's not like /m⎯⎯→m/. /m⎯⎯→m/ is quiet. /a⎯⎯→a/ is loud. Let's all say that sound together. /a⎯⎯→a/. Put your hand on your mouth to feel how wide it is. Let's stretch it again, /a⎯⎯→a/.**

Making the Sound—Ask students to say /n/. **When I say /n⎯⎯→n/, the tip of my tongue goes behind my top teeth and I send air through my nose. Let's all stretch that sound. /n⎯⎯→n/.**

Making the Sound—Ask students to say /c/. **When I say /c...c...c/, I can feel the sound way in the back of my mouth. It sounds a lot like another sound we know, /g/. But /c/ is a little different. When I say /c...c...c/, I can feel air coming out. I can put my hand in front of my mouth and feel the air. Let's say this sound together.** Bounce the /c/ sound three times with the students. Make sure that they do not add a vowel sound and say "cuh."

The letter itself is printed on the back of the Key Card so students can make an easy transition from responding to the picture cue to responding to the actual letter (as shown in Figure 4.4).

When a letter shape is introduced, students are taught a rhythmic writing cue related to the Key Card picture. The writing cue for the letter "a," for example, is "Left around the apple and down the leaf. /aaa/." Students recite this writing cue while writing the letter—an activity that connects the visual image, the sound, and the shape of the letter at the same time, ensuring a strong connection between a sound and the letter that represents it. The letter shape is reinforced with a quick multisensory practice. Students "write" the letter in the air, on their hands, and on a partners' hand.

To make the presentation even more memorable, a one-minute animation of the Key Card that dramatizes the associated sounds is presented. For "a," a child is sitting under an apple tree, and an apple drops on his head. He yells /aaaaa/, making the letter sound. All of the animations used have a twist that makes them funny and more memorable. In the "a" animation, after three apples drop on the child (and he yells /aaaa/ three times), he gives the tree a shake in frustration. Of course, all of the apples fall on him at that point. These activities create visual and auditory mnemonics that help develop an instant connection between the letter and its sound.

Because an automatic association between the phoneme and grapheme is desired for rapid decoding of words, many practice opportunities are provided using quick routines

Figure 4.4   A Letter "a" Key Card

that can be frequently repeated. As a whole group, students review the letters previously presented in a pocket chart at the beginning of each class. Students say the sounds together as the teacher points to the Key Cards, so every student is involved. Students practice further in partnerships using Partner Practice books, taking turns being the reader and listener. This activity is quite different from reinforcement using a worksheet. Partners are responsible for monitoring each other's progress, helping as needed, and initialing their partners' books when they have identified all of the sounds quickly and correctly. The teacher's role in this practice step is key, as the teaching is not finished when the presentation is completed—only when all students have mastered the content. Teachers move among the partners as they work, and initial students' books as they verify the success. Certificates of success go home with students as they successfully demonstrate success with each of seven groups of graphemes, to celebrate their mastery. A section from a lesson showing the introduction of a letter/sound and related partner practice is shown in Figure 4.5 (FastTrack Lesson 16).

Word-Level Blending

Word-level blending is the ability to look at a word, recognize the graphemes, make the sound for each grapheme, and then put the sounds together to say the word. The understanding and use of letter-sound correspondence, auditory blending, and auditory segmenting are prerequisite skills that enable students to perform this more complex task. Using letter-sound correspondence knowledge, students are able to look at the different graphemes in a word and make the sound for each one. Auditorily blending previously practiced skills enables students to blend sounds together to form words. Students combine these skills to begin to read words.

However, reading does not happen automatically when students learn letter-sound correspondences and auditory blending and segmenting skills. The jump from auditory blending to visual blending to recognizing a familiar spoken word is a complicated one, and therefore is carefully scaffolded. Students are directly taught to blend sounds and make words. To start, the teacher chooses letter cards from a deck of 3" x 4" cards ("m," "a," and "n," for example) and displays the cards spaced apart in a pocket chart. As the teacher points to each card, the students make the sound for that letter. As the activity continues, the teacher moves the cards closer together, so students say the sounds faster, stretching the stretchable sounds. The cards are finally pushed together completely, and students blend the sounds into a recognizable word and say it in a sentence (see Figure 4.6).

Thus, the blending deck provides the bridge between students' knowledge of letter-sound correspondence (certain letters make certain sounds) and their auditory blending experience (sounds blend into words) so they can read words. The word-level blending process is referred to as Stretch and Read. This reminds students that they need to "stretch" words by saying each sound, then put the sounds together to read them.

Blending is sometimes more challenging for students when a word begins with a short sound like /k/ and /p/. Figure 4.7 shows how teachers address this issue in Reading Roots.

To foster mastery, partner practice again follows the direct teacher instruction. Students work with their partners to gain individual fluency and mastery of the blending process. The Stretch and Read process is an easy one to describe, but for many students, the ability to use the process automatically when reading takes months of practice. Repetition and reinforcement of Stretch and Read takes place with the introduction of each new letter/sound combination. The cycle of presentation, guided practice, partner

Figure 4.5 Introduction of a Letter Sound

Hear Sounds

Show each Phonics Picture Card below, name the picture, and ask students to say the name after you. Then cue students to tell you the initial sound in each word.

bed   rope   up   key

Hear the New Sound

Key Card

Key Picture—Have Alphie introduce the Key Card and the alliterative phrase: **The floppy flower falls.** Say the phrase with the students, stretching the /f/ sound in each word.

Pictures and Objects—Use My Turn, Your Turn to review the names of the pictures on the Phonics Picture Cards. Say the name and have students say it after you. Stretch the initial sound in each word.

fire   fish   fan   five

Making the Sound—Ask students to say /f/. **When I say /f——→f/, my teeth touch my bottom lip.** Put your teeth in the /f/ position and point to them. **I make the /f——→f/ sound by pushing air between my teeth. /f——→f/. Let's say that sound together. /f——→f/**

Think-Pair-Share

Students' Words—Use Think-Pair-Share to have students share words that begin with /f/.

Introduce the New Shape

📺
Animated Alphabet: /**f**/

Video Option: Animated Alphabet—Introduce and play the Animated Alphabet segment. **Let's see our Key Card in action. This will help us remember how the shape and sound go together.** After playing the segment, ask the students what sound the letter makes.

Write the letter "f," and show students how the letter looks like the picture. Build a strong connection between the picture and the letter.

f

Write Letters

New—Trace your finger over the picture as you recite the writing cue three times: **Curve down the flower and then across the leaves, /f———→f/.**

Have students write the letter in the air while they recite the cue.

Have students write the letter on a partner's hand, arm, or back.

Have students write the letter in their Partner Writing Books and check each other's work.

Familiar—Choose five previously learned letters, based on student need, or use the list below. Say the sound for each letter. Have students write those letters in their Partner Writing Books.

> **/a/** as in apple   **/u/** as in ugly   **/b/** as in back
>
> **/s/** as in simple   **/i/** as in igloo

Have partners check each other. When they have finished, write any letters that students need to review on the board, going over the Key Card and writing cue.

Review the letter cues for three letters of your choice or use the list below. Have students write each letter several times using the letter cue.

> **/m/** as in Maria   **/d/** as in Dan   **/t/** as in Tom

Lesson 16

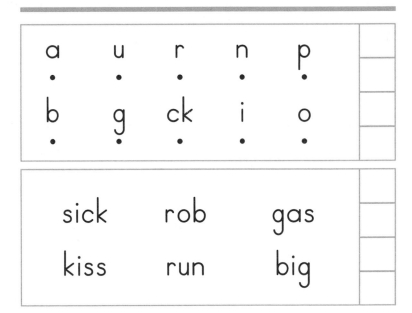

Figure 4.6   The Blending Deck

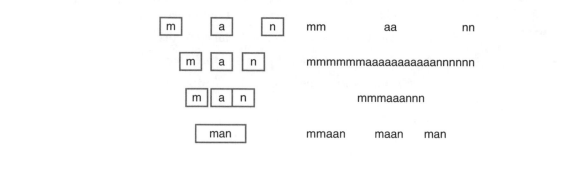

Figure 4.7   Blending Word Model

Teacher Note: Blending words with an initial sound that is bounced is more difficult than blending a word that starts with a stretched sound. Model like this, moving the blending cards closer together with each step:

/c…a——→a…t/
/c..a——→a..t/
/c.a——→a.t/
/ca→at/
cat

If students have difficulty, cover up the final "t" card and have students work with the first two cards. Tell your students: **The /c/ sound is so short it needs a piggyback ride on the /a/. Get your mouth ready to say the /c/ but don't say it. Now say them right together without stopping in between. /ca——→a/.** Use this process when students have difficulty blending any bounced sounds at the beginning of words.

practice with teacher monitoring, and feedback is repeated many times, and students gain confidence with each cycle. An example of the partner practice activity for Stretch and Read from FastTrack Phonics Lesson 16 is shown in Figure 4.8.

Students' blending skills are developed further using an activity called "Quick Erase," which focuses students on the importance of each sound in the word (as shown in Figure 4.9).

Figure 4.8 Stretch and Read

Stretch and Read

With the teacher—Choose three to five Green Words from previous lessons for students to Stretch and Read.

With a partner—Have students turn to Lesson 16 in their Partner Practice Booklets, and read the words together and make up sentences. Partnerships who successfully read the words fluently can make up sentences using the words. Then they can move on to the challenge words in the following box.

Move around the class to observe, provide positive feedback, and assist as needed. Initial partner books when **both** partners can read the words successfully. When finished, have the class read the words together (or randomly select a partnership to read them). Ask a partnership to share a sentence they have made up. Ask another partnership to read the challenge words.

sick	rob	gas
kiss	run	big

*runs	*dogs	*pats

fun	fit	fan

Figure 4.9   Quick Erase

Quick Erase

Today we're going to play a new reading game.

Write the word "sad" on the board. Put your finger under the first letter. Say: **Make the sound for each letter as I touch it.** Slowly touch each letter, and make the sounds with the students. Then, sweep your finger under the entire word, and read it with the students.

Now I want to see if I can trick you. I'm going to change one letter in this word. Do you think you can read it if I change one letter? Change the letter "d" to "t." Sound out the word by touching each letter and making its sound. Then, read the whole word. Continue to change one letter at a time and read the words with the students. Gradually reduce your support so that students can read on their own. Use the following word sequence:

sad...sat...sit...bit...bat

Sound Spelling

Students have been using Stretch and Read to help them understand the concept that words are made up of separate sounds that can be identified, then blended together to read words. Now they are ready to build on that concept to *write* words. Students learn to identify the separate sounds in words, then write the letters for each of the sounds they hear. Two activities allow students to learn and practice these concepts.

The first activity is a game called Stretch and Count. In Stretch and Count, the teacher says a word, and the students use Alphie Talk to break it down into its separate sounds and count the sounds on their fingers as they do this. Students will use the fingers of one hand to count the sounds in words and use the other hand to hide their fingers. When the entire class has had a chance to stretch and count the word, the teacher has students check with their partner, and then finally asks the class to show their count all together. Students then "write" (using an index finger) the grapheme that represents each phoneme on one of the fingers that have counted.

When students know how to use Stretch and Count to segment a word, they are ready to learn the second activity. Stretch and Spell is a continuation of Stretch and Count; students count the sounds they hear in words, then write the letter for each sound in their Partner Writing Books. Students check each other's work to provide feedback and assistance to each other.

As with Stretch and Read, Stretch and Spell may take some time to develop at first. Reading Roots teachers provide extensive modeling in the early stages, and make sure that students are participating in *each part* of the process—from repeating the word, to stretching and counting the sounds, to writing the letters. Developing skill using Stretch and Spell gives a powerful boost to students' confidence in decoding, as it reinforces letter/sound correspondences using a variety of modalities. Examples of instructional segments for sound spelling are shown here to demonstrate the progression of skills from simple to more and more complex. In each segment, the teacher provides modeling, partner practice, peer assessment and support, and whole class review (as shown in Figure 4.10).

Students practice writing words using sounds as a daily activity to reinforce previously learned skills while acquiring new ones. By the end of the Reading Roots sequence, students have learned that sounds can sometimes be represented by more than one

Figure 4.10 Sound Spelling

Example A—FastTrack Phonics Lesson 17

Stretch and Count

Model using Alphie Talk to Stretch and Count to say the word **mad.** Show students how to feel the sounds by putting their hands on their lips. Then have students use Stretch and Count to identify and count the sounds in the word. Be sure to have students

- count to themselves hiding their fingers,
- check with their partners,
- then show their fingers as a class.

Then have students use their magic pencils to write each letter on one of their fingers.

Continue the activity with the following words:

    not   **it**   **man**

Example B—FastTrack Phonics Lesson 21

Stretch and Count/Stretch and Spell

Have students use Stretch and Count to identify and count the sounds in the word "mat." Students will write the letters on their fingers with their magic pencils. Say: **Now that you can count the sounds and make the letter shapes, you are ready to write the words. Watch me as I Stretch and Spell /m——→m/.** Write the letter "m" on chart paper or a chalkboard. **The next sound is /a——→a/. I can write the letter for /a——→a/.** Write the letter "a" on the board. **The last sound is /t/. I can write the letter for /t/.** Write the letter "t" on the board. Touch each letter, make the sound for that letter, and then say the word. **/m——→ma——→at/. I just wrote the word "mat."**

Example C—FastTrack Phonics Lesson 29

Stretch and Count/Stretch and Spell

Have students use Stretch and Count, then Stretch and Spell, to sound out and write the following words.

With the new letter:

    quit   **quiz**   **quack**

With familiar letters:

    bath   **yet**   **sing**

Whole Group Response

After partners have checked each other's work, have the whole class dictate how to spell the words as you write them on the board.

Figure 4.11 FastTrack Phonics Lesson 56

Write Words and Sentences

Write Words—Have students use Stretch and Spell to write the words below. Use words in a simple sentence, if necessary, to make sure students hear the word correctly. Have partners check each other's work after you have finished the list. Have the class Stretch and Spell the words together.

Tell students to use /ou/ as in shout.

> **loud**
>
> **proud**
>
> **found**

Tell students to use /ow/ as in cow.

> **now**
>
> **brown**
>
> **frowned**

Write a Sentence—Tell students that Cami has brought a sentence that she thinks they can write. Have Cami read this sentence.

> **Henry saw a brown cow.**

Discuss the meaning of the sentence briefly. Have partners work **separately** and write the sentence in their Partner Writing Books. Have the sight word posted. When everyone is finished, have a partnership tell you how to write this sentence on the board. Celebrate everyone's growing skills.

---

grapheme, and they need to learn the customary spelling of individual words. Long vowel sounds are frequently represented by more than one grapheme. For instance, the long "o" sound can be written, "oa," "ow," or "o_e." Students first practice writing groups of words like bone, home, rope, and note, or grow, show, and own, or boat, toad, coat, and groan, which all use the same grapheme for the sounds. After these groups are firmly established, the teacher tells the students which "o" grapheme to use when using Stretch and Spell to write a word. An example of this process is shown in Figure 4.11.

Still later, students are asked to choose which of two graphemes they think is right for each of several words containing the long "o" sound to demonstrate that there is a customary spelling that can be learned. The goal at this point is not to teach students to spell a specific group of words correctly, but to teach the skill of using grapho-phonemic knowledge to work out a very limited number of choices and then to select the customary spelling. An example of this process appears in Figure 4.12.

Assessment of Progress

Individual student progress on six phonics-related skills is assessed about every two weeks using brief oral and written activities incorporated into the lesson sequence. The data are used to plan for review lessons for the class as a whole as well as for planning extra instructional time that may be needed for individual students to ensure that they do not fall behind. A sample of the assessment record form that follows FastTrack Phonics lesson 20 is shown in Figure 4.13.

Figure 4.12   Promoting Grapho-Phonemic Knowledge

Alphie's Story

What do (we)* see when we go to the sea? (We) see seashells, seagulls, green crabs, and seaweed. If you look in the sand, you may find the real teeth of a shark. Sometimes (we) see seals. I feed them (bread) and peanuts with my brother, Neal.

The sea is easy to reach. Just walk three blocks to the end of our street. The breeze from the nearby sea blows each leaf on the big oak trees. It is a (great) place to (be)*!

List Words on the Chart

When partners have completed the task, ask them to identify the different ways they saw the long e sound spelled ("ee" and "ea"). Tell the students that you will make a chart for Alphie that shows the different spellings.

Make a chart with two columns on a piece of chart paper. Label one column "ee" and the other column "ea." Then divide the chart paper into three rows. Your chart paper will look like this:

	ee	ea
①		
②		
③		

The students have this chart in their Partner Practice Booklets. Have them label the columns "ee" and "ea."

Reread the passage with the students a sentence at a time. Stop at the end of each sentence and ask: **Did you find any /ē/ words in that sentence?** Use Think-Pair-Share to call on a partnership to share their answer. Remind the students to check their papers to see if they have identified and circled the word in their books.

As the students share long /ē/ words, you will write them on the chart paper as follows:

Alphie's Words

	ee	ea
①	see, green, teeth, feed, three, street, breeze	sea, real, Neal, reach, each, leaf
②	trees	seals, easy
③		seashells, seaweed, seagulls, peanuts, nearby

Underline the base word and circle the ending for the row 2 words.

Place the Alphie card on top of the chart paper. **These are Alphie's spelling words. Alphie's spelling words have the /ē/ sound spelled with "ee" or "ea."**

Figure 4.13 Sample Assessment Record

Fast Track Phonics for Roots, Volume 1 | **Class Assessment Form**

Student	Break-It-Down Say-It-Fast		2nd Assessment												Stretch and Read Total	
	Out of 5	Out of 5	c	k	ck	u	r	b	f	e	l	h	ng	Out of 21	Out of 10
1															
2															
3															
4															
5															
6															
7															
8															
9															
10															
11															
12															
13															
14															
15															
16															
17															
18															
19															
20															
Class Total															

Date _____

Shared Stories

Learning to use the alphabetic principle to unlock words is only one step in the process of reading, as the goal of reading is not to identify a word, but to understand a written communication. In Reading Roots, students start creating meaning as they read as soon as they have learned enough letter-sound correspondences to make words. After learning the sounds for "m," "a," "s," and "d," students and teacher together read a Shared Story in which text read by the teacher sets the stage for student-read, phonetically regular text. The page shown in Figure 4.14 illustrates the use of teacher text to create a more interesting story at this very early stage. In addition to teacher text, "readles" (simple line drawings used to substitute for words) provide additional meaning. Students discover that they have the power to read something on their own and understand its meaning.

Partner reading is used to guide the reading of all stories in Reading Roots. The process is introduced in a step-by-step process in the early Reading Roots lessons, using puppet videos to model the process. Students learn how to take turns reading, and how to play roles as reader and listener. As the reader reads the student text, the listener assists if the reader struggles, and then restates what was read. Students then switch roles and reread the page.

The partner reading process is carefully taught, modeled, and reinforced throughout the sequence of Reading Roots lessons. It is a powerful tool that engages all children actively in reading new text on their own daily, and in responding to another student's reading as well. The partnership requires students not only to read, but to think about their reading and provide explanations about both meaning and decoding to each other as they work together. Errors become learning experiences rather than public failures, allowing confidence and skill to grow.

As students learn systematic strategies for finding the meaning of words, sentences, and stories, they take increasing responsibility for their reading. As students are able to read more and more words, the need to use teacher text to create an interesting story is decreased, and the use of teacher text and "readles" diminishes. The pages in Figures 4.15 and 4.16 are from stories read during the second and third quarters of the program.

During the last quarter of the Shared Story sequence, readles and teacher text are no longer used. A page from a story used in the last quarter is shown in Figure 4.17. Figures of complete shared stories appear in Appendices 4.1 and 4.2.

The Shared Stories in Reading Roots are organized into four thematically related sections. Level 1, Stories 1–15, is built around a first grader named Matt, his dog Sad Sam, and his friends in the neighborhood. Level 2, Stories 16–25, describes the experiences of a group of students in Ms. Stanton's first grade class. Level 3, Stories 26–37, focuses on a group of city children and their visits to relatives in the country as the seasons change throughout the year. Level 4, Stories 38–48, takes students around the world introducing both traditional folk and fairy tales, along with informational text. Expository narratives present information about Sweden, Nigeria, China, Colombia, and the U.S. Each factual story is followed by a tale from that country. Level 4 presents a very challenging reading experience that is designed to make a transition between the carefully sequenced Reading Roots lessons and the novels or basals that students will use in Reading Wings.

Parallel stories are provided for Reading Roots Shared Stories 4–37, for use by teachers and tutors to reinforce the skills in the initial story. A parallel story uses the same letters and sight words, but introduces additional phonetically regular words in different stories.

Figure 4.14   Sample Page From Level 1—*The Ice Cream Man*

Tim gets another ice cream cone. He gives his first one to Sad Sam.

Sad Sam likes ice cream!

Tim is ☺ (happy).

Sad Sam is ☺ (happy).

The ice cream man is ☺ (happy)!

The ice cream man is not mad anymore. He is glad that Sad Sam is cleaning up the mess. And Sad Sam is glad to get a treat!

Figure 4.15   Sample Page From Level 2—*Bug Alert*

By now, all the children are standing and yelling. Mr. Cob stops the bus and comes to look.

The bus stops.

Mr. Cob stands up.

He says, "Kids, stop and sit!"

Tanya sobs, "But my bug!

I cannot see it!"

Figure 4.16   Sample Page From Level 3—*Cupcakes*

Granddad led the way into the kitchen.

Deena got a bowl, spoons, a cup, and the cake tin.
Then Granddad read the list:
"Two eggs, milk, and butter."
Jim got the eggs. Fran got the milk. Jack got the butter.
"We have all that we need to bake," said Granddad.

Figure 4.17   Sample Page From Level 4—*Anansi, the Spider*

When the three spiders were alone, Anansi sniffed.
He could smell chicken with peanuts. It was coming from
the East Village. Anansi was delighted!
    He said,
        "I *would* like to go to the feast.
        I *should* go, but I don't know when it is.
        I *could* go if . . ."
    Anansi stopped.

Figure 4.18   Guided Partner Reading

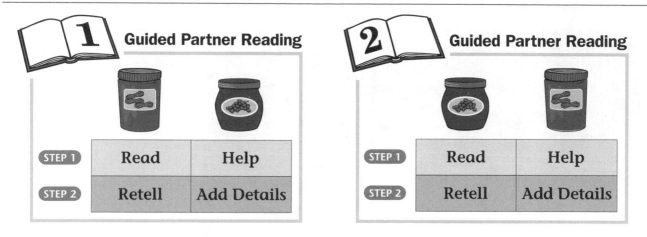

Reading for Comprehension

The focus of a Shared Story lesson is to engage students in using their phonics skills to read meaningful text, so the presentation of a Shared Story begins with a preview of the story to invite a discussion about what will be coming. After introducing important story vocabulary using the process described in the next section, guided reading of the story begins. On each page, the teacher reads the teacher's text to create student interest in finding out what comes next. Then students read the page with their partner using the process shown on the cue card in Figure 4.18. Each student is designated as either "peanut butter" or "jelly." First, the partner designated "peanut butter" reads the page and retells what he or she read. The "jelly" partner helps if "peanut butter" gets stuck, and then adds details to the retelling. Then, "jelly" reads and retells, and "peanut butter" helps with problems and adds details to the retelling.

As students are reading, the teacher moves from pair to pair, listening, guiding students in helping one another, and reteaching as needed.

When both partners have read the page, the teacher pulls the class together to discuss the page to ensure that students understand what they read, make predictions about what will happen, and enjoy the story as it unfolds. Comprehension is further reinforced as students write the answers to comprehension questions at the end of each story.

Story Vocabulary

Story vocabulary is introduced to ensure that the meaning of words key to the story is understood. Phonetically regular words, called "Green Words," are introduced using the sound blending process used in the FastTrack Phonics segments. Words students cannot decode using known sounds are presented as "Red Words," which students need to know by sight. Red Words are presented using a routine called "Say-Spell-Say" in which the teacher shows the word, says it, and has the students say it as a group, spelling it letter by letter while they clap once for each letter. After spelling it, the class says it together once again.

The meaning of words that might be new to some students is illustrated using picture cards, objects, pantomime, demonstration, or in a sentence. Additional supports are provided to help ensure that English language learners know words that might be difficult

Figure 4.19   Word Play

Lisa enters.

Lisa: Hi Lynn.

Lynn: Hi Lisa. Watch out for the mud! Watch out for the suds!

Lisa: Can I mop? I want to mop!

Lisa pulls mop.

Lynn: Stop! Don't tug my mop!

for them, so that word meaning does not hinder their understanding. Short video segments called "Word Plays" show a skit in which characters use the key story words in a memorable context. For instance, the words "mop" and "suds" are introduced in a brief humorous sequence showing two sisters who argue over the privilege of mopping the kitchen floor on a rainy day (as shown in Figure 4.19).

Partner practice once again follows teacher instruction to ensure that every student can decode the Green Words, and remember the Red Words. Students practice reading words in word lists and then in sentences with their partners before they begin to read the story. To provide additional reinforcement, the entire class reads the "Word Wall," a collection of current and previous story words, at the end of each lesson.

Fluency

The development of fluent reading is also strongly supported by the partner reading process. Rereading for fluency is an explicit part of the lesson sequence, and partners help ensure that fluency is achieved. Partnerships are rewarded for joint success with celebratory notes home. Fluency is first measured and celebrated at the word level, then the sentence level, and finally the page level.

The concept of fluent reading of text is introduced in four stages as the lessons progress. First, students are introduced to reading with accuracy, then smoothly using sentence punctuation as a guide, then with expression, and finally at an appropriate rate. Each stage is introduced with a puppet video (see Figure 4.20) that explains and models the skill, to provide explicit examples as well as motivation.

In the final quarter of the Reading Roots sequence, reading rate is highlighted in the Reading Olympics. Students work to build accuracy, smooth reading, expression, and rate and to achieve the expected rate of sixty words correct per minute by the end of first grade. Two-minute, partner-supported practice sessions are conducted daily. During these practices, one partner reads a teacher-selected section of about sixty words from a Shared Story while the other student listens for errors. When students can read a section with two or fewer errors, they are eligible to read for the teacher and receive an Olympic medal if they succeed at reaching the goal for that story. The teacher gradually shortens

Figure 4.20   Puppet Video for Fluency

Alphie is in training for the Reading Olympics. He is wearing sweats, with a towel around his neck. He is in the alley. There is a table and chair in the background. The monster and Cami are his assistants. Bob Barker is interviewing him.

BOB: Welcome back. Once again we're visiting with Alphie as he gets ready for the Reading Olympics. Alphie, how's the fluency practice going?

Alphie is bobbing up and down as if he is jogging in place.

ALPHIE: It's going great Bob. I'm getting all the words right. I'm reading smoothly. But to really read fluently I also have to read with expression and at the right speed.

BOB: What will you practice today, Alphie?

ALPHIE: I'm ready to work on reading with expression, Bob.

BOB: Reading with expression? Never heard of it. What does that mean?

CAMI: Reading with expression means to read like you're telling a good story. You don't want to sound like a robot.

BOB: No, of course not. It would be boring to sound like a robot while you were reading a story. Can you share one of your training tips for reading with expression?

the practice time as student fluency grows, until students are successfully reading at a rate of sixty words correct per minute.

The use of this highly structured partner-based practice routine to develop fluency has many advantages for both the reader and the listener. As readers, students get many opportunities to receive feedback on their fluency, and to see their skills grow. As listeners, students learn to evaluate accuracy in their partner's reading, which develops their understanding of the definition and importance of accuracy. Frequent celebration of growth in fluency motivates students to work actively to improve, both in class and at home. An example of the monitoring and celebration notes is shown in Figure 4.21. This note is sent home to parents when students have successfully completed the tasks listed.

Each Shared Story lesson for Levels 1, 2, and 3 in Reading Roots takes three days. A sample three-day lesson sequence for the Shared Story segment of a Reading Roots lesson is shown in Figure 4.22.

Figure 4.21 Fluency Flyer

LEVEL 3 **Fluency Flyer** for Reading Roots

Name_____

Story	Title	My partner and I can read a page accurately.	My partner and I can read a page smoothly and with expression.
32	Home with a Cold		
33	Slippery Steps		
34	The Ice Storm		
35	Did That Tree Eat My Kite?		
36	Who Is Wilfred?		
37	Planting Seeds in May		

Dear Parents: The mark beside the story title shows that your child has read the story successfully.
Be sure to celebrate this progress!

Figure 4.22 Shared Story Lessons

Lesson 18 Shared Story Sequence
Day 1

YOU WILL NEED

Shared Story 18: *Fang*

Picture Cards *(See margin list.)*

Key Card: "f"

Word Cards

Readles

DVD/Video *(optional)*

Reading Strategies

Previewing

Predicting

Key Card

"f"

Animated Alphabet

The Sound and the Furry

Green Words

fun	fangs	sniffs
fast	bumps	will
off	stack	fat
ruff	gasp	fit

Red Words

go	rolls	say

Readles

leaves   jungle gym

Monitor

Shared Story

Previewing

- **Let's preview the story by thinking about the title and the cover picture. Remember, that will help us understand the story better when we read it.**

- Display the book. **The title of this story is *Fang*. I see a girl, Lana** (point), **on the cover of the book. I also see a dog.** (Point.) **I think Fang must be the name of the dog. I know that fangs are long teeth that animals have. I can see two fangs on the dog.** (Point.)

Word Presentation

- **Let's practice the special letter we'll see a lot of in today's story.** Display the Key Card for "f," or play the Animated Alphabet segment(s) for Lesson 18 of *Reading Reels*. (optional) Have students review the alliterative phrase and practice the sound.

- **Now let's practice reading some words.** Show the video segments for Finger Detective and Sound It Out for Lesson 18. (optional)

- Select three to five Green Words to Stretch and Read with students.

- Use Say-Spell-Say to introduce the Red Words. Post the words on the Word Wall; then review all of the Red Words with the class. Keep the Red Words posted until students learn them.

NOTE: *If any letter sounds appear to be especially difficult for the students to remember in the context of words, make a note of them, and spend extra time on those letter sounds in tomorrow's phonics lesson.*

- Present the story's Readles one at a time, stating the words and asking students to repeat them.

Partner Word and Sentence Reading

- Have students sit with their partners. Distribute the Shared Stories and have partners turn to the inside front cover. Partners will take turns reading story words and sentences to each other.

- If partners have finished reading the words to each other, have them continue and read the sentences to each other.

- Monitor partners and assist with Stretch and Read or partner work behaviors as necessary. Remind students to say every sound in the Green Words.

Teacher Shared Story

Guided Partner Reading

- **Now we're ready to read the story with our partners.**

- Make sure each partnership has a Reading Strategy Card to refer to while they are reading.

- Have partners turn to the first page of the book. Make sure that partners are prepared to read, with their books open to the first page.

- Follow the Guided Partner Reading steps to lead the class through a reading of the entire book.

  1. The teacher reads the teacher text at the top of the page.
  2. Partner A reads the first sentence of the student text. Partner B helps.
  3. Partner B reads the next sentence of the student text. Partner A helps.
  4. Partners continue to alternate sentences until they have read the entire page.
  5. The partners reread the entire page in unison.
  6. The teacher leads a short discussion of the page to check comprehension.
  7. The whole class reads the page in unison. (optional)

- Repeat steps 1–7 for the remainder of the pages. Monitor the partner reading to make sure partners continue to alternate reading sentences on each page and help one another effectively.

Discussion Questions

> After you have read the story, review the Picture Cards (or selected cards) with students. Display each card, name each, and have students name each card with you.

Think–Pair–Share

- Ask the discussion questions listed on the inside back cover of the Teacher Shared Story. Have students use the Think-Pair-Share strategy to discuss and listen to each other's responses. Call on different partnerships to share their answers with the class.

  1. Why does Tanya fall in the mud? *[Tanya falls in the mud because Fang bumps into her.]*

  2. Why is Paco scared? *[Paco is scared because the dog has fangs.]*

  3. What did Fang do to help the children? *[Fang found the ball in a stack of leaves.]*

- Ask whether their predictions were accurate or the book surprised them.

- **Let's talk about the characters in the story. Characters are people, or even animals, in a story. This story had a new character, a character we had never seen before. Who was the new character in this story?** (T-P-S)

Reading Celebration

- Have two students read a page or two of the story for the whole class. Have the entire class provide applause and praise. Present students with Reading Celebration certificates. Choose two students to read for tomorrow's Reading Celebration.

- Close with a quick review of the Word Wall.

Figure 4.22 (Continued)

Day 2

YOU WILL NEED

Shared Story 18:
Fang
DVD/Video
(optional)

Think-Pair-Share

Shared Story

Story Review

Yesterday we read a new story. I want to see how much you remember about that story. Review the title of the story and the characters with students. Ask the following review questions. Call on different partnerships to share their answers with the class. (T-P-S)

1. **What are the children doing at the beginning of the book?** *[The children are playing during recess.]*

2. **Why is Tanya mad at Fang?** *[She is mad because Fang pushed her into the mud.]*

3. **How does Fang help the children?** *[Fang finds the ball for them.]*

4. **Who are the new characters in the story?** *[The new characters are Fang and Lana.]* **How would you describe them?** (T-P-S)

Partner Reading

The Sound and the Furry

- Show the video segment for Fluency: Smooth. (optional) **Let's see how Alphie practices reading smoothly as he trains for the Reading Olympics.**

- Have partners turn to the first page of the book. Make sure that the partners are prepared to read, with their books open to the first page.

Focus on Accuracy →

- Have students practice reading the story together. Partners should take turns reading each page aloud and monitoring for accuracy. Have students reread the page until they read every word correctly.

Monitor →

- Monitor students as they practice Partner Reading. Listen as students read, prompting and reinforcing accurate reading.

- After Partner Reading, choose a partnership or two to read one page of the book with accuracy. Have the class congratulate the team on the students' success.

Partner Story Questions

- Have students turn to the inside back cover of the Shared Story. Discuss and model how students will read and answer the comprehension statements and questions with their partners. Model writing an answer with the class before students begin writing individually. Do not complete the activities as a class.

Monitor →

- Circulate to monitor partner work.

Reading Celebration

- Have two students read a page or two of the story for the whole class. Have the entire class provide applause and praise. Present students with Reading Celebration certificates.

Day 3

YOU WILL NEED

Shared Story 18:
Fang
DVD/Video
(optional)

Shared Story

Partner Word and Sentence Reading

- Have students sit with their assigned partners. Distribute the Shared Stories and have students turn to the list of story words on the inside front cover.

- **We're going to practice reading words and sentences from the story together. Take turns reading each of the words with your partner. When you and your partner are finished, I want you to think about which word was easiest to read and which word was hardest to read. Then you can read the sentences.**

- Visit partnerships as they read together and listen for pairs of students who can read the entire list of story words accurately. Place a sticker on each student's Fluency Flyer beside the story title.

- Call on partnerships to tell you which words were easy to read and which words were hard. Review reading strategies to sound out difficult words or to read sight words.

Focus on Expression →

Partner Reading

- **Now we're going to read the story with our partners, just like we did yesterday. Since we already know what happens in the story, we can use this time to practice reading in our best storytelling voices. A storytelling voice is nice and smooth. Let's practice that today as we read the story together.**

Monitor →

- Monitor students as they participate in Partner Reading. Make sure that students are taking turns and reading with expression.

- Model specific reading strategies and reading with expression as necessary.

- Allow students to read previous Shared Stories. Record mastery as students demonstrate it on any Shared Story.

All Together Now

- **You did a great job reading! Now we'll all read the story together so we can show how well we can read. Let's use a nice, clear voice that sounds as though we're telling a story.**

- Lead a Guided Group Rereading of the story. Focus on reading the story with rich expression. Celebrate by leading a class cheer. Choose two students to read for tomorrow's Reading Celebration.

- Show the second *Between the Lions* segment for Lesson 18. (optional)

Story Telling and Retelling (StaR)

Children's literature opens a world of imagination and information that delights and engages students. It also provides a rich opportunity to expand students' vocabulary as well as their understanding and use of complex language. The Story Telling and Retelling (StaR) lesson engages students in lively and interactive twenty-minute readings of stories selected from children's literature that are thematically linked to the Shared Stories.

A simple cooperative learning tool, Think-Pair-Share (T-P-S), is used to involve students in the reading. In T-P-S, the teacher poses a question, gives students a few seconds of think time, and then asks them to discuss their thinking with a partner. After a brief partner discussion, the teacher asks several pairs to share with the class. This simple technique increases the engagement of all students in the reading of the story, as it requires that every one of them must put into words a response to what has been read. Students cannot be passive listeners.

Other tools are used to elaborate vocabulary in the story, especially for English language learners. Cues for the use of pointing, pantomime, Total Physical Response (TPR), and use of objects to define a word are included in the lesson.

STaR lessons are structured to model the use of background knowledge, reasoning, prediction, and higher-order thinking skills to increase story comprehension. STaR books are read using a two-day lesson plan. An example of the STaR process for the reading of a story called *A River Dream* is shown in Figure 4.23.

As shown in the lesson example, Day 1 of the lesson focuses on activating students' background knowledge related to the story and models the use of previewing to build comprehension. Then the teacher reads the story interactively with the class. Teacher questions focus on ensuring that students understand the characters, setting, and plot of the story. On Day 2, teacher and class reread and retell the story, extending children's understanding. Teacher questions on the second day of each STaR cycle challenge students to identify and discuss characters' feelings and motivations, and connections of the story to other events and books. Retelling takes many forms. Students may sequence cards showing major events in the story, may take the roles of characters and act out a key scene, or may invent a new ending for the story.

Writing activities are an integral part of each STaR lesson. In Level 1, students use sentence stems and other scaffolding methods to write short, complete sentences that express their ideas about the stories or story themes. In Level 2, students gradually progress to thinking about and discussing their ideas with partners to write their own descriptive sentences. In Level 3, students become adept at writing their own sentences and are introduced to graphic organizers as a way to think about and organize their writing ideas. In Level 4, Adventures in Writing takes place over a two-day period. The first day comprises prewriting and drafting activities, and the second day comprises editing and polishing activities. A sample from Level 3 is shown in Figure 4.24.

Language Links

Language Links lessons are designed to promote students' oral-language development. Students learn and practice new vocabulary, practice using varied sentence structures, and learn effective ways to communicate ideas, feelings, and experiences in complete sentences with partners, team members, and the class.

Each Language Links lesson requires students to work with partners or teams on a content-based language function engaging every student in active use of language. The range of activities in Level 2 is shown in Figure 4.25.

These peer activities ensure that authentic communication is taking place, that students are challenged, and that a variety of language models are available to encourage development of speaking and listening skills; they encourage students to use elaborated language in complete sentences rather than single words or short phrases. The lessons are carefully scaffolded to support the success of all students whether they are articulate speakers or English language learners. An example of a Language Links lesson is shown in Figure 4.26.

Figure 4.23 The StaR Process

Day 1

STaR Story:
A River Dream
Picture Cards
(See margin list.)

Objective

Students will look for story clues to determine if the main characters' experiences are real or just a dream.

Think-Pair-Share →

Think-Pair-Share →

Think-Pair-Share →

STaR

A River Dream By Allen Say

Summary: *A young boy named Mark is sick with a fever. While he is resting at home, a package arrives from his Uncle Scott. It is a metal box used to hold trout flies for fishing. The trout flies appear to be magical; they fly out of the box and lead Mark to the river for an exciting fishing adventure with his uncle. Several clues in the story help the reader conclude that this colorful fishing adventure is just a dream.*

Before Reading: Story Preview

- Display the front cover of the book and read the title, author, and illustrator. Use the following text as a guide to preview the story.

- **This story tells about a fishing trip. Let's pretend that our class is going on a fishing trip. What kinds of things will we need to bring with us on our trip? Let's talk to a partner about the things we will need to go fishing.** (T-P-S)

During Reading: Interactive Story Reading

Read the story interactively, discussing the vocabulary words in context and asking the comprehension questions listed below.

page 5	**This is Mark.** Point.
page 6	**Mark is looking out the window. He sees a river.** Point to the river. **Let's look back at the first picture of Mark's room.** Turn to page 4. **In this picture, is there a river outside of Mark's window? No. It looks like a neighborhood outside of his window. What do you think is happening outside?** (T-P-S)
page 9	Point to the boat. **Here is a boat. What do you think Mark is going to do?** (T-P-S)
page 10	Point to Uncle Scott. **Here is Mark's uncle. What is he doing?**

page 13	**Look at Uncle Scott. He has a fishing rod** (point) **and a net** (point) **to help catch fish.**
page 16	**What do you think will happen?** (T-P-S)
page 19	**What do you think Mark has caught?** (T-P-S)
page 24	**If Mark wants to keep the fish, he needs to kill it with the knife.** Point to the knife. **What do you think Mark will do?** (T-P-S)
page 26	**Why do you think Mark put the fish back in the water?** (T-P-S)
page 31	**Look out the window. Do you see the river anymore? What do you think happened?** (T-P-S) Display the cover of the book. **The title of this book is *The River Dream*. Do you think this title gives us a clue about the book? What does it tell us?** (T-P-S)

After Reading: Story Structure Review

- Ask students the following questions. Guide students to answer questions using complete sentences.

(Continued)

Figure 4.23 (Continued)

Day 2

STaR

Story Review

- Review the title and author of the story as you display the book. **I am going to see how much you remember about this book**. Ask the following questions. Encourage students to answer in complete sentences.

Whole Group Response

Think-Pair-Share

- **Let's remember some things that happened in the story *The River Dream*. Did Mark really go fishing with his uncle?** (WGR) **How do you know?** (T-P-S)
- **Did Mark catch a fish in his dream?** (WGR) **What did he do with it? Why?** (T-P-S)

Interactive Story Retell

Reread the story with students, stopping to review as necessary, and ask the following comprehension questions:

page 5	**Is this part real or is it a dream?** *[It is real.]*

Whole Group Response

Think-Pair-Share

page 7	**Is this part real or is it a dream?** (WGR) **How do you know?** (T-P-S)
page 12	**Why did Uncle Scott let the fish go?** (T-P-S)
page 15	Point to each of the vocabulary items in the picture and have students name them. *[hat, rod, vest, net, line, boat]*
page 18	**What happens next?** (T-P-S)
page 26	**What would you do if you were Mark? Why?** (T-P-S)

Story Critique

- **I want to know if you would recommend this book to a friend. If you would recommend it, that means you like it and you think someone else would like it too. Raise your hand if you would recommend this book to a friend.** Call on some students to tell why they would recommend the book.

- **If you would NOT recommend this book to a friend, raise your hand.** Call on some students to tell why they would not recommend the book.

To start, the teacher models the desired language activity as well as the peer-centered activity. Students then talk with their partners so that all are actually speaking and using the desired activity. All students are encouraged to develop their language step by step. An expressive student would be encouraged to be precise, while a student who routinely spoke in one- or two-word sentences would be encouraged to speak in three- or four-word sentences.

Students' language development is assessed throughout the program with the SOLO, an acronym for Structured Oral Language Observation. It is a quick and informal assessment tool used to measure growth in students' oral language.

Each SOLO assessment is based on a STaR book, and assesses receptive vocabulary, expressive vocabulary, and oral expression in a brief one-to-one discussion of the story

Figure 4.24   Level 3—Lesson 36, Day 3

Writing

Planning

- Have students return to their seats. Distribute writing paper to each student. Students should copy the six questions (Who? What? Where? When? Why? How?) onto their papers. Have students plan their writing with their partners. Their first sentence should be about <u>what</u> their partner plans to do. Make sure that they also name their partner in the first sentence (to answer the question "Who?"). Point to "Who" and "What" on the chart and say: **What sentence can you use to tell <u>what</u> your partner is going to do this summer? Remember to also tell <u>who</u> your partner is in this first sentence. <u>Think</u> about it. <u>Say</u> it to a partner. Then <u>practice</u> it a few times.** Share a sentence of your own (Example: **Tim plans to go fishing.**), and then call on several partnerships to share their ideas with the class. Have them make a note on the scratch paper to help them remember their ideas.

Think, Say, Practice ⟶

- Go over the rest of the questions in the same way, giving students an opportunity to Think, Say, Practice the sentences that they will write and to make a note on their lists to help them remember.

Drafting

Think, Say, Practice ⟶

- Have students write three to six sentences for a newspaper article about their partners' summer plans. (If they write only three sentences, they can just include information about who, what, where, why, and when.) Remind students to use the Think, Say, Practice process to write their sentences.

- Circulate as they work, assisting with writing strategies as needed. Encourage students to write as much as they can.

- Bett's version of Adventures in Writing represents the minimum expectation for the writing assignment. Challenge students to describe their ideas fully and write as much as they can.

SOLO ⟶

- After students are engaged in their writing, administer the SOLO to two students.

Checking

Think-Pair-Share ⟶

Display the chart-paper version of Bett's Adventures in Writing. Tell students that Bett interviewed her friend Sam. Read each sentence slowly, and ask students: **Does that sound right to you?** Have students use the Think-Pair-Share strategy to discuss what changes need to be made. Use a colored pencil to make the changes directly on the chart paper.

Adventures in Writing

Prewriting

- Have students gather in front of the chart paper. Introduce the activity. **We have been reading and talking about newspapers. Today we are going to pretend to be newspaper writers. We are going to interview our classmates for a newspaper article about their plans for the summer. After we write our articles, we will put them in a class newspaper.**

- **First, let's think about the six important questions that we need to ask when we interview someone for a newspaper article.**

(Continued)

Figure 4.24 (Continued)

Objective

Students will interview classmates and write an article.

- Discuss the kind of information that you need to write a newspaper article. On the chart, write:

  Summer Plans

  Who?

  What?

  Where?

  When?

  Why?

  How?

- Have students sit with their partners.

- Invite students to interview their partners about their summer plans. They should ask their partners the six questions on the chart paper.

- Call on partnerships to share their information with the class. Jot down a few ideas on the chart to show how making a list can help you to prepare for writing. Model using partial sound spelling or placeholders for difficult words.

- **We have lots of ideas for our newspaper articles. Now let's try to write these ideas in sentences.**

Bett's Adventures in Writing

> # Summer Plans
>
> (Who & What)
> Sam plans to stay wet this summer.
> (When)
> He will swim this summer
> (Where)
> he will swim at the pool.
> He will play in the sprnklr at home.
> (Why)
> Sam like to swim a lot.

Corrections:

Sentence 1: No changes.
Sentence 2: Add a period to the end of the sentence.
Sentence 3: Capitalize the "h" in the word "he."
Sentence 4: Note that Bett didn't know all of the letters in "sprinkler," but you are glad that she included that word in her writing. Don't forget to change it.
Sentence 5: Add "s" to the end of the word "like."

- Have students read their writing to their partners to check it.

Celebrating Writing

- Select examples of students' work that demonstrate the different stages of writing. Share each piece with the class and point out the specific writing skills that the students are using.

Celebrate Progress

- Have students share their writing with new partners. Make sure students are responding to each other's work by making constructive comments and asking each other questions. Model this behavior if necessary.

- Select one or two students to share their writing with the class.

- Students who gain confidence in their writing will write longer and longer pieces. Celebrate growing confidence.

Figure 4.25 Language Links Activities

Reading Roots 3rd Edition Scope and Sequence

Language Links																		
Lessons	1	2	3	4	5	6	7	8	9	10	11	12	13	14	15	16	17	18
Oral Language Skills																		
Brainstorming	✔		✔							✔		✔						✔
Classifying									P									✔
Comparing		✔	✔						P	✔					✔			✔
Describing	P	✔	P	P		P	P	P		P	P	P	P	P	✔	P	P	P
Discussing		P		P	P			P		P	P	P	P	P	P	✔	✔	
Identifying	P	✔	P	✔	✔	✔		✔	✔		P	P	✔		✔	P	P	✔
Imagining							P	✔		✔		P			P			
Labeling									✔									✔
Pantomiming		✔				P				✔					P	✔		
Problem Solving															✔	✔		
Questioning	✔	✔	✔	✔	✔		P			✔		P	✔					
Reasoning		✔					✔	✔	✔		✔	✔	✔		✔	✔		✔
Remembering	✔		✔		✔					✔			P				✔	✔
Sequencing																		
Theorizing															✔			
Vocabulary Building	✔		✔	✔		✔	✔	✔		✔	✔	✔	✔	✔	✔	✔	✔	P	✔

P = Primary focus   ✔ = Covered   **+** = Optional skill

conducted by the teacher with one or two students a day. This informal approach allows students to feel comfortable enough to express themselves and gives teachers an opportunity to observe and track language growth and development with a simple tool. An example for the SOLO for Lesson 18 is shown in Figure 4.27.

The SOLO starts slowly and comfortably as the teacher and student look though the STaR book. The teacher asks the student to point to five items on the pages, and then asks the student to say the name of the five items. Finally, the teacher asks the students several questions related to the story and rates the response.

SOLOs have a simple scoring system, and each question contains sample answers to help teachers determine how to score student responses. SOLO scores are recorded on the Reading Roots Assessment Summary for the Quarterly Planning form (see Chapter 2). They can also be recorded in the teacher's grade book or in student portfolios to provide a log of students' language development over a period of time.

SOLOs are administered on Day 3 of each lesson. While the class is engaged in their Adventures in Writing assignment, the teacher spends a few minutes with two students to complete the assessment.

Figure 4.26   Lesson 18, Day 2

Index cards*
Marker*

* Teacher acquired

Objective

Describe classmates.

Language Links

Modeling

- Write the following words on separate index cards:
  green   long tail   big teeth   friendly   swim

- **Today we are going to learn to play a new game called Who Am I? We can play this game by thinking about words that describe different people.**

- **I'm going to say some words that describe someone you know. When you think you know whom I'm talking about, raise your hand.**

- Show each index card and use the words in a sentence. (Example: **I am green. I have a long tail. I have big teeth. I am friendly. I can swim. Who am I?**) When students have raised their hands, invite them to respond in unison. *[Alphie]*

Guided Group Practice

- **Now we're going to think of some more words that describe students in the class.** Invite a student to sit or stand in the middle of the group. Ask the rest of the class to think of three or four words that describe the student. (Example: long hair, brown eyes, tennis shoes, earrings.) Write each word or words on a separate index card.

- Shuffle the cards and invite all of the students to stand up. **I am going to read each card. If the card tells something about you, you can remain standing. If the card does NOT tell something about you, you will sit down.**

- Read the cards, using each word in a sentence. (Example: **I have long hair. I have brown eyes. I have tennis shoes. I have earrings.**) Make sure that students remain standing or sit down as necessary. When you have finished reading the cards, ask the class: **Who am I?** Encourage the class to respond in unison: **I am _____.**

NOTE: *More than one student may remain standing.*

- Continue playing the game until you have created a set of cards for each student in the class (if time permits).

Partner Practice

- Collect all of the description cards and shuffle them. Have students sit with a partner and designate an A and a B in each pair. **I am going to read each of these cards. You need to decide if the card I read tells about your partner.**

- Read one of the cards (without a complete sentence this time.) **This card says "brown shoes." A's, look and see if your partner has brown shoes. If he does, you'll say: You have brown shoes. If he doesn't, you'll say: You don't have brown shoes.** Have A's talk to their partners.

- **Now B's, look and see if your partner has brown shoes.** Have B's talk to their partners.

- Continue to read the index cards to students. A's and B's will take turns telling each other if the phrase on the card describes them or not.

Review/Extension *If time permits*

Play another round (or more) of Who Am I? with the whole class as time permits.

Figure 4.27   Structured Oral Language Observation (SOLO) for Lesson 18

STaR Story   *SOLO—18*

I Miss Franklin P. Shuckles by Ulana Snihura and Leane Franson

Receptive Vocabulary

Display the illustrations on the pages listed below. Ask the students to point to the:

page 2	page 5	page 7	page 9	page 10
ball	**glasses**	**lunch**	**backpack**	**note**

Use this information as an informal tool to gauge how well the student is learning new story vocabulary.

Expressive Vocabulary

Display the illustrations on the pages listed below. As you point to each illustration ask: **What is this?**

page 1	page 2	page 13	page 14	page 15
door	**legs**	**cookie**	**tree**	**street**

Use this information as an informal tool to gauge how well the student is learning new story vocabulary.

Oral Language Production

Ask the students the following questions and score each one according to the 5-point rubric. Average the student's score on the Oral Language Production questions. Take this score into consideration when completing the Oral Language column of the Assessment Summary Form.

	Display	Ask	Sample Response
1.	page 2	**What is Franklin P. Shuckles doing?**	1. *No response* 2. *Franklin.* 3. *Franklin talking.* 4. *Franklin tells stories.* 5. *Franklin is telling stories to his friend Molly.*
2.	page 10	**What is Molly doing?**	1. *No response* 2. *Molly.* 3. *Molly. Note.* 4. *Molly writes a note.* 5. *Molly is writing a note to her friend Franklin.*
3.	page 21	**What happened in this picture?**	1. *No response* 2. *Molly. Franklin.* 3. *Molly. Franklin. Friends.* 4. *Molly and Franklin are friends.* 5. *Molly and Franklin are friends again. She wrote him another note and now everything is OK.*

SOLO 5-POINT RUBRIC 5–Student gives elaborated responses that use a variety of structures and frequently uses high-level vocabulary from lessons taught. **4**–Student gives complete, yet unelaborated responses and uses some high-level vocabulary. **3**–Student gives short responses with limited use of vocabulary. **2**–Student gives a limited or one-word response. **1**–Student gives no response.

Daily Schedules

The activities and time allocations for the activities described above in a lesson cycle are as follows.

Lesson Activities for Reading Roots—Levels 1–3

Day 1	Day 2	Day 3
FastTrack Phonics (20 min.)	FastTrack Phonics (20 min.)	FastTrack Phonics (20 min.)
Shared Story (30 min.)	Shared Story (30 min.)	Shared Story (30 min.)
STaR (20 min.)	STaR (20 min.)	Adventures in Writing (40 min.)
Language Links (20 min.)	Language Links (20 min.)	

Lesson Activities for Reading Roots—Level 4

Day 1	Day 2	Day 3	Day 4
Goal Setting (20 min.)	FastTrack Phonics (Optional—20 min.)	Fast Track Phonics (Optional—20 min.)	FastTrack Phonics (Optional—20 min.)
Shared Story (50 min.)	Shared Story (50–70 min.)	Shared Story (50–70 min.)	Shared Story (40–50 min.)
STaR (20 min.)	STaR (20 min.)	Adventures in Writing (20 min.)	Adventures in Writing (30–40 min.)

A teacher's guide to the full Reading Roots Lesson 18 is included in Appendix 4.1 on pages 131–151. Lesson 18 would be taught in the second or third month of the program.

LEE CONMIGO

Lee Conmigo ("Read with Me"), the Spanish beginning reading approach used in Success for All, is built on the same principles as Reading Roots and uses the same lesson structure and instructional processes. The reading materials used are created according to the same logic as the English materials, except that they follow a sequence of letter presentation appropriate to the Spanish language. The stories are again enhanced by context provided in a teacher-read portion of the story. Lee Conmigo lessons built around these stories teach both metacognitive and word attack skills using the same presentations, games, routines, and strategies as Reading Roots.

The one significant difference between Lee Conmigo and Reading Roots lies in the frequent use of syllables (rather than individual letters) as the major unit of sound in Lee Conmigo. Within the Spanish language, words are essentially made up of groups of syllables rather than groups of individual letters. The games and activities in Lee Conmigo have been adapted to take advantage of this. For instance, in Stretch and Spell, words are stretched a syllable at a time (lla ma) rather than a letter at a time as in English (c a t). Lesson 19 of Lee Conmigo is shown in Appendix 4.2 on pages 152–180.

Reading Roots

· · Lesson **18**

At a Glance

FastTrack Phonics

Refer to Phonics Manual.

Shared Story

Shared Story 18:
Fang

Letter Sound: /f/

Strategies/Skills:
Previewing
Predicting
Identifying and
describing new
characters

STaR

STaR Story:
*I Miss Franklin
P. Shuckles*

Objective:
Identify the story
problem and solution.

Background Words:
throw, catch, glasses,
sneeze, note, backpack,
lunch, seat

Story Words:
shares, recess, wave

Language Links

Describing:
Describe different
characters in the stories.
Describe classmates.

Adventures in Writing

Create a character
web. Write descriptive
sentences about a
person.

Homework

Read and Respond

Structured Oral Language Observation

Administer the SOLO to
two students on Day 3.

DAY 1

FastTrack Phonics

Refer to the *FastTrack Phonics Teacher's Manual.*

Complete a phonics lesson that is matched to your class assessment/skill level.

YOU WILL NEED

Shared Story 18:
Fang
Picture Cards
(See margin list.)
Key Card: "f"
Word Cards
Readles
DVD/Video
(optional)

Reading Strategies

Previewing
Predicting

Shared Story

Previewing

- **Let's preview the story by thinking about the title and the cover picture. Remember, that will help us understand the story better when we read it.**

- Display the book. **The title of this story is *Fang*. I see a girl, Lana (point), on the cover of the book. I also see a dog. Point. I think Fang must be the name of the dog. I know that fangs are long teeth that animals have. I can see two fangs on the dog.** Point.

Reading Roots

Story Skill

Identifying and describing new story characters. *(See Story Discussion.)*

Picture Cards

ball	fangs
dog	ground
hero	jungle gym
leaves	mud
recess	playground
teeth	St. Bernard
bushes	

Video Words 📺

go	fast
field	stack
rolls	bumps

Key Card 🗂

"f"

Animated Alphabet 📺

The Sound and the Furry 📺

Green Words

fun	fangs	sniffs
fast	bumps	will
off	stack	fat
ruff	gasp	fit

Red Words

go	rolls	say

Readles

leaves   jungle gym

---

*For students who need additional language development, choose **one** of the following options to continue previewing. If you do not have the video Word Plays for the Shared Stories, use Option A. If you plan to use the video, skip Option A and move on to Option B.*

Option A: Teacher Overview

- **Now let's look through the book to see if we can find out more of what this story is going to be about.**

- Display page 2. **I see children playing. It looks like Fang wants to play too.** Display page 3. **Fang is a big, big dog. It looks like he has knocked Tanya down! I wonder if Fang is a good dog or a bad dog?** (T-P-S) **We'll have to read the story to find out more about Fang.**

- **Let's review some words we will see in the story.** Display each Picture Card (or select Picture Cards from the list that you think will be most helpful to your students), name each, and have students repeat. Give a brief explanation of each card.

Option B: Video Word Play

- **Now we're going to watch a video that will help us find out more about the story.** Show the video Word Play for Shared Story 18 to introduce the story theme and vocabulary. Have students say the vocabulary words with the video during the "Do You Remember?" section.

- **Let's review some words we will see in the story.** Display each Picture Card (or select Picture Cards from the list that you think will be most helpful to your students), name each, and have students repeat. Give a brief explanation of each card.

Word Presentation

- **Let's practice the special letter we'll see a lot of in today's story.** Display the Key Card for "f," or play the Animated Alphabet segment(s) for Lesson 18 of *Reading Reels*. (optional) Have students review the alliterative phrase and practice the sound.

- **Now let's practice reading some words.** Show the video segments for Finger Detective and Sound It Out for Lesson 18. (optional)

- Select three to five Green Words to Stretch and Read with students.

- Use Say-Spell-Say to introduce the Red Words. Post the words on the Word Wall; then review all of the Red Words with the class. Keep the Red Words posted until students learn them.

NOTE: *If any letter sounds appear to be especially difficult for the students to remember in the context of words, make a note of them, and spend extra time on those letter sounds in tomorrow's phonics lesson.*

- Present the story's Readles one at a time, stating the words and asking students to repeat them.

Reading Roots   Lesson 18 • Day 1

Monitor

Partner Word and Sentence Reading

- Have students sit with their partners. Distribute the Shared Stories and have partners turn to the inside front cover. Partners will take turns reading story words and sentences to each other.

- If partners have finished reading the words to each other, have them continue and read the sentences to each other.

- Monitor partners and assist with Stretch and Read or partner work behaviors as necessary. Remind students to say every sound in the Green Words.

Teacher Shared Story

Guided Partner Reading

- **Now we're ready to read the story with our partners.**

- Make sure each partnership has a Reading Strategy Card to refer to while they are reading.

- Have partners turn to the first page of the book. Make sure that partners are prepared to read, with their books open to the first page.

- Follow the Guided Partner Reading steps to lead the class through a reading of the entire book.

  1. The teacher reads the teacher text at the top of the page.
  2. Partner A reads the first sentence of the student text. Partner B helps.
  3. Partner B reads the next sentence of the student text. Partner A helps.
  4. Partners continue to alternate sentences until they have read the entire page.
  5. The partners reread the entire page in unison.
  6. The teacher leads a short discussion of the page to check comprehension.
  7. The whole class reads the page in unison. (optional)

- Repeat steps 1–7 for the remainder of the pages. Monitor the partner reading to make sure partners continue to alternate reading sentences on each page and help one another effectively.

Discussion Questions

After you have read the story, review the Picture Cards (or selected cards) with students. Display each card, name each, and have students name each card with you.

Think–Pair–Share

- Ask the discussion questions listed on the inside back cover of the Teacher Shared Story. Have students use the Think-Pair-Share strategy to discuss and listen to each other's responses. Call on different partnerships to share their answers with the class.

  1. **Why does Tanya fall in the mud?** *[Tanya falls in the mud because Fang bumps into her.]*

  2. **Why is Paco scared?** *[Paco is scared because the dog has fangs.]*

  3. **What did Fang do to help the children?** *[Fang found the ball in a stack of leaves.]*

Reading Roots   Lesson 18 • Day 1

- Ask whether their predictions were accurate or the book surprised them.

- **Let's talk about the characters in the story. Characters are people, or even animals, in a story. This story had a new character, a character we had never seen before. Who was the new character in this story?** (T-P-S)

Reading Celebration

- Have two students read a page or two of the story for the whole class. Have the entire class provide applause and praise. Present students with Reading Celebration certificates. Choose two students to read for tomorrow's Reading Celebration.

- Close with a quick review of the Word Wall.

YOU WILL NEED

STaR Story:
I Miss Franklin P. Shuckles

Objective

Students will identify the problem and solution in the story.

Background Words

throw	catch
glasses	sneeze
note	backpack
lunch	seat

Story Words

shares	recess
wave	

STaR

I Miss Franklin P. Shuckles By Ulana Snihura and Leane Franson

Summary: *Franklin P. Shuckles is a young boy who moves in next door to a girl named Molly Pepper. They become friends over the summer, but only because she doesn't have anyone else with whom to play. She is initially put off by his funny glasses and his skinny legs. She also notices that he isn't good at playing sports. Over time though, she realizes that he has other admirable qualities such as being a great storyteller. She comes to enjoy spending time with him. When school starts the following fall, the other kids see only a shy, uncoordinated, and awkward boy. She's suddenly embarrassed to have him for her friend and eventually ends their friendship. It isn't long before she realizes that she has made a terrible mistake. She has to work very hard to get Franklin P. Shuckles to speak to her again. When he finally agrees to be her friend, she knows this time it will be forever.*

Before Reading: Story Preview

- Display the front cover of the book, and read the title, author, and illustrator. Use the following text as a guide to preview the story.

TPR

- **We are going to read a story about this girl. Her name is Molly. She is sad.** Point to the girl's face on the front cover. **See how sad she looks? Can you show me how you look when you are sad?**

- **Molly is sad because she misses her friend Franklin. I wonder where he is. What do you think has happened to Franklin?** (T-P-S)

Reading Roots

During Reading: Interactive Story Reading

Read the story interactively, discussing the vocabulary words in context and asking the comprehension questions listed below.

page 2   Point to the picture of Franklin trying to catch the ball. **It doesn't look like Franklin is good at playing baseball. Is it hard to make friends if you aren't good at playing games?** (T-P-S)

Think-Pair-Share   page 4   **Molly is friends with Franklin because there is no one else around. Do you think they will still be friends when school starts?** (T-P-S)

Think-Pair-Share   page 6   **Why did the kids at school laugh at Franklin?** (T-P-S) **What would you have done if they had laughed at your friend just because of the way he looked?** (T-P-S)

page 10   Point to the picture of Franklin. **How do you think he feels?** (T-P-S) **Can you show me what that feeling looks like?** (TPR)

What do you think will happen next? (T-P-S)

Think-Pair-Share   page 16   **Molly misses Franklin, doesn't she? What can she do to get him to talk to her again?** (T-P-S)

TPR   page 18   **How do you think Franklin will feel when he gets the note?** (T-P-S) **Can you show me what that feeling looks like?** (TPR)

After Reading: Story Structure Review

- Ask the students the following questions. Guide the students to answer the questions using complete sentences.

Whole Group Response   Display pages 1 and 2. Point to the picture of Molly on page 1. **Who is this?** (WGR) Point to the picture of Franklin on page 2. **Who is this?** (WGR)

Think-Pair-Share   - Invite the students to recall the story title, setting, story problem, and solution. Use a piece of chart paper, and list each heading down the left-hand side of the paper. Point to each heading, and then ask the students to recall the information using the Think-Pair-Share strategy.

YOU WILL NEED

Shared Story 18:
Fang

STaR Story:
*I Miss Franklin
P. Shuckles*

Chart paper*

Marker*

* Teacher acquired

Whole Group Response

Objective

Describe different
characters in two
stories.

Language Links

Modeling

- Draw a line down the center of a piece of chart paper. Write *"Fang"* at the top of one side and *"I Miss Franklin P. Shuckles"* at the top of the other side.

- **We are going to talk about the characters in both of the stories that we read. We will remember the characters in the story *Fang*** (display the book) **and the story *I Miss Franklin P. Shuckles*.** Display the book. **Remember, a character is a person, or sometimes an animal, in a story.**

- **I'm going to name a character. Then I'm going to think: Was that a character in *Fang* or a character in *I Miss Franklin P. Shuckles*?**

- **Paco. Let's see…Paco was a character in *Fang*, wasn't he?** (WGR) **I'm going to write Paco's name on the side of the paper that says *"Fang."***

Guided Group Practice

- **Now I'm going to say the names of more characters. When I say a name, think about which story the character was in. Raise your hand when you know the answer. Then you can all tell me your answer as a group. Let's try one for practice.**

- Say the name **"Franklin."** When students have raised their hands, guide them to say: **Franklin was a character in *I Miss Franklin P. Shuckles*.** Write the name "Franklin" in the appropriate column on the chart paper.

Whole Group Response

- Read the remaining list of characters in random order, and guide students to use Whole Group Response to tell you which story they belong in. Write the name of each character in the proper column on the chart paper.

Fang	*I Miss Franklin P. Shuckles*
Lana	Franklin
Fang	Molly
Paco	School Children

Partner Practice

- On a new piece of chart paper, draw a diagram like the one shown below. **We are going to choose one character from the two stories we read. We'll write the name of the character here in the middle of the circle.** Point. **Then we'll talk to our partners to think of words that describe the character.**

- Select a student to choose one character from the list you just made. Write the character's name in the circle, then allow partners some time to think of words to describe the character. Write their responses around the circle, adding more lines to the circle if necessary.

Reading Roots   Lesson 18 • Day 2

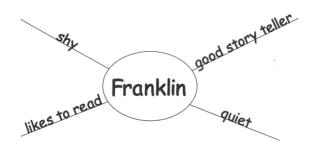

* Continue to have students select characters and discuss them. Complete a new character web for each character.

Review/Extension *If time permits*

Remove the character webs you completed with the class. Without showing students the webs, read the list of descriptive words. Challenge students to recall which characters you are describing.

Homework

Have students read the words and sentences on the inside front cover of the Shared Stories to family members several times. Ask them to return the Shared Story and the Read and Respond forms to school with signatures and comments from their listeners.

D A Y   2

FastTrack Phonics

Refer to the *FastTrack Phonics Teacher's Manual*.

Complete a phonics lesson that is matched to your class assessment/skill level.

Shared Story 18:
Fang
DVD/Video
(optional)

Think-Pair-Share ⟶

Shared Story

Story Review

Yesterday we read a new story. I want to see how much you remember about that story. Review the title of the story and the characters with students. Ask the following review questions. Call on different partnerships to share their answers with the class. (T-P-S)

Reading Roots

1. **What are the children doing at the beginning of the book?** *[The children are playing during recess.]*

2. **Why is Tanya mad at Fang?** *[She is mad because Fang pushed her into the mud.]*

3. **How does Fang help the children?** *[Fang finds the ball for them.]*

4. **Who are the new characters in the story?** *[The new characters are Fang and Lana.]* **How would you describe them?** (T-P-S)

Partner Word and Sentence Reading

- Have students sit with their assigned partners.

- Distribute the Shared Stories and have partners take turns reading the words and sentences on the inside front cover.

- Monitor the partners as they read to each other. Make sure the partners trade places so each has a chance to read while the other listens and monitors.

- As you visit partnerships, listen for pairs of students who can read the entire list of story words accurately. Place a sticker on each student's Fluency Flyer beside the story title.

Partner Reading

The Sound and the Furry

- Show the video segment for Fluency: Smooth. (optional) **Let's see how Alphie practices reading smoothly as he trains for the Reading Olympics.**

- Have partners turn to the first page of the book. Make sure that the partners are prepared to read, with their books open to the first page.

Focus on Accuracy →

- Have students practice reading the story together. Partners should take turns reading each page aloud and monitoring for accuracy. Have students reread the page until they read every word correctly.

Monitor →

- Monitor students as they practice Partner Reading. Listen as students read, prompting and reinforcing accurate reading.

- After Partner Reading, choose a partnership or two to read one page of the book with accuracy. Have the class congratulate the team on the students' success.

Partner Story Questions

- Have students turn to the inside back cover of the Shared Story. Discuss and model how students will read and answer the comprehension statements and questions with their partners. Model writing an answer with the class before students begin writing individually. Do not complete the activities as a class.

Monitor →

- Circulate to monitor partner work.

Reading Celebration

- Have two students read a page or two of the story for the whole class. Have the entire class provide applause and praise. Present students with Reading Celebration certificates.

Reading Roots   Lesson 18 • Day 2

Between the Lions

- Conduct a rapid review of the Word Wall.
- Show the first *Between the Lions* segment for Lesson 18. (optional)

STaR Story:
I Miss Franklin P. Shuckles

Story Map Poster

Think-Pair-Share ⟶

STaR
Story Review

- Encourage the students to recall the story problem and solution in *I Miss Franklin P. Shuckles.*

Interactive Story Retell

- Reread the story with the students, stopping to review as necessary, and ask the following comprehension questions:

page 1   **Why did Molly play with Franklin in the beginning of the story?** (T-P-S)

page 4   **Why does Molly like to play with Franklin now?** (T-P-S)

page 11   **Why did Molly write that note to Franklin?** (T-P-S)

page 21   **How did Molly fix her problem?** (T-P-S)

- **One of the things I learned from this book is that we should be nice to people, no matter what they look like. Do you agree?** (WGR) **Let's listen to a song that tells about something nice we could say to our friends at school.**

- Play "Hello, Good Morning" from the *Songs and Sounds* CD. Encourage the students to listen and sing along.

Story Critique

Encourage the students to think of reasons why they would or would not recommend the story. Have them write a story recommendation as a class.

Index cards*
Marker*

* Teacher acquired

Objective
Describe classmates.

Language Links
Modeling

- Write the following words on separate index cards:
  green   long tail   big teeth   friendly   swim

- **Today we are going to learn to play a new game called Who Am I? We can play this game by thinking about words that describe different people.**

- **I'm going to say some words that describe someone you know. When you think you know whom I'm talking about, raise your hand.**

- Show each index card and use the words in a sentence. (Example: **I am green. I have a long tail. I have big teeth. I am friendly. I can swim. Who am I?**) When students have raised their hands, invite them to respond in unison. *[Alphie]*

Reading Roots   Lesson 18 • Day 2

Guided Group Practice

- **Now we're going to think of some more words that describe students in the class.** Invite a student to sit or stand in the middle of the group. Ask the rest of the class to think of three or four words that describe the student. (Example: long hair, brown eyes, tennis shoes, earrings.) Write each word or words on a separate index card.

- Shuffle the cards and invite all of the students to stand up. **I am going to read each card. If the card tells something about you, you can remain standing. If the card does NOT tell something about you, you will sit down.**

- Read the cards, using each word in a sentence. (Example: **I have long hair. I have brown eyes. I have tennis shoes. I have earrings.**) Make sure that students remain standing or sit down as necessary. When you have finished reading the cards, ask the class: **Who am I?** Encourage the class to respond in unison: **I am _____.**

NOTE: *More than one student may remain standing.*

- Continue playing the game until you have created a set of cards for each student in the class (if time permits).

Partner Practice

- Collect all of the description cards and shuffle them. Have students sit with a partner and designate an A and a B in each pair. **I am going to read each of these cards. You need to decide if the card I read tells about your partner.**

- Read one of the cards (without a complete sentence this time.) **This card says "brown shoes." A's, look and see if your partner has brown shoes. If he does, you'll say: You have brown shoes. If he doesn't, you'll say: You don't have brown shoes.** Have A's talk to their partners.

- **Now B's, look and see if your partner has brown shoes.** Have B's talk to their partners.

- Continue to read the index cards to students. A's and B's will take turns telling each other if the phrase on the card describes them or not.

Review/Extension *If time permits*

Play another round (or more) of Who Am I? with the whole class as time permits.

Homework

Ask students to read the comprehension questions and discuss the answers with family members several times. Have them return the Shared Stories and Read and Respond forms to school with signatures and comments from their listeners.

D A Y 3

FastTrack Phonics

Refer to the *FastTrack Phonics Teacher's Manual.*

Complete a phonics lesson that is matched to your class assessment/skill level.

Shared Story

YOU WILL NEED

Shared Story 18:
Fang
DVD/Video
(optional)

Partner Word and Sentence Reading

- Have students sit with their assigned partners. Distribute the Shared Stories and have students turn to the list of story words on the inside front cover.

- **We're going to practice reading words and sentences from the story together. Take turns reading each of the words with your partner. When you and your partner are finished, I want you to think about which word was easiest to read and which word was hardest to read. Then you can read the sentences.**

- Visit partnerships as they read together and listen for pairs of students who can read the entire list of story words accurately. Place a sticker on each student's Fluency Flyer beside the story title.

- Call on partnerships to tell you which words were easy to read and which words were hard. Review reading strategies to sound out difficult words or to read sight words.

Partner Reading

Focus on Expression →

- **Now we're going to read the story with our partners, just like we did yesterday. Since we already know what happens in the story, we can use this time to practice reading in our best storytelling voices. A storytelling voice is nice and smooth. Let's practice that today as we read the story together.**

Monitor →

- Monitor students as they participate in Partner Reading. Make sure that students are taking turns and reading with expression.

- Model specific reading strategies and reading with expression as necessary.

- Allow students to read previous Shared Stories. Record mastery as students demonstrate it on any Shared Story.

Reading Roots   Lesson 18 • Day 3

All Together Now

- **You did a great job reading! Now we'll all read the story together so we can show how well we can read. Let's use a nice, clear voice that sounds as though we're telling a story.**

- Lead a Guided Group Rereading of the story. Focus on reading the story with rich expression. Celebrate by leading a class cheer. Choose two students to read for tomorrow's Reading Celebration.

Between the Lions

- Show the second *Between the Lions* segment for Lesson 18. (optional)

Objective

Students will create a character web to help them write descriptive sentences about someone they know.

Adventures in Writing

Prewriting/Group Practice

- Have students gather in front of the chart paper. Draw a blank character web on the chalkboard or on a piece of paper. **I am going to write some words around this web that tell about someone we know. I wonder if you can guess who it is?**

- Write the words "brown," "fuzzy," "four paws," and "friendly" on the character web. Read the words to the students and have them guess about whom you are writing. When students have guessed the character Bett, write her name in the middle of the web.

- Repeat the activity above using Cami as the character. Use the words "small," "insect," "has wings," and "yellow."

- **These webs tell something about Bett and Cami. Now I want you to help me make one that tells about the dog Fang. We'll use the web to help us write some sentences about Fang.**

- Draw another character web and write "Fang" in the middle. **Let's think of some words that describe Fang.** Call on students to share their words with you and write them on the web. Model using sound spelling and other writing strategies as you write the words. When you have recorded several ideas on the web, say: **Now I have lots of ideas to help me write some sentences about Fang. I can use the words to think of sentences.** Point to a word on the web (Example: "big"). **Here is the word "big." I can make a sentence with this word that tells about Fang. I can say: "Fang is big."** Have the class repeat. **Here are some more words: "bushy tail." I can make a sentence with those words too. I can say: "Fang has a bushy tail."** Have the class repeat. Continue to demonstrate how to take the words and use them to make complete sentences. Have the class repeat each sentence. Model writing one or two sentences below the web.

Partner Practice

Planning

- Have students return to their seats. **Now it's your turn. You're going to start by making a web that tells about Fang.** Distribute copies of the blackline master to the students. Have them write the word "Fang" in the middle of the web. If you are not using the blackline master, have students draw their own webs.

- **Think of some words that describe Fang. Write each word at the end of one of the long lines on the web.** Give students some time to write descriptive words about Fang. (Make sure that you have removed your chart-paper web so students will write their own words rather than copy yours.)

- When students have finished writing, say: **Now I want you to choose one of the words on your character web. Put your finger on the word you chose.**

- **Now I want you to think about how you would use that word in a sentence. Say the sentence softly to yourself; then say it to a partner.**

- Pause while students practice their sentences. Continue the process two or three more times.

Drafting

- **Now you're ready to begin writing some sentences about Fang.** Circulate as students are writing to assist and encourage them. Remind them of different writing strategies and model them if necessary. Encourage and guide students to use sound spelling. Remind students to start their sentences with a capital letter and to end them with a period.

SOLO

- After students are engaged in their writing, administer the SOLO to two students.

Checking

Have students check their sentences by reading them to themselves and then to their partners. Encourage students to comment and ask questions about their partners' sentences.

Celebrating Writing

- Select examples of students' work that demonstrate the different stages of writing. Share each piece with the class and point out the specific writing skills that students are using.

- Have students share their writing with new partners. Make sure students are responding to each other's work by making constructive comments and asking each other questions. Model this behavior if necessary.

- Select one or two students to share their writing with the class.

Homework

Students should take the Shared Stories home and read them to family members several times. Have them return the Read and Respond forms to school with signatures and comments from their listeners.

Name_____

STaR Story
SOLO—18

I Miss Franklin P. Shuckles by Ulana Snihura and Leane Franson

Receptive Vocabulary

Display the illustrations on the pages listed below. Ask the students to point to the:

page 2	page 5	page 7	page 9	page 10
ball	**glasses**	**lunch**	**backpack**	**note**

Use this information as an informal tool to gauge how well the student is learning new story vocabulary.

Expressive Vocabulary

Display the illustrations on the pages listed below. As you point to each illustration ask: **What is this?**

page 1	page 2	page 13	page 14	page 15
door	**legs**	**cookie**	**tree**	**street**

Use this information as an informal tool to gauge how well the student is learning new story vocabulary.

Oral Language Production

Ask the students the following questions and score each one according to the 5-point rubric. Average the student's score on the Oral Language Production questions. Take this score into consideration when completing the Oral Language column of the Assessment Summary Form.

	Display	Ask	Sample Response
1.	page 2	**What is Franklin P. Shuckles doing?**	1. *No response* 2. *Franklin.* 3. *Franklin talking.* 4. *Franklin tells stories.* 5. *Franklin is telling stories to his friend Molly.*
2.	page 10	**What is Molly doing?**	1. *No response* 2. *Molly.* 3. *Molly. Note.* 4. *Molly writes a note.* 5. *Molly is writing a note to her friend Franklin.*
3.	page 21	**What happened in this picture?**	1. *No response* 2. *Molly. Franklin.* 3. *Molly. Franklin. Friends.* 4. *Molly and Franklin are friends.* 5. *Molly and Franklin are friends again. She wrote him another note and now everything is OK.*

SOLO 5-POINT RUBRIC 5–Student gives elaborated responses that use a variety of structures and frequently uses high-level vocabulary from lessons taught. **4**–Student gives complete, yet unelaborated responses and uses some high-level vocabulary. **3**–Student gives short responses with limited use of vocabulary. **2**–Student gives a limited or one-word response. **1**–Student gives no response.

Fang

Story by Laura Burton Rice
Illustrations by Jennifer Clark

Green Words (Phonetic):

fangs	bumps	fat	off
stack	ruff	sniffs	gasp
fit	will	fast	fun

Red Words (Sight):

go	rolls	say

Practice reading these sentences.

Tanya kicks the ball.

She runs fast to get it.

A fat dog bumps into Tanya.

Paco says, "The dog has fangs!"

Scott, Tanya, and Lana are playing with a ball during recess.

Scott rolls the ball.
BAM!
Tanya kicks it.
She runs fast.
Lana says, "I will get the ball."

Scott and Tanya look for the ball in the bushes. Suddenly, Scott sees something.

"Look, Tanya!" gasps Scott.
Tanya looks.
She sees a big, fat dog.
The dog runs fast.
It bumps into Tanya.
She falls in the mud.

"Ick!" says Tanya. "Mud is not fun.
Go, dog!"
The big dog sits.
He pants.

Paco sees something that scares him.

Paco says, "See the dog's fangs!"
"FANGS!!" says Tanya.
The big dog says, "RUFF!"
The kids get on the [jungle gym].
"Can we fit?" asks Paco.

Lana runs fast.

"Fang!" Lana says.

"Fang is my dog.

He is not bad," says Lana.

Lana explains that Fang is gentle, even though he has big teeth.

Lana says, "Fang is a fun dog.

He likes kids."

The kids get off the  .

jungle gym

All of a sudden, Derrick has an idea.

Derrick says, "Can Fang get the ball?"
Lana nods.
"Get the ball, Fang!" says Lana.

Fang puts his nose to the ground. He sniffs everything, trying to find the ball.

Fang runs.
He sniffs.
He digs in a stack of .
The kids say, "Fang got the ball back!"

Fang is a hero. He has found the missing ball!

1. Did the dog have fangs?

_____

_____

2. Was the dog big and fat?

_____

_____

3. Did the kids like Fang?

_____

_____

4. Did Fang like the kids?

_____

_____

_____

Lee Conmigo   **Lección 19**

Vistazo de la lección

Oídos y Sonidos	Leamos juntos	Hablemos juntos	Escritura compartida
Referirse al Manual del maestro.	**Cuento** *Sapo y Sepo son amigos*	**Objetivos** Discutir diferentes razones para escribir una carta y explicar el porqué. Identificar	**Objetivo** Escribir una carta de tres oraciones en la que se comunique a un amigo
Cuento compartido	**Objetivo** Establecer	semejanzas y diferencias entre uno	porqué su amistad es especial.
Cuento compartido 19 *La nueva alumna*	comparaciones y contrastes entre dos personajes.	mismo y los amigos.	**Tarea**
Sonido de la letra /l/	**Palabras del cuento**	Describir en detalle porqué un amigo es	Leer y responder
Sílabas /la/, /le/, /li/, /lo/, /lu/	sendero, imaginar, reojo, desgraciado	alguien especial.	**Sistema de observación del lenguaje oral**
Estrategias/Destrezas Referirse a la lección.			Aplicar el SOLO a dos alumnos el Día 3.

D Í A   1

Oídos y Sonidos

- Referirse al Manual del maestro de *Oídos y Sonidos*.
- Completar la lección que corresponda al nivel de habilidades de sus alumnos.

Cuento compartido

Materiales
- Cuento compartido: *La nueva alumna*
- Tarjeta clave: /l/
- Tarjetas de dibujo: lago, leche, libro, lobo, luna
- Rueda de sílabas: "l"
- Tarjetas de palabras: lado, Lupita, listos, pelotita, dale, altísimo, meterla, muletas, palmas, palmitas, saluden, hola

Estrategias/Destrezas
- Destrezas de contexto: Uso del diminutivo (—itas) como sufijo; uso del superlativo (—ísimo) como sufijo; uso del texto
- Destreza de ortografía: Uso de letras mayúsculas en los nombres de lugares
- Destreza de lectura: Comparación y contraste entre dos personajes

Conocimiento previo del cuento

- Muestre la cubierta del libro y lea el título del Cuento compartido. Diga: **El título de este cuento es *La nueva alumna*. ¿Qué significa ese título?** *(Respuestas de los alumnos).* **Me imagino que este cuento relatará una serie de sucesos que ocurren cuando una nueva alumna llega a una clase. Voy a observar la ilustración de la cubierta para ver si me ayuda a comprender el título. Veo a una niña saludando a los niños del aula.**

LeeConmigo   **Lección 19**

• •

Seguramente, ella es la nueva alumna. ¿En qué se ve diferente esta niña de los demás? *(Respuestas de los alumnos).* **Es probable que este cuento nos narre las experiencias de esta niña en su primer día en la escuela. Voy a leer para ver qué pasa.**

- Comente con los alumnos las siguientes preguntas de conocimiento previo utilizando la estrategia Piensen-Únanse-Compartan:

> **¿Alguna vez han convivido con alguien que usara muletas, o que tuviera algún tipo de impedimento físico?**
>
> **¿Cómo creen que debemos comportarnos con las personas que tienen un impedimento físico? ¿Por qué?**
>
> **¿Cómo creen que debemos comportarnos con los compañeros que llegan a nuestro grupo cuando el año escolar ya ha comenzado?**
>
> **¿Alguno de ustedes ha sido "el nuevo alumno" alguna vez? ¿Qué les pasó durante esa experiencia?**

- Haga las siguientes preguntas de predicción utilizando la estrategia Piensen-Únanse-Compartan:

> **¿Cómo se sentirá la nueva alumna en su primer día de clases?**
> **¿Qué harán sus compañeros?**
> **¿Cómo le darán la bienvenida?**

- Explique a los alumnos que van a aprender todos los sonidos, letras y palabras que necesitan saber para leer este cuento.

Repaso de la letra y las sílabas

- Guíe a los alumnos a repasar el sonido de la letra "l" y la frase aliterada, utilizando la Tarjeta clave correspondiente.

- Repase con los alumnos cómo pronunciar las sílabas de la letra "l", utilizando la Rueda de sílabas y las cinco Tarjetas de dibujo correspondientes.

li	**li**bro	**lilili**bro
la	**la**go	**lalala**go
lo	**lo**bo	**lololo**bo
lu	**lu**na	**lululu**na
le	**le**che	**lelele**che

Presentación de las palabras del cuento

- Muestre cómo usar Cubrir y descubrir para leer la palabra **altísimo**. Al leerla, indique cómo el acento muestra dónde poner el énfasis al leer esta palabra. Luego, al utilizar la palabra en una oración, haga hincapié en el sufijo "—ísimo" que indica el superlativo (muy alto).

Lea la primera parte:	**a**■
Lea ésta y agregue la siguiente:	**al**■
Lea ésta y agregue la siguiente:	**al tí**■
Lea ésta y agregue la siguiente:	**altí si**■
Lea ésta y agregue la siguiente:	**altísi mo**
Lea la palabra completa:	**altísimo**
Diga una oración:	Pepe dio un salto **altísimo** y metió la pelota.

Ayude a los alumnos a leer de la misma manera las palabras: **palmas** y **palmitas**. Al leer la palabra "palmitas", haga hincapié en el sufijo "—itas" como diminutivo (palmas pequeñas) y utilícela en una oración para mostrar su significado por medio del contexto .

Elija una o dos otras palabras para demostrar cómo leerlas.

- Después de presentar cada una de las palabras del cuento, ubíquela en el Tren de palabras.

Lee Conmigo

Lectura de palabras y oraciones en parejas

- Pida a los alumnos que se sienten junto a su compañero de trabajo. Repártales los Cuentos compartidos y pídales que se detengan en la lista de palabras y oraciones escritas dentro de la cubierta anterior.

- Pida a los alumnos que se turnen con su compañero para leerse mutuamente las palabras. Cuando terminen, pídales que se turnen nuevamente para leerse las oraciones que se encuentran a continuación de las palabras.

Lectura guiada del cuento en parejas

- Asegúrese de que cada pareja tenga una Tarjeta de las estrategias de lectura, para consultarla mientras leen, de ser necesario.

- Pida a las parejas de compañeros que se preparen para la lectura del cuento. Asegúrese de que tengan sus libros abiertos en la primera página.

- Utilice la version duplicada del Cuento compartido que se encuentra a continuación en esta lección y siga los siguientes pasos para la Lectura guiada del cuento en parejas, ayudando a la clase en la lectura de todo el libro.

  1. Lea el texto que se encuentra en la parte superior de la página.
  2. El compañero "A" lee la primera oración del texto del alumno. El compañero "B" le ayuda.
  3. El compañero "B" lee la primera oración del texto del alumno. El compañero "A" le ayuda.
  4. Ambos compañeros continúan alternándose para leer las oraciones de una página, hasta terminar de leerla.
  5. Los compañeros leen toda la página, al unísono.
  6. Dirija una breve discusión sobre esa página para verificar que todos hayan comprendido lo que leyeron.
  7. Toda la clase lee la página entera, al unísono (opcional).

- Repita los siete pasos anteriores para las páginas restantes del cuento. Supervise la lectura de las parejas para asegurarse de que los compañeros continúan alternándose en la lectura de las oraciones, en cada página, y de que se ayudan mutuamente de manera efectiva.

- Por medio de la estrategia de Pensar en voz alta presente las palabras de contexto durante la lectura del cuento: **cesta**, **aula**, **Lima, Perú** y la onomatopeya ¡**pom**!

---

1. Empieza el día y todos los niños de la clase de la señorita Peña miran con curiosidad a una niña que está en medio del salón. ¿Quién es?

> La señorita Peña dice:
>
> —Esta es Lupita, de Lima, Perú.
>
> Este año Lupita estará con nosotros.

Pensar en voz alta: "Lima, Peru". No estoy segura(o) qué significa esto. ¿Qué creen ustedes que signifique? *(Respuestas de los alumnos).* ¡Muy bien! Es el nombre del lugar de donde viene o donde nació Lupita. Lo sé porque los dos nombres comienzan con mayúscula. Quizás Lima es el nombre de la ciudad, y Perú es el nombre del país. ¿Dónde creen ustedes que quede este lugar? *(Respuestas de los alumnos).* ¡Muy bien! Lima, Perú queda en America del Sur. **Muestre un mapa de America del Sur si lo considera necesario, pero no se extienda mucho tiempo en la explicación.**

Lee Conmigo

Lección 19

· ·

2. La señorita Peña se da cuenta de que Lupita es un poco tímida y quiere que se sienta más comoda, así es que les pide a los niños:

>—Niños, saluden a Lupita
>
>>—dice la señorita Peña.
>
>Los niños gritan:
>
>—¡Hola, Lupita!
>
>Lupita dice:
>
>—¡Hola, niños!

3. Con mucho cariño la señorita Peña sienta a Lupita junto a una de las niñas.

>Lupita se pone al lado de Lola.
>
>Pero Lupita es tímida.
>
>Lola le dice:
>
>—No seas tímida.
>
>>Todos somos tus amigos.

4. Lola explica a Lupita que en la escuela todas las personas, incluyendo a la señorita Peña, son sus amigos. La señorita Peña, al oír esto, sonríe y dice:
—¡Es cierto! Nosotros somos amigos que siempre jugamos.
Entonces, ¿qué hace ella?

>La señorita Peña les enseña una pelota.
>
>Dice:
>
>—Amigos del aula! Hay que meter la pelota
>
>>en la cesta. ¿Están listos?
>
>—Sí, estamos listos—dicen todos.

<u>Pensar en voz alta</u>: "aula" y "cesta". **No estoy segura(o) si entiendo estas palabras. Voy a mirar el dibujo. La señorita Peña está con todos sus alumnos en una cancha de baloncesto. ¿A quién se está dirigiendo la señorita Peña al hablar?** *(Respuestas de los alumnos)*. **Ella se está dirigiendo a todos los niños del salón. Entonces "aula" tiene el mismo significado que salón o clase. ¿Dónde tienen que meter la pelota los niños?** *(Respuestas de los alumnos)*. **¡Muy bien en la canasta o cesta! Cesta tiene el mismo significado que canasta ¿Conocen ustedes otro nombre para la cesta? ¿Cuál es?** *(Respuestas de los alumnos)*.

5. Varios niños quieren ser los primeros.
—Yo primero, señorita —dice Dani.
—Después sigo yo —dice Paco.

>La señorita Peña le da la pelota a Paco.
>
>—¡Dale, Paco, dale! —lo animan entre todos.
>
>Paco toma la pelota en las manos.
>
>Da un salto altísimo y . . .
>
>¡POM! Mete la pelota.

Lee Conmigo

• •

Hacer una predicción: ¿A quién le tocará ahora lanzar la pelota? ¿Será una buena idea de la maestra poner a participar a Lupita en este juego? **Escuche con atención las respuestas de los alumnos. Pídales que discutan sus respuestas. Estimúlelos para que sustenten sus predicciones con evidencias del cuento.**

6. —¡Canasta!—grita Paco muy contento.

—Toma, Lola. Te toca —dice Paco.

Lola toma la pelota en las manos.

Dice:

—Palmas, palmitas, entra, pelotita.

Lola da un salto y tira la pelota.

—¡Metí la pelota! —dice Lola.

7. Feliz con su triunfo, Lola vuelve a la fila y le da la pelota a su nueva amiga.

—Tu turno, Lupita —dice Lola.

Lupita mira la pelota.

Dice:

—No me des la pelota, Lola.

No podré meterla.

8. Lupita está a punto de llorar y su nueva amiga quiere saber qué le pasa.

—¿Por qué, Lupita? —pregunta Lola.

—Tengo muletas.

No podré usar las manos —responde Lupita.

Lupita está triste.

9. Cuando la señorita Peña se da cuenta de que Lupita llora, siente pena.

—¿Qué te pasa, Lupita?

—dice la señorita Peña.

—No podré meter la pelota.

Tengo muletas —dice Lupita.

—Sí podrás —la anima la señorita Peña.

Todos los niños animan a Lupita.

—¡Lupita! ¡Lupita! ¡Ra, ra, ra! —dicen todos.

10. Entonces Lupita, al oír a los niños, se anima. ¿Qué hace?

—Dame la pelota, Lola —dice Lupita.

Lupita toma la pelota y . . .

¡POM! Lupita mete la pelota.

—¡Metí la pelota, la metí! —dice Lupita.

Lee Conmigo   **Lección 19**
• •

> **Pensar en voz alta:** "**¡Pom!**" ¿Qué creen ustedes que signifique "¡pom!"? (***Respuestas de los alumnos***). Voy a leer nuevamente. Lupita mete la pelota en la cesta. ¡Ah! "¡Pom!" es el sonido que hace la pelota al golpear contra el tablero donde está la cesta.
>
> **Lupita está muy contenta porque los niños y la maestra de su nueva escuela son muy buenos con ella. Y todos los niños están contentos porque pudieron ser los campeones del baloncesto.**

Comentario del cuento

- Haga las siguientes preguntas de discusión y trate de orientar las conclusiones de los alumnos a las comparaciones contrastes entre los personajes:

  ¿Quién era Lupita? ¿Cómo era Lupita?
  ¿Cómo trató a Lupita Lola? ¿Cómo era Lola?
  ¿Por qué los niños decidieron darle muchos ánimos a Lupita?
  ¿Qué pasó cuando Lupita se decidió a hacer el intento?

- Pida a los alumnos que utilicen la estrategia Piensen-Únanse-Compartan para comentar las respuestas con su compañero. Luego, pida a varias parejas que compartan sus respuestas con el resto de la clase.

- Pregunte a los alumnos si sus predicciones fueron acertadas o si los sucesos del cuento los sorprendieron.

Celebración

- Pida a dos alumnos que lean una o dos páginas de un cuento conocido. Haga que todo el grupo los aplauda y aliente, y otorgue los Certificados de lectura a los lectores. Elija a dos alumnos para que se preparen para leer el próximo día durante la celebración.

Leamos juntos

Sapo y Sepo son amigos de Arnold Lobel

Materiales
- Cuento: *Sapo y Sepo son amigos* de Arnold Lobel (Capítulos: "La primavera", "El cuento" y "La carta")
- Diagrama de Venn*
  *Adquirido por el maestro

Objetivo
- Establecer comparaciones y contrastes entre dos personajes del cuento.

Palabras del cuento
sendero   imaginar

Resumen del cuento

- Sapo y Sepo eran muy buenos amigos. Cuando llegó la primavera, Sapo fue a buscar a Sepo para que disfrutaran juntos de las cosas del mundo. Sin embargo, Sepo no quería levantarse sino hasta que llegara el mes de mayo. Para convencerlo de que caminara junto a él, Sapo arrancó todas las páginas del calendario; desde noviembre hasta mayo, y se lo mostró a Sepo, quien convencido se levantó a caminar. Luego, cuando Sapo estuvo enfermo, Sepo le pidió que se acostara y le hizo una taza de té, pero no pudo imaginarse ni un solo cuento a pesar de haberse puesto de cabezas, echado agua en la cara y golpeado contra la pared. Enfermo de intentarlo tanto, Sepo se acostó y Sapo, que ya se sentía mejor, le contó un cuento. Una vez, Sepo se sentía

LeeConmigo

• •

muy desgraciado porque nunca había recibido una carta. Para alegrarlo Sapo le escribió una y se la envió con el caracol. En su carta Sapo le decía lo feliz y agradecido que estaba de que Sepo fuera su mejor amigo.

Antes de la lectura: Presentación

• Muestre la cubierta del libro, lea el título y el nombre del autor e ilustrador. Comente con las alumnos las siguientes preguntas y guíelos a responder usando oraciones completas. De ser necesario, ejemplifique y amplíe las respuestas para ayudar a enriquecer la expresión oral de los alumnos.

• Diga: **El cuento que vamos a comenzar a leer hoy se llama** *Sapo y Sepo son amigos* **de Arnold Lobel. Hoy leeremos dos capítulos del cuento, uno se llama "La primavera" y el otro "El cuento". Vamos a observar la cubierta y las primeras páginas. ¿Quiénes aparecen en ella?** *(Aparecen dos sapos, tal vez uno sea Sapo y el otro sea Sepo).* **¿Dónde se encuentran los sapos?** *(Los sapos parecen estar en el bosque).* **¿De qué creen ustedes que se trate este cuento?** *(De las cosas que hacen los amigos para divertirse y entretenerse).* **¿Cómo son sus amigos? ¿Qué hacen ustedes con sus amigos?** Permita que los alumnos expresen sus ideas a través de oraciones completas. **¿Qué hacen durante la primavera? ¿Cuál es la estación del año anterior a la primavera? ¿Cuál es la estación del año que viene después de la primavera? ¿Cómo es el clima durante la primavera? ¿Cómo cambia el ambiente durante la primavera? ¿Qué prefieren ustedes, el invierno o la primavera? ¿Cómo se sienten en general durante la primavera**? Permita que los alumnos comenten estas preguntas y compartan sus ideas. **A mi me encanta la primavera, especialmente porque escucho el canto de los pájaros y veo renacer los colores de las plantas y las flores. Vamos a leer este cuento para enterarnos de qué es lo que hacen Sapo y Sepo en la primavera.**

Durante la lectura: Lectura interactiva

• Presente el objetivo de la lectura. Diga: **Recuerden que una de las estrategias que nos permite entender mejor los cuentos es comparar a los personajes de un mismo cuento. En el cuento** *La nueva alumna*, **vimos que Lupita tenía algo diferente a los demás niños, sin embargo esto no le impidió a compartir la misma actividad que hacían los alumnos. ¿En qué se diferenciaba Lupita de los demás alumnos de la clase de la señorita Peña? ¿En qué le afectaba esta diferencia?** Permita que los alumnos respondan usando oraciones completas. **Ahora comenzaré a leer nuestro cuento de hoy. Escuchen con atención. Piensen en lo que les dice el cuento, identifiquen a los personajes y comparen sus diferencias.**

• Comience a leer el capítulo "La primavera" haciendo las pausas necesarias para resumir y hacer preguntas de predicción e inferencias que motiven a los alumnos a interactuar con el cuento. Asegúrese de alentar a los alumnos a usar oraciones completas al responder acerca de lo que ha pasado en cada una de las páginas que se encuentran indicadas a continuación.

Página 11:   **¿Por qué fue Sapo a despertar a Sepo? ¿Qué hizo Sepo?** *(Cuando llegó la primavera, Sapo subió corriendo por el* <u>sendero</u> *a la casa de Sepo. Sapo quería recorrer el mundo junto a su amigo por eso fue a llamarlo. Sepo no quiso salir y regresó de nuevo a la cama).*

<u>Pensar en voz alta</u>: **¿Dónde viven Sapo y Sepo?** *(Ellos viven en un bosque).* **En el bosque hay muchos caminos o** <u>senderos</u>. **Seguro que fue por uno de esos caminos que Sapo subió para llegar a casa de Sepo. ¿De qué otra manera se le pueden llamar a los caminos o** <u>senderos</u>? **¡Muy bien! También se los pueden llamar veredas, sendas o rutas.**

Lee Conmigo   Lección 19

· ·

Página 13: **¿Por qué no se quería levantar Sepo? ¿Cuándo quería hacerlo?**
(Sepo no quería levantarse porque le parecía que aún era muy temprano para que fuera la primavera. Él quería seguir durmiendo hasta el principio de mayo).

Hacer una predicción: **¿Qué hará Sapo ahora? ¿ Logrará disfrutar de la primavera en compañía de su mejor amigo?**

Página 17: **¿Cómo convenció Sapo a Sepo de que era ya tiempo de levantarse?** *(Sapo se dio cuenta de que en el calendario de Sepo todavía estaba la página de noviembre y arrancó las páginas hasta mayo. Luego se lo mostró a Sepo para que se diera cuenta de que ya era hora de disfrutar la primavera. Sepo se levantó contento y salió con Sapo a ver el mundo en primavera).*

- Comience a leer el próximo capítulo "El cuento" haciendo las pausas necesarias para resumir y hacer preguntas de predicción e inferencias que motiven a los alumnos a interactuar con el cuento. Asegúrese de alentar a los alumnos a usar oraciones completas al responder acerca de lo que ha pasado en cada una de las páginas que se encuentran indicadas a continuación.

Página 19: **¿Qué hizo Sepo cuando Sapo estaba enfermo? ¿Qué hizo Sapo?**
(Cuando Sapo se enfermó, Sepo le pidió que se metiera en la cama y descansara. Además le hizo una taza de té bien caliente. Sapo le pidió a Sepo que le contara un cuento para escucharlo mientras descansaba).

Página 22: **¿Qué hizo Sepo para intentar <u>imaginar</u> un cuento?** *(A Sepo no se le ocurría nada para contar a Sapo. Entonces salió al porche y paseó de un lado a otro para ayudarse, pero no se le ocurría nada. Luego entró a la casa y estuvo cabeza abajo durante mucho rato, pero nada. Después se echó agua en la cabeza y se golpeó la cabeza contra la pared. Sepo no pudo <u>imaginarse</u> nada).*

Pensar en voz alta: **¿Qué es la imaginación?** *(Respuestas de los alumnos).* **Cuando queremos contar algo o escribir algo siempre vemos en nuestra mente como una película mental con imágenes. A eso le llamamos <u>imaginación</u>. Debe ser por eso que Sepo intentó hacer tantas cosas para poner a funcionar su <u>imaginación</u>. ¿Qué hacen ustedes para intentar imaginar un cuento?**

Hacer una predicción: **¿Cómo se sentirá Sapo? ¿Creen que ya no le haga falta escuchar el cuento?**

Página 29: **¿Qué hizo Sapo cuando Sepo se sintió fatal?** *(Sapo ya se sentía mejor y le dejo la cama a Sepo para que se acostara. Sepo se sentía fatal por todas las cosas que había intentado hacer al tratar de imaginar un cuento para Sapo. Entonces Sapo le contó un cuento a Sepo sobre dos amigos y Sepo se quedó dormido).*

Lee Conmigo   Lección 19

• •

- Comience a leer el capítulo "La carta" haciendo las pausas necesarias para resumir y hacer preguntas de predicción e inferencias que motiven a los alumnos a interactuar con el cuento. Asegúrese de alentar a los alumnos a usar oraciones completas al responder acerca de lo que ha pasado en cada una de las páginas que se encuentran indicadas a continuación.

Página 56: **¿Por qué se sentía Sepo tan <u>desgraciado</u>? ¿Cuál era su rato triste del día?** *(Sepo se sentía desgraciado porque no tenía nadie que le escribiera cartas. Todos los días se sentaba a esperar a la hora que llegaba la correspondencia y ese era su rato más triste del día. Su buzón siempre estaba vacío).*

<u>Pensar en voz alta</u>: **Sepo se sentaba a ver pasar el correo y nunca había ni una carta para él. Era por eso que se sentía tan <u>desgraciado</u>, es decir tan infeliz, triste y desafortunado. ¿Han recibido alguna vez ustedes una carta? ¿De quién? ¿Cómo se sintieron?** (Permita que los alumnos expresen sus experiencias).

Página 66: **¿Qué hizo Sapo para ayudar a su amigo? ¿Cómo se sintió Sepo?**
(Sapo sintió que tenía que hacer algo. Entonces fue a su casa y escribió una carta para Sepo en la que le decía lo contento que estaba por ser su amigo. Sapo y Sepo esperaron la carta juntos. Sepo se sintió muy feliz de haber recibido una carta de su amigo).

Después de la lectura: Repaso

- Haga a los alumnos las siguientes preguntas y anímelos a responderlas usando oraciones completas. Promueva en ellos la expresión oral ampliando sus respuestas y pidiéndoles que desarrollen las ideas que expresan.
Pida a los alumnos que describan las semejanzas y las diferencias entre los personajes. Añada estos detalles en un Diagrama de Venn.

1. **¿Dónde ocurren los dos acontecimientos entre los amigos? ¿Quiénes son los personajes?** (*Ambos acontecimientos ocurren en la casa de Sepo. Los personajes son Sapo y Sepo).*

2. **¿Cómo reaccionó Sapo cuando llegó la primavera? ¿Cómo reaccionó Sepo?** (*Sapo quería salir a pasear con su amigo Sepo. Sepo no quería dejar su cama para salir. Sapo tuvo que convencerlo para que saliera mostrándole las páginas del calendario).*

3. **¿Qué hizo Sepo cuando Sapo se enfermó? ¿Qué hizo Sapo cuando Sepo se sintió pésimo?** (*Sepo le pidió a Sapo que se acostara en la cama y le hizo una taza caliente de té, pero no pudo imaginar un cuento para contarle a Sapo. Cuando Sepo se sintió pésimo por todo lo que hizo para tratar de imaginar un cuento, Sapo lo consoló y le contó el cuento de dos buenos amigos).*

4. **¿Cómo se sentía Sepo mientras esperaba que llegara el correo? ¿Cómo se sentía Sapo?** (*Sepo se sentía muy triste mientras esperaba que llegara el correo. Él no había recibido ni una carta nunca. A Sapo no le importaba no recibir ni una carta, pero también se sintió triste por su amigo).*

5. **¿En qué se parecen y en qué se diferencian Sapo de Sepo?** (*Sapo y Sepo se parecen porque ambos son sapos y son muy buenos amigos. Siempre tratan de buscar algo que haga feliz al otro. Se diferencian en que a Sepo no le resulta fácil encontrar soluciones y le gusta permanecer en casa sin hacer muchas*

Lee Conmigo   **Lección 19**

· ·

cosas al aire libre. A Sapo le gusta salir y jugar al aire libre. También, rápidamente encuentra soluciones simples).

Hablemos juntos

Materiales
- Cuento: *Sapo y Sepo son amigos* de Arnold Lobel (Capítulo, "La carta")
- Títere: Alfi

Objetivos
- Pensar y explicar diferentes razones para escribir una carta.
- Nombrar las personas a quienes le escribirían una carta.
- Completar las siguientes frases como base para construir el conocimiento:

  ¿A quién le escribirás una carta?
  Voy a escribir una carta a_____.
  ¿Por qué vas a escribir la carta?
  Voy a escribir la carta porque_____.

Demostración

- Repase brevemente el capítulo "La carta" del cuento *Sapo y Sepo son amigos*. Diga: **¿Recuerdan quién escribió la carta en este cuento? ¿Qué le escribió Sapo a Sepo? ¿Por qué le escribió Sapo a Sepo?** (Permita que uno de los alumnos responda).

- Discuta con los alumnos las diferentes razones que existen para escribir una carta. Diga: **Existe muchas razones para escribir una carta a alguien. Puede escribirse una carta a un familiar que vive en otra ciudad o país para saludarlo y saber de él. Puede escribirse una carta para felicitar a un amigo por su cumpleaños o graduación. Puede escribirse una carta para invitar o enviar agradecimientos a un tío o cualquier otra persona ¿Qué otras razones existen para escribir una carta?** Permita a los alumnos que discutan e intercambien sus ideas.

- Use a Alfi para demostrar a quién le escribirá una carta.

  Maestro: **Alfi, ¿a quién le escribirás una carta?**
  Alfi: **Voy a escribir una carta a mi amiga Berta.**

- Diga: **¡Muy bien! Alfi nos ha dicho que escribirá una carta a su amiga Berta. Ahora veamos a quién le escribirían ustedes una carta. ¿Están listos?**

Práctica guiada en grupo

- Invite a los alumnos a que se sienten formando un círculo para compartir sus ideas.

- Comience diciendo a quién usted le escribiría una carta, luego pregúntele al alumno que esté sentado a su derecha. Diga: **Yo voy a escribirle una carta a mi tío Antonio. ¿A quién le escribirás tú la carta?**

- Permita que los alumnos se turnen para que pregunten y respondan a quién le escribirán una carta. Anímelos a expresar sus ideas con una oración completa:

  Voy a escribir una carta a _____.

- Si los alumnos quieren explicar porqué quieren escribir la carta, dígales que tendrán oportunidad de hablar de esto más adelante en la práctica en parejas.

LeeConmigo   **Lección 19**

• •

Práctica en parejas

• Use a Alfi para demostrar cómo explicar el propósito de escribir una carta. Diga: **Ahora vamos a pensar en las razones para escribir una carta a la persona que hayan escogido. ¿Cuál es el propósito de la carta? Vamos a escuchar a Alfi quién nos va a demostrar cómo explicar esto.**

Maestro:	**Alfi, ¿por qué le vas a escribir una carta a Berta?**
Alfi:	**Voy a escribirle una carta a Berta para invitarla a mi fiesta.**

• Diga: **¡Muy bien, Alfi! Esa es una excelente razón para escribirle una carta a una amiga. Ahora es el turno de ustedes para hablar con su compañero y explicarle las razones por la que escribirán la carta.**

• Pida a los alumnos que se sienten junto a sus compañero y que discutan acerca de las razones para escribir una carta a la persona que hayan escogido.

• Diga a los alumnos que tomen turnos para preguntar y responder:
  ¿Por qué vas a escribir la carta?
  Voy a escribir la carta porque_____.

Anímelos a que añadan tantos detalles como puedan para elaborar el propósito de escribir una carta a la persona que ellos hayan escogido.

• Cuando los alumnos hayan terminado, pídales a tres o cuatro alumnos que compartan sus ideas con la clase.

Actividades de extensión

• Si el tiempo lo permite, pida a los alumnos que hablen con su compañero acerca de lo que escribirían en la carta y de qué estrategias usarían para escribir las palabras con sonidos de letras que aún no conozcan.

Tarea

• Pida a los alumnos que lean a los miembros de la familia las palabras y oraciones que se encuentran dentro de la cubierta anterior del cuento. Recuérdeles que deben regresar a la escuela los formatos de Leer y responder con la firma y los comentarios de los oyentes.

Lee Conmigo   **Lección 19**

. . . .

D Í A   2

Oídos y Sonidos

- Referirse al Manual del maestro de *Oídos y Sonidos*.
- Completar la lección que corresponda al nivel de habilidades de sus alumnos.

Cuento compartido

Materiales
- Cuento compartido: *La nueva alumna*

Estrategias/Destrezas
- Destreza de comprensión: Elegir respuestas múltiples y escribir respuestas a preguntas de comprensión

Repaso del cuento

Repase con los alumnos el título del cuento y los nombres de los personajes. Diga: Ayer leímos un nuevo cuento. Me gustaría que me contaran lo que recuerdan. Haga las siguientes preguntas:

¿Quién era la nueva alumna?
¿En qué se parecían Lupita y Lola? ¿En qué eran diferentes?
¿Por qué Lupita pensó que no podría meter la pelota?
¿Por qué Lupita se animó a hacer el intento?

Lectura de palabras y oraciones en parejas

- Pida a los alumnos que se sienten junto a su compañero.

- Reparta los Cuentos compartidos y pida a los alumnos que se turnen para leer las palabras y oraciones que se encuentran dentro de la cubierta anterior del cuento.

- Supervise a las parejas mientras se leen mutuamente las palabras y las oraciones. Asegúrese de que los compañeros se turnen para que ambos tengan la oportunidad de leer mientras el otro escucha.

- Cuando visite a cada pareja, asegúrese de que ambos alumnos puedan leer correctamente toda la lista de palabras del cuento. Cuando sea así, ponga una calcomanía en la Tabla de fluidez de cada alumno, al lado del título del cuento.

Lectura del cuento en parejas

- Pida a las parejas que abran su libro en la primera página y asegúrese de que todos estén preparados para leer.

- Pida a los alumnos que lean el cuento con su compañero. Los compañeros deben alternarse para leer cada página. Supervise si ambos leen en forma correcta. Pida a los alumnos que relean la página hasta que lean correctamente todas las palabras.

- Supervise a los alumnos mientras practican la Lectura en parejas. Escúchelos mientras leen, promoviendo y reforzando que lo hagan correctamente y asegurándose de que comprendan lo que están leyendo.

- Después de la Lectura en parejas, elija a una o dos parejas para que lean una página del cuento correctamente. Invite al resto de la clase a felicitar a la pareja por su éxito.

Lee Conmigo

Lectura y comentario de preguntas en parejas

- Pida a los alumnos que observen dentro la cubierta posterior del cuento. Comente y ejemplifique cómo deben leer y responder, en parejas, a las preguntas de comprensión.

- Luego, ejemplifique cómo responder por escrito a una de las preguntas, antes de que los alumnos comiencen a escribir individualmente. No realice la escritura de todas las respuestas en grupo.

- Circule alrededor del salón para ayudar a los alumnos, de ser necesario, y para asegurarse de que hayan comprendido la actividad.

Celebración

- Pida a dos alumnos que lean una o dos páginas del cuento. Haga que todo el grupo los aplauda y aliente, y otorgue los Certificados de lectura a los lectores. Elija dos alumnos para prepararse a leer el próximo día durante la Celebración.

- Haga un breve repaso de las palabras en el Tren de palabras.

Leamos juntos

Sapo y Sepo son amigos de Arnold Lobel

Materiales
- Cuento: *Sapo y Sepo son amigos* de Arnold Lobel (Capítulos, "Un botón perdido" y "El baño")
- Diagrama de Venn*
  *Adquirido por el maestro

Objetivo
- Establecer comparaciones y contrastes entre dos personajes.

Palabras del cuento

reojo   desgraciado

Resumen del cuento

- Un día en el que los amigos estuvieron dando un largo paseo, Sepo perdió un botón. Sapo y otros animales del bosque intentaron encontrarlo, pero sólo hallaron otros botones distintos al que Sepo había perdido. Cuando Sepo regresó a casa descubrió que su botón había estado siempre en el piso de su casa. Sepo cosió en su chaqueta todos los botones que encontró Sapo y se la regaló a Sapo al día siguiente. El día en que Sapo y Sepo salieron a nadar, Sapo intentó evitar que los animales del bosque se rieran de lo ridículo que se veía Sepo en traje de baño. Pero no pudo y Sepo tuvo que pasar la vergüenza en frente de todos.

Lee Conmigo   **Lección 19**

. . . .

Antes de la lectura: Repaso/Presentación

- Muestre el libro. Diga: **Me gustaría saber qué recuerdan de los capítulos que leímos ayer**. Señale a los personajes en la ilustración de la cubierta del libro. Guíelos a recordar el título, el autor el ilustrador, y los nombres de los personajes. Ayúdelos a identificar el escenario, el problema y la solución de cada capítulo. Anime a los alumnos a reconocer los elementos importantes de los dos capítulos usando oraciones completas para describir las semejanzas y diferencias entre los personajes del cuento.

- Comience a leer el capitulo "Un botón perdido" haciendo las pausas necesarias para resumir y hacer preguntas de predicción e inferencias que motiven a los alumnos a interactuar con el cuento. Asegúrese de alentar a los alumnos a usar oraciones completas al responder acerca de lo que ha pasado en cada una de las páginas que se encuentran indicadas a continuación.

  Página 31:   **¿Por qué estaba tan enojado Sepo?** *(Sepo estaba tan enojado porque estaba muy cansado del paseo. Le dolían mucho los pies y además había perdido el botón de su chaqueta).*

  Página 41:   **¿Cómo era el botón que había perdido Sepo? ¿Qué hizo con los botones que encontraron sus amigos?** *(El botón que había perdido Sepo era redondo, gordo, blanco, grande y con cuatro agujeros. Cuando llegó a casa lo encontró en el piso. Entonces decidió coser en la chaqueta los otros botones que habían encontrado sus amigos, y luego se la regaló a Sapo).*

- Comience a leer el capitulo "El baño" haciendo las pausas necesarias para resumir y hacer preguntas de predicción e inferencias que motiven a los alumnos a interactuar con el cuento. Asegúrese de alentar a los alumnos a usar oraciones completas al responder acerca de lo que ha pasado en cada una de las páginas que se encuentran indicadas a continuación.

  Página 44:   **¿Por qué no quería Sepo que lo mirarán de <u>reojo</u> cuando fue a nadar con Sapo?** *(Sepo no quería que Sapo lo viera en traje de baño. Él decía que se veía ridículo, por eso no quería que Sapo lo mirara ni de <u>reojo</u>).*

  <u>Pensar en voz alta</u>: **Sepo tenía mucha vergüenza de que Sapo lo viera en traje de baño. Tal vez por eso Sapo quiso ver cómo se veía Sepo sin que este se diera cuenta y por eso lo vio de <u>reojo</u>, es decir, con disimulo.**

  Página 54:   **¿Quiénes se rieron de Sepo? ¿Por qué Sapo no pudo evitarlo?**
  (Cuando Sapo intentó evitar que la tortuga viera a Sepo, el lagarto, la serpiente, dos libélulas y un ratón escucharon y se quedaron esperando hasta que Sepo saliera. Cuando Sepo salió, todos se rieron y hasta Sapo que era su amigo se rió).

Después de la lectura: Repaso

- Haga a los alumnos las siguientes preguntas y anímelos a responderlas usando oraciones completas. Promueva en ellos la expresión oral ampliando sus respuestas y pidiéndoles que desarrollen las ideas que expresan.

- Pida a los alumnos que describan las semejanzas y las diferencias entre los personajes. Añada estos detalles en el Diagrama de Venn.

Lee Conmigo

• •

1. **¿Dónde ocurren los sucesos de los cuentos "Un botón perdido" y "El baño"?** *("El botón perdido" ocurre durante un paseo por el bosque. "Un baño" ocurre en un lago del bosque).*

2. **¿Cómo era el botón que había perdido Sepo? ¿Cómo eran los botones que habían encontrado Sapo y sus amigos?** *(El botón que había perdido Sepo era blanco, grande y grueso, no era ni negro, ni pequeño, ni fino como los que encontró Sepo. Tenía cuatro agujeros, no dos como el botón que encontró el gorrión. Era redondo y no cuadrado como el que encontró el mapache).*

3. **¿Cómo nadó Sapo y cómo nadó Sepo cuando fueron al lago?** *(Sepo usó traje de baño para nadar. Él nadaba despacio y levantaba poco agua. Sapo no usó traje de baño. Él nadaba rápido y levantaba mucha agua).*

5. **¿Quién tenía más problemas, Sapo o Sepo?** *(Sepo era quien tenía más problemas de los dos amigos. Primero perdió su botón, luego se sentía ridículo al usar su traje de baño para nadar. Sapo era más tranquilo y ayudaba a su amigo a solucionar los problemas).*

Evaluación del cuento

• Pida a los alumnos que trabajen en equipos. Asigne a cada equipo una de las categorías de evaluación del cuento que se listan a continuación. Invite a los alumnos a discutir con sus compañeros de equipo cuántas estrellas asignarán a la categoría que les tocó evaluar. Anímelos a usar oraciones completas y a elaborar razones que justifiquen sus decisiones.

> Pensar en voz alta: **Los capítulos de este cuento han sido muy divertidos. En cada uno de ellos vemos las cosas que los amigos hacen para ayudarse mutuamente. Especialmente vemos que Sapo siempre trata de solucionar los problemas en que se mete Sepo. Me gustó mucho la manera en que ambos se demuestran cariño y respeto. Los dibujos del cuento son un poco descoloridos y pequeños, pero la trama de cada uno de los cuentos fue muy interesante. Yo le otorgaría cuatro estrellas a cada una de sus categorías excepto a la de los dibujos.**

• Pida a un voluntario de cada equipo que comparta su evaluación con el resto de la clase. Categorías:

> Escenario
> Título
> Personajes
> Ilustraciones
> Trama

• Cuente el número de votos y de acuerdo a la mayoría, obtenga la evaluación total de la clase. Pida a los alumnos que discutan los motivos de sus evaluaciones.

Lee Conmigo   **Lección 19**

• •

Hablemos juntos

Materiales
- Cuento: *Sapo y Sepo son amigos* de Arnold Lobel
- Títere: Berta

Objetivos
- Usar oraciones completas para identificar en que se parecen o se diferencian de sus amigos.
- Describir los detalles de porqué un amigo es alguien especial.
- Completar las siguientes frases como base para construir las ideas:

    Me parezco a mi amigo(a) en_____.
    Pero, no me parezco a mi amigo(a) en_____.
    Mi amigo(a) es muy especial porque_____.

Demostración

- Repase brevemente las semejanzas y diferencias de los personajes del cuento *Sapo y Sepo son amigos*. Explique a los alumnos que entre los amigos hay siempre cosas en común pero que también hay otras que son diferentes. Diga: **¿Recuerdan lo que les gustaba hacer juntos a Sapo y a Sepo? A Sapo y a Sepo les gustaba caminar por el bosque y nadar en el lago. ¿Recuerdan que cosas los diferenciaba? Sepo siempre se quejaba de estar cansado y nadaba con traje de baño. Además Sapo nadaba rápidamente y salpicaba mucho y Sepo nadaba lentamente y salpicaba poco. Hoy vamos a pensar en las cosas en las que nos parecemos a nuestros amigos y en las que nos diferenciamos.**

- Dé a los alumnos unos minutos para que piensen y discutan acerca de las cosas en las que ellos se parecen a sus amigos y en las que se diferencian.

- Use a Berta para demostrar cómo hablar acerca de las cosas comunes entre los amigos y las que son diferentes.

    Maestro: **Berta, ¿en qué te pareces a tu amigo(a)?**
    Berta: **Me parezco a mi amiga en <u>que a las dos nos gusta bailar.</u> Pero, no me parezco a mi amiga porque <u>yo bailo con ritmo diferente.</u>**

- Diga: **¡Excelente! Berta nos ha expresado en dos oraciones completas en qué se parece y en qué se diferencia de su amiga. Ahora será el turno de ustedes. ¿Están listos?**

Práctica guiada en grupo

- Invite a los alumnos que se sienten formando un círculo. Comience diciendo en qué se parece usted a su amigo y en qué se diferencia. Diga: **Me parezco a mi amigo en que a ambos nos gusta ir al cine. Pero, no me parezco a mi amigo porque a mi no me gustan las películas de "terror".** Pregunte al alumno que esté sentado a su derecha: **¿En qué te pareces a tu amigo(a)?**

- Permita a los alumnos que tomen turnos para decir en qué se parecen y diferencian de sus amigos. Use oraciones completas para parafrasear las preguntas y las respuestas de los alumnos, cuando sea necesario. Anime a los alumnos a usar oraciones completas para expresar sus ideas:

    Me parezco a mi amigo(a) en_____.
    Pero, no me parezco a mi amigo(a) en_____.

- Felicite a los alumnos por su participación y por la forma en que se han expresado sus ideas. Diga: **¡Muy bien! Han dicho claramente en qué se parecen y diferencian de sus amigos, además han usado oraciones completas para expresarlo. ¡Los felicito!**

Lee Conmigo

Práctica en parejas

• Diga: **Ahora hablaremos más acerca de nuestros amigos. Vamos a pensar en las cosas que los hacen ser tan especial. ¿Recuerdan cómo Sepo y Sapo se ayudaban mutuamente? Ellos siempre trataban de solucionar los problemas juntos, por eso eran tan especiales. Vamos a ver qué nos dice Berta acerca de su amiga.**

• Use a Berta para demostrar cómo hablar acerca de un amigo muy especial.

> Maestro: **Berta, ¿por qué tu amigo es alguien especial para ti?**
> Berta: **Mi amigo es muy especial porque <u>siempre nos divertimos juntos</u>.**

• Pida a los alumnos que se sienten junto a su compañero para que cada uno tenga la oportunidad de explicar porqué su amigo(a) es especial. Diga: **Piensen en porqué sus amigos son especiales y coméntenlo entre compañeros.**

• Anime a los alumnos a describir los detalles que expliquen porqué sus amigos son especiales. Dígales que traten de recordar las cosas que hayan pasado juntos, no solamente los gratos momentos sino aquellos en los que juntos hayan podido superar algún conflicto. Asegúrese de que los alumnos usen oraciones completas para expresar sus ideas de forma clara.

> **¿Por qué tu amigo es alguien especial para ti?**
> **Mi amigo es muy especial porque _____.**

• Cuando los alumnos hayan terminado sus descripciones, pídales a uno o a dos que compartan sus ideas con el resto de la clase.

Actividades de extensión

• Si el tiempo lo permite, pida a los alumnos que continúen hablando acerca de las cosas que hacen con sus amigos, no solamente los juegos o las salidas sino también aquellos momentos en los que han tenido que animarlos o darles algún consejo.

Tarea

• Pida a los alumnos que lean a varios miembros de la familia las preguntas de comprensión y las respuestas que escogieron. Pídales que regresen a la escuela los formatos de Leer y responder con la firma y los comentarios de los oyentes.

Lee Conmigo   **Lección 19**

· ·

D Í A   3

Oídos y Sonidos

- Referirse al Manual del maestro de *Oídos y Sonidos*.
- Completar la lección que corresponda al nivel de habilidades de sus alumnos.

Cuento compartido

Materiales
- Cuento compartido: *La nueva alumna*

Estrategias/Destrezas
- Destreza de comprensión: Recapitular el cuento

Lectura de palabras y oraciones en parejas

- Pida a los alumnos que se sienten junto a su pareja. Reparta los cuentos compartidos y pídales que localicen la lista de las palabras que se encuentra dentro de la cubierta anterior del cuento.

- Pida a las parejas que lean las palabras y las oraciones. Diga: **Vamos a leer las palabras y oraciones del cuento. Túrnense con su compañero para leer cada una de las palabras y oraciones. Cuando terminen de leerlas, me gustaría que piensen en qué palabras les resultaron fáciles de leer y en cuáles tuvieron dificultades. Después, pueden pasar a leer las oraciones.**

- Visite a cada pareja mientras leen juntos e identifique a aquellas parejas de alumnos que puedan leer toda la lista de palabras del cuento sin errores. Ponga una calcomanía en la Tabla de fluidez de cada alumno, junto al título del cuento correspondiente.

- Cuando las parejas hayan terminado de leer e identifiquen las palabras que les resultaron difíciles de leer, repase su lectura por medio de la estrategia de Cubrir y descubrir.

Lectura del cuento en parejas

- Pida a los alumnos que lean el cuento con su compañero. Diga: **Vamos a practicar la lectura del cuento con nuestros compañeros de trabajo como lo hicimos ayer. Como ya entendimos lo que pasa en el cuento, ahora nos concentraremos en practicar cómo leerlo con nuestra mejor voz narrativa. La voz que narra un cuento debe ser clara y agradable.**

- Observe a los alumnos mientras participan en la Lectura del cuento en parejas. Asegúrese de que los alumnos se turnen para leer con expresión y recapitular cada página.

- Ejemplifique estrategias de lectura específicas y cómo leer con expresión, si lo considera necesario. Permita que los alumnos lean Cuentos compartidos previos. Registre su dominio de la lectura conforme los alumnos los lean.

Celebremos juntos

- Pida a los alumnos que lean el cuento todos juntos. Diga: **Todos han hecho un excelente trabajo leyendo este cuento. Ahora me gustaría que lo leyéramos juntos para celebrar. Este es el momento de mostrar cuánto hemos aprendido. Vamos a leer este cuento con una voz narrativa agradable y clara.**

Lee Conmigo   **Lección** 19

· ·

Nota: Los alumnos del Nivel 1 pueden leer todo el cuento. Los alumnos de niveles más altos leerán una página o dos páginas del cuento.

• Festeje el esfuerzo con un caluroso aplauso para toda la clase.

• Elija a dos alumnos para que lean en la próxima Celebración que tenga planeada.

Escritura compartida

Materiales
• Cuento compartido: *La nueva alumna*
• Cuento: *Sapo y Sepo son amigos* de Arnold Lobel
• Útiles de escritura: Hojas de papel rayado o en blanco, cartulina, lápices, crayones*
  *Adquirido por el maestro

Objetivos
• Escribir una carta de tres oraciones en la que comuniquen a un amigo porqué su amistad es especial.

• Aprender cómo escribir el saludo y la despedida de una carta:

> **Querido(a) _____:**
>
> **Tu amigo(a), _____**

Ensayo de la escritura
• Presente la actividad. Diga: **Hoy vamos a escribir una carta a un amigo para expresarle nuestro afecto. Estoy segura de que todos ustedes tienen a un amigo o amiga a quien consideran especial. ¿Qué les gustaría decirle?** *(Respuestas de los alumnos).* **La idea principal de nuestra escritura será: "¿Qué me gustaría decirle a mi mejor amigo(a) para expresarle que su amistad es especial?"**

• Repase con los alumnos algunos de los aspectos más importantes del cuento *La nueva alumna*. Pregunte a los alumnos: **¿Cómo se portó Lola cuando Lupita se sentó a su lado?** *(Lola trató de ser amigable. Le dijo a Lupita que no fuera tímida, que todos los compañeros eran sus amigos).* **¿Creen que Lola y Lupita podrían llegar a ser las mejores amigas? ¿Por qué?** (Las respuestas varían). Comente brevemente con los alumnos que en el cuento *Sapo y Sepo son amigos* encontramos un capítulo llamada "La carta", en la que Sapo decide expresarle a Sepo lo que siente, precisamente por medio de una carta. Pregunte a los alumnos: **¿Qué mensaje contenía la carta de Sapo?** *(En la carta, Sapo le dijo a Sepo que estaba muy contento de que fuera su mejor amigo).* **¿Por qué Sapo decidió escribirle una carta a Sepo?** *(Sapo quería que su amigo ya no se sintiera triste a la hora de esperar el correo. Sepo se ponía triste a esa hora porque nunca recibía cartas).* Guíe a los alumnos a discutir y concluir que en ambos cuentos, los personajes tienen relaciones amistosas entre sí y que se proporcionan ayuda, apoyo y consuelo durante los momentos difíciles.

Lee Conmigo   **Lección 19**

. . . .

- Diga: **Ahora vamos a pensar en nuestra idea principal: "¿Qué me gustaría decirle a mi mejor amigo(a) para expresarle que su amistad es especial?"** Sobre una cartulina o en el pizarrón escriba el siguiente esquema:

  Querido(a) _____:

  _____

  _____

  _____

  Tu amigo(a),_____

- Explique: **Ahora yo les voy a mostrar cómo le escribiría una carta a mi mejor amiga. Comenzaré completando el primer planteamiento para escribir el saludo de mi carta** (escriba en el diagrama de su cartulina o del pizarrón):

  Querida Marta:

- Pida a dos o tres alumnos que le proporcionen información para completar la carta. Es muy importante que usted demuestre cómo escribir una o varias oraciones completas para escribir el mensaje central de la carta. Diga: **¿Cómo le dirían a su amigo(a) que su amistad es especial? ¿Qué les gustaría decirle a su mejor amigo(a)?** *(Respuestas de los alumnos).* Se recomienda que, por medio de un torbellino de ideas, los alumnos suministren información para que usted escriba dos o tres ejemplos de cartas en el pizarrón, y las repita, de ser necesario, de tal manera que los mensajes de amistad de los alumnos se expresen por medio de oraciones completas. Es muy importante que haga hincapié en la relación que existe entre el sentimiento que tenemos por nuestros amigos y el mensaje que queremos expresar. Por ejemplo:

  Nuestra amistad es especial porque compartimos muchas cosas.

- Luego, muestre cómo completar la carta. Diga: **Finalmente, voy a completar la última parte de mi carta añadiendo mi nombre** (añada esta última parte a su esquema):

  Tu amiga, Rosa

- En voz alta lea toda la carta.

Práctica de la escritura

Planificar

- Pida a los alumnos que se sienten con sus compañeros de equipo para continuar comentando las ideas que quieran expresar en su carta.

- Luego, pídales que escriban el saludo de su carta. Recuérdeles que cuando hayan terminado su carta deban firmarla.

- Diga: **Me gustaría que todos guardáramos silencio para pensar en lo que vamos a escribir.** Haga una breve pausa para que los alumnos se concentren. Asegúrese que ellos hayan pensado, comentado y armado toda la información que necesitan para escribir su carta completando un esquema similar al que usted ha reproducido frente al grupo.

- Diga: **Compartan con sus compañeros las ideas y oraciones que pensaron.** Haga una pausa mientras los alumnos comparten sus pensamientos. Diga: **Saquen sus oraciones del puño de sus manos y ¡escríbanlas!**

Lee Conmigo   **Lección 19**

• •

Escribir

- Circule alrededor del salón mientras los alumnos escriben, si lo considera conveniente, ayúdelos y estimúlelos. De ser necesario, haga un breve recordatorio de las diferentes estrategias de escritura y ejemplifíquelas. Estimule y guíe a los alumnos a deletrear o a separar las palabras por sílabas.

Revisar

- Pida a los alumnos que verifiquen sus oraciones leyéndoselas a ellos mismos y a sus compañeros de equipo.

- Pida a los alumnos que verifiquen que sus oraciones comiencen con mayúscula y que no se les haya olvidado colocar el punto final.

- Pida a los alumnos que verifiquen que su carta haya empezado con un saludo y terminado con su firma.

Celebremos juntos

- Reparta a cada equipo una hoja de papel para que elaboren su carta. Se sugiere que pida a los alumnos que ilustren alguna de las ideas que escribieron, si el tiempo se los permite.

- Exhiba las cartas en un lugar privilegiado del salón de clases. Estimule a los alumnos a leerlas espontáneamente o cuando tengan algún tiempo disponible durante el receso.

Tarea

- Los alumnos deben llevar los Cuentos compartidos a sus casas y leerlos ante los miembros de su familia varias veces. Pídales que regresen a la escuela los formatos de Leer y responder con la firma y los comentarios de los oyentes.

Cuento de Leamos juntos   SOLO—19

Sapo y Sepo son amigos de Arnold Lobel

Vocabulario receptivo

Muestre y nombre los dibujos de estas páginas. Pida al alumno que los indique.

página 8	página 9	página 19	página 52	página 66
Sapo	**Sepo dormido**	**Sapo enfermo**	**Sepo ridículo**	**carta**

Utilice esta información como una evaluación informal de la comprensión del vocabulario del alumno.

Vocabulario expresivo

Muestre los dibujos de estas páginas. Al indicar cada dibujo, pregunte: **¿Qué es?**

página 15	página 39	página 43	página 52	página 66
calendario	**botón**	**traje de baño**	**río**	**carta**

Utilice esta información como una evaluación informal de la comprensión del vocabulario del alumno.

Producción del lenguaje oral

Haga al alumno las siguientes preguntas y evalúelas de acuerdo a la Guía para evaluar de 5 puntos. Promedie la calificación del alumno con las preguntas de la sección del Lenguaje oral. Tome en consideración esta calificación cuando llene la columna del Lenguaje oral en el formato Resumen de valoración.

	Mostrar	Preguntar	Respuestas posibles
1.	páginas 14 y 15	**¿Por qué arrancó Sapo las páginas del calendario?**	*1. No hay ninguna respuesta.* *2. Era mayo.* *3. Sapo le mostró a Sepo el calendario.* *4. Sapo quería mostrarle a Sepo que era mayo.* *5. Sapo las arrancó para mostrarle a Sepo que ya era mayo y había llegado la primavera para salir a jugar juntos.*
2.	páginas 44 y 45	**¿Cómo nadaban Sapo y Sepo?**	*1. No hay ninguna respuesta.* *2. Sapo y Sepo nadaban juntos.* *3. Sepo usaba un traje de baño para nadar y Sapo no.* *4. Sapo nadaba rápido y Sapo nadaba despacio.* *5. Sapo no usaba traje de baño, nadaba rápido y salpicaba mucho. Sepo usaba traje de baño nadaba despacio y salpicaba poco.*
3.	páginas 64 y 65	**¿Qué le escribió Sapo a Sepo en la carta?**	*1. No hay ninguna respuesta.* *2. Amigo.* *3. Sepo, eres mi amigo.* *4. Querido Sepo, eres mi mejor amigo.* *5. Querido Sepo, estoy contento de que tu seas mi mejor amigo. Tu mejor amigo, Sapo.*

Guía para evaluar (5 puntos):
5—Responde en forma elaborada, usa una variedad de estructuras del lenguaje y usa frecuentemente el vocabulario de alto nivel que aprendió de la lección.
4— Responde en forma completa pero simple y usa algunas palabras del vocabulario de alto nivel.
3—Responde en forma corta y con un uso limitado del vocabulario.
2—Responde en forma limitada o formulando respuestas de pocas palabras.
1—No responde.

Cuento compartido 19   LeeConmigo

La nueva alumna

Autora: Ursula Sayers-Ward
Ilustradora: Deborah Sassali

Leer las palabras del cuento:

lado	listos	pelotita	meterla
Lupita	palmitas	dale	muletas
palmas	saluden	altísmo	hola

Leer las oraciones del cuento:

Lupita es una niña con muletas.

La señorita Peña da la pelota a Lupita.

Lupita dice:

—No podré meter la pelota.

  Tengo muletas.

Todos los niños animan a Lupita.

¡Lupita mete la pelota!

La señorita Peña dice:
—Esta es Lupita, de Lima, Perú.
  Este año Lupita estará con nosotros.

La señorita Peña se da cuenta de que Lupita es un poco tímida y quiere que se sienta
más cómoda, así es que les pide a los niños:

—Niños, saluden a Lupita
  —dice la señorita Peña.
Los niños gritan:
—¡Hola, Lupita!
Lupita dice:
—¡Hola, niños!

Con mucho cariño la señorita Peña sienta a Lupita junto a una de las niñas.

Lupita se pone al lado de Lola.
Pero Lupita es tímida.
Lola le dice:
—No seas tímida.
  Todos somos tus amigos.

Lola explica a Lupita que en la escuela todas las personas, incluyendo a la señorita Peña, son sus amigos. La señorita Peña, al oír esto, sonríe y dice:
—¡Es cierto! Nosotros somos amigos que siempre jugamos.
Entonces, ¿qué hace ella?

La señorita Peña les enseña una pelota.

Dice:

—¡Amigos del aula! Hay que meter la pelota
en la cesta. ¿Están listos?

—Sí, estamos listos —dicen todos.

Varios niños quieren ser los primeros.
—Yo primero, señorita —dice Dani.
—Después sigo yo —dice Paco.

La señorita Peña le da la pelota a Paco.

—¡Dale, Paco, dale! —lo animan entre todos.

Paco toma la pelota en las manos.

Da un salto altísimo y ...

¡POM! Mete la pelota.

—¡Canasta! —grita Paco muy contento.

—Toma, Lola. Te toca —dice Paco.

Lola toma la pelota en las manos.

Dice:

—Palmas, palmitas, entra, pelotita.

Lola da un salto y tira la pelota.

—¡Metí la pelota! —dice Lola.

Feliz con su triunfo, Lola vuelve a la fila y le da la pelota a su nueva amiga.

—Tu turno, Lupita —dice Lola.

Lupita mira la pelota.

Dice:

—No me des la pelota, Lola.

  No podré meterla.

Lupita está a punto de llorar y su nueva amiga quiere saber qué le pasa.

—¿Por qué, Lupita? —pregunta Lola.

—Tengo muletas.

No podré usar las manos —responde Lupita.

Lupita está triste.

Cuando la señorita Peña se da cuenta de que Lupita llora, siente pena.

—¿Qué te pasa, Lupita?

—dice la señorita Peña.

—No podré meter la pelota.

Tengo muletas —dice Lupita.

—Sí podrás —la anima la señorita Peña.

Todos los niños animan a Lupita.

—¡Lupita! ¡Lupita! ¡Ra, ra, ra! —dicen todos.

Entonces Lupita, al oír a los niños, se anima. ¿Qué hace?

—Dame la pelota, Lola —dice Lupita.

Lupita toma la pelota y . . .

¡POM! Lupita mete la pelota.

—¡Metí la pelota, la metí! —dice Lupita.

Lupita está muy contenta porque los niños y la maestra de su nueva escuela son muy buenos con ella. Y todos los niños están contentos porque pudieron ser los campeones del baloncesto.

Responde las preguntas del cuento:

1. ¿Es Lupita de Lima?

   sí   no

2. ¿Qué pide la señorita Peña a los niños?

   _____

   _____

3. ¿Da Lola un salto?

   _____

   _____

4. ¿Dónde mete Lupita la pelota?

   _____

   _____

5

Intermediate Reading

Reading Wings

Reading Wings is the reading approach used in Success for All from the second grade level to the end of elementary school. The key to its effectiveness is the powerful cooperative learning process that it uses to engage students in meaningful and challenging discussions of their reading with their teammates and classmates. Every day, students explain their understanding of their reading to their teammates, and teammates question and explain their thinking to each other to ensure that every student on the team has a deep understanding of the reading. To ensure that the team takes responsibility for the learning of all of its members, the teacher randomly chooses a team member to report for the team in class discussions. Teams must be sure that all members are prepared to answer questions about a reading and to explain what evidence from the reading or from their background knowledge supports their answer because any one of the team's members could be asked to represent the team during the class discussion. In addition, teams can earn recognition as a group for successfully demonstrating strong text comprehension, use of comprehension strategies, mastery of vocabulary, and writing skills in written assessments. Reading Wings is an adaptation of Cooperative Integrated Reading and Composition (CIRC), a cooperative learning program that encompasses both reading and writing/language arts. Studies of CIRC have shown it to be effective in increasing students' reading, writing, and language achievement (e.g., Stevens et al., 1987).

The curricular focus of Reading Wings is primarily on building comprehension and thinking skills, fluency, vocabulary, and pleasure in reading. Reading Wings assumes that students coming out of Reading Roots have solid word attack skills, but need to build on this foundation as they learn to understand and enjoy increasingly complex material. As in Reading Roots, students in Reading Wings are regrouped for reading across grade lines, so a class reading texts at a third grade reading level could be composed of second, third, and fourth graders.

Students use their regular basal readers, novels, or anthologies, or they may purchase trade books specifically for Reading Wings. Guides, called *Targeted Treasure Hunts*, have been developed to accompany a large number of current basals and novels, including Spanish basals and novels.

Stories are introduced and discussed by the teacher. During these lessons, teachers elicit and provide background knowledge, set a purpose for reading, introduce new vocabulary, review old vocabulary, discuss the story after students have read it, and so on. Presentation methods for each segment of the lesson are structured. For example, teachers use a vocabulary presentation procedure that requires a demonstration of understanding word meaning by each individual, a review of methods of word attack, repetitive oral reading of vocabulary to achieve automaticity, and use of the meanings of the vocabulary words to help introduce the content of the story. Story discussions are structured to emphasize such skills as making and supporting predictions about the story and understanding major structural components of the story (e.g., problem and solution in a narrative).

COOPERATIVE LEARNING STRUCTURES

In Reading Wings, students are assigned to four- or five-member learning teams that are heterogeneous in performance level, sex, and age. These teams choose team names and work together for six to eight weeks. Each week, students take a set of quizzes that assess text comprehension, use of comprehension strategies, and vocabulary. Quiz scores contribute to a team score, and the teams can earn certificates and other recognition based on the team's average quiz scores. Students also contribute points to their teams by completing book reports and writing assignments, and by returning completed forms initialed by parents indicating that they have been reading at home each evening.

Teams also receive points for effective teamwork. Team members learn to work together using a set of team cooperation goals, as follows:

Practice active listening.

Help and encourage each other.

Everyone participates.

Explain your answer/tell why.

Complete tasks.

Teachers choose a specific teamwork focus each week, briefly introduce the goal with a discussion of what it looks like, sounds like, and feels like, and then provide feedback by giving points that count toward team certificates.

Teams are recognized as SuperTeams, GreatTeams, or GoodTeams with certificates that can be posted on class bulletin boards and sent home for celebration by parents. Teachers often celebrate team success in a variety of other ways to develop excitement and motivate teams. Each week, successful teams might be named in a schoolwide announcement, allowed to eat lunch in a special place, or offered other activities to celebrate their success. Since all teams have equal opportunities to succeed, the desire to achieve recognition can motivate students to work harder, help their teammates, accept help from teammates, and learn more as individuals.

Two simple cooperative learning techniques are used frequently during the lesson to build high-quality team interaction into the daily Reading Wings process. Think-Pair-Share is used in Reading Wings to engage students in brief partner discussions that require all students to put their thinking about a portion of the lesson into words on the spot. In this simple technique, the teacher poses a question, allows ten to twenty seconds of think time, and then asks students to tell a partner their thinking. After a brief partner discussion, the teacher asks several pairs to share their ideas with the class. The teacher uses the responses to move the discussion forward, or to spend more time on a portion of the lesson if students' responses indicate the need.

Numbered Heads is used to involve a team in a longer discussion of lesson content, and creates a clear expectation that the team members are responsible for the learning of every student on the team. In Numbered Heads, each member of each team receives a number from one to four (or five if the team is a five-member team). The teacher poses a question for team discussion, and allows the team time to work through and discuss the problem. Students know that a number will be chosen at random, and that the team member with that number will respond for the team, so they are responsible for preparing all team members to answer and explain the question posed. Teams can earn points based on their successful responses.

CYCLE OF EFFECTIVE INSTRUCTION

The Cycle of Effective Instruction is the teaching model that drives Reading Wings instruction and learning by combining the best direct instructional practices with cooperative learning.

Active Instruction

Every instructional cycle begins with active instruction in which the teacher teaches, demonstrates, models, and guides student practice of the targeted objective. For instance, a teacher developing her students' comparing and contrasting skills might first model the skill by having the class describe similarities and differences between an elephant and a mouse while she records using a Venn diagram. She would then give teams a few minutes to talk together to compare and contrast baseball and basketball using a Venn diagram. As they worked, she would listen in to assess needs for further teaching, and might interrupt the discussion if needed to clarify the concepts presented previously. To extend the concept, she might have students read a short compare/contrast passage and complete a Venn diagram as a team. Finally, the teacher would pull the class together and randomly choose several students from different teams to report the results of their discussion, again taking the opportunity to note good use of the Venn diagram and to reteach as needed so that students are prepared for an effective Team Practice.

Teamwork

In the Active Teaching phase of the lesson, students should develop enough understanding of the objective to enable them to practice effectively as teams. During the Team Practice phase, students work together in pairs or as a full team to ensure that *every* individual in the team masters the skill. To start, team members coconstruct responses to the practice tasks, and then, as confidence builds, the activity gradually transitions into independent practice with peer assessment and feedback to prepare students for individual assessments of the targeted skill or strategy.

In the example above, students work in their teams with more passages during Team Practice, providing suggestions and explanations to one another as they work together on comparisons and contrasts. After working through one or two passages together, they try their hands individually, and then compare Venn diagrams to ensure that everyone has a clear enough understanding to allow them to succeed on the individual assessment. As students work together, the teacher moves around the class, recognizing both effective use of the Venn diagram for compare and contrast and recognizing the use of the cooperation skills used to increase learning.

At the end of team practice, the teacher again pulls the class together to debrief the teams, and again randomly chooses a few students using Numbered Heads to report for their team by showing their work. The team receives points for their team score sheet if the work of the student randomly chosen is well done. This feedback rewards students for paying close attention to the learning of their teammates, and gives students permission both to ask for help and give help to ensure the success of the team.

Assessment

During the assessment phase, each student is individually assessed to make sure that he or she has mastered the targeted skill or strategy. Assessment can consist of informal or formal measures such as observations, written tests, and timed oral reading. The assessment used in the example above would be for each student to use a Venn diagram independently to make a comparison. Each student's score on the assessment is recorded on the team score sheet, and averaged in with other points earned to help determine whether the team is a SuperTeam that week. The assessment information is also used by the teacher to determine whether additional teaching is needed and to record individual progress in the grade book. A sample Team Score Sheet is shown in Figure 5.1. Scores are collected and recorded on the Team Score Sheet throughout the cycle of activities. Points for team cooperation are also recorded daily on the score sheet.

Celebration

During Celebration, teams are recognized as a group for their success. Keeping the focus on group success is critical in order to develop a classroom culture in which students can be true partners in learning. Successful teams will figure out how to ask their teammates the right questions to find out whether they know what they should know, and will reteach, encourage, and provide the concrete practice that teachers cannot provide for every student individually. In a traditional classroom in which students are only responsible for themselves, it is often considered rude or intrusive to ask another student to explain themselves, and it can feel demeaning to have another student offer an explanation. These barriers fall when the goal is team success.

Celebration takes many forms, and the more creative and varied it is, the more fun students have and the stronger their teams become. Certificates awarded to SuperTeams can be backed by cheers, stickers, privileges, small snacks, or whatever the teacher and students find fun and workable in the classroom. Reading Wings classes have developed many forms of celebration. Team cheers have become a trademark of Reading Wings,

Figure 5.1 Reading Wings Team Score Sheet

Team Cooperation	1	2	3	4	5	6	7	8	9	10	11	12	13	14	15	16	17	18	19	20

Team Name *Flying Falcons*   **Reading Wings Team Score Sheet**   Strategy Target _____

Start Date *12/4*   Unit Title *Uncle Jed's Barbershop* _____

Team Members	Comprehension Score	Vocabulary Score	Fluency	Strategy Use	Adventures in Writing	Word Power (if used)	Team Cooperation	Subtotal	(÷ by # of columns used)	Individual Average	Goal Met	Vocabulary Vault	Read and Respond	Book Response	Individual points
1. Julio	80	70	90	80) 90	90	—	97	517	÷ 6	=86	+ __	+ 5	+ 5	+ 5	101
2. Kenzie	80	80	90	80) 90	100	—	97	537	÷ 6	=90	+ __	+ 5	+ 5	+ —	100
3. Max	70	80	70) 70	90	100	—	97	507	÷ 6	=85	+ __	+ 5	+ 5	+ 5	100
4. Sofia	80	80	100	70) 90	90	—	97	537	÷ 6	=90	+ __	+ 5	+ 5	+ 5	105
5.									÷	=	+	+	+	+	

Total **406**

÷ by # of team members

Team Score **102**

Team Cooperation Points (20 points daily)

	Day 1	Day 2	Day 3	Day 4	Quality Pts. or Day 5	Total
	20	19	18	20	20	97

Good Team _____   Great Team _____   Super Team _____

01712
HBP0507

with new cheers shared among schools each year. Samples of some of the favorite cheers for successful teamwork are shown in Figure 5.2.

Targeted Treasure Hunts

Targeted Treasure Hunts provide teachers with materials for instruction and cooperative practice built around a wide variety of student readings, including most basal series

Figure 5.2 Samples of Reading Wings Cheers

Arctic Shiver

Cross hands and place on shoulders. Rub your hands up and down your upper arms and shiver as you say "Ooooooh, so cool!"

Firecracker

Clap twice, then stretch arms out, wiggle fingers and let arms fall downward. Make a "shhhhhhhh" sound as your arms fall.

Shine Your Halo

Pretend to "shine" an invisible halo over your head by rubbing it in a circular motion.

as well as a rich selection of trade book titles. The process is used with students at reading Levels 2 through 6 and builds in the Cycle of Effective Instruction. Targeted Treasure Hunts provide specific materials for teacher instruction and cooperative practice in the essential outcomes for students at this level, including the development of comprehension skills and strategy use, word recognition and vocabulary, fluency, and writing skills. The combination of the Cycle of Effective Instruction with Targeted Treasure Hunt lessons creates a dynamic classroom, as teachers model, prompt, reinforce, and assess the goals established for their students, and students are actively engaged in working through texts as partners and teams and on their own.

In order to keep the sometimes elusive goals of reading instruction front and center, teachers assess strategy use and skill development with various assessment tools such as rubrics, checklists, and student tests. To help students monitor their progress, feedback is provided frequently and with celebrations of both team and individual progress. For instance, after comprehension monitoring (or clarification) is introduced through direct instruction, video modeling, and partner practice, teachers monitor student growth using the "Charting Progress" form shown in Figure 5.3.

The key comprehension strategies are introduced using a sequence of lessons called The Savvy Reader. These lessons are interspersed throughout the year, and then practiced in teamwork in every Treasure Hunt. Four main skills are directly taught and practiced: Clarifying, Questioning, Summarizing, and Predicting. The summarizing component includes a strategy for reading expository text called SQRRRL (Survey, Question, Read and Restate, Review, and Learn), described in more detail later in this chapter. Video vignettes help teachers introduce these skills and build motivation for using their comprehension strategies as they read their texts and other materials. The use of the four core reading strategies (clarifying, predicting, questioning, and summarizing) is embedded in the Targeted Treasure Hunt. Once students learn these strategies, they become a routine part of the students' reading-comprehension monitoring.

A tool for monitoring growth in fluency similarly keeps students and teachers focused, and provides a basis for celebrating progress.

Active Instruction

A Targeted Treasure Hunt cycle is completed over about a week. Each cycle begins with Active Instruction, designed to introduce the targeted strategy or skill targeted in the cycle and prepare students for the text they will read. In Active Instruction, teachers explain and model these skills or strategies. Targeted skills include cause and effect, main idea and supporting details, plot, characterization, problem and solution, sequencing, and theme. The teacher first presents the vocabulary words, models the targeted skill or strategy, and then reinforces the skill or strategy as she or he reads aloud. During each part of the process, students are actively engaged as they practice vocabulary, review with partners, and participate in learning the targeted skill/strategy. The subcomponents of Active Instruction are described below.

Set the Stage

Teachers use Set the Stage each day of the cycle to introduce and review the title and author of the student text and the reading goal. On Day 1, students take time to write their vocabulary words and rate their knowledge of them. Students also set goals as a class, team, or as individuals based on the previous lesson's team score sheet.

Figure 5.3   Charting Progress Form

Clarifying: Setting Goals and Charting Progress

OUTCOME: Stop when you don't understand what you have read. Identify what you do not understand with a sticky note.

Class: _____   Date: _____ to _____

Update this form during each quarter using a different-colored pen or pencil each time. Record dates below in color used on update.

Marking Key *(See back of form for details.)*   **P:** Prompted   **I:** Independent

Students	Stop when you can't pronounce a word and then...					Stop when you don't know a word's meaning and then...						Stop when you don't understand a sentence(s) and then...							
	Sound Blend	Chunk familiar word parts	Look for base word	Reread	Ask for help	Describe strategy clearly	Use context	Reread	Read on	Use other resources (Dictionary/Thesaurus)	Ask for help	Describe strategy clearly	Use background knowledge	Use context	Reread	Read on	Use narrative text structure(s)	Use expository text structure(s)	Ask for help	Describe strategy clearly

Figure 5.4   Vocabulary Sequence Sample Lessons

TP **Teacher Procedure**

Active Instruction

Vocabulary Presentation and Review

▶ Point to and read each word on your chart, explaining how to use the identification strategy. Ask the students to repeat each word. (This step becomes optional after Day 2.)

▶ Assign teammates as Partners 1 and 2 for reviewing the vocabulary words. Teach or model this Student Routine **SR** as necessary before having the students begin.

Note: *Level B (2) students should try to give their own definition and sentence if possible. You may allow them to read the definition and sentence at first but by the end of the week, they should be able to give their own.*

How to Review Vocabulary With Your Partner

You	Your Partner
Using your journal list:	Using the vocabulary chart:

+ Words
 • Say the word, tell what it means, and use it in a sentence.
 • Add another "+" if you are correct!
 • Add a "?" if you needed help.
	+ Words
	 • Say "yes" for correct answers.
	 • Help your partner if he or she needs it.
	   • Suggest an identification strategy.
	   • Read a definition or a sentence.
	 • Ask your teammates or teacher for help if you need it.

? Words
 • Read the word if you can.
 • Tell the definition and sentence if you can.
 • Ask your partner for help if you don't know.
 • Add another "?" if you needed help.
 • Add a "+" if you are correct!
	? Words
	 • Say "yes" for correct answers.
	 • Help your partner if he or she needs it.
	   • Suggest an identification strategy.
	   • Read a definition or a sentence.
	 • Ask your teammates or teacher for help if you need it.

Review these vocabulary words with your partner each day:

Four-Day Lessons

Day 1	Day 2	Day 3
Partner 1: Words 1–3 Partner 2: Words 4–6	Partner 1: Words 4–6 Partner 2: Words 1–3	Partners review all words together

Five-Day Lessons

Day 1	Day 2	Day 3	Day 4
Partner 1: Words 1–4 Partner 2: Words 5–8	Partner 1: Words 5–8 Partner 2: Words 1–4	Partner 1: Words 1–4 Partner 2: Words 5–8	Partner 1: Words 5–8 Partner 2: Words 1–4

▶ Use Numbered Heads to review the word pronunciations, meanings, and sentences. Allow the students to use their lesson charts on Day 1 if they do not know a word or its meaning.

▶ Review, as necessary, the directions for finding the vocabulary words in the daily reading (Levels C–F, 3–6) and for adding words to the Vocabulary Vault.

Directions for finding vocabulary words in the daily reading (Levels C–F, 3–6)

1. As you read on instructional days, when you find a vocabulary word, write the page number where you found it in your journal, next to the word.

2. Record only one page number, even if you read the word again.

3. On the assessment day, your teacher will look at your journal to check your words.

Directions for using the Vocabulary Vault

1. If you read or hear a vocabulary word somewhere other than in your assigned reading, remember or write down the word and how it was used.

2. Write the word and your name on a Vocabulary Voucher and put the slip in the Vault.

3. When you are called on to explain your Voucher, you will earn team bonus points if you can say the word and how it was used. You must say or paraphrase the sentence in which the word was used, using the word correctly and demonstrating its meaning.

Vocabulary

Key vocabulary for the story is introduced before the story is previewed, so that students can move directly from previewing to reading. During vocabulary presentation and review, students develop word strategies to help with word pronunciation, word meaning, and word use within context. Students are introduced to vocabulary words from the text they are about to read. After the teacher presents the vocabulary words, students review these words with their partners. Teachers also remind students to look for these words and to list them in their journals during Partner Reading. The vocabulary component of the process provides instruction in word-recognition skills and also prepares students to encounter these words within the context of their reading. An example of a vocabulary sequence for the first day of the sample lesson and then for Days 2, 3, and 4 of the five-day cycle is shown in Figure 5.4. The words presented in *Kids Are Citizens* are shown in Figure 5.5.

As shown in the example, vocabulary routines maximize the student's exposure to words and word meanings by specifying a variety of activities that use the words during a five-day lesson cycle. The activities combine to form the entire Cycle of Effective Instruction for key vocabulary words. In Active Instruction, the teacher presents the words using suggested strategies (including affixes, words parts, and sound blending), and gives the meaning as used in the selection with definitions and example sentences. Vocabulary charts with the words, definitions, and sample sentences are in the teacher and student materials. The teacher materials also include identification strategies and the page numbers for words in the student text.

Students write the vocabulary words in their journals on the first day and rate their knowledge of these words. On subsequent days, they use these journal lists to review the words with partners and in teams; as they review the words, they rate the words again. This allows them to identify and record their progress. Continuous rating of their word knowledge helps focus the class on the words that they have not yet learned, and the teacher uses the ratings to gauge what reinforcement is needed.

Figure 5.5 Vocabulary Introduction

Introduce Vocabulary TP

▶ Introduce the vocabulary.

▶ Have the teams review the vocabulary words. SR

▶ Follow up the team review using Numbered Heads.

▶ Review the procedures for the students finding words in their daily reading and for adding words to the Vocabulary Vault.

Word and Page Number	Identification Strategy	Definition	Sentence
citizen p. 9	chunk: cit-i-zen	resident of a country having rights by birth or by law	Paul was a *citizen* of South Africa, where he was born.
trigger p. 14	chunk: trigg-er	start, set off	The park ranger feared that the campfire would *trigger* a larger forest fire.
position p. 14	chunk: pos-i-tion	belief, point of view	Cory used facts to support his *position* that school lunches should be healthier.
judge p. 14	blend	decide, form an opinion	The jury would *judge* the case after they heard all of the facts.
present p. 15	stress the second syllable chunk: pre-sent	show, give	Ellie used a film and charts to *present* her research on recycling.
approved p. 20	base word + ending approv(e) + ed	accepted, agreed to	The principal *approved* the proposed list of guest speakers to attend Career Day.
harm p. 21	blend	hurt	Ken gently picked up the baby bird so he would not *harm* it.
contact p. 26	chunk: con-tact	get in touch with, communicate with	Lydia planned to *contact* her group members by e-mail.

Students are motivated to find the selected words outside the classroom using a routine called "Vocabulary Vault," in which students earn team points for finding their vocabulary word in their environment, in either written or spoken form. When this occurs, the words are put in the class Vocabulary Vault. Each day the teacher opens the Vault during Active Instruction, takes out its contents one at a time, and asks contributing students to explain how their words were used.

During Teamwork, teams review word pronunciations, meanings, and sample sentences, and note when they find the selected vocabulary in the week's reading by recording page numbers on which the words are found in their journals. In addition, team members develop their depth of knowledge through specially constructed practice activities using multiple choice and cloze items. They also learn to create "meaningful sentences" to express the meaning of the selected vocabulary word.

Informal assessment goes on throughout the lesson cycle as students rate their words and as they work with their teammates. More formal assessment occurs in the test at the end of the cycle. End-of-cycle tests may include multiple choice and cloze items, as well as the construction of new sentences that show word meaning. Progress is celebrated with points earned on the team score sheet.

Build Background

The reading that forms the basis of the cycle is previewed on Day 10 of a lesson cycle in the Build Background section of the lesson. In addition, students are introduced to necessary background information in preparation for reading the text. During Build Background, the teacher teaches, explains, and/or demonstrates the targeted skill or strategy. On the remaining instructional days, students work in teams to review the main events/ideas of the previously read material and discuss strategic use. On test day, students work together to organize the story elements from that week's reading onto a story map for narrative texts. Build Background not only prepares students to apply the targeted skill and strategy in their reading, but it also activates their prior knowledge, helping them to establish a context for their reading.

Listening Comprehension

Listening Comprehension is an interactive part of the lesson that motivates students by generating interest and helping them make connections to the text, their prior knowledge, and text ideas picked up through the readings. Listening Comprehension also teaches and scaffolds understanding of the reading goal across the week. On Day 1, students preview the text; on subsequent instructional days, they review the text. Each day, students make predictions using evidence from the text and background knowledge when new information is presented in the text. The teacher also uses Think Alouds to teach and model the reading goal within the context of the story, and Team Talk questions are reviewed to draw attention to the reading goal as well as to set the purpose for student reading. Listening Comprehension further prepares students for partner and silent reading by allowing them to see the targeted skills and strategies applied to the text.

An example from the Listening Comprehension portion of a lesson built around *Kids Are Citizens,* an expository text for sixth graders, is shown in Figure 5.6. The goal of this lesson is to introduce the use of a graphic organizer, an Idea Tree, in the reading of expository text.

Teamwork

Teamwork consists of Partner Reading, Team Discussion, and Class Discussion. During this part of the process, students read with partners and then silently discuss strategy use and answer Team Talk questions. Partner Reading and Team Discussion are student-led activities. During this time, students work with partners and then teams as the teacher monitors and reinforces their discussions. Class Discussion is teacher-led and serves as a time to review partner and team discussions at the class level. During Teamwork, students receive ample opportunity to discuss and extend their comprehension of the text while focusing on the keys to unlocking their comprehension: the core reading strategies.

(Text continued on page 196.)

Figure 5.6   Sample Listening Comprehension Lesson

Day 1

Active Instruction

Timing Goal:
25 minutes

Preparation: Write the vocabulary words on chart paper.

Set the Stage

▶ Using your vocabulary chart, have the students copy the words into their journals and rate their knowledge of each as they arrive for class.

▶ Introduce the text, author, and reading goal.

> *This week, we will read* Kids Are Citizens, *an expository text by Ellen Keller. As we read, we will look for main ideas and supporting details using a process called SQRRRL. Good readers identify the main ideas and supporting details, especially when they read expository texts, to make sure they learn and remember the important information.*

▶ Establish, or have the students establish, the purpose for reading (e.g., to be informed, to follow directions, to be entertained). Discuss with the students ways to adjust their reading to fit the purpose.

▶ Explain the student assessments: Fluency, Adventures in Writing, and the Student Test. Tell the students there will be questions on the Student Test that are related to the reading goal.

Build Background

▶ Remind the students that *Kids Are Citizens* is an expository text. Ask them to examine a few pages to see how it looks different from a narrative text. If necessary, summarize the difference between narrative and expository texts.

> *Narrative texts tell stories and include characters, settings, problems, and solutions. The stories can be real, such as those about the lives of famous people, but often they are fictional: made-up stories about made-up people. Expository texts are not made up. They describe, explain, or otherwise give information, through the use of titles, chapters, headings, definitions, charts, photographs and captions, and other tools, to help readers learn and understand the information.*

▶ Explain that since we read expository texts to learn about things, we want to be sure that we figure out, and remember, the important information. Tell the students that SQRRRL will help them do that. Tell what the SQRRRL letters stand for, and explain that they will use the process while reading this week's text.

> *SQRRRL stands for Survey, Question, Read and Restate, Review, and Learn. We will do each of these things this week as we read to make sure we understand the main ideas and supporting details. SQRRRL will help us remember this information too.*

▶ Explain that the SQRRRL Process is used with an Idea Tree, which has a "big topic" trunk and main idea branches coming out of it. Draw an Idea Tree with eight branches on chart paper, and have the students do the same on their papers, leaving room to add more branches.

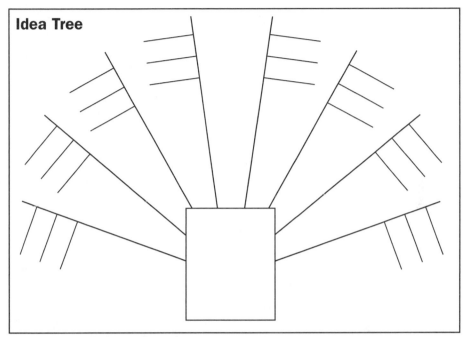

Idea Tree

▶ Tell the students that when using the SQRRRL Process, they must first survey the text to figure out the "big topic." Explain how to survey, and then model with a Think Aloud, using *Kids Are Citizens.*

> *To survey, I'll preview the text before I read, which will help me figure out what the book is about. I'll look at the title, table of contents, pictures, headings, and other text features that stand out on the pages.*

> (Model surveying the book with a Think Aloud.) *The title of the book is* Kids Are Citizens. *As I look at the table of contents, I see the words "rights," "take action," and "responsibilities." As I look at the pictures, I see several of the American flag, presidents of the United States, and people who look like they are giving speeches. The pictures show American things, and the title tells me the book is about citizens, so I think this book is about being a citizen of the United States.*

▶ Write the "big topic" (being a citizen of the United States) on the trunk of your Idea Tree, and ask the students to do so also.

▶ Explain and model the Question part of SQRRRL. Write your questions on chart paper so you can model how to answer them on Day 5.

Figure 5.6 (Continued)

> *The next part of SQRRRL is Question. Questions give us a purpose for reading. Even though you have Team Talk questions to answer, it's important to think of your own questions to give you your own purpose for reading.*
>
> *When I surveyed the text, I saw a chapter titled "Becoming a Good Listener." I don't know what being a good listener has to do with being a citizen of the United States, so I'll write a question about that. My question will be, "Why do citizens of the United States have to be good listeners?"* (Write this question on chart paper.)
>
> *I also saw a picture of a woman. Beneath her picture was the name Sandra Day O'Connor. I don't know who she is, so my other question will be, "Who is Sandra Day O'Connor?"* (Write this question on chart paper.)

▶ Have the students survey the text and write two questions on the back of their Idea Trees that they would like answered as they read.

Listening Comprehension

▶ Tell the students that you're going to show them how to do the next two parts of SQRRRL—Read and Restate the main ideas. This is what they will do with their partners to identify the main ideas for the branches of their trees.

▶ Explain to the students that, as you read, you are going to stop after each page to see if you can restate the main ideas and write them on your Idea Tree. Point out that some pages, such as those that introduce chapters, may not have main ideas to add to your Idea Tree. Tell the students that some pages may have more than one main idea.

▶ Read page 5. Use a Think Aloud to model finding the main idea.

> *I'm going to stop and think about what I have read. This page is about the ways a person can become a citizen of the United States. I see the title "Who Is a Citizen?" I think that is the main idea, so I'll write the title as a main idea on my Idea Tree. I want to remember where I found that idea, so I'll write "page 5" next to it.*

▶ Model checking the main idea by finding supporting details. Write these details next to the main idea on your Idea Tree.

> *Now I'll check my main idea by finding supporting details. I said that my main idea is "Who Is a Citizen?" I read that someone born in the United States is a citizen, so I'll write that on the Idea Tree. (Add this detail to the Idea Tree.) I also read that if you were born in another country and then moved to the United States, you can take a test to become a citizen of the United States. I'll write "people from other countries who pass a test" as another detail on my Idea Tree. (Add this detail to the Idea Tree.)*

Active Instruction
continued

▶ Point out that you used a text feature to help you find the main idea.

> *Earlier we said that expository texts have features, such as titles and headings, that can help us learn and understand the information that authors want us to know. I just used a text feature to do that: I used a title to identify a main idea.*

▶ Read page 6. After reading, stop and point out that this page introduces Chapter 1 and does not have a main idea to add to the Idea Tree.

▶ Read pages 7–8. After reading each page, stop and summarize the main ideas and details from your reading, and write these on an Idea Tree. See the sample Idea Tree for possible main ideas and details.

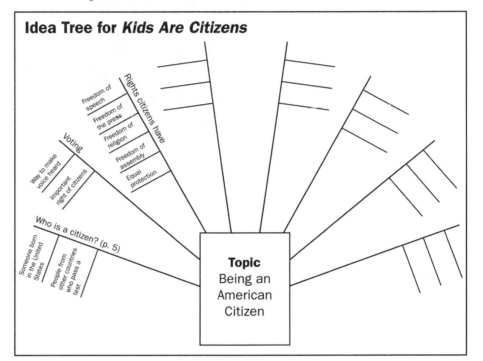

Idea Tree for *Kids Are Citizens*

Topic
Being an American Citizen

▶ Have the students preview pages 9–11. Remind them to look at pictures and headings to help them predict what they will read about. Then use Think-Pair-Share to ask the students to make their predictions. Make sure they tell why they made those predictions.

▶ Point out that the headings and subheadings on these pages can help them to identify main ideas and supporting details.

▶ Preview the Team Talk questions with the class. Tell the students that they will write out the answers to Questions #2 and #3 independently, after they talk in their teams. Point out that Question #1 is a main idea question.

(Continued)

Figure 5.6 (Continued)

Active Instruction
continued

**Student Edition,
page 3**

> **Team Talk**
> 1. Which of the following is the main idea of the section titled "Responsibilities"? [Main Idea]
>   a. Good citizens have no responsibilities.
>   b. A responsible citizen should think only of himself.
>   *c. Citizens have responsibilities as well as rights.*
>   d. Citizens have many rights and no responsibilities.
>   What are some details the author uses to support this main idea?
>   *[Possible details: Be informed. Respect the law. Make your voice heard. Show your respect to others.]*
> 2. What is an informed opinion? (Write)
>   *[An informed opinion is an opinion that is based on facts.]*
> 3. Why does Sandra Day O'Connor need to be a good listener? (Write) [Cause and Effect]
>   *[Sandra Day O'Connor needs to be a good listener so that she can make good decisions. Her decisions affect all citizens.]*

Partner Reading

Students read and restate with partners and then read silently, while applying the comprehension strategies.

- Each day the students begin by taking turns reading pages aloud; then they continue, but silently. As instructed, partners learn the following procedures:
  o If you don't understand a word, try to figure it out.
  o If you can't figure it out, ask your partner for help.
  o If your partner can't help you, put a sticky note in the margin next to the word.
- Before Partner Reading, the teacher reviews the procedures for strategy use, passes out a limited number of sticky notes to each student, and tells the students to begin reading. Both the student and teacher materials contain the page numbers to be read.
- Once the students begin to read, the teacher circulates to explain, model, prompt, and reinforce the students in their strategy use. During this time, the teacher also uses the Setting Goals and Charting Progress tools to record individual student progress on the selected goal. This record helps provide guidance to the teacher as she or he models and reinforces strategy use, and selects strategies to focus on in future lesson cycles.

Team Discussion

After partners read, the team comes together for the team discussion. On the first day of each lesson cycle, the teacher randomly assigns a Team Leader for each team for the week. This student is responsible for making sure that the team completes all activities and that each member is prepared for the class discussion. The agenda for Team Discussion includes reviewing strategy use during partner reading, discussing answers to Team Talk questions, writing answers to Team Talk questions if indicated, and preparing for Class Discussion by making sure all teammates can share successful strategy use, and can relate the team's consensus answers to the Team Talk questions.

During Team Discussion, students take turns discussing their strategy use and answers to the Team Talk questions. To ensure equal team participation, turn-taking procedures are used to guide discussion. When students are finished discussing their strategy use and answers to Team Talk questions, they independently write their responses to the designated questions.

The teacher's role during Team Discussion is to circulate to explain, model, prompt, and reinforce the students in their discussions. It is particularly important for the teacher to model the asking of challenging questions, and to show how to follow up answers with requests for evidence so that team members learn that these are the expectations for discussion. Students are asked to answer questions for the team and describe the evidence they have used, so the team must prepare every student to report for the team.

Students may find it helpful to use role cards (shown in Figure 5.7) to structure the team discussion. The use of role cards helps ensure that every student participates in the discussion, and helps students learn how to discuss their reading together as a team. As students become more experienced, they may no longer need this scaffolding.

A sample of Team Talk questions from *Kids Are Citizens* is shown in Figure 5.8.

Class Discussion

Class Discussion is a whole-class, teacher-led discussion that serves as a critical follow-up to Team Discussion. The teacher reinforces and rewards effective thinking, discussion, and team cooperation at this time. During the Class Discussion, teachers choose students randomly, using Numbered Heads, to share with the class their team's discussion of strategy use and Team Talk questions during partner reading. Because students know that one teammate often will be chosen to speak for their team, they know that each one must be prepared to speak. The routine use of Numbered Heads during Class Discussion creates powerful motivation for students to work effectively during Teamwork.

Teams receive points on their Team Score Sheets based on their team discussion of their strategy use while reading. Teachers or students and teachers together select a strategy to focus on each week, and students write it on the team score sheet. The same strategy should be the focus for eight to sixteen weeks so that students can see growth in their use of the strategy. During Class Discussion, the teacher gives points based on one of the rubrics shown in Figure 5.9 to celebrate students' effective use of strategies and effective team discussion.

Class Discussion also provides the teacher with additional opportunities to teach, model, prompt, and reinforce skills. After discussing the students' strategy use and answers to Team Talk questions, the teacher extends the discussion with a thought-provoking question known as an Extender that grows from the students' comments related to the reading. The Extender challenges the students' thinking about the passage that they read and discussed that day, and allows them to share the connection they have made to their own experiences.

Figure 5.7   Sample Role Cards

A.

Read the Question

1. Read in a voice that can be heard only by your teammates. Be sure everyone is practicing "Active Listening."
2. Check to be sure everyone heard and understands the question.

B.

Answer the Question

1. Restate the question in your own words.
2. Restate part of the question in your answer.
3. Give your answer and explain why you think it is correct.
4. Check to be sure everyone heard.

C.

Agree and Add or Disagree Because...

Restate your teammate's answer and:
1. Agree and add additional information from your text or experience or ...
2. Disagree and support your answer from the text or your experience.

D.

Summarize and Check for Understanding

1. Restate the group's agreed-upon answer.
2. Check with each teammate to be sure everyone understands and agrees.

Figure 5.8   Team Talk Questions

Day 2

Team Talk

1. What do you think the phrase "foreign-born" means? What clues from the text help you figure out the meaning? (Write)

2. Which of the following is a detail about "loaded language"?

   a. Loaded language has nothing to do with point of view.

   b. Loaded language is a part of the English language.

   c. Word choices do not matter in trying to persuade someone.

   d. Word choices can affect how someone feels about an issue.

3. On page 14, which speaker opposes this position: "Provide a safe place for young people to socialize. Keep the new youth center open." Explain how you know. (Write)

Figure 5.9   Strategy Rubrics

Strategy Rubrics

Clarifying

100 points	A team member* can identify a word that the team clarified, say the word, explain what it means, and explain how they clarified the word, identifying specific clarifying strategies they used (i.e., sound blending, chunking, base words, rereading).
90 points	A team member* can identify a word that the team clarified, say the word, and explain what it means.
80 points	A team member* can identify a word that the team clarified and say the word.

Questioning

100 points	A team member* earns 90 points AND can describe whether the question is a Right There or Think question and can explain why.
90 points	A team member* asks a question, answers it correctly, and points to supporting information in the text or describes background knowledge used.
80 points	A team member* asks a question and answers it correctly.

Predicting

100 points	A team member* tells about a prediction that the team made, provides support for their prediction, and can explain if it has been confirmed or disproved.
90 points	A team member* tells about a prediction that the team made and provides support for the prediction.
80 points	A team member* tells about a prediction that the team made.

Summarizing

100 points	A team member* restates main idea(s) and can give reasons for the team's selection of the main idea(s).
90 points	A team member* restates the main idea(s).
80 points	A team member* restates some important ideas, but includes some less important details as well.

* The teacher uses Numbered Heads to select a team member to respond for the team. Teams must be sure that ALL team members are able to respond for the team.

Team Practice

During this time, students practice vocabulary words and fluency to gain mastery. This is a student-led instructional process. Students complete the activities, with the help of their partners and/or teams as the teacher monitors and reinforces student work. Team practice assists students in their comprehension and reading skills by providing more practice with their vocabulary words in context and by giving students the opportunity to gain feedback in fluency.

Fluency Practice

Students develop fluency through teacher modeling and partner practice. The teacher first introduces and models fluency skills (i.e., accuracy, smoothness, expressiveness, and rate) using a fluency rubric. The teacher demonstrates fluent reading first and then demonstrates a lack of fluency by rereading the same page several times without each skill in the rubric. After modeling, the teacher guides the students in providing feedback using the rubric. Each day, students practice fluent reading using pages from the text they have already read. Students do not score each other but use the rubric to give feedback to their partners. After Day 1, students deemed by their partners to be ready read aloud to the teacher for a score. The teacher uses the rubric to score fluency, provide targeted feedback, and guide students in setting goals. Students are also introduced to reading at an appropriate rate. The teacher explains and models reading fluently and identifying the use of a count of words read correctly per minute (WCPM). Then students practice reading for fluency while working toward their WCPM goal. The fluency rubric is shown in Figure 5.10.

Teachers formally assess fluency rate using a "cold" read once or twice a quarter as a benchmark for growth. Expectations for fluency in terms of "words correct per minute" at different points in the schools year and at different reading levels are shown below. Students not reaching these levels are encouraged to set a goal for improvement, practice with their teammates and at home, and celebrate growth at the next measurement.

Targeted Fluency Rates

Level 2	60 (Fall) to 90 (Spring) WCPM
Level 3	90 (Fall) to 120 (Spring) WCPM
Level 4 and above	120+ WCPM

Vocabulary Practice

Students apply their knowledge of their vocabulary words and their meanings through one of three activities (cloze, multiple choice, or meaningful sentences). Students receive practice in the same format across the week. On Day 5, students are assessed using the same format they practiced throughout the week.

The teacher procedures for Vocabulary Practice are shown in Figure 5.11.

Adventures in Writing

Adventures in Writing activities are linked to the student texts. They are designed to extend students' thinking about certain concepts and skills. Adventures in Writing activities concentrate on developing well-constructed responses to questions related to the text that students are reading. Each instructional day, students respond to a question using an abbreviated writing process. A scoring guide is provided to guide the development of students' responses. Students have an opportunity to discuss their ideas with partners before they write independently. After students write their responses, they work with

Figure 5.10 Fluency Rubric

Fluency Rubric

100 points

Expressiveness ☐

The reading shows emotion and changes with punctuation, such as question marks, exclamation points, and quotation marks.

Word Errors:

- Skips a word
- Mispronounces the word
- Has word read by listener

90 points

Smoothness ☐

The reading is smooth and includes pauses for periods and commas.

Smoothness ☐

The reading is smooth and includes pauses for periods and commas.

80 points

Rate and Correctness ☐

Most of the words are correct (not more than four errors). The student reads at the targeted rate.

Targeted Rate:

_____

Rate and Correctness ☐

Most of the words are correct (not more than four errors). The student reads at the targeted rate.

Targeted Rate:

_____

Rate and Correctness ☐

Most of the words are correct (not more than four errors). The student reads at the targeted rate.

Targeted Rate:

_____

70 points

Correctness ☐

Most of the words are correct (not more than four errors).

---

partners to discuss and give feedback before revising their work. As students work, the teacher prompts, monitors, and reinforces their ideas and writing skills. At the end of the cycle, students select one of their written products to turn in for a score. The teacher uses the same scoring guide to rate each student's Adventures in Writing piece.

The student routines for Adventures in Writing are shown in Figure 5.12, with an example from *Kids Are Citizens*.

Assessment Day

Assessment day provides teachers and students with an opportunity to assess their understanding of the targeted strategy/skill, their vocabulary words, and their overall comprehension of the text. On assessment day, the teacher guides the students as they build background and prepare for the test. During the test, students read independently as they apply their strategy use and add relevant information to the story map/idea tree. Students then complete the comprehension test and vocabulary test. When they are finished, the teacher collects their answers, but students retain their test questions and story

Figure 5.11 Vocabulary Practice Procedure

Vocabulary

▶ Explain, or have the Team Leaders review, as necessary, the directions for the vocabulary practice activity before having the students begin. (Directions for the different activities follow.)

▶ Follow up vocabulary practice by checking one teammate's answers for consensus on multiple-choice or cloze activities or individual sentences for meaningful sentence activities.

▶ Remind the students to look for their vocabulary words outside reading class, so they can add them to the Vocabulary Vault tomorrow.

Cloze Practice

Students: Number your papers according to the number of underlined words in the activity for that day. Read the passage or sentences. Pick the word that best completes each sentence. Write your answers next to the matching numbers on your papers.

Teams: Take turns reading the sentences, including the missing words. Tell your teammates one clue that helped you find the answer. If you disagree on an answer, discuss it until all teammates agree.

Partners: Quiz your partner on the meanings of the words that he or she missed on the practice activity.

Multiple-Choice Practice

Students: Number your papers according to the number of underlined words in the activity for that day. Read the passage or sentences. Pick the word(s) that means the same thing or almost the same thing as the underlined word. Write your answers next to the matching numbers on your papers.

Teams: Take turns reading the sentences. Tell the definition you chose for the underlined word and at least one clue that helped you find the answer. If you disagree on an answer, discuss it until all teammates agree.

Partners: Quiz your partner on the meanings of the words that he or she missed on the practice activity.

Meaningful Sentence Practice

1. On Day 1, divide the vocabulary list with your partner evenly so each of you has your own list of words. Make sure that you use all the words and that you and your partner have different words.

2. Choose a new vocabulary word from your list each day to use in a meaningful sentence.

3. Use an organizer to plan your meaningful sentence and write a first draft.

4. Share your draft with your partner, and provide feedback for his or her sentence.

5. Revise your meaningful sentence based on your partner's feedback.

Vocabulary Practice

Students apply their knowledge of their vocabulary words and their meanings through one of three activities (cloze, multiple choice, or meaningful sentences). Students receive practice in the same format across the week. On Day 5, students are assessed using the same format they practiced throughout the week.

- Vocabulary practice gives the students an additional opportunity to work with their vocabulary words in their teams.
- This practice gives the students more exposure to the words in activities that are similar across one week, but vary from week to week.
- The different types of activities provide practice in standardized-test formats and in creating meaningful sentences.
- The procedures for the different types of activities—meaningful sentences, cloze, and multiple choice—are shown below.
- All activities and directions are in the Teacher Procedures and Student Routines pages.

Figure 5.12   Student Routines for Adventures in Writing

Adventures in Writing · · · · · · · · ·

> **Writing Prompt**
>
> Should the town council pass a law that makes it illegal to publicly express hateful things about others, or should people be allowed to publicly express messages of hate? Take a position on this issue. Write a speech that you will deliver to your town council, persuading them to accept your point of view. Your speech must tell your listeners how you feel about this issue and give at least three reasons that will persuade them to accept your point of view.

> **Scoring Guide**
>
> | | |
> |---|---|
> | An introductory paragraph that states the issue and how you feel about it | 10 points |
> | A paragraph with at least three supported reasons that will persuade your listeners | 15 points for each (60 points maximum) |
> | A concluding paragraph that restates how you feel about the issue | 20 points |
> | Ideas in complete sentences | 10 points |

maps/idea trees. During Teamwork, students participate in Team Discussion. Teams discuss strategy use, answers to the test questions, and any additions to the story map/idea trees.

An example of the written assessment for *Kids Are Citizens* is shown in Figure 5.13.

Independent Reading

Every evening, students are asked to read a trade book of their choice for at least twenty minutes, and write a one-sentence response to their reading. In most schools, classroom libraries of paperback books are established for this purpose. Parents initial a Read and Respond form (shown in Figure 5.14) nightly, indicating that students have read for the required time, and students contribute points to their teams if they submit a completed form each week. In a twice-weekly "book club," students discuss the books they have been reading and present more formal book reports, trying to entice others to take home the same book. "Book reports" can take many forms, from the completion of a brief written summary form to an oral summary, advertisement, puppet show, or whatever other form the reader and teacher wish to use. Independent reading and book reports replace all other homework in reading and language arts. If students complete their story-related activities or other activities early, they may also read their independent reading books in class.

Mastering Expository Text

Special attention is paid to the development of strategies to be used with expository text to enable readers to identify main ideas and details, and therefore understand and retain the information provided. A series of Savvy Reader lessons that introduce tools for the reading of expository text are an important part of Reading Wings at every reading level. Different text structures are explored, and graphic organizers useful in organizing the information presented are introduced. Brief video vignettes provide engaging examples of how these tools are used. Specific tools for monitoring the use of prediction, questioning, and summarization with expository text are used by the teacher during reading of expository text in content area classes as well as reading classes to track and encourage the use of strategies whenever informational text is read.

The instructional process for addressing expository text differs little from the process for narrative text. Both utilize the Cycle of Effective Instruction, target a skill or strategy, and include vocabulary, fluency, and writing structures. The targets in expository lessons focus on understanding the purpose and structure of expository text. Students use the SQRRRL process whenever they read informational text. The steps of SQRRRL are:

Survey. Survey the text to identify the main topic. Begin an Idea Tree to record main ideas and supporting details.

Question. Develop personal questions about the text that are likely to be answered during the reading.

Read. Read the text from start to finish.

Restate. Restate the main ideas and supporting details.

Review. Reread the text to answer the questions formulated.

Demonstrate **L**earning. Summarize the information in a written form to demonstrate what was learned.

Figure 5.13 Written Assessment

Student Test

Kids Are Citizens

Story Questions

Read pages 29–30 of *Kids Are Citizens*, and answer the following questions:

1. What are at least two responsibilities that citizens of the United States have?

2. Which of the following is a detail that supports the main idea "Giving a speech is a way to share your viewpoint."

    a. Famous people don't write their own speeches.

    b. Make sure you are nice to your audience in your speech.

    c. You need to work hard to write a good speech.

    d. Candidates give speeches to tell how they feel about issues.

3. Why did Susan B. Anthony give speeches and speak to Congress?

4. What did Anita do after she found the accident reports?

5. Which of the following is the main idea from the section titled "Write Your Speech"?

    a. Fall asleep after you write a speech.

    b. how to involve your audience in your speech

    c. how to organize your ideas

    d. Your speech should be easy for your audience to follow.

    What are some details that the author uses to support this main idea?

6. This text is an example of

    a. nonfiction.

    b. poetry.

    c. drama.

    d. fiction.

    Explain how you know.

(Continued)

Figure 5.13 (Continued)

Student Test

Kids Are Citizens

Vocabulary Items

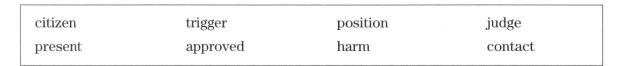

citizen	trigger	position	judge
present	approved	harm	contact

1. Choose two vocabulary words from the box above.
2. Write a Meaningful Sentence for each word. You may draw an organizer to help you if you wish.
3. If you choose words that you wrote Meaningful Sentences for earlier this week, make sure you write new sentences for those words.

Students are taught to use the Idea Tree graphic organizer, discussed earlier and similar to a web, to organize ideas as they read. Other graphic organizers, such as Venn diagrams, are introduced for use with specific text structures such as compare-contrast essays.

Knowledge of Word Structure Tools for Word Recognition

Special attention is paid at the second grade reading level to the development of students' knowledge of specific word structures that can help them break down unknown words and figure out their pronunciation and meaning. A variety of strategies are taught over a series of forty-eight lessons called Sail Along. To start, students are taught to break words into base words and endings, and to recognize the changes in spelling that can occur when endings are applied. Mnemonic cues are provided, and a cue card is made available to students to use as they read any text in which they need to work out unfamiliar words. The cue card is shown in Figure 5.15. Lots of structured practice is provided through team practice so that students become fluent with the use of the strategies. As always, students are awarded team points for success, and know they are responsible for ensuring that every member of the team learns to use the strategies.

Other strategies for breaking up words are introduced in subsequent lessons. Strategies for breaking up compound words, separating base words from prefixes and suffixes, and recognizing contractions are taught, modeled, and practiced, and then applied during the reading of all text. "Chunking" is introduced to give students a strategy for breaking up long words into chunks approximating syllables if no base words can be found. Visual cues that connect to the nautical theme of Reading Wings are introduced to make the strategies more concrete. Base words are represented by the mainsails of a sailboat. Endings,

Figure 5.14   Sample Read and Respond Form

Read and Respond

I have read for 20 minutes at home today. I read some of the time silently and the rest of the time out loud to:

_____   _____   _____
Student   Date   Listener

_____

_____

_____

I have read for 20 minutes at home today. I read some of the time silently and the rest of the time out loud to:

_____   _____   _____
Student   Date   Listener

_____

_____

_____

I have read for 20 minutes at home today. I read some of the time silently and the rest of the time out loud to:

_____   _____   _____
Student   Date   Listener

_____

_____

_____

I have read for 20 minutes at home today. I read some of the time silently and the rest of the time out loud to:

_____   _____   _____
Student   Date   Listener

_____

_____

_____

Figure 5.15 Cue Card

Figure 5.16 Reader Tools

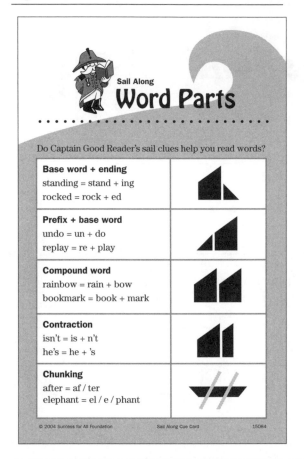

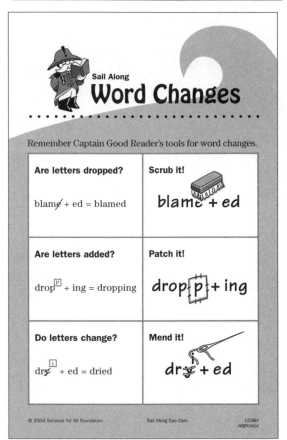

suffixes, and prefixes are represented by a small triangular sail preceding or following the mainsail, and compound words are represented by two mainsails. These and other cues are summarized on the flip side of the cue card, shown in Figure 5.16.

Teachers recognizing that students reading above the second grade level have not mastered these skills can choose to provide this instruction during vocabulary presentation, and to encourage their students to use the cue cards to assist them as they read.

The Power of Reading Wings

The structure provided in Reading Wings focuses both student and teacher on mastering the critical strategies in reading, and gives them opportunities to work with the support of their teammates to discuss and refine their comprehension. The weekly feedback on team success motivates students to pay close attention to the learning of every team member in each of the areas on the team score sheet. These areas are the goals of reading instruction. The constant feedback on each of these goals over time reminds everyone that their job is not only to understand and enjoy their reading, but also to become better readers.

6

Middle School Reading

The Reading Edge

There is a national crisis in the reading achievement of disadvantaged students in the middle grades. On the National Assessment of Educational Progress (NCES, 2007), 42 percent of eighth graders who qualified for free lunch scored below the basic reading level, compared to only 18 percent of their nonqualifying peers. This situation is not new, but by any standard, the reading scores of disadvantaged and minority students at the end of the middle grades is unacceptable (see Alvermann, 2001; Cooney, 1998; Jackson & Davis, 2000). Clearly, there is a need for well-evaluated programs capable of significantly accelerating the achievement of young adolescents. Yet, there are very few replicable interventions available to improve the reading achievement of students in these grades, and fewer still that have strong evidence of effectiveness. The Reading Edge was designed to fill this gap, building on Reading Wings to create a reading program capable of accelerating the reading performance of a broad range of students in the middle grades.

The Reading Edge is a comprehensive literacy program for all middle grades students, from struggling to advanced, with the goal of preparing them to be strategic, independent, and motivated readers and learners. The Reading Edge combines effective instructional practices, a coherent curriculum, and frequent informal assessment and feedback to students with extensive professional development for teachers and instructional leaders. This enables middle school teachers to provide intensive reading instruction that emphasizes four key areas: metacognitive strategy use, cooperative learning, goal setting and feedback, and classroom management (Slavin, Daniels, & Madden, 2005). The following sections describe how each of these is used in The Reading Edge. Appendices 6.1 (pages 218–231) and 6.2 (pages 232–240) show examples of Reading Edge student materials.

METACOGNITION

Numerous studies show that metacognition plays an important role in both learning to read and in learning new content through reading (Gertz, 1994). Research suggests that students who can assess their own knowledge and interest in a topic, and choose and apply effective strategies to understand unfamiliar text on that topic, can control their learning environment and successfully make meaning from what they read (Pressley & Woloshyn, 1995).

Use of metacognitive strategies is related to age and experience. By middle school, successful readers will have developed enough background knowledge, vocabulary, and experience with both narrative and expository text to take the next step in their reading development. Skilled readers develop the thinking skills necessary to grapple with the difficult text presented in content-area classes, and to acquire the study skills needed to store, retrieve, and use information after they achieve comprehension. However, not all students enter middle school reading fluently or widely. If early adolescence is the time during which students lay the groundwork for more mature ways of thinking and rigorous coursework in high school, then it is essential that students do more than just "catch up." Students need the opportunity to set goals, experiment with new skills and strategies, and learn that persistence leads to success. All students, including those who are reading on or above grade level by middle school, can benefit from instruction in recognizing various text structures and practicing strategies to help them make meaning from text.

Early in every Reading Edge lesson, students are presented with "The Big Question," a provocative question that they ponder and discuss over the course of the day's activities. With stems such as "Have you ever . . . " or "How would you handle this character's challenge . . . " or "Based on what you know about . . . ," students must draw upon their own experiences and beliefs as well as details from the text they are reading in order to formulate their answer. This question often leads to student-generated questions of the same kind, and enriches team and partner discussions about the text. It also requires students to paraphrase or summarize what they have read, and encourages students to monitor their comprehension as they read.

Also in the beginning of every lesson, teachers complete a "Building Background" segment in which they activate prior knowledge with "KWL" charts that ask students to summarize what they know about the topic (K), what they want to know (W), and then what they learned (L). Teachers make connections to student interests, and hold conversations in which they discuss vocabulary important to the understanding of the text. They preview the text, and then discuss text features that prompt students to make predictions about the main idea, topic, or theme, depending on the nature of the text.

During the "Active Instruction" portion of the lesson, the teacher engages students in targeted instruction on how to use a particular strategy or skill. Metacognitive strategies for comprehension are explicitly modeled and practiced. For example, the teacher will read aloud a passage from the text and stop and "think aloud" about something significant, perhaps an example of foreshadowing, and how it influences her thinking as she reads. As she does this, she is breaking down a larger strategy into smaller steps so students can understand the otherwise invisible tools that good readers use. Now that this strategy has been modeled and discussed, students practice using it as they read, and later reflect upon whether or not it helped them.

During Teamwork, students read some text silently and some aloud with a partner. They stop regularly to paraphrase what they just read, share insights, ask questions, clarify understanding, and summarize using graphic organizers such as Idea Trees (see Chapter 5) or story maps, shown in Figure 6.1. After reading, each team of four or

Figure 6.1   Graphic Organizers

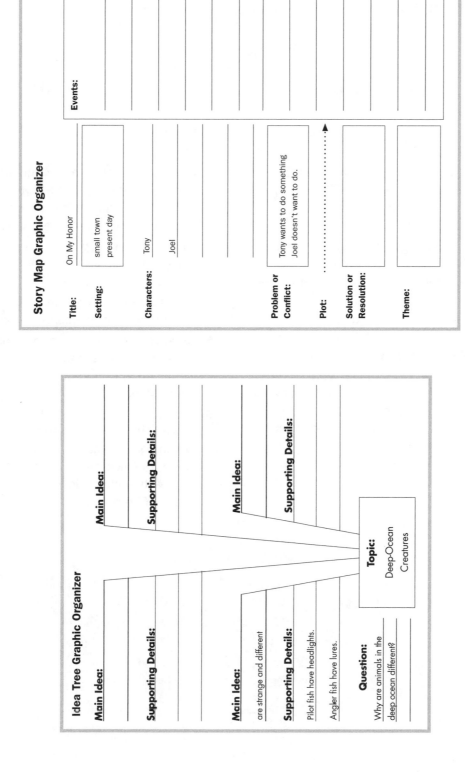

Story Map Graphic Organizer

Title: On My Honor

Setting: small town
present day

Characters: Tony

Joel

**Problem or
Conflict:**   Tony wants to do something
Joel doesn't want to do.

Plot:

**Solution or
Resolution:**

Theme:

Events:

Idea Tree Graphic Organizer

Main Idea:

Supporting Details:

Main Idea:

Supporting Details:

Main Idea: are strange and different

Supporting Details: Pilot fish have headlights.

Angler fish have lures.

Question: Why are animals in the
deep ocean different?

Topic: Deep-Ocean
Creatures

Figure 6.2   Guidelines for Partner Reading

Student Reference Sheet, Levels 4–6

Teamwork

Partner Reading

Informational Text	Narrative Text
1. Take turns reading aloud a page or paragraph of text.	1. Take turns reading aloud the assigned pages.
2. With your partner, clarify confusing words and passages. What you cannot clarify, mark with a sticky note to discuss with your team.	2. With your partner, clarify confusing words and passages. What you cannot clarify, mark with a sticky note to discuss with your team.
3. After each page or paragraph, identify the main ideas with your partner. Write these on your graphic organizers (Idea Trees).	3. When the reading partner has finished a page, the listening partner retells the main events of that page.
4. Review the page and discuss the supporting details. Add these to your graphic organizers.	4. During silent reading, continue to silently restate the main events from each page.
5. Choose a section (several paragraphs) of the day's reading that you think was exciting or that makes a great mind movie. Practice rereading it and have your partner check your fluency. (See Fluency Checklist.)	5. When you are both finished reading, record the main events and important elements on your graphic organizers (Story Maps).
	6. Choose a section (several paragraphs) of the day's reading that you think was exciting or that makes a great mind movie. Practice rereading it and have your partner check your fluency. (See Fluency Checklist.)

Fluency Checklist

Your partner's reading is correct, smooth, and expressive.

☐ Your partner pronounces most of the words correctly (no more than four errors).

☐ Your partner's reading is smooth and includes pauses for periods and commas.

☐ Your partner's reading is expressive. It shows emotion and changes with punctuation such as question marks, exclamation points, and dialogue.

five students uses another routine to discuss what they have read, and "Discuss and Defend" their answers to prepared "Team Talk Questions." Students have the opportunity to clarify their thinking, try out new ideas, use new vocabulary, and help someone else understand the text, all in the safety of a small collaborative group. During Teamwork time, the teacher circulates around the room to check for understanding, prompts and reinforces positive behavior, and conducts quick, informal conferences with partners or teams called "One-to-One's." During these interactions, the teacher can informally assess the students' grasp of the targeted strategy or skill. Teamwork guidelines for partner reading are shown in Figure 6.2. Guidelines for team discussion are shown in Figure 6.3.

COOPERATIVE LEARNING

Cooperative learning refers to a wide variety of methods in which students work in small groups (usually four members) to help one another learn. Extensive experimental research on cooperative learning methods has found that these strategies increase student achievement if they incorporate group goals and individual accountability (Slavin, 1995; Slavin, Hurley, & Chamberlain, 2003; Webb & Palincsar, 1996). Cooperative learning has been particularly effective and extensively researched in middle schools. Cooperative learning methods in which students have regular opportunities to discuss ideas with partners, to help each other study, and to provide formative feedback to each other have been successfully evaluated in several randomized evaluations in elementary and middle schools (Slavin, 1995, in press). Cooperative learning has also been successfully evaluated many times as a means of introducing and practicing metacognitive skills (e.g., Meloth & Deering, 1994).

In The Reading Edge, students work in teacher-assigned, cooperative teams of four or five students. Each student is individually accountable for his or her own learning and there are no group grades. However, teams are recognized when all members improve their performance compared to their past performance. Students set goals together, and with the support of practiced routines, they help each other learn new content; use, evaluate, and personalize strategies; and remain attentive to the task at hand. Teams also provide a safe environment for individuals to try out new ideas or admit when they are confused. Each team works to help each member achieve his or her "personal best," so there is always an equal opportunity for success—teams are not in competition with each other. Teams strive to improve upon past performance.

STUDENT GOAL SETTING AND FEEDBACK

Research demonstrates that students who perceive a classroom emphasis on meeting mastery goals rather than on ability and performance goals are more likely to take on challenging tasks, use effective strategies, and have a positive attitude in class. These students are also more likely to believe that effort brings success (Ames & Archer, 1988).

Built into the Reading Edge are several unique components that engage students in the learning process: goal setting, peer support, and frequent assessment and feedback. These powerful motivators provide the impetus for increased metacognitive strategy use and student achievement.

Goal Setting

The most important aspect of the first three weeks of reading instruction in The Reading Edge is to engage students in the learning process. Teachers engage students in straight talk about reading difficulties they may have had in the past, especially related to work in their content area classes. Students engage in activities that help them identify

Figure 6.3 Guidelines for Team Discussion

Team Talk Discussion Guidelines

Read a Question

1. Each person reads the question silently. Select the key words in the question.

2. Taking turns, each team member reads a question aloud. Be sure everyone practices active listening.

3. Partners check to be sure they understand the question.

Answer the Question

1. Taking turns, one team member answers the question. (Be sure to restate part of the question in the answer.)

2. Explain why you think this answer is correct.
- Find evidence in the text to support your answer.
- Make sure you have answered all parts of the question.

Agree and Disagree

1. Taking turns, each team member states why he or she agrees with the answer given and adds supporting evidence from the text OR

2. States why he or she disagrees and adds supporting evidence from the text for a different answer.

Summarize

1. Summarize the answers that have been given.

2. Check to see that all team members understand the answers discussed.

Go on to the next question.

Peer Feedback for Writing Project

1. Read your writing project to your teammates. Remember to read with expression.

2. Ask each of the questions below. Write your teammates' suggestions in the margin of your writing project.
- Did I include the elements listed in the scoring guide?
- Is it easy to identify the topic? Is there anything that does not fit with this topic?
- Do the details help you make a mind movie? What details make the picture clear? Do you have to guess other details? If so, what areas are unclear?
- Is the writing organized so you can see how the pieces are connected? Are the ideas in a logical order?

3. Make a revision plan. On the back of your paper, list one or two of the most important changes you could make based on the feedback from your teammates.

goals that are important to them, and to learn how to work collaboratively to reach those goals. During the first two weeks of school, students take an initial or baseline reading assessment. Students learn how they scored on the initial reading assessment and are placed in an appropriate reading class. All reading levels begin with a Foundation Unit designed to demonstrate how strategies students already use in everyday situations (making predictions, asking questions, etc.) can also be applied to learning problems, such as understanding their science textbook. Connecting with students' prior knowledge and experience with problem-solving strategies launches the overarching investigation into how to choose and apply multiple, effective strategies for success in reading.

Peer Support

Placing students in reading classes by instructional level gives students a safe place to work on the issues that are most difficult for them. By the middle grades, most students who are reading below grade level are painfully aware of their deficiencies, and most have learned how to hide them. Early in The Reading Edge, students learn that everyone has something to learn, including their teacher, and that in this reading class they will work with their teammates to fill in gaps and build on their strengths. Not only is it acceptable to talk about what stumps them when they are reading, it is part of the everyday routine. Teaching students how to work well with partners and teammates to enhance everyone's learning is an explicit part of the Reading Edge program.

Frequent Assessment and Feedback

At the beginning of every cycle (six days of instruction ending with a curriculum-based assessment), students receive a Learning Guide. On it, students record reading goals for each lesson and points they earn for classwork, homework, and tests that make up their grade for the cycle. The Learning Guide is a self-assessment tool that helps the students identify strengths and weaknesses and set personal goals. It also helps students stay organized. Students keep track of their work as they complete it, and identify the work they still need to master. As the teacher visits each team during one-to-one conferences, she initials work that students have done well, and helps them identify next steps. A sample Learning Guide is shown in Figure 6.4.

Teams can earn bonus points for demonstrating extra effort by participating in activities such as Book Club, in which students share their critiques of books they have read outside of school. In "Word Wise," students share how they have used their vocabulary words in new contexts. Students also learn to use a Team Mastery Process to prepare for the end of cycle test. This gives students time to try out new study skills in a personally meaningful context.

At the end of each cycle, students compare their current total score to their previous work. Teams receive "Improvement Points" for each member who increases his or her score. Improvement Points are averaged across students and combined with points for cooperation to form a team score for the cycle. Teams scoring between 90 and 100 are "SuperTeams," while those scoring between 80 and 89 are "GreatTeams," and those below 80 are "GoodTeams." There is not one winning team. All teams can be SuperTeams if they work hard. Team success is recognized in a whole class celebration. This celebration of team rather than individual success is key to the power of the Reading Edge program, and changes the culture of a middle grades classroom from one focused on individual competition for good grades (or tacit agreement to avoid good grades) to peer cooperation focused on increasing the learning of every member of the team.

Figure 6.4   Sample Learning Guide Used to Guide Teamwork During a Lesson Cycle

Learning Guide

Name _____   Date _____

Title _____   Cycle _____

Objectives: Reading Goals

Day 1 _____

Day 2 _____

Day 3 _____

Day 4 _____

Day 5 _____

Activities:

1. Team Talk Questions

Day 1 [ ] + Day 2 [ ] + Day 3 [ ] + Day 4 [ ] = [ ] (20 pts.)
(5 pts.) (5 pts.) (5 pts.) (5 pts.)

2. Cycle Test

Day 5   [ ] + [ ] = [ ] (40 pts.)
Vocabulary   Story Test
(16 points) (24 points)

3. Homework (Read, Reflect, Respond)

Day 5   [ ] (20 pts.)

4. Writing Project

Day 6   [ ] (20 pts.)

5. Book Club

[ ] (Bonus pts.)

(To get total, add the points from the Team Talk questions, cycle test, homework, writing project, and Book Club.)   **Total** → [ ] (100 pts.)

To calculate improvement points:

If your total is...	Improvement points
■ more than 10 points below base score	70
■ 10 points to 1 point below base score	80
■ same to 10 points above base score	90
■ more than 10 points above base score	100
■ 100	100

[ ]   **Base score** (last cycle's total)

[ ]   **Total** (this cycle)

[ ]   **Improvement points**

How did the Reading Goals help you in your reading this week?

_____

_____

Every quarter, students take a standardized reading assessment such as the Gates MacGinitie Reading Tests, or the Scholastic Reading Inventory. This information is added to the set of data about how students are performing. Students know that as soon as they show sufficient improvement in reading, they will move up to the next level, or even skip a level. Regular and frequent assessment and feedback routines include the student as an equal partner in the process. Students learn that hard work and persistence will pay off.

CLASSROOM MANAGEMENT

Research indicates that a rapid pace of instruction, consistent with high student comprehension, both maintains students' attention and increases students' achievement (e.g., Emmer, Evertson, & Worsham, 2006). In addition, classroom management methods based on cooperative learning have both immediate and lasting impact on students' behavior and achievement. The Reading Edge teachers begin each school year with a conflict-resolution and academic problem-solving unit called "Getting Along Together." In this unit, students learn how to use effective social, communication, and problem-solving skills to maintain positive social and academic relationships. These skills are then referenced and practiced in reading lessons. During Setting the Stage, the teacher and students discuss and set a cooperation goal for the day. Teams can earn bonus points and recognition for meeting goals such as active listening, explaining their thinking to a teammate, helping and encouraging each other, or 100 percent team participation.

During Active Instruction, teachers use techniques for keeping the lesson moving at a brisk pace by posing important questions to the entire class and randomly calling on students to answer. Teachers use routines such as Think-Pair-Share and Numbered Heads to allow students time to examine their thinking and then try it out in a brief team discussion. Students learn that any team member could be called upon to answer for their team, so they must help each other prepare to answer every question. For quick checks for understanding, teachers use whole-class responses such as Thumbs-Up/Thumbs Down to keep the pace of instruction brisk, and every child involved.

Reading Edge Levels

Because students coming into middle schools are at widely varying levels of achievement in reading, the Reading Edge provides materials for groups of students at instructional levels ranging from beginning reading to beyond grade eight. The focus of the instruction varies by level. Levels 4 through 8 use short stories, novels, poetry, and nonfiction to help students learn and apply effective comprehension strategies and build their vocabularies through their reading. Levels 2 and 3 use high-interest fiction, nonfiction, and reader's theater to reinforce basic decoding skills, and build fluency, vocabulary, and comprehension. Level 1 focuses on giving beginning readers the tools they need to develop the basic skills of decoding and understanding print. It uses a sequence of illustrated stories written specifically for this age group with phonetically regular text that becomes rapidly more challenging as students master letter/sound relationships and build blending and word structure skills. See the appendices for this chapter for sample lessons.

The Reading Edge for High School

In 2007, the Success for All Foundation received a grant to develop and evaluate a form of The Reading Edge for high school students that focuses on the development of critical reading skills needed for success in content area classes. This project is just getting under way at this writing.

Great Speeches

Summary

The following speeches are included in this unit:

"Ain't I a Woman?" by Sojourner Truth

> This speech, delivered to the Woman's Convention in Akron, Ohio, in 1851, is an argument in favor of equal rights for women.

"Pearl Harbor Speech" by President Franklin Delano Roosevelt

> In this speech, delivered on December 8, 1941, the President asked the Congress to declare war on Japan in response to its attack on Pearl Harbor and other sites throughout the Pacific.

"I Have a Dream" by Reverend Martin Luther King, Jr.

> Delivered on the steps of the Lincoln Memorial during the 1963 March on Washington, this speech has become a classic for its eloquence and passion.

"The Gettysburg Address" by President Abraham Lincoln

> This famous speech was given on November 19, 1863, at the dedication of a cemetery for Civil War soldiers who died at the battle of Gettysburg in Pennsylvania.

Instructional Goals

Reading

Identify persuasive techniques.

As they read, the students will identify how speakers persuade their audiences.

Writing

Write a persuasive speech.

The students write a persuasive speech on a contemporary topic.

Cycle 1 | Day 1

Listening Comprehension: Day 1 "Ain't I a Woman?"
Partner Reading: Day 1

Preparation: Materials
• Transparency of Idea Tree
  graphic organizer
For each student
• Copy of the book
• Student pages
• Learning Guide
For each team
• Team Score Sheet

Timing Goal: 5 minutes

Teacher Background

At the 1851 Woman's Convention in Akron, Ohio, Sojourner Truth—a former slave and active abolitionist—gave a speech in support of women's suffrage. It is important to recall that at the time, women did not have the same rights as men in the United States, for example, the right to vote. In her speech, Sojourner uses her personal experience to argue against the sexist notions of the time.

Set the Stage

1. Post and present the Reading Goal and Today's Big Question.

> **Reading Goal:**
> As we read, we will identify how a speaker uses personal experience to persuade.
>
> **Today's Big Question:**
> How can you persuade someone to agree with you?

2. Remind the students that you will award team cooperation points to teams whose members complete all tasks.

Timing Goal: 25 minutes

Active Instruction

Build Background

1. Create interest in the reading by discussing why people make speeches. Use **Think-Pair-Share** to ask:

> **Have you ever heard someone give a speech, either in person or on television?**
> *Answers will vary. Some students may have witnessed political campaign speeches or speeches during ceremonies at school.*

> **Why do people give speeches?**
> *Accept reasonable responses. For example, people give speeches to inform or persuade.*

Remind the students that the text of a speech is informational, so it is different from narrative texts. Narrative texts, both fiction and nonfiction, tell stories. The author's purpose for writing this text is to inform or persuade the reader about a topic.

2. Have partners preview the speech and predict what it is about. Allow 1 minute for this activity. Debrief the activity. Use **Numbered Heads** to ask:

> **What do you think this speech will be about?**
> *Answers will vary.*

> **What can you predict about the speaker, Sojourner Truth, from her name? Explain.**
> *Accept supported answers. Some students may recognize that the words* sojourner *and* journey *have the same base words. They may guess that Sojourner Truth is someone who travels around and speaks the truth.*

Explain that this speech was given in 1851 at a women's rights convention.

> **What rights did women want at that time in our history?**
> *Accept reasonable responses. For example, the students may mention voting rights or the right to own property.*

> **Would you predict that this speech about women's rights was made for the purpose of informing people or persuading them? Explain.**
> *Accept supported answers. Some students may think that everyone already had enough information about which rights women wanted, so it must have been intended to persuade opponents of women's rights.*

3. Distribute Idea Tree graphic organizers or have the students draw Idea Trees on which they will record the main ideas and details of this speech as they partner read.

4. To establish a purpose for their reading, ask the students to think about one or two questions that they expect the text of the speech to answer. Have them write these questions on the trunk of their Idea Trees. Model this step if necessary. Allow 1 minute for this activity.

Skill Instruction

1. Explain that during this unit the students will be looking closely at the different techniques speakers use to persuade their audience. Use **Think-Pair-Share** to ask:

> **What does it mean to persuade someone?**
> *Accept reasonable responses. For example, you try to get them to agree with your opinion about something.*

> **How can you convince someone that your opinion is based on good reasons?**
> *Accept reasonable responses. For example, you could explain what you have learned or experienced that caused you to form your opinion.*

Active Instruction
continued

2. Explain that describing your personal experience is one of the most effective ways to persuade someone to listen to your opinion. Describe the following situation for the students:

    > Suppose you and a friend are looking at video games in a store, and your friend is about to buy one. You try to stop him or her by saying, "That game is no fun. It's way too easy to win."

    Use **Think-Pair-Share** to ask:

    > **How could you use your personal experience to back up your opinion about the game?**
    > *Accept reasonable responses. For example, you could tell your friend that you won in 15 minutes the first time you played.*

    Point out that we use this technique very frequently in everyday life. For example, we say: "You should see that movie. I saw it last weekend, and it was great!" or "I listened to that band's new CD at my friend's house, and it is not as good as its first one." Often, before we will listen with respect to other people's opinions, we first ask what personal experience they have with the subject. We say, "How do you know that she is a strict teacher? Were you ever in her class?" Common sense tells us that we should not listen to people who have no personal experience to back up their opinions.

3. Tell the students that as we read we will look for ways that Sojourner Truth uses her personal experience to back up her opinions about women's rights.

Listening Comprehension

1. Read aloud the first paragraph of the speech in the Listening Comprehension reading for Day 1. Then, use a Think Aloud to model identifying how a speaker uses personal experience to persuade an audience:

    > This part of the speech seems to be a sort of introduction to the topic of rights. The speaker says that both southern Negroes and northern women are making a lot of "racket"— that means noise—about rights and that this shows that there's something "out of kilter." That's an old slang phrase! It means that there is some imbalance in the system, so it's not working right. She says she's going to explain what all the talking is about. I guess that means she will discuss some of the arguments about rights. It sounds odd to hear her use the term *Negro*. But, at the time, the term *Negro* was a respectful way to refer to African Americans.

    Read the rest of the Listening Comprehension for Day 1 aloud and continue with the Think Aloud:

    > Hmm. I wonder when she says "that man" if she's talking about a particular man or the "white men" she mentioned in

Active Instruction
continued

To identify the main idea of a paragraph or page ask, "What is the most important information the author wants me to know from my reading?" or "What is the idea that everything else talks about?"

Student Edition, Cycle 1 | Day 1

the first paragraph. Whoever he is, he has made the argument that women can't be equal, that they are so weak they need to be helped into carriages and over puddles. Then, she uses her own personal experience to show that not all women get that kind of help—certainly not poor women like herself! She's saying that no one can generalize like that about all women. Her own experience proves that their definition of "a woman" is wrong.

2. Summarize the main ideas and details from your reading and write these on an Idea Tree.

Vocabulary Introduction

1. Introduce the vocabulary for this cycle. Using the chart below, read the vocabulary word, the definition, and the sentence. Ask the students to repeat the words as you read the list a second time. Allow about 2 minutes for this activity.

Word	Identification Strategy and Pronunciation	Definition	Sentence
intellect (noun) PR | Day 1	chunk: in-tel-lect (IN-tehl-lehkt)	the ability to think on an advanced level	As a woman of great *intellect*, Denise loved to read and talk about ideas.
intervening (adjective) LC | Day 2	chunk: in-ter-ven-ing (in-tuhr-VEEN-ing)	occurring between two events, placed between two things	Once school ends, I can use the *intervening* days before vacation to pack.
onslaught (noun) PR | Day 2	chunk: on-slaught (ON-slawt)	a massive attack	The *onslaught* of the rebel armies left our forces outnumbered and without hope for victory.
seared (verb) LC | Day 3	blend: seared (SEERD)	burned, scorched	The plants were *seared* by the desert sun.
fatigue noun PR | Day 3	chunk: fa-tigue (fuh-TEEG)	a state of being very tired	The *fatigue* was obvious on the faces of the long-distance bicycle racers.
exalted (verb) PR | Day 4	chunk: ex-al-ted (ig-ZAWL-ted)	raised high; elevated	The coach's reputation was *exalted* by news of the team's victory.
resolve (verb) Day 5	chunk: re-solve (ree-ZAHLV)	to make a firm decision	I *resolve* to keep trying until I get it right.

Active Instruction
continued

Word	Identification Strategy and Pronunciation	Definition	Sentence
perish (verb) Day 5	chunk: per-ish (PEHR-ish)	to be destroyed, to die off	If I don't water these plants soon, they will *perish* in the hot sun.

2. Read the Team Talk questions aloud. Tell the students that they will answer these questions during Team Discussion.

Teamwork

Partner Reading

Timing Goal: 15 minutes

For a description of Partner Reading, see the Routines teacher reference sheet.

1. Partners read and restate the text. Review the Partner Reading routines for informational text.

Clarifying: When partners come to anything confusing or unclear in their reading, they first try to make sense of it through discussion. If there is still a problem, they place a sticky note in the margin to mark it. Then they can come back to the problem and try to solve it with the help of the rest of their team during Team Discussion.

2. Review what partners should do when they come to a word they don't know or a passage that they don't understand.

3. Have the students read:

> Partner Reading | Day 1 aloud with partners.

4. As partners work together, circulate and check for comprehension and fluency. Prompt and reinforce their discussions. An example follows:

> Make sure you and your partner agree on the main idea. Look back at the text to find supporting details that prove the main idea. If you can't find any supporting details on the page you just read, continue reading. Maybe you will find some on the next page. If you still can't find supporting details, you need to rethink your main idea.

Team Discussion

Teams discuss all questions. The students individually write the answer to the marked skill question. You may choose to have your students write answers to more than one question.

1. Explain that teams will discuss the main ideas on their Idea Trees and try to solve any problems marked with sticky notes. Then they will go on to a discussion of the Team Talk questions. The students will write the answer to the marked skill question following Team Discussion.

Student Edition, Cycle 1 | Day 1

> **Team Talk Questions**
> 1. What ideas did most men apparently have about women at that time?
>   *Accept reasonable responses. For example, most men apparently thought that all women were weak.*

Teamwork
continued

2. Why did Sojourner Truth and the other women at the conference want to change these ideas?

Accept reasonable responses. For example, they wanted to prove that they were strong enough to make their own decisions and take charge of their own possessions.

3. How does Sojourner Truth use her personal experience to persuade her audience that women can be very strong? (write)

Accept reasonable responses. For example, to prove her strength, she gives vivid examples of the hard work she has done in her life and the suffering she has endured.

4. If you were a man living at that time, would this speech persuade you that women were stronger than you thought? Why or why not?

Accept supported answers.

Use One-to-One conferences to show the students how to search for clues to a word's meaning using its context. Also try to show the students that they can often understand the author's meaning without knowing a particular word or phrase.

Timing Goal: 15 minutes

2. Circulate through the classroom and check for comprehension. Listen to team discussions, and offer hints and suggestions. To encourage further discussion, ask questions such as:

Why does Sojourner Truth keep repeating "Ain't I a woman?"

Who does Sojourner Truth mean by "the first woman God ever made"?

Time for Reflection

Class Discussion

1. Use **Numbered Heads** to have teams share and compare responses to the Team Talk questions and explain their thinking. Allow 2 minutes for this activity.

2. Refer the students to Today's Big Question: "How can you persuade someone to agree with you?" and ask:

Do you think Sojourner Truth's speech was persuasive? Why or why not?
Accept supported answers.

Is it difficult to persuade someone to think or act in a certain way? Why?
Accept supported answers.

Have you ever used your personal experience to persuade someone to accept your opinion? Explain.
Accept supported answers.

Time for Reflection
continued

Student Edition, Cycle 1 | Day 1

What other techniques have you used to persuade someone to agree with you?
Answers will vary.

Vocabulary Review

1. Review the directions for the vocabulary activity. Have partners work together to complete the activity.

> **Vocabulary Activity**
>
> **Directions:** Choose the word from the word bank that best completes each sentence.
>
> 1. I can't give up ice cream, no matter how often I *resolve* to.
> 2. My dog would *perish* from disappointment if I didn't take him with me to the lake.
> 3. He was *exalted* by all the praise he received for saving the drowning boy.
> 4. My fever and *fatigue* told me that I was coming down with the flu.
>
> **Word Bank**
>
> | exalted | fatigue | resolve | perish |
> |---------|---------|---------|--------|

Cycle 1 | Day 2

Listening Comprehension: Day 2 "Pearl Harbor Speech"
Partner Reading: Day 2

Teacher Background

On December 7, 1941, Japanese bombers attacked the American naval base in Pearl Harbor, Hawaii. On December 8, President Franklin Delano Roosevelt went before Congress to ask them to declare war on Japan. Roosevelt's speech is a famous example of how evidence can be used to move an audience to action.

Set the Stage

Timing Goal: 5 minutes

1. Post and present the Reading Goal and Today's Big Question.

> **Reading Goal:**
> As we read, we will identify how a speaker uses factual evidence to persuade.
>
> **Today's Big Question:**
> How does using evidence help you persuade someone to take action?

2. Remind the students that you will award team cooperation points to teams whose members complete all tasks.

Active Instruction

Timing Goal: 20 minutes

Build Background

1. Ask teammates to review the main idea and details recorded on their Idea Trees from the speech they read the previous day. Use **Numbered Heads** to ask the students to share these with the class.

2. Remind the students that Sojourner Truth made use of her own experience to persuade her audience. Explain that today they will discuss another technique that is used to persuade others.

Point out that when people make speeches, they frequently want their audience to do more than just agree with them. Often the goal of a speech is to convince audience members to take a particular action. This type of speech is often heard in the halls of Congress and in state legislatures. Use **Think-Pair-Share** to ask:

What are members of Congress typically trying to persuade their colleagues to do?
Accept reasonable responses. For example, they want them to vote a certain way.

Why would the president speak to the Congress?
Accept reasonable responses. For example, he could be trying to persuade them to do something or vote a certain way.

If you were a representative in Congress, what would you need to know before you could decide how to vote?
Accept reasonable responses. For example, you would need factual evidence that proved that the speaker's idea was a good one.

3. Tell the students that in today's lesson they will read one of the most famous speeches a president of the United States ever made to Congress in an emergency. He appeared before Congress to ask them to declare war on another country. Use **Think-Pair-Share** to ask:

If you were a member of Congress, what would you want to know before you would vote to go to war with another country?
Accept reasonable responses. For example, most students will probably mention the need for reasons or facts about what the other country has done.

4. Have the students create a new Idea Tree for this speech. To establish a purpose for their reading, ask the students to think about one or two questions that they expect the text of the speech to answer. Have them write these questions on the trunks of their Idea Trees.

Skill Instruction

1. Discuss what qualifies as evidence. Ask teams to brainstorm a list of the types of information they would consider to be good evidence. Use **Numbered Heads** to ask the students to share these with the class.

What do we mean when we ask for good evidence?
Accept reasonable responses. For example, we want facts— not rumors: statistics, places, dates, eyewitness accounts, and photographs.

Would one piece of evidence be enough to persuade you, or would you need more? Explain.
Accept supported answers.

2. Explain that the speech that they will read today was given by President Franklin Delano Roosevelt on December 8, 1941. Ask the students to think about the kinds of evidence Roosevelt uses to persuade the Congress to take action, as you read the beginning of this speech.

Active Instruction
continued

To identify the main idea of a paragraph or page ask, "What is the most important information the author wants me to know from my reading?" or "What is the idea that everything else talks about?"

Timing Goal: 20 minutes

For a description of Partner Reading, see the Routines teacher reference sheet.

Clarifying: When partners come to anything confusing or unclear in their reading, they first try to make sense of it through discussion. If there is still a problem, they place a sticky note in the margin to mark it. Then they can come back to the problem and try to solve it with the help of the rest of their team during Team Discussion.

Teams discuss all questions. The students individually write the answer to the marked skill question. You may choose to have your students write answers to more than one question.

Listening Comprehension

1. Read aloud the Listening Comprehension reading for Day 2. Use a Think Aloud to model identifying evidence that the speaker uses to persuade his audience to take action:

> Let me see how the president uses evidence in this part of his speech. The first evidence he supplies is the date of the attack and the identity of the attackers. Then, he cites the fact that the U.S. was not at war with Japan. In fact, the two countries were engaged in peace talks at the time of the attack. I think he must be using these facts to prove that the U.S. did nothing to provoke the attack.
>
> I think the next piece of evidence he presents is very effective. The Japanese ambassador delivered a formal note to the Secretary of State ending the peace talks—an hour after Japan began bombing in Hawaii. The President argues that, considering the distance between Japan and Hawaii, the Japanese would have been planning the attack at the same time they were having peace talks with us. This proves that the negotiations were simply a trick to keep the U.S. from suspecting that a sneak attack was being planned.

2. Summarize the main ideas and details from your reading and write these on the Idea Tree.

3. Read the Team Talk questions aloud. Tell the students that they will answer these questions during Team Discussion.

Teamwork

Partner Reading

1. Partners read and restate the text. Review the Partner Reading routines for informational text.

2. Review what partners should do when they come to a word they don't know or a passage that they don't understand.

3. Have the students read:

> Partner Reading | Day 2 aloud with partners.

4. As partners work together, circulate to prompt and reinforce the students' efforts to clarify what they read. Refer them to the clarifying strategies.

Team Discussion

1. Remind the teams that they will discuss the main ideas on their Idea Trees and try to solve any problems marked with sticky notes. Then they will go on to a discussion of the Team Talk questions. The

Teamwork
continued

Student Edition, Cycle 1 | Day 2

students will write the answer to the marked skill question following Team Discussion.

> **Team Talk Questions**
>
> 1. What specific damage to American lives and property does President Roosevelt cite as evidence of the effects of the Japanese attack? Why do you think he doesn't feel the need to go into the gory details about this?
>
>   *Accept reasonable responses. For example, he mentions damage to military forces and the death of Americans, but he probably has no numbers available yet. Plus, he knows that everybody in the country has been listening to vivid news reports on the radio about the attack.*
>
> 2. Why do you think Roosevelt lists in his speech all the other places that Japan has just attacked? Do you think it strengthens or weakens his case for going to war? Why? (write)
>
>   *Accept reasonable responses. For example, the list strengthens his speech because it shows that Japan is not just hurting our country, but many others as well. By listing them, Roosevelt makes Japan seem like a threat to the world in general, so that fighting them seems less about personal revenge and more about the common good.*
>
> 3. Roosevelt says that "the people of the United States have already formed their opinions and well understand the implication to … our nation." Does he offer evidence of this? What kind of evidence might have supported this statement?
>
>   *Accept supported answers. For example, no, he doesn't offer any evidence. It is a best guess about how the American people were feeling. An opinion poll or survey, if it had been available at the time, might have supported this statement.*
>
> 4. If you were a member of Congress listening to this speech, would you have voted to go to war? Why?
>
>   *Accept supported answers.*

2. Circulate through the classroom and check for comprehension. Listen to team discussions, and offer hints and suggestions. To encourage further discussion, ask questions such as:

> **What does Roosevelt say in the speech to encourage his listeners to believe that they can win this war?**
>
> **Why does he emphasize that the attack was unprovoked?**

Time for Reflection

Class Discussion

1. Use **Numbered Heads** to have teams share and compare responses to the Team Talk questions and explain their thinking. Allow 2 minutes for this activity.

2. Refer the students to Today's Big Question: "How does using evidence help you persuade someone to take action?" and ask:

   Do you think that Roosevelt's speech was effective in using evidence to persuade the Congress that they must act? Why or why not?
   Accept supported answers.

   In what kinds of situations have you needed to get someone to take action?
   Answers will vary. Some students may mention persuading others to go somewhere or to help with a job.

   Did you use evidence to help persuade them? How?
   Accept supported answers.

   Why does using evidence help you persuade someone to take action?
   Accept reasonable responses. For example, evidence gives your listener a real reason to do something by proving that the action is needed.

   Are you more likely to take action if someone gives you factual evidence that shows why they need you to act? Why or why not?
   Accept supported answers.

Vocabulary Review

1. Do a 1-minute review of the vocabulary words. Read each sentence from the vocabulary chart, and have the students respond by reading the word and its definition.

   > **Vocabulary Highlight:** Our vocabulary word *intervening* begins with the prefix *inter-*, which means between, among, or together. Consider several other words that use the same prefix: *interact, intercept, interfere, interject,* and *interrupt.* How are the meanings of all these words related?

APPENDIX 6.1 **231**

continued

Student Edition, Cycle 1 | Day 2

2. Review the directions for the vocabulary activity. Have partners work together to complete the activity.

Vocabulary Activity

Directions: Choose the word from the word bank that best completes each sentence.

1. I love the taste of chicken _seared_ on the grill.
2. I tried to head from my car to the box office, but I ran into an _intervening_ barrier.
3. The _onslaught_ of the hurricane's high winds caught us all by surprise.
4. His powerful _intellect_ helps him to win many debates.

Word Bank

intellect	seared	onslaught	intervening

Appendix 6.2   Sample Reading Edge Student Material

Martin Luther King, Jr. and the March on Washington

By Frances E. Ruffin

Summary

A moving speech by Martin Luther King, Jr., at the March on Washington in 1963 resulted in important civil rights legislation.

The following background information can help enrich your students' experience with this book.

1. **The geography and significance of Washington, D.C.**

   This book abounds in references to and images of the nation's capital and asserts (page 25) that the protest leaders chose the District of Columbia because it is the place where the nation's laws are made.

   The founders of the United States created an entirely new city as its seat of government, which resulted, for the first time in history, in a capital that was intentionally built to reflect the design of its government and to represent its prestige and ideals. Unlike other large U.S. city centers—which are typically characterized by high skyscrapers and narrow streets—the District of Columbia is a city of wide boulevards, green parks, solemn monuments, and classically inspired buildings.

   The March on Washington takes place near the Lincoln Memorial (page 8) featuring a 19-foot-high statue of Abraham Lincoln by sculptor Daniel Chester French (a detail of the statue is featured on page 10). Visitors to the Memorial can read the Great Emancipator's most famous speeches (the Gettysburg Address and his second inaugural address) on tablets within the monument. The memorial, completed in 1922, had already become a significant symbol for the civil rights struggle in 1939. The famous black singer Marian Anderson sang there to a huge crowd after the Daughters of the American Revolution refused to let her sing in Constitution Hall.

   The Washington Monument, honoring the nation's first president, is also featured prominently in the book's illustrations. It is one of the most visible D.C. landmarks and the largest masonry structure in the world. Builders began working on the Monument in 1838, but did not complete it until 1884 because of the Civil War and lack of funding. Visitors to D.C. can climb up inside the structure, which was designed to resemble an Egyptian obelisk, and view the surrounding city.

2. **Marches and other protests in Washington, D.C.**

The 1963 March on Washington drew on past protests in the nation's capital for inspiration, and provided inspiration for future protests. Drawing attention to protests in D.C. that your students or their parents have heard about in the news can help them relate to how the March on Washington was perceived in 1963. Your students or their parents may have heard, for example, of the Million Man March, designed to draw attention to the plight of black men, which took place on October 16, 1995. The organizers of this march explicitly used the 1963 march as a model.

3. **The tragic side of the civil rights struggle**

Since this book is intended for younger students, it goes to great lengths to omit the fact that both Martin Luther King, Jr., and John F. Kennedy were assassinated. John F. Kennedy was shot on November 22, 1963, while campaigning for reelection in Dallas, Texas. The book thus creates the impression (pages 42–44) that Kennedy signed the Civil Rights Act of 1964, when in fact, the act was signed into law by Lyndon Johnson after Kennedy's death. Martin Luther King was killed on April 4, 1968, while supporting a strike by sanitation workers in Memphis, Tennessee. These deaths were part of a turbulent period in American history that showed the United States at its worst as well as its best.

Reading Goal

Discover strategies for clarifying difficult words.

The students will learn how to identify strategies—such as sounding it out, using context clues, looking at the pictures, and asking for help—that will help them clarify difficult words.

Cycle 1 | Day 1

Listening Comprehension: pages 4–7
Partner Reading: pages 8–13

Preparation: Materials

For each student
• Copy of the book, with several sticky notes inside the front cover
• Learning Guide
• Notebook paper
• Homework pages

For each team
• Team Score Sheet

Timing Goal: 10 minutes

Take it up a notch: Replace this question with one that is open-ended. Allow the students to discuss it during Teamwork.

Timing Goal: 20 minutes

Teacher Background

In today's reading, more than 250,000 people take part in the 1963 March on Washington. A century after Lincoln helped free the slaves, blacks and whites are still not treated equally, and those who take part in the March are speaking out against something they see as wrong.

Set the Stage

1. Post and present the Reading Goals and Today's Big Question.

> **Reading Goals:**
> As we read, we will think about what we do to figure out difficult words.
>
> **Today's Big Question:**
> Why were the people in this book coming to Washington, D.C.?

2. Remind the students that you will award team cooperation points to teams whose members complete their tasks.

Review

1. Do a quick review of the last unit's skill or strategy.

Active Instruction

Build Background

1. Introduce a KWL chart to help the students access their prior knowledge. Display the chart on the chalkboard or a blank transparency.

> We are going to read a book called *Martin Luther King, Jr. and the March on Washington.* As we read, we are going to use sticky notes to identify words we don't understand.

Active Instruction
continued

Ask questions such as the following:

> **What do you remember about Martin Luther King, Jr.?**
> *Accept reasonable responses. The students may remember that he was a prominent civil rights leader, that he gave the famous "I Have a Dream" speech, and that he was assassinated. Write the students' answers in the K column of the chart.*

> **What else do you know about Martin Luther King, Jr.?**
> *Accept reasonable responses. Write them on the chart.*

> **Have you heard of the March on Washington? What do you remember about it?**
> *Accept reasonable responses. Write them on the chart.*

> **What else would you like to know about Martin Luther King, Jr. and the March on Washington?**
> *Accept reasonable responses. Write the answers in the W column of the chart.*

> **What do you know about the struggle for civil rights and how blacks were mistreated? What else would you like to know?**
> *Accept reasonable responses.*

Strategy Instruction

1. Pass out copies of the book. There should be several sticky notes inside the front cover of each book. Have the students look at the book's cover and predict what it will be about.

   > **What are some of the things you notice on this book's cover?**
   > *Accept reasonable responses. The students will probably recognize that the cover features Martin Luther King, Jr. They will notice that he is standing before a large crowd. Some students may recognize the Reflecting Pool and the Washington Monument in the distance.*

   Sometimes when you are getting ready to read a book, it's a good idea to leaf through it and look at the illustrations. Let's do that now.

Using **Think-Pair-Share**, ask:

> **What is an illustration that you see, and what does it tell you about this book?**
> *Accept reasonable responses.*

> **Is there anything else that you would like to learn from this book?**
> *Accept reasonable responses. Write the answers in the W column of the KWL chart.*

Active Instruction
continued

2. Present the Reading Goal:

> Today I would like to hear from you about what you do when you read. What do you do when you come to a word you don't recognize?
>
> *Answers may vary.*

Without evaluating the students' answers, make a list of them on the board or a blank transparency. After the students have suggested as many strategies as possible, consult the list below to add any that they have omitted.

sound it out	read the whole sentence
think about it	use the dictionary
ask your partner	look at other words for clues
keep reading	use the pictures
ask the teacher	

Using Thumbs Up/Thumbs down, ask:

> **Do all of these strategies work just as well for every difficult word?**
>
> *Expected response is no.*
>
> Let's read the book and see.

Read pages 4–7 of the book aloud. Be sure to read expressively, obeying punctuation and emphasizing important words. Using Think Alouds, talk about words that might be unfamiliar and how to figure them out.

Stop when you get to the word *summer*. Act as if you don't quite recognize the word and sound it out. "August 28, 1963. It is a hot s-s-uh-mm-mm-err, summer, day in Washington, D.C."

> The word *summer* was a little difficult for me, but I got it by sounding it out. I will put a sticky note on this word.

In the next sentence, stop at the word *people* and try to sound it out as it is spelled. "More than two hundred and fifty thousand p-p-ee-oh-p-leh, peeohpleh?"

> That word's not right. Maybe it's a word that doesn't sound exactly the way it's spelled. I will put a sticky note next to it, too, and see if any of the other words help me figure it out.

"—are pouring into the city."

> Well, the book is about a protest march, which usually involves a lot of people … oh, maybe the word is *people*.

Reread the sentence, this time pronouncing *people* correctly. "More than 250,000 people are pouring into the city."

> I wasn't able to get the word *people* by sounding it out, but I kept reading and used the context, the other words around it, and that helped me figure the word out.

Active Instruction
continued

Keep reading until you get to the word *roller-skated*. Stop at this word as if you are having trouble recognizing it.

> This word is a bit long and complicated-looking, but the picture shows a man on roller-skates. So it would make sense for it to be *roller-skated*. I will put a sticky note on that word, too.

Using **Think-Pair-Share**, ask:

> **What are the strategies I used to figure out these words?** *Answers should include sounding it out, using other words as clues, and looking at the pictures.*

Listening Comprehension

1. After you have finished modeling the strategy, reread the entire passage without any breaks to model fluency and so the students can focus on comprehension.

Vocabulary Introduction

1. Display all the lists you plan to present in this cycle, and introduce the first Word Mastery List. The starred words are for vocabulary-building activities.

List 1 read and spell	List 2 read	List 3 challenge list
more	laws	gathered
people	restaurants	president
miles	separate*	slavery
morning	public	nation
crowd*	change	speakers
narrow*	grandchildren	memorial
place	protests*	fighter
helped	refuse*	silence
slaves	hotels	civil
equally*	theaters	rights

Explain to the students that they will need to know how to read and spell all the words on List 1 and read all the words on List 2 by the end of the cycle. They can get bonus points for spelling the words on List 2 and for reading the List 3 (challenge) words.

Point to and read each word on List 1 as the class reads each word after you in unison. Then, point to each word in random order as the class reads it aloud. Distribute the homework pages so the students will have the word lists in front of them.

Take it up a notch: Point to and read both List 1 and List 2.

2. Have partners take turns reading the words aloud. Partners should listen for correctness and initial each other's Learning Guides when they can read all the words on a list. Circulate to assess the students'

Active Instruction
continued

1 = This word is totally new to me;
2 = The word looks familiar, but I don't know what it means;
3 = I know this word when I'm reading it, it has something to do with...;
4 = I know the word and can use it.

If possible, display this list of definitions for the entire cycle, hiding it only during the cycle test.

Timing Goal: 20 minutes

understanding and to provide pronunciation for any words the students have difficulty reading.

When the students are finished practicing the words, ask:

> **Was learning to read these words easy or hard?**
> *Answers will vary.*
>
> **Did you learn anything new about reading these words?**
> *Answers will vary.*
>
> **How will knowing these words help you in your reading today?**
> *Accept reasonable responses.*

Vocabulary Development

1. Point to the starred words on List 1. Ask the students to rate their knowledge of each word on their homework sheets.

   Ask the students to guess at the meaning of the words. Using **Numbered Heads**, allow a few of the students to share their guesses while you write them on the board or on chart paper. Read the definitions and the model sentences below, or create your own student-friendly definitions and sentences.

   > **crowd:** a large group of people
   > *The crowd cheered for the winning runner.*
   >
   > **narrow:** of very small width; not wide
   > *The large man had trouble climbing the narrow staircase.*
   >
   > **equally:** in the same manner or in the same amount
   > *The two dancers were equally good.*

   Allow the students the opportunity to adjust their own definitions if necessary. Write the students' definitions next to each word.

   Tell the students they will have an opportunity to refine their definitions after reading the passage.

2. Read the Team Talk questions aloud. Tell the students that they will answer these questions during Team Discussion.

Teamwork

Partner Reading

1. Have the students read:

   pages 8–13 aloud with partners.

   Have partners read the passage several times, alternating pages. Review word strategies that partners can use when they come to a word in the book they don't know: sound it out, look for context clues, look at the pictures, or ask for help.

Teamwork
continued

Take it down a notch: Have the students read the entire passage one time only, then repeat-read a single page or a 90-word selection.

Teams discuss all questions. The students individually write the answer to the marked question.

For now, I want you to focus on getting the words. The first time you read the passage, I want you to pay attention to the words you don't know or don't understand, and then talk with your partners about how to figure them out. Use sticky notes to identify unfamiliar words. Each time you reread the passage, remove the sticky notes next to words that you now understand and are able to read smoothly. Your goal is to read the entire passage smoothly and without making mistakes.

As partners work together, circulate to prompt and reinforce the students' efforts to clarify what they read. Remind them to sound words out, look for context clues, look at the pictures, or ask for help. Partners initial each other's Learning Guides when they can read the passage without mistakes.

2. When the students are finished reading and clarifying the passage, use **Think-Pair-Share** to ask:

> **What was a word you figured out? What strategy did you use?**
> *Answers will vary.*

> **Did you find the starred words in your reading?**
> *The students should answer yes.*

> **Based on your reading, do we need to refine our definitions of the starred words?**
> *Accept reasonable responses.*

Team Discussion

1. Display the Team Talk questions and read them aloud again. Remind the students to take turns reading the questions with their team and talking about the answers.

> **Team Talk Questions**
> 1. What important thing happened one hundred years ago?
>   *One hundred years ago, President Lincoln helped free the slaves.*
> 2. Why were the people in this book coming to Washington, D.C.? (write)
>   *The people were coming to Washington, D.C. to protest that black people and white people were still not treated equally.*

As the students discuss the questions, circulate through the classroom to conduct informal comprehension checks. Listen to team discussions and offer hints and suggestions.

2. Using student suggestions for the answer, model for the class how to write a good answer to the unmarked question. Emphasize the need to restate part of the question and to follow capitalization and punctuation rules.

Teamwork
continued

Timing Goal: 10 minutes

Take it up a notch: Ask for a volunteer to provide his or her own sentence for a Two-Minute Edit.

If possible, return the sentences to the students tomorrow.

Have the students write the answer to the marked question only.

Check your partner's answer. Is it a complete sentence that answers the question and repeats part of the question?

Time for Reflection

Class Discussion

1. When the students have completed their work, review the answers with the class. Use **Numbered Heads** to elicit an answer, and ask if anyone answered differently.

2. Do a Two-Minute Edit, using either the following sentence or a sentence of your own invention that highlights a grammar mistake that many of your students are making.

    the people were coming to Washington to protest.

Write the sentence on the board. Explain that there is one thing wrong. Using **Think-Pair-Share**, ask:

What would you do to make this sentence right?
The sentence can be made right by capitalizing the first word.

Remind the students that all sentences must start with a capital letter.

Have partners check each other's work to correct errors. When they are done, have them turn in their work. Explain that they will be awarded 1 point for giving the answer in complete sentence form and 1 point for having the correct answer.

Fluency Practice: Word Lists

1. Have the students practice reading and spelling List 1. When they can read the words accurately, have them check off each other's Learning Guides. Circulate to conduct informal word fluency checks and to correct mistakes.

Homework

1. Have the students pull out the homework passage. Explain that they will practice this passage at home each night until they can read it correctly and smoothly.

    The first time you read the passage, underline any words you have trouble with. You will then use strategies, such as sounding out the word, looking at context clues, and asking a friend or an adult for help, to figure out the words you have underlined. Then reread the passage until you can read it smoothly without making mistakes. Part of your test at the end of this unit will be to read a similar passage with some of the same words and answer questions about it.

7

Tutoring Programs

Tutoring is the most important means by which Success for All ensures that *all* students will succeed in reading. It is one of the most expensive elements of the program, but also probably one of the most cost-effective, since it is tutoring, more than any other feature, that enables the school to reduce retentions and special education placements (see Chapters 10 and 11).

Ideally, tutors in Success for All are certified teachers with a background in reading or early childhood education. These teacher-tutors have a dual role. During reading period (usually ninety minutes per day), certified teachers teach a reading class, both to reduce class sizes for reading and to give them a thorough idea of what the regular reading program is. The rest of the day, they work one-on-one with children who are having the greatest difficulties learning to read. In some schools moving away from traditional Title I pullout models, the Title I remedial teachers are now used as tutors. Special education teachers frequently serve as tutors as well, in which case they primarily tutor special education students or students at risk for special education placement. Some tutors are bilingual or ESL teachers, and specialize in English language learning. In many schools, highly trained paraprofessionals are also used. The Success for All tutoring model is designed to provide the necessary support and structure that enables less experienced staff to deliver effective supplementary reading instruction, while allowing certified teachers and skilled paraprofessionals the flexibility to take advantage of their valuable experience as they tutor struggling readers.

Decisions about which students need tutoring are made based on students' scores on quarterly assessments (see Chapter 4), plus teacher recommendations. First graders receive priority for tutoring, although second and third graders can be tutored if enough tutoring services are available. In high-poverty schools, we recommend providing enough tutoring for 30 percent of first graders, 20 percent of second graders, and 10 percent of third graders. With this, a number of first, second, and third grade tutoring "slots" are set aside based on the number of tutors available and scheduling constraints, and then the lowest-achieving students at each grade level are assigned a tutor. Students leave tutoring when their performance no longer places them among the lowest achievers in their grade. The average student who receives any tutoring will meet with a tutor every day for a semester (eighteen weeks), but individual first graders have stayed in tutoring for as long as one and a half years, into mid-second grade.

Tutors meet with children for twenty minutes each day. The school's schedule is set up so that tutors can work all day without ever taking students from reading, language arts, or math periods. Many schools reorganize their days to add twenty minutes each day to social studies, and then those students who receive tutoring are taken from social studies. In this arrangement, social studies periods are placed at different times for different classes and grades. Some schools have special resource periods or find other ways to schedule tutoring with minimum impact on students' other subjects. Before and after-school tutoring can sometimes extend the hours available for tutoring if transportation is not a problem.

BASIC PRINCIPLES OF TUTORING IN SUCCESS FOR ALL

The tutoring program in Success for All is based on a set of fundamental principles. These are as follows.

Tutoring Is One-to-One

One-to-one tutoring is the most effective form of instruction, especially for students with reading problems (Wasik & Slavin, 1993; Slavin, 1994). One reason for the effectiveness of one-to-one tutoring is that it allows tutors to teach to the individual student's needs. Tutors can make individual learning plans that fit the student's needs and can spend as much time as needed to teach a particular sound-blending or comprehension strategy.

Also, in one-to-one tutoring, tutors have the opportunity to give constant, immediate feedback to a student. If a student makes an error when reading, immediate corrective feedback can be provided along with the instruction needed to prevent further errors. This immediate diagnostic assessment and feedback is not possible when working with an entire class, or even a small group.

Because tutors have the opportunity to provide intensive instruction to each student, they learn a lot about the student's strengths and weakness, and which approaches work best with each. Tutors capitalize on this knowledge and use it to present material in the best way that will help students learn and remember the information.

One-to-one tutoring increases the opportunity for reading. When it is just one tutor and one student, the student can read and reread until he or she has mastered words, comprehended the story, and can read fluently. These opportunities are typically limited for poor readers during group instruction.

Tutoring Supports Classroom Instruction

Tutoring is closely coordinated with classroom instruction. The tutor works to support student success on the material that is presented in class, rather than teaching a separate program. For example, the same stories, letter-sound cues, and comprehension strategies are used in reading class and tutoring. This helps students keep up with class instruction and helps accelerate their learning. The repeated practice with, and exposure to, the material and methods presented in the classroom helps students solidify their reading knowledge.

Students Learn to Read by Reading

Students learn to read by reading. Reading is a complex process which involves decoding of words, tracking of words across the page, and constructing meaning from individual words as well as sentences and paragraphs. Success in reading requires the coordination of these complex activities. Therefore, teaching each of these activities in isolation will not teach a student to read and comprehend text. Reading connected text helps develop decoding skills, helps with fluency, and facilitates reading comprehension. Tutoring provides an opportunity for students to read and get immediate feedback on their reading.

Communication Between Tutors and Classroom Reading Teachers Is Essential

Tutors must communicate with the reading teacher of the students they are tutoring. It is essential that the tutors know how the students they are tutoring are performing in the classroom. They need to adapt their tutoring plan to the specific areas in which the student is having problems. The teacher also needs to be informed of the student's progress and other specific information that the tutor can provide that would help the teacher work better with the student.

THE TUTORING PROCESS IN READING ROOTS

The primary goal of tutoring is to help the student learn to create meaning from the printed word. The tutor reinforces the Reading Roots lessons presented in the reading classroom, providing students with a number of skills and strategies to figure out unknown words and to understand the meaning of sentences and paragraphs. Some of the most critical skills and strategies include:

1. Mastering letter/sound relationships and using phonics to sound out unknown words.
2. Using context and pictures to figure out unknown words.
3. Using context and pictures to obtain meaningful information about what is happening in the story.
4. Using comprehension-monitoring strategies to become active, engaged readers.

To help struggling readers become skilled readers, the Success for All tutoring model leads tutors and students through a cycle of assessment, planning, and active instruction.

Assessment

Before the tutor begins working with a student, he or she administers the Tutoring Assessment (see Figure 7.1). The Tutoring Assessment helps tutors determine the specific problems and strengths of a student and to tailor the tutoring session to meet the specific needs of the student. The tutor can determine if the student is having problems with phonemic awareness, sounding out words, recognizing specific letter sounds, understanding connected text, or more basic problems with concepts about print or tracking.

Tutors use the data from the Tutoring Assessment to select a Tutoring Plan template that will provide a framework for developing the instructional plan, and will be used during active instruction. The Tutoring Assessment provides novice tutors with guidance in choosing which of four elaborated templates is most appropriate based on their students' reading levels (see Figure 7.2).

Figure 7.1   Sample Assessment Sections of Tutoring

The Tutoring Assessment Part 1

Part 1 consists of three sections: Phonemic Awareness, Concepts About Print, and Letter Skills. The first two sections are for Reading Roots students ONLY. Reading Wings students begin with the third section: Letter Skills.

Phonemic Awareness (PA)

Administer the Phonemic Awareness section to Reading Roots students only.

Materials:

Student Record Form, word lists from Student Assessment Pages, paper, pen or pencil

Directions:

Administer the objectives in the **Phonemic Awareness** section to Roots students who have been identified for tutoring. Read the items for each objective from left to right. Circle correct responses, and write nothing for incorrect responses. If the student misses four items within a group, proceed to the next objective. When you have completed the **Phonemic Awareness** section, proceed to **Concepts About Print.**

PA–1. Identifies initial sounds in spoken words

- Tell the student that you will say a word, and you want him or her to listen carefully and tell you what sound the word starts with. Model an example for the student.

    Say: **If the word were *ten*, you would say /t/ because that's the first sound in *ten*.**

dive	call	sun	fin	pig
tank	hot	grape	thumb	chalk

Scoring Sample: The student identified the first sound in all words but *fin*.

dive	call	sun	fin	pig

PA–2. Blends sounds together to say a word

- Tell the student that you will say some letter sounds. Explain that you want him or her to listen carefully to all the sounds and then put them together to make a word. Model an example.

Say: **If I said the sounds /s/ /i/ /t/, you would put them together to make the word *sit*.**

/m/ /e/ me	/n/ /o/ /t/ not	/s/ /ee/ see	/r/ /a/ /m/ ram	/m/ /u/ /g/ mug
/s/ /t/ /o/ /p/ stop	/f/ /ee/ /t/ feet	/m/ /ai/ /n/ main	/ph/ /o_e/ /n/ phone	/n/ /a_e/ /m/ name

Scoring Sample: The student correctly blended the words *me*, *not*, and *ram*.

/m/ /e/ me	/n/ /o/ /t/ not	/s/ /ee/ see	/r/ /a/ /m/ ram	/m/ /u/ /g/ mug

PA–3. Breaks down a word and says each sound separately

- Tell the student that you will say a word, and you want him or her to listen carefully and then say each sound very slowly. Model an example, and then have the student repeat the sounds slowly.

  Say: **If the word were *man*, you would say each sound that you hear in that word - /m/ /a/ /n/. Can you say those sounds?** (Wait for the student's response.)

in /i/ /n/	red /r/ /e/ /d/	sun /s/ /u/ /n/	leg /l/ /e/ /g/	shop /sh/ /o/ /p/
rich /r/ /i/ /ch/	neat /n/ /ea/ /t/	chin /ch/ /i/ /n/	frog /f/ /r/ /o/ /g/	slam /s/ /l/ /a/ /m/

Scoring Sample: The student correctly segmented the words *red* and *leg*.

in /i/ /n/	red /r/ /e/ /d/	sun /s/ /u/ /n/	leg /l/ /e/ /g/	shop /sh/ /o/ /p/

Letter Skills (LS)

Reading Wings students start here.

Please Note: If the reading teacher has already tested the student and has these results, you may transfer that information onto the Student Record Form.

Materials:

Student Record Form, Letter Chart from Student Assessment Pages, paper, and pen or pencil

(Continued)

Figure 7.1 (Continued)

Directions:

Administer Set 1 from the Letter Chart for each of the three objectives that follow. Circle correct responses on the Student Record Form as indicated. (Do not mark incorrect responses.)

LS–1. Identifies (reads) letter sounds

- Point to the first letter on the list, and ask the student to tell you the sound that the letter makes.

- If the student tells you the name of the letter, say: **That's the name of the letter. What sound do you make when you read that letter?**

- If the student tells you a different sound that the letter makes, such as the long vowel sound instead of the short one, say: **Yes, that's one sound that this letter makes. Can you think of another sound that it makes?**

- Continue with the other letters in the set, moving left to right.

- Circle correct responses.

- Stop if the student misses four in a set. Go on to Objective 2.

Set 1	FTP 1–10	m	a (mad)	s	d	t	i (pin)	n	p	g	o (dot)	
Set 2	FTP 11–20	c (cup)	k	ck	u (rug)	r	b	f	e (net)	l	h	ng
Set 3	FTP 21–30	sh	z	w	ch	j	v	y (yell)	th	q	x	
Set 4	FTP 31–35	a_e	ee	i_e	o_e							
Set 5	FTP 36–40	oo (moon)	ar	c (mice)	ou (shout)	ay						
Set 6	FTP 41–45	ea (bean)	or	ie (pie)	_y (happy)	oy						
Set 7	FTP 46–50	er	ue	ai	igh	ow (snow)						
Set 8	FTP 51–55	aw	oi	oa	ur							
Set 9	FTP 56–60	ow (cow)	oo (book)	u_e	ir	_y (try)						

WS–2. Spells a word by breaking it into separate sounds

- Give the student a piece of paper, and explain the activity.

  Say: **I will say a word and then use it in a sentence. I want you to repeat the word and say the sounds you hear in the word. Then, write the word on the paper.**

- Begin with the first word from the chart. Give the student time to write each word before saying the next one.

- For letter sounds with more than one spelling, if the student uses a real combination that is not correct, prompt him or her to try and spell the word a different way. An example appears below:

  Student wrote *pale*.

  Say: **That's one way to spell *pail*. Can you try and spell *pail* another way?"**

- Retain the student's paper for his or her file.

Set 1	FTP 1–10	sip	mat	top
Set 2	FTP 11–20	cat	bed	lock
Set 3	FTP 21–30	fox	ship	math
Set 4	FTP 31–35	rake	cone	queen
Set 5	FTP 36–40	ice	stay	bark
Set 6	FTP 41–45	toy	dream	puppy
Set 7	FTP 46–50	pail	blue	night
Set 8	FTP 51–55	hurt	paw	boil
Set 9	FTP 56–60	plow	stir	brook

Scoring Sample: Student correctly wrote all words in Set 1.

Set 1	FTP 1–10	sip	mat	top

(Continued)

Figure 7.1 (Continued)

Comprehension and Writing – Expository – Level 2 (CWE2)

Materials:

Student Record Form, expository (nonfiction) text the student has not read before, Shared Story or Treasure Hunt questions, paper, pen or pencil, sticky notes

CWE2–1. Retells what was read (paragraph or page)

- Ask the student to read the text aloud. When the student has read one complete paragraph or page, ask him or her to tell you what he or she has read in his or her own words.

- If the student is able to tell you what the text is about in his or her own words, write the date in the Mastered column of the Student Record Form.

- If the student has trouble retelling what he or she read, ask the student questions about what he or she has read. Some sample questions follow.

  Ask: **What is hibernation? Why do bears hibernate?**

- If he or she is able to answer questions about the reading, write the date in the Developing column. If the student is still unable to tell you what he or she read, do not write anything.

CWE2–2. Answers literal questions about a text (oral)

- Have the student continue to read. Stop him or her periodically to ask literal questions about the text (information that appears in the text). Some sample questions follow.

  Ask: **Where do bears hibernate? What season do they sleep through?**

- If the student is able to tell you the correct answer, write the date in the Mastered column of the Student Record Form.

- If the student cannot tell you an answer, ask more questions to help him or her think of the answers. Some sample questions follow.

  Ask: **Do bears sleep in open fields? Do they sleep during the summer?**

- If the student is able to answer the question with prompting, write the date in the Developing column. If he or she is still unable to tell you what he or she read, do not write anything.

CWE2–3. Recognizes when sentence or passage does not make sense and attempts to clarify

- Give the student three or four sticky notes.

- Explain to the student that you want him or her to continue reading and if he or she comes to a part of the text that he or she does not understand, he or she can put a sticky note next to that part.

- Have the student continue reading, and when he or she places a sticky note on the text, ask why.

  Say: **I noticed you stopped reading and put a sticky note there. Why did you put it there? What didn't make sense to you?**

- If the student realizes that a part that he or she read does not make sense, write the date in the Mastered column of the Student Record Form.

- If the student continues to read, even though he or she has made a mistake, stop the student and ask if he or she understands everything that he or she has read. If the student says that he or she was confused by something, write the date in the Developing column of the Student Record Form. If the student does not realize that he or she has made an error, do not mark anything.

CWE2–4. Answers Shared Story or Treasure Hunt questions with evidence (oral)

- Choose a Shared Story or Treasure Hunt question that correlates with what the student has just read and read it aloud.

- Ask the student to tell you the answer. If the student is able to answer the question using information from the text, write the date in the Mastered column of the Student Record Form.

- If he or she tells you an answer, but does not support it with information from the text, ask him or her to tell you more.

  Say: **That's a good answer. What did you use in the text to help you figure that out?**

- If he or she is able to answer the question with prompting, write the date in the Developing column. If he or she is unable to tell you a correct answer, do not write anything.

Figure 7.2   Tutoring Plan Outlines

Tutoring Plan Outlines

Phonemic Awareness/Phonics Tutoring Plan Outline 1

Session Structure	Objectives
Goal Review (1–2 minutes) Student and tutor set or review the instructional goal for the week.	Together the student and tutor will review the Goal Setting/Progress Chart. They will chart any new progress and set a new goal or review the current goal.
Phonemic Awareness (4 minutes) Student develops phonemic awareness through rhyming and sound-identification activities.	Phonemic Awareness Objectives 1–3
Phonemic Awareness (4 minutes) Student develops phonemic awareness through rhyming and sound-identification activities.	Phonemic Awareness Objectives 1–3
Phonemic Awareness (4 minutes) Student develops phonemic awareness through rhyming and sound-identification activities.	Phonemic Awareness Objectives 1–3
Letter Skills (7 minutes) Student learns the relationship between letters and sounds by reading and writing letter sounds.	Letter Skills 1–3

Phonemic Awareness/Phonics Tutoring Plan Outline 2

Session Structure	Objectives
Goal Review (1–2 minutes) Student and tutor set or review the instructional goal for the week.	Together the student and tutor will review the Goal Setting/Progress Chart. They will chart any new progress and set a new goal or review the current goal.
Phonemic Awareness (5 minutes) Student practices blending sounds into words and breaking words into separate sounds.	Phonemic Awareness Objectives 2–3
Letter Skills (5 minutes) Student learns the relationship between letters and sounds by reading and writing letter sounds.	Letter Skills Objectives 1–3
Word Reading (5 minutes) Student reads words using blending.	Word Skills 1
Spelling (2 minutes) Student spells words by breaking them into separate sounds.	Word Skills 2
Sight Words (2 minutes) Student memorizes sight words.	Sight Words 1

Phonemic Awareness/Phonics Tutoring Plan Outline 3

Session Structure	Objectives
Goal Review (1–2 minutes) Student and tutor set or review the instructional goal for the week.	Together the student and tutor will review the Goal Setting/Progress Chart. They will chart any new progress and set a new goal or review the current goal.
Letter Skills (3 minutes) Student learns the relationship between letters and sounds by reading and writing letter sounds.	Letter Skills 1–3
Word Reading (4 minutes) The student reads words using blending.	Word Skills 1, 3, 4, 5
Spelling (3 minutes) The student spells words by breaking them into separate sounds.	Word Skills 2
Story Preparation Word Review (2 minutes) The student reviews Green Words, Red Words, and important vocabulary from the story.	Word Skills 1 Sight Words 1 Vocabulary 1
New Story (7 minutes) Student reads from current story and develops fluency and comprehension skills.	Vocabulary 1 Concepts about Print 1–6 Tracking 1–3 Fluency 1–4 Comprehension and Writing – Levels 1–5

Phonemic Awareness/Phonics Tutoring Plan Outline 4

Session Structure	Objectives
Goal Review (1–2 minutes) Student and tutor set or review the instructional goal for the week.	Together the student and tutor will review the Goal Setting/Progress Chart. They will chart any new progress and set a new goal or review the current goal.
Familiar Story (4 minutes) Student reads from a familiar story and develops fluency skills.	Tracking 1–3 Fluency 1–4
Word Reading (4 minutes) Student reads words using blending.	Word Skills 1, 3, 4, 5
Spelling (3 minutes) Student spells words by breaking them into separate sounds.	Word Skills 2
Story Preparation Word Review (2 minutes) Student reviews Green Words, Red Words, and important vocabulary from the story.	Word Skills 1 Sight Words 1 Vocabulary 1
New Story (6 minutes) Student reads from current story and develops fluency and comprehension skills.	Vocabulary 1 Tracking 1–3 Fluency 1–4 Comprehension and Writing - Levels 1–5

Experienced tutors have the flexibility of selecting one of the four elaborated templates or using a blank template to develop the student's tutoring plan.

Planning

After tutors have selected a Tutoring Plan template for a student, they identify the student's reading objectives and record them on the plan. If the student is at the most basic reading level, the tutor will select objectives that cover skills such as phonemic awareness, letter/sound correspondence, and word-level blending. If the student is a more advanced reader, the tutor will select objectives and activities that develop the student's ability to decode multisyllabic words, read connected text fluently, and use a variety of strategies to increase reading comprehension.

If a tutor is using one of the four elaborated templates, the template provides support for the planning process by defining the broad skill areas that will be covered during the tutoring session and lists a range of objectives that address skill development in each area (see Figure 7.3).

Once tutors have selected the reading objectives the student will work on, they consult the tutoring manual to choose the specific activities that will be used to practice each objective. These activities are recorded on the tutoring plan, along with the time the tutor and student will devote to each activity.

The final step of the planning process is goal setting. This step is completed in consultation with the student. During the first weekly session, the tutor and student discuss the objectives and activities they will be working on. The tutor helps the student to develop a personal goal to achieve. This goal is simple, concrete, and directly related to the skills the student will be practicing.

The tutor and student also agree on a small reward that the student will earn if the goal is achieved. Setting personal goals motivates students and prompts them to think consciously about their learning.

Active Instruction

After the Tutoring Plan is complete, the tutor and student are ready to begin active instruction.

In the Success for All tutoring model, instructional activities are organized into the following broad areas:

Phonemic Awareness

Concepts About Print

Letter Skills

Sight Words

Word Skills

Vocabulary

Tracking

Fluency

Comprehension and Writing

A description of each broad area and an example activity from each area are provided beginning on page 254.

Figure 7.3   Sample Tutoring Plan

Tutoring Plan 3

Student's Name: Jenny	Homeroom Teacher: Mr. Hill	Reading Teacher: Ms. Banks	Start Date: 10/10/04	Suggested Times LS: 3 minutes WR: 4 minutes SPL: 3 minutes SP: 2 minutes NS: 7 minutes

Student Goal – Week 1: Met?   Yes   No

My goal is to *stop when I come to words I don't know and try to figure them out.* If I am able to do this 8 times per week I will get a sticker.

			End Date: 10/22/04

Student Goal – Week 2: Met?   Yes   No

Lesson Plan Week 1

	Sessions		Progress/Notes		

Letter Skills (LS 1, 2, 3)

Objective: LS 1 – Will identify letter sounds.

Activity: C – Letter Blending Card – Letter Sound Match

Time: 3 minutes

| 1. Intro. activity. Worked on sounds from FTP lessons 17–20. (D) | 2. Cont. working on sounds from FTP lessons 17–20. (D) | 3. Worked on sounds from FTP lessons 17–20. (M) | 4. Worked on sounds from FTP lessons 21–24. (D) | 5. Worked on sounds from FTP lessons 21–24. (D) | Objective Met? Yes No |

Word Reading (WS 1, 3, 4, 5)

Objective: WS 1 – Will use blending to read words.

Activity: A – Blending Sounds into Words

Time: 4 minutes

| 1. Intro. activity. Worked on words from FTP lessons 15–18. (D) | 2. Working on words from FTP lessons 15–18. (D) | 3. Working on words from FTP lessons 15–18. (D) | 4. Worked on words from FTP lessons 15–18. (M) | 5. Worked on words from FTP lessons 19–23. (D) | Objective Met? Yes No |

Spelling (WS 2)

Objective: WS 2 – Will spell words by breaking them into sounds.

Activity: C – Spelling Words

Time: 2 minutes

| 1. Intro. activity Worked on words from FTP lessons 15–18. (D) | 2. Working on words from FTP lessons 15–18. (D) | 3. Working on words from FTP lessons 15–18. (D) | 4. Working on words from FTP lessons 15–18. (D) | 5. Working on words from FTP lessons 15–18. (D) | Objective Met? Yes No |

Story Preparation (SW 1 | WS 1 | V 1)

Objective: SW 1 – Will read sight words.

Activity: A – Reading Red Words in Shared Stories

Time: 2 minutes

| 1. Kim's Visit. (D) Problem word–give | 2. Kim's Visit. (M) | 3. The Field Trip. (D) Problem word–out | 4. The Field Trip. (D) | 5. The Field Trip. (M) | Objective Met? Yes No |

New Story {CP 1–6 | V 1 | T 1–3 | F 1–4 | C1 | W1 | CWN 2–5 | CWE 2–5}

Objective: C1–3 – Will sound out unknown words in her reading.

Activity: A – Sound Blending Words in a Sentence

Time: 7 minutes

| 1. Kim's Visit. (D) Needed prompting. | 2. Kim's Visit. (M) | 3. The Field Trip. (D) Needed prompting | 4. The Field Trip. (D) Needed prompting. | 5. The Field Trip. (M) | Objective Met? Yes No |

Phonemic Awareness

Phonemic awareness is the ability to discriminate, identify, and manipulate individual speech sounds. These skills support a student's ability to sound out words in print, the most useful word-identification strategy. Before children can learn to identify and blend letter sounds to read words, they must be able to hear these sounds in speech.

Say-It-Fast. The tutor teaches the student to blend discrete sounds into words by saying the sounds of a simple word such as "hot" with a pause between each sound: /h/ /o/ /t/. Then the teacher models "saying the sounds fast" or blending them into a word.

Next the teacher will present words as segmented sounds for the student to blend into words. Gradually, the tutor will increase the number of sounds until the student is blending four-phoneme words.

Concepts About Print

Concepts about print are basic to learning to read. Before the students can construct meaning from print, they must know why people read; the right way to hold a book; where the title is; that the message is in the print, rather than in the pictures; that there are spaces between the words; and that reading print occurs from left to right. These, and similar concepts, are the foundation for learning to read.

Identifying the Title of a Book. The tutor points to the title of a book and reads it for the student. Then, the tutor explains that the title tells the name of the story and is found on the cover of the book. The tutor also explains that the title is usually written in larger letters than other words on the cover because it contains the most important words. During later sessions, the tutor will ask the student to point to the title and will provide support until the student can do this independently.

Letter Skills

Students need to get to the point where knowledge of the letter sounds is automatic, so that their attention can be free to focus on comprehension.

Identifying Letter Sounds. Tutors teach these letter sounds using letter key cards that include a picture cue and alliterative phrase that reinforces the letter sound. For example, tutors teach the sound for the letter "m" by linking it to a picture of a man marching on a mountain and the phrase "The man marches on mountains." Students learn to say the sound /mmm/ when the tutor presents the M-picture key card. Next they learn to say the sound when the tutor presents a letter card without the picture cue. If the student has difficulty remembering the letter sound, the tutor will prompt the student to think of the picture or phrase that goes with the letter.

Sight Words

Sight words are words that cannot be sounded out because they do not follow the straightforward decoding rules the students learn early in their reading class. The students must learn to recognize these words in their reading, and they need repeated exposure to become familiar with them.

Reading Sight Words. The stories used in the Roots curriculum list the sight words, called Red Words, inside the front cover. Tutors teach the Red Words by pointing to each word and asking the students to read it. If the student can't read the word, the tutor will relay the word and ask the student to repeat it. The tutor repeats this process until the student can read all of the sight words for the story automatically.

Word Skills

Students need to develop word skills to identify and figure out words as they read and spell. These skills range from reading simple, phonetically regular words—using sound blending—to chunking and other strategies for reading more complex and difficult words.

Blending Sounds Into Words. Using letters that the student has already mastered, the tutor writes a short word, such as "man," at the top of a small piece of paper and spaces the letters far apart to look like this:

m . . . . a . . . . .n

Then the tutor will touch each letter and have the student make the letter sound. Next the tutor will write the word again and put the letters closer together to look like this:

m . . . . a . . . . n

The tutor and student will repeat the routine, but the student will have to say the sounds faster. Finally, the tutor will write the word underneath the other two rows of letters like this:

man

The tutor will then repeat the pointing routine at a fast pace and then ask the student to say the word he or she has read.

Vocabulary

Understanding important vocabulary words that appear in text is a key part of reading comprehension. Students must learn the meaning of unknown words if they are going to fully understand what they are reading.

Learning Important Vocabulary. As the student reads, the tutor monitors for signs that the student does not understand the meaning of words. If the tutor finds a word the student doesn't know, he or she will provide a simple definition and sample sentence. Then the tutor will ask the student to use the word in a sentence and the meaning of the word in the student's own words. The tutor can also have the student keep a list of these words for review at a later time.

Tracking

Tracking refers to the ability to follow the print on each page efficiently. At first, some students need help tracking a line of print from left to right smoothly, without losing their place, or jumping back and forth. Sometimes students need help learning where one word stops and another starts.

Reading From Left to Right. The tutor explains and models how to read print from left to right and how to continue to the next line of print. Then the tutor asks the student to show the direction he or she will read. If necessary, the tutor will guide his or her finger under the words.

Fluency

Fluency is the ability to read words accurately, smoothly, with expression, and at an appropriate rate. Developing reading fluency helps students practice familiar words and familiar sentence patterns, and gives the student repeated opportunities to comprehend the material. Being able to read fluently and with expression also indicates that the student comprehends what is being read. Fluency practice also has additional benefits, as each time the student reads the story, the student focuses on different parts of the reading process, which reinforces word recognition strategies and comprehension skills.

Reading With Expression. Students reread a familiar story during this activity and, with it, the tutor explains reading with expression. The tutor also demonstrates how reading a sentence differently can send different messages. Then, the tutor models reading with expression from a page in a familiar story. The student reads the same page with expression. The student continues reading the story as the tutor prompts to focus on reading with expression and to pretend to be the characters or to talk like the characters would.

Comprehension and Writing

The Success for All tutoring model links reading comprehension and writing. Working on comprehension skills—like previewing and predicting or identifying the most important details from a text—helps students become better readers. Writing skills help students learn to answer different kinds of comprehension questions, communicate their thoughts in sentences that make sense, and write summaries of different kinds of texts.

Rereading and Thinking When Reading a Story. The purpose of this activity is to teach the student how to read for meaning and monitor comprehension at the same time. Often a student will read the words in a story but not understand the message being communicated in the text. For students with reading problems, comprehension monitoring is not a skill that comes automatically with reading. The tutor needs to teach this skill. There are two parts to teaching comprehension monitoring skills. One is to help the student know whether or not he or she understood the text. The second is to teach the student what to do when he or she does not understand.

The tutor begins by teaching the student to ask questions that determine understanding. First, the tutor models self-monitoring strategies. The first is for the tutor to read a passage and act as if a word or section has arisen that is not understood. Then the tutor models rereading the passage and using different strategies to figure out the meaning of the word or words. Next the tutor will look for opportunities to prompt the student to check comprehension. The tutor may ask questions that will assess the student's understanding, such as "Does what you have just read make sense to you? Do you understand what happened in the story?" Lastly, the student is asked to summarize in his or her own words what he or she just read.

The idea is to get students into a routine of asking themselves comprehension-check questions. The students get to the point where they know what questions to ask. If a student cannot answer the comprehension-check questions correctly, or does not provide information to show that the reading is understood, the tutor demonstrates how to find the answer. The tutor may begin by instructing the student to reread the section out loud, explaining that rereading the story will improve understanding so the student will be able to tell if what was read makes sense.

After the student has reread the section of a story, the tutor may ask another comprehension-check question. If the student is still unable to answer the question, the tutor may assess other obstacles that might be interfering with comprehension, such as inadequate vocabulary knowledge, word recognition skills, or background knowledge. Once assessed, the tutor may help the student with any of these.

THE TUTORING PROCESS IN READING WINGS

Because the emphasis of tutoring is on children in the primary grades who are having difficulties with reading, almost all tutoring involves Reading Roots, the first grade model. However, sometimes children receive tutoring in Reading Wings. The tutoring cycle (Assessment, Planning, Active Instruction) remains the same for Reading Wings students, but there is a greater focus on fluency, comprehension, and writing skills.

TUTORING WITH ALPHIE'S ALLEY (COMPUTER-BASED TUTORING)

Alphie's Alley is a computer-based tool designed to help tutors carry out the tutoring cycle: Assessment, Planning, and Active Instruction (see Figure 7.4). Success for All developed Alphie's Alley to capitalize on the computer's ability to facilitate the complex task of analyzing assessment data to create tutoring plans, while at the same time providing effective, compelling, and fun computer activities to practice reading skills.

Alphie's Alley guides the tutor and student through a computer-based assessment, which automatically identifies which objectives the student has mastered and which ones require additional work. Then the program selects a Tutoring Plan template *and* activities based on the assessment results. Novice tutors can simply accept this suggested plan and begin tutoring, while experienced tutors have the flexibility to modify the plan. The Activities Module in Alphie's Alley contains seventeen interactive computer-based activities and more than one hundred paper-and-pencil activities that help students develop the skills that are crucial for their success in learning to read.

Figure 7.4 Alphie's Alley

Alphie's Alley also contains an online tutorial, which provides the tutor with detailed information on the three components of the tutoring cycle, including video segments of expert tutors working with students and describing best practices.

TUTORING WITH TEAM ALPHIE (COMPUTER-BASED SMALL GROUP TUTORING)

As noted earlier, tutoring is one the most expensive elements of the Success for All model. It is difficult to staff tutoring positions with certified teachers. Yet, providing tutoring for struggling readers is a key factor in bringing them up to grade level and reducing special education placements. In response to these conditions, Success for All has begun the development of Team Alphie, a computer-based, small group tutoring program, so that schools can provide supplemental reading instruction to more students with fewer staff.

Team Alphie is based on Alphie's Alley, and the Assessment and Planning components of the tutoring cycle in the two programs are almost identical. However, during Active Instruction in Team Alphie, students are grouped into teams of two to three students, with each team working on one computer (see Figure 7.5). The students work together to complete the computer activities. For most of these activities, one student plays the role of "Player" and responds to items presented by the computer, while the other student(s) play the role of "Ref" and evaluates whether the Player's response was correct or incorrect. After several items (or minutes), the students switch roles. While students are working on the activities, the tutor rotates among teams and provides support or instruction as needed, and conducts brief assessments to ensure that the students are mastering the reading skill they are working on. Using Team Alphie, tutors are able to work with groups of four to eight students at a time, rather than the one tutor to one student ratio of conventional tutoring.

Figure 7.5   Team Creator Screen Shot, Alphie's Alley

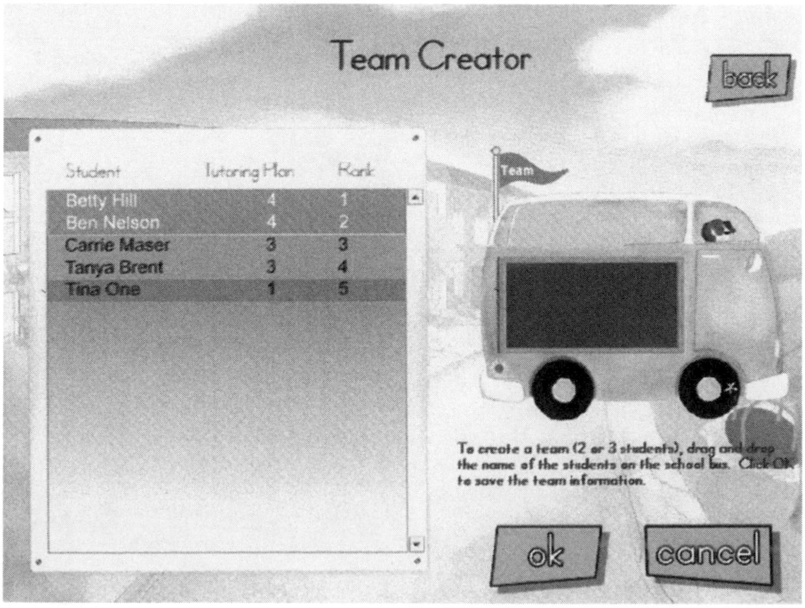

Writing, Math, and Data-Driven Reform

Other SFA Programs

While all Success for All elementary schools use KinderCorner, Reading Roots, and Reading Wings, there are additional programs in writing/language arts and mathematics that are optional, and are used in some but not all SFA schools. Also, the Success for All Foundation provides a number of stand-alone programs that are based on SFA components but may be used in non-SFA schools, including an SFA afterschool program, separate reading and math programs, benchmark assessments, and professional development programs to help districts interpret their own data and choose effective programs (which may or may not be SFA programs). This chapter briefly describes all of these and other programs that go beyond the SFA comprehensive reform model.

WRITING AND LANGUAGE ARTS

Writing and language arts are critical elements of the Success for All programs, particularly because writing is the opposite side of the reading coin. In prekindergarten, kindergarten, and first grade, emergent literacy strategies such as journal writing, shared writing, and sound-based spelling are used to build students' interest in expressing their ideas in writing. In Reading Roots and Lee Conmigo, students regularly write to respond in some way to the story or to give their answers to questions about the story. In Reading Wings, students exercise their writing skills in responses to Treasure Hunt questions and in creative story-related writing activities.

All of these activities use writing to support the learning of reading while providing opportunities to write. However, students also need specific instruction in how to improve their writing. A formal writing/language arts instructional program is usually introduced in Success for All once most teachers are comfortable with the reading program. In practice, this usually means that the writing/language arts program is introduced in the spring of the first implementation year or in the fall of the second year.

Writing/language arts instruction in Success for All is usually provided to students in their heterogeneous homerooms, not in their reading groups. The basic philosophy behind the writing/language arts programs is that writing should be given the main emphasis and that language arts, especially mechanics and usage, should be taught in the context of writing, not as a separate topic.

There are two levels in the Success for All writing and language arts approach. Both are based on the ideas of writing process (Calkins, 1983; Graves, 1983), which emphasize writing for a real audience, writing for revision, and gradually building spelling and mechanics in the context of writing. Writing From the Heart, used in Grades 1–2, uses an informal version of writing process, while the Cooperative Integrated Reading and Composition (CIRC) program, Writing Wings, used in Grades 3–6, uses a more formal writing process model with regular four-member peer response groups and students working compositions through from plan to draft to revision to editing to publication. These programs are described below.

Writing From the Heart

A young child thinks of writing as an extension of oral communication. Most, given the undivided attention of an audience, will talk endlessly about their experiences. Young authors rarely have a problem of too little to say; their problem is overcoming the barriers they perceive to putting their ideas down on paper.

The goal of Writing From the Heart, the writing/language arts program used in Grades 1–2 in Success for All, is to tap students' innate desire, energy, and enthusiasm for communication and to move them to the next step of sharing their ideas with others through writing. When writing is seen as mastery of spelling and mechanics, it is a formidable task. Students will ultimately need to master these skills, but first they need to develop pleasure and fluency in putting their thoughts on paper. Most importantly, students need to see writing as a personal expression, not an ordinary school task. They must put their hearts into their writing, not just their minds.

Writing From the Heart uses a writing process model, which means that students write for a real audience and learn to revise their writing until it is ready for "publication." Students do not work in formal writing teams (that will come in third grade), but they do work informally with partners while they are writing.

The main elements of Writing From the Heart are as follows:

1. *Modeling and Motivating Writing.* At the beginning of each lesson, the teacher provides a model or motivator for writing. For example, the teacher may read a story that is like what students will be writing, or may ask students to describe experiences that relate to a particular kind of writing. The teacher may introduce formats to help students plan their writing. For example, in writing about "myself," students are given a set of questions to answer about themselves, which they then use to put into a story.

2. *Writing a "Sloppy Copy."* Students are encouraged to write a "sloppy copy," a first draft of their composition. They are taught to use "sound spelling" (invented spelling) if they cannot spell a word. For example, "dinasr" is a way a student might write "dinosaur."

3. *Partner Sharing.* At several points in the writing process, students share their writing with partners and receive feedback and ideas from them.

4. *Revision.* Students learn to revise their compositions using feedback from partners and from the teacher. Specific revision skills are taught and modeled in the lessons. Students learn to add the information necessary to help their audience follow and enjoy their story.

5. *Editing.* In preparation for publication, the teacher helps each child prepare a perfect draft of his or her composition, complete with pictures. This is when "dinasr" becomes "dinosaur."

6. *Publication.* Final drafts of students' writings are "published" in a class book, read to the class, and recognized in as many ways as the teacher can think of.

7. *Sharing and Celebration.* At many points in the writing process, students have opportunities to share their writing with the class. The teacher sets up a special "author's chair" from which the "authors" present their latest works. Authors are taught to ask three questions of their audience:
   - What did you hear? Can you tell me about my story?
   - What did you like about my story?
   - What else would you like to know about my story?

   The teacher models use of the author's chair by presenting his or her own writing, and models answers to the author's questions.

Writing From the Heart prepares students for the Writing Wings program starting in Grade 3 by convincing students that they are authors and have something to say, by teaching them that writing is a process of thinking, drafting, revising, and polishing ideas, and by letting them know that writing is fun. They are then ready to learn more about the craft of writing with more formal instruction in tricks of the trade, style, mechanics, and usage.

Writing Wings

The writing/language arts program used in the upper elementary grades is one developed earlier as part of CIRC for Grades 3 and up (Stevens et al., 1987). In this program, students are assigned to four- or five-member heterogeneous writing teams. Writing Wings has two major instructional formats. About three days each week are used for writing process activities, and two for language arts instruction.

Writing Concept Lessons

Each writing process day begins with a brief lesson on a writing concept. For example, the first lesson is on "mind movies," visualization of events in a narrative to see where additional detail or description is needed. Other lessons include organizing imaginative narratives, using observation to add life to descriptions, writing personal narratives, mysteries, persuasive arguments, explanatory writing, and so on. The writing concept lessons are meant to spark ideas and help students expand upon their writing and evaluate their own and others' compositions.

Writing Process

Most of the writing/language arts period is spent with students writing their own compositions while the teacher circulates among the teams and conferences with individual students. Students draft many compositions and then choose a smaller number they would like to carry all the way through the steps to publication. The steps are as follows:

1. *Prewriting.* Students discuss with their teammates topics they would like to address and audiences for their writing. They each then draft a plan, using a "skeleton planning form," an "idea net," or other forms to organize their thinking.

2. *Drafting.* After the student prepares a plan in consultation with teammates, he or she writes a first draft, focusing on getting ideas on paper rather than spelling and mechanics (they will come later).

3. *Team Response and Revision.* Students read their drafts to their teammates. The teammates are taught to rephrase the main idea of the story in their own words, to mention two things they liked about the story, and to note two things they'd like to hear more about. The teacher may also conference with students at the revision stage to applaud students' ideas and suggest additions and changes. Revision guides for specific categories of writing assist students in responding usefully to their teammates' writing. For instance, as students learn to enrich their narratives with rich description, they use a team response guide that asks them to tell the author (their teammate) their favorite descriptive words. As they look at the writing of their teammates, they learn to look for those features in their own writing. Students make revisions based on their teammates' responses.

4. *Editing.* Once the author is satisfied with the content of the writing, he or she is ready to correct the mechanics, usage, and spelling. Students work with a partner to go through an editing checklist. The checklist starts with a small number of goals (e.g., correct capitalization and end punctuation), but then adds goals as students complete language arts lessons. For example, after a lesson on subject-verb agreement or run-on sentences, these skills may be added to the checklist. The author first checks the composition against the checklist, then a teammate does so, and finally the teacher checks it.

5. *Publication.* Publication involves the creation of the final draft and celebration of the author's writing. Students carefully rewrite their work incorporating all final corrections made by the teacher. They then present their compositions to the class from a fancy "author's chair," and may then contribute their writing to a team book or a team section of a class book. These books are proudly displayed in the class or library. In addition, students may be asked to read their compositions to other classes, or to otherwise celebrate and disseminate their masterpieces!

A sample presentation guide for a writing lesson focusing on rich expression in a personal narrative is included in Appendix 8.1 on pages 271–304. This guide covers the development of the concept and the planning, drafting, and team response sections of the writing process. The other steps would be completed later.

Revision and Editing Skills Lessons

About two days each week, the teacher teaches structured lessons on language mechanics skills. These are presented as skills for revision and editing, because their purpose is to directly support students' writing. The teacher determines the order of lessons according to problems students are experiencing and skills they will need for upcoming writing. For example, the teacher may notice that many students are having problems with complete sentences, or may anticipate that since students are about to write dialogue they may need to learn how to use quotation marks.

Students work in their four-member writing teams to help one another master the skills taught by the teacher. The students work on examples, compare answers with each other, resolve discrepancies, explain ideas to each other, and so on. Ultimately, students are quizzed on the skill, and the teams can earn certificates or other recognition based on the average performance of all team members. As noted earlier, immediately after a revision and editing skills lesson, the new skill is added to the editing checklist, so language arts skills are immediately put into practice in students' writing.

Video-Enhanced Writing Wings

A longstanding problem in the use of all writing process models is that students may not know what effective writing teams should look like. As a result, members of writing teams may be too critical of each other, or alternatively may give very little help or advice to their partners. Teachers may also be unsure about writing process approaches. Recently, we have introduced a series of videos (usually used on DVDs or electronic whiteboards) that show students and teachers how the writing process works and, most importantly, give them models of effective teamwork. The main element of the videos is a series of skits in which a writing team, "The Write-On Dudes," works together to learn to write. The "Dudes" are puppets, each of whom has a characteristic writing problem that their partners help with. Mona, a bit of a goth, thinks she has nothing to say and is very unsure of herself. Ricardo, the class poet, is overly florid. Tasha, a sports nut, tends to write all the facts with little description. Flash, a sci-fi fan, has wonderful ideas and great enthusiasm but is disorganized. The Dudes model a kind and helpful tone as well as specific strategies, beginning with elements of the writing process (e.g., planning, revising, editing), and then showing how these elements play out in various writing genres (e.g., personal narratives, factual stories, persuasive essays, and business letters). In addition, a series of live action skits, usually including animations, introduces the "Language Mechanics," who work in a garage fixing up sentences. These videos segments introduce grammar, punctuation, usage, and other mechanics skills.

MATHWINGS

MathWings, the Roots & Wings mathematics program for Grades 1–6, is based on the standards of the National Council of Teachers of Mathematics (2000), and is consistent with Focal Points (NCTM, 2006). A program to prepare students for mathematics in the twenty-first century needs to actively involve students in the conceptual development and practical application of their mathematics skills. The MathWings program reflects a balance of solid mathematical conceptual development, problem solving in real world applications, and maintenance of necessary mathematics skills.

Students enter school with a great deal of mathematical knowledge. They know about combining and separating, halves and wholes, and so on. What they need is a bridge between their preexisting knowledge and the formal representation of this knowledge in mathematical symbols. This requires the use of manipulatives, demonstrations, and discovery to help students build mathematical understanding. MathWings uses cooperative learning at all age levels while incorporating problem solving in real situations, skill practice and reinforcement for efficiency in application, calculator use, alternative assessments, writing, connections to literature and other disciplines, and application to the students' world and personal experiences. Although students help each other learn, they are always individually accountable for their own learning, and are frequently assessed on their progress in understanding and using math (see Slavin, 1995).

Critical Components of MathWings

The NCTM Standards advocate emphasizing problem solving rather than rote calculation with algorithms. MathWings lessons involve the students in problem solving in "real" situations to give validity and purpose to their mathematics explorations, and in daily problem solving as part of the routine of math class. MathWings lessons also make connections to literature, science, art, and other subjects as well as students' experiences to provide this real world problem-solving context.

Another strand of the NCTM Standards is mathematical reasoning. Students develop their ability to think through and solve mathematical problems when they use manipulatives to develop concepts and then represent what is actually happening with symbols. MathWings units are constructed to develop concepts from the concrete to the abstract so that each step of the reasoning is clarified. The Standards also promote the use of calculators for developing concepts and exploring advanced problem-solving situations rather than checking answers or replacing skills and mental math. MathWings students use calculators in this way to increase both their mathematical reasoning skills and the scope and complexity of the problems they can solve, and to focus their energy on mathematical reasoning rather than mere mechanical calculation.

The NCTM Standards emphasize communication, both oral and written, to clarify, extend, and refine the students' knowledge. MathWings students constantly explain and defend their solutions orally, and regularly write in their logbooks. This emphasis on communication extends to the assessments as well. The Standards suggest the use of alternative assessments, which incorporate communication as well as calculation. MathWings units involve the students in many different types of ongoing formal and informal assessment. Intermediate students complete "Concept Checks" in which they explain their thinking as they solve problems after every few lessons. They work on performance tasks at the end of each unit to use the skills they have learned to solve practical real world situations and explain and communicate about their thinking. Primary students complete a written assessment at the end of each unit. Teacher observations—of both primary and intermediate students at work with manipulatives, collecting data, etc., and students' written and oral communications—are also used to assess understanding.

The use of cooperative learning in MathWings is based on years of research regarding effective strategies for classroom instruction. This research has shown that the cognitive rehearsal opportunities presented by cooperative learning, as well as the opportunities for clarification and reteaching for students who do not catch a concept immediately, have positive effects on academic achievement (Slavin, 1995). In cooperative learning, students work together to learn; the team's work is not complete until all team members have learned the material being studied. This positive interdependence is an essential feature of cooperative learning.

Research has identified three key components that make cooperative learning strategies effective: team recognition, individual accountability, and equal opportunities for success. In MathWings, students work in four-member, mixed-ability teams. Starting in second grade, teams may earn certificates and additional means of recognition if they achieve at or above a designated standard. All teams can succeed because they are working to reach a common standard rather than competing against one another. The team's success depends on the individual learning of all team members; students must make sure that everyone on the team has learned, since each team member must demonstrate his or her knowledge on an individual assessment. Students have an equal opportunity for success in MathWings because they contribute points to their teams by improving over their own individual performance, by bringing in their homework, and by meeting particular behavior goals set by the teacher; these are accomplishments that are within the capabilities of every student but that are also demanding for every student. Students who are typically seen as lower achievers can contribute as many points to the team as high achievers.

The MathWings program is designed to use the calculator as a tool, not a crutch. Calculators enable the students to explore and demonstrate concepts in an appealing way. Students discover that they need to check their calculator answers for accuracy since the calculator is only as accurate as the information and process that is keyed into it. Thus, students develop their skills in estimating and predicting outcomes. Students also spend more time actually thinking about math and the processes that will most efficiently solve a given problem rather than focusing completely on tedious and lengthy calculations. Because of the speed of calculation with calculators, students are more willing to try several approaches to solving a problem situation or to reevaluate their answers and try a different method of solution. Finally, calculators build students' confidence in mathematics as they receive much positive reinforcement from correct solutions. This leads, in turn, to a greater willingness to tackle more challenging mathematical situations in the belief that they have the ability and the tools to solve them.

Manipulative use is a basic building block of the MathWings program at all levels. Students construct understanding and develop original methods for solving problems using manipulatives. As they work with manipulatives and discuss and defend their thinking, they gradually make the concepts their own. Once a problem can be solved with manipulatives, students draw a picture and then write a number sentence to represent what was happening with the manipulatives as they solved the problem. This gradual progression from concrete to pictorial to abstract provides a solid foundation of understanding upon which the students can build. Every method or algorithm can be understood, and even reinvented, with manipulatives, thus replacing rote learning of algorithms with understanding of concepts and ways to efficiently apply them. Once the concepts have been firmly established and students understand how the algorithms work, they move away from using concrete manipulatives. However, manipulatives can be revisited at any time to remediate or extend a concept as needed.

Most MathWings Action Math units have a literature connection, which is an integral part of the concept development. Literature provides a wonderful vehicle for exploring mathematical concepts in meaningful contexts, demonstrating that mathematics is an integral part of human experience. The use of literature incorporates the affective elements and demonstrates the aesthetic aspect of mathematics. Finally, the use of literature encourages students to pose problems from real and imaginary situations and to use language to communicate about mathematics.

MathWings involves the students in daily routines that frame each lesson and are efficient ways to provide for team management, problem solving, and skill practice and reinforcement to facilitate efficiency in calculation and application. Once the students have mastered the facts and basic algorithms, they become tools for the students to use as they develop concepts and problem solving. These routines include facts practice at both levels. In Intermediate MathWings there are weekly timed-facts tests to encourage mastery of the basic facts, and then practice problems at varying difficulty levels to provide for fluency in the use of the essential algorithms. There are also daily real-world applications in Primary MathWings and daily problem solving in Intermediate.

MathWings has two major forms. Primary MathWings is used in Grades 1–2 and Intermediate MathWings is used in Grades 3–5. The MathWings program is quite similar at the two levels, with one key exception. In Primary MathWings, the main element of daily lessons, called Action Math, is taught every day to the entire class and an additional interactive bulletin board activity called 15-Minute Math is included daily. Intermediate MathWings also uses Action Math, but intersperses Action Math Units with Power Math, which provides individualized work to help students gain facility and confidence in algorithms, remediate gaps in prior skills and concepts, master grade level material, or accelerate their mathematics skill development. Otherwise, Primary and Intermediate MathWings use similar routines, procedures, and teaching methods, as appropriate to children's age levels.

Primary MathWings

In Primary MathWings, students spend seventy-five minutes in math daily. There are two start-up routines: 15-Minute Math and Check-In. The 15-Minute Math routine can be done at the beginning of the lesson or at any other time during the school day. It uses an interactive bulletin board that contains activities based on everyday mathematical experiences. Students use a calendar, look at patterns, create a weather graph, keep a tally to show the number of days they have been in school, and do many other "thinking tasks." The activities are revisited repeatedly to provide opportunities for developing fluency with basic math skills. During 15-Minute Math, students also practice their basic facts during a daily three-minute facts practice session. With a facts partner, students work on a weekly facts game or activity. There is a menu of different games and activities for facts practice.

The lesson begins with Check-In, which lasts approximately five minutes. The teacher quickly collects the Home Connection from the night before and assigns partners for the day. A "Review to Remember" activity gives students a chance to practice their basic facts and other skills that were introduced earlier in the year. Skills and concepts are reviewed and spiraled throughout the school year. "Flashback" follows the Review to Remember activity and is a time for students to recall mathematics concepts and activities from the previous lesson to build on in the new lesson.

The Primary MathWings lesson is made up of Active Instruction, Teamwork, and Direct Instruction. Active Instruction provides a springboard for new ideas, concepts, terminology, etc. It is the part of the lesson that invites students to draw from their background knowledge while discussing new ideas and concepts. This part of the lesson might contain a new literature piece or poem, the teacher might introduce a new problem situation, or the students might brainstorm ideas, create a web, make a list, make observations about something, predict outcomes, or estimate.

Teamwork is intended to provide students with an opportunity to test their ideas, practice what they have discussed in Active Instruction, generate and organize data, and communicate about mathematics. Students in first grade most often work in pairs, especially in the earlier parts of the year. Students in second grade work in pairs or teams, with a greater emphasis on teamwork during the second half of the year. Teachers begin the Teamwork phase of the lesson by clearly explaining and modeling the team or paired activity. In most lessons, students work with manipulatives. Prior to using these manipulatives, students are given approximately two minutes to explore. Students then work with a partner or with their team to complete the mathematics activity while the teacher circulates to assist and informally assess them. During Teamwork, students may complete handouts, collect and record data, draw illustrations, or write about the activity.

Direct Instruction is the part of the lesson where the whole class shares the results of Teamwork, analyzes data, and discusses what they have learned. This is also a time for the teacher to clarify confusions, review any terms that have been introduced, and ask specific questions to ensure that the mathematics concepts involved in the lesson activities become clear to students. Sometimes students write in their Mathematics Log during this part of the lesson.

The closure routines are included in Reflection. During Reflection, students discuss what they have just done. They share what they liked about the lesson, what they have learned, and where they are confused. Then the teacher summarizes the key concepts, reviews vocabulary, and explains the Home Connection assignment. Reflection ends with Team Wrap-Up to have the students get ready for the next class.

Intermediate MathWings

In Intermediate MathWings, students spend at least sixty minutes daily in their mathematics class, although seventy-five minutes is recommended. Daily lessons consist of three components: Check-In, Action Math or Power Math, and Reflection.

The first fifteen-minute segment is Check-In, an efficient class start-up routine in which the teams regularly complete one challenging real-world problem and then discuss their various strategies together. They also complete a facts or fluency study process twice a week, and check homework briefly every day.

The next forty to fifty-five minutes in either Action Math or Power Math is the heart of the lesson. When the class is doing an Action Math unit, the lesson involves the students in Active Instruction, Teamwork, and Assessment. During Active Instruction, the teacher and students interact to explore a concept and its practical applications and skills. The teacher may present a challenging problem for students to explore with manipulatives to construct a solution, may challenge the teams to use prior knowledge to discover a solution, and may ask the teams to find a pattern to develop a rule.

During Teamwork, the students come to consensus about their solutions to problems, their understanding of concepts, and their thinking. A team member is chosen randomly to share his or her ideas with the class. Then students individually practice similar problems with teammates available for support. The team members check answers with each other and rehearse to be sure that every team member can explain them.

At the end of the teamwork, there is a brief feedback opportunity. The teacher randomly chooses a team member to share the ideas or solutions of the team, and to explain their thinking. This enables the teacher to assess the understanding of the group as a whole and ensures that teammates are invested in making sure that all members of the team are mastering the concepts.

The final portion of an Action Math lesson is Assessment. One or more brief problems are used as a quick individual assessment of mastery of the concept or skill explored in the lesson.

Intermediate classes intersperse one- to two-week Power Math units among Action Math units. During these units, the forty- to fifty-five minute heart of the lesson involves each student in remediating, refining, or accelerating his or her skills. This component is an adaptation of Team Accelerated Instruction, an individualized math program found to be effective in several studies (Slavin, Leavey, & Madden, 1984). Power Math covers a range of skills from basic addition to statistics and algebra. Students work at their own pace on the skill which they need to practice, completing check outs and mastery tests successfully to move to another skill they need to practice. Teammates check each other's work and provide help as needed. Students who have mastered the basic skills explore accelerated units at their own pace. The teacher teaches mini-lessons to small groups of students (working on the same skills) gathered from various teams while the other students continue to work individually.

The last five-minute segment of class is Reflection. This is an efficient routine to bring closure to the class time. During Action Math units, Reflection involves a quick summary of the key concepts by the teacher. During both Action Math units and Power Math units, homework sheets are passed out, and a short entry is written in the MathWings Logbook in response to a writing prompt about the lesson.

All students should not only be given the opportunity to establish a solid foundation in mathematics, but also the opportunity to extend and stretch their knowledge and experience in mathematics. Thus, a program of mathematics should include a structure to accommodate diverse abilities and prior mathematical knowledge, while ensuring that *all* students experience the depth, breadth, and beauty of mathematics. The MathWings curriculum incorporates this philosophy in its development.

Samples of Primary and Intermediate MathWings lessons are included in Appendix 8.2 on pages 305–325.

SUCCESS 360

Success for All was initially designed as a comprehensive, whole-school reform model, and that is how it is primarily used. However, there are many situations in which schools want or need less than the entire model. They may not be able to afford the full model, or may not be ready for that much change, or may have localized problems that require tailored solutions rather than comprehensive reform. The Success for All Foundation has created stand-alone modules, collectively called Success 360, based on many of the components of Success for All. Each of these has its own materials, training, and (usually) technology supports, so in no case are these any less intensive than the full model, but they do touch on particular grades or objectives that involve parts of the school rather than the whole school. In many cases, schools adopt one of the Success 360 elements and then add elements over time until they become full-scale Success for All schools. Currently available Success 360 programs include the following:

Success 360 Programs and the Groups of Students They Benefit

KinderCorner—comprehensive kindergarten program

KinderRoots Phonics—phonics curriculum for kindergarten students

Reading Roots 3rd Edition—reading curriculum for first grade students

FastTrack Phonics—phonics curriculum for first grade students

Reading Wings 3rd Edition—reading curriculum for second through sixth grade students

The Savvy Reader—comprehension strategy instruction for second through sixth grade students

Adventure Island—reading intervention/afterschool program for first through sixth grade students

Cooperative Learning—for first through eighth grade students

Reading Edge—reading intervention for middle school

DATA-DRIVEN REFORM

Success for All has always been focused on data-driven reform. It uses formative assessments daily and weekly, culminating in quarterly assessments, which are used to guide instruction and to suggest grouping, needs for tutoring, and other assistance. As No Child Left Behind has increased accountability pressures, leaders in many Success for All schools asked us to develop benchmark assessments keyed to their state assessments, and we did so, ultimately creating 4Sight assessments for the twenty-five states with the largest numbers of SFA schools. We then realized that 4Sight would also be useful in non-SFA schools, and began to disseminate it in this way. In 2004, Johns Hopkins University received a grant to develop and evaluate a district reform strategy to help district and building leaders use data intelligently to identify key problems and their root causes and then to adopt research-proven programs known to enhance achievement in the areas in which help is needed. Our Center for Data-Driven Reform in Education (CDDRE) is currently working in sixty districts in seven states to help district leaders reform their entire district by using data and proven programs.

4Sight Benchmark Assessments

4Sight benchmark assessments are used to help schools predict their state test scores in reading and math up to five times per year. The assessments are made from scratch for each state, to match state standards and assessments. Each 4Sight assessment looks exactly like the state test, using identical item formats, proportion of open-ended items, graphics, and even fonts, but the tests require only an hour each. 4Sight assessments are piloted in a sample of schools before being generally released, both to validate them and to determine their correlations with state assessments. In general, these correlations are very high, averaging +0.80.

4Sight benchmark assessments are used to tell schools where they are strong and weak early enough for schools to take appropriate action, if needed. They tell school leaders which subgroups are likely to have problems on which types of items and objectives. After schools adopt research-proven interventions (SFA or other programs), 4Sight is used to tell school leaders whether the program is working yet, so they can make appropriate adjustments.

Center for Data-Driven Reform in Education (CDDRE)

The Center for Data-Driven Reform in Education was established at Johns Hopkins University in 2004 to develop statewide and districtwide reform approaches that can be used on a very broad scale to help many schools at risk of failing to meet their adequate yearly progress goals.

Under NCLB, state departments of education have responsibilities to help schools struggling to meet adequate yearly progress standards. In most states, however, the numbers of schools not meeting AYP or at risk of not meeting AYP is too large to justify one school at a time solutions, yet surface changes are not sufficient to bring about the fundamental changes in teaching and learning needed to turn around schools that have often been failing for many years.

The CDDRE strategy focuses on helping schools and districts to: 1) understand and enrich their data; 2) understand where intervention is necessary; and 3) choose among research-proven programs known to enable schools to improve student achievement. Helping schools and districts select research-proven programs includes providing tools that simplify the search for programs that have been rigorously evaluated in random or matched control studies and have shown significant positive effects. For this purpose, CDDRE created a Web site, the Best Evidence Encyclopedia (the BEE), www.bestevidence.org, to summarize evidence from rigorous evaluations of practical programs.

The main elements of the CDDRE approach are as follows:

Study

- Identify states and districts willing to implement the CDDRE core strategy.
- Integrate the core strategy to meet the needs of the existing state system of support (e.g., support teams, intermediaries, distinguished educators).
- Convene data exploration meetings with state, district and school leaders.
- Model and arrange walk-through process and hypothesis testing.

Plan

- Use data gathered to meet with school, district, and SEA leaders to identify key areas for intervention.
- Review research on proven interventions that target key areas (using the BEE).
- Support districts and schools during the intervention selection process.

Evaluate

- Evaluate implementation of ongoing reform efforts using benchmark assessments (usually 4Sight).

Early results and observations have suggested that district and state leaders welcome and make good use of benchmark assessments and assistance with data-based planning, but that making the transition from knowing what needs to be done to implementing proven programs requires time and strong leadership. However, early-implementing districts have shown gains in their self-selected initial improvement areas.

Appendix 8.1   Writing Lesson Focusing on Rich Expression in a Personal Narrative

Unit Four

Personal Writing

Background

Personal writing overlaps descriptive, narrative, and informative writing. The difference is that the writer is producing writing for himself, or herself, or for a friend. The form of personal writing might be notes from a class; records of experiences, observations, or ideas and thoughts in a journal or diary; private letters or e-mail. For many people, personal writing becomes a lifelong custom and a source of pleasure. For some published authors, personal writing is a resource of ideas for their published work.

Activities and Craft Lessons

Unit Four

- **Personal Journals**
  Craft Lesson: Free Writing
- **Response Journals**
  Craft Lesson: Responding to Literature
- **Personal Stories**
  Craft Lesson: Dialogue

Notes About Instruction

In the first activity, Personal Journals, the students will learn that people write in diaries or journals for different reasons. They can write about events, interesting observations, or experiences in which they felt a certain way. The students will have the opportunity to write at least one entry for each purpose. During the Response Journals activity, the students will record personal responses to a story. A list of response suggestions is provided to model ways readers respond to literature and to help prompt the students' ideas as they write. In the third activity, Personal Stories, the students will combine what they know about writing a story (has a beginning, middle, and end and includes the story elements) with what they know best—themselves.

Two of the activities in this unit, Personal Journals and Response Journals, deviate from the established writing process. These activities do not include revising, editing, and publishing. These two activities also strive to encourage the students to feel confident in expressing their thoughts, feelings, and opinions through writing, regardless of conventions such as spelling and grammar. Because of this, the scoring guides do not contain Editing Checklists, and no language mechanics lessons are taught during these two activities.

How to Introduce the Unit

- Tell the students that the next type of writing they will compose is called personal writing.

- Tell the students that sometimes people like to write their thoughts and feelings and keep them to themselves or share them with a very small group of people. Use Think-Pair-Share to have the students think of where people might write their private thoughts or feelings. *[Diaries, journals, personal letters, etc.]*

- Explain that writing for yourself or a very small audience is called personal writing. Point out that personal writing can include opinions, reactions, and descriptions as well as thoughts and feelings.

- Tell the students about the writing activities in which they will participate in this unit.

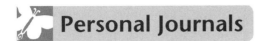 **Personal Journals**

Summary

The students will experience writing about events, observations, and feelings in personal journals, also known as diaries. In the Craft Lesson, they will practice free writing to express their thoughts and ideas more fluently.

Preparation

- Make transparencies and copies of materials found at the end of the activity.

- **Note:** Because of the nature of the activity, the Craft Lesson does not contain a Quick Check. **CL**

Teacher Presentation: Set the Stage

- Ask the students what a diary, or a personal journal, is and what it is used for. Explain, if necessary, that these are terms for the same thing. Ask them if they have diaries of their own or know people who write in diaries.

- Display the Dear Diary transparency and read it aloud.

Dear Diary

June 12, 2009

I'm so mad I could scream at the top of my lungs! Ryan Westcott! At school Ryan pulled my hair, stole my pencil, and repeated everything I said. I told him to cut it out, but he didn't listen. When I told Miss Potter, he called me a tattletale and then had the whole class saying it with him. I wish he would just move away from here, and then I would never have to see him again. Isha told me that he's just kidding around, but she doesn't get it.

- Use Think-Pair-Share to ask the students about its topic, audience, purpose, and form.

   Who is the author's expected audience? Usually the only person who reads a diary is the person who writes in it. Why did the author write in her diary? What did she write about? How does the author feel about the situation that she wrote about in her diary?

- Tell the students that they will experiment with writing different kinds of diary entries this week.

- Explain that the students will not revise, edit, or publish their diary entries because the writing is personal. Point out that we revise and publish writing when we write for larger or less familiar audiences.

- Tell the students that because diaries are personal and not written for audiences other than the writer, the authors are able to write more freely.

 **Free Writing**

Craft Lesson

Teacher Presentation

- Give the students three minutes to talk to their partners about anything they like. Tell them they can have three minutes of *free talking*.

- At the end of three minutes, ask the students what they talked about and if they were able to make vivid mind movies.

    What were some things you and your partner discussed? Did you and your partner talk about the same topic the entire time? Were you able to make vivid mind movies while your partner talked?

- Tell the students that the free talking they did is very similar to the free writing they will do when they write to express their own ideas.

- Distribute the Writing Examples handout. Have the students read Example 1. Tell the students that a third grader named Zack wrote this when his teacher told him to write about what happened last Saturday.

Writing Examples

Example 1

This past Saturday we had a family reunion at Key Park. My whole family was there! We had a barbecue. My cousin ate four hot dogs! My Uncle Ray brought his guitar and played it. We all sang along with him. My grandmother cried because she was so happy that we were all together. It was a lot of fun.

- Have the students read Example 2. Tell the students that Zack wrote this as an entry in his journal about the same topic.

Example 2

This past Saturday was our family reunion. We had to drive all the way to Key Park. What a long drive! I was so sick of being in the car! Thank goodness I had the video game that DeRon lent me. That game is awesome! I got really good at it.

We got to Key Park at about 11:30. A lot of my family was there, but Uncle Ray and Aunt Patty weren't there yet.

Grammy kept saying, "I can't believe everyone is coming! I can't believe we'll all be together." She even cried when we took our family picture.

Finally Uncle Ray and Aunt Patty got there and we could eat. I was starving! Grampy cooked the lunch on the grill. Rex ate four hot dogs! That's nasty! His mom was so mad at him! She thought he would get sick. Aunt Dora made chocolate pie. I wanted to eat the whole thing! She said she would make another when we see her this summer.

Anyway, after lunch Uncle Ray took out his guitar. I wish I could play guitar! I would play that awesome song by The Hammers called "If Only You Knew What I Knew." Hey, I think I'm going to sing that for the talent show this year. Well, Uncle Ray doesn't know any songs by The Hammers. I asked. He played songs, and we all sang along with him.

Then we all played kickball. I really wanted to be on Nessa's team, but I was on Felix's team instead. I knew we would get demolished, and I was right. I think the score was 12 to 2. We stunk!

I can't wait for another reunion. Maybe next year.

- Have the students work in teams to discuss how Example 2 is different from Example 1 *[It is longer; it contains more information; sentences are not complete; it changes topic; it sounds as if he is talking.]* and which example helped them create better mind movies. *[Example 2.]* Use Numbered Heads to share responses.

- Tell the students that Example 2 is a sample of free writing. Explain the concept of free writing.

> **The second example is what we call free writing. Zack put down everything that came to his mind about what happened last Saturday. As one thought led to another, he just wrote it all down. He has lots of interesting details about what happened and what he thought and felt. It sounds like he might be talking to a good friend rather than writing for his teacher.**
>
> **Writing like this is called free writing because your mind is free of the things you often try to remember when you want to write correctly. In school you often try hard to write what the teacher wants, to make complete sentences, and to spell your words correctly. When you write just for yourself, you don't think about these things as much. You write whatever comes to mind and often capture great mind movies with wonderful details of your thoughts and feelings.**

- Explain to the students that writers often free write as a way to plan or draft a story; they free write to get ideas, thoughts, and feelings on paper, then choose an idea from their free writing and develop it into a story by revising and editing it.

- Tell the students that they will write freely when they communicate to their teammates in their journal writing.

Team Practice

- Tell the students that you want them to practice free writing, letting their thoughts flow onto the paper.

- Explain to the students that to free write, they need to do the following:
  - Make a mind movie about their topic before they write.
  - Write as much as they can about their subject, whatever comes to mind.
  - Do not try to correct errors.
  - Write as if they were describing the subject in detail to a best friend, rather than explaining an event to someone they did not know well.

- Use Think-Pair-Share to ask the students about a recent experience they had that was a lot of fun. Tell the students that this is what they will free write about. If necessary, brainstorm with the students for writing ideas.

- Explain that you want them to close their eyes for one minute (you will tell them when to start and stop) and remember all they can about the experience. Tell them to think about what happened in detail, how they felt, and why.

- When the minute is up, tell the students that they will write about this experience for two full minutes. Explain that they may not stop or pause before the two minutes are up.

- Time the writing. Remind those who stop or pause frequently to write for the full two minutes.

- Tell the students to stop at the end of the two minutes. Have them read their papers aloud in teams.

- Talk with the class about their free-writing experience. Ask questions such as: Did you reach a point when you had written everything you planned to say before the time was up? What kinds of things did you add then? Did you discover new details that you had not thought of earlier? Were there moments when you wanted to pause because you were not sure how to spell a word? What did you do?

- Ask several volunteers to read their papers aloud for the class.

Team Mastery

- Use Think-Pair-Share to have the students select another experience about which to write. This experience should be one they remember with strong emotions, good or bad. Tell them they may also write to extend what they just wrote.

- Have the students close their eyes again and make a mind movie of the experience for one minute. Tell them to be aware of their feelings and thoughts as they see the events.

- Tell the students to free write about the experience for two minutes until you tell them to stop. Remind the students that they should write as if they are talking to a good friend and that they should not be concerned about errors.

- At the end of the two minutes, have the students share their writing with teammates and discuss whether the activity was easier the second time. Have the students explain their answers.

- Ask for volunteers to share their answers with the class.

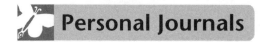
Personal Journals

Teacher Presentation: Writing Instruction

- Tell the students that they are ready to use free writing as they write their diary entries.

- Explain that people write in journals for different purposes: to write about events, to write interesting observations, or to write about experiences that were especially emotional. Write the various purposes on the board.

- Display the diary entry from Set the Stage. Have a student reread it. Model identifying the purpose of the entry (writing about an emotional time) and the emotion that the author was probably feeling (anger).

- Tell the students that there are more entries that you would like them to read and for which you would like them to determine the author's purpose.

- Distribute the Diary Entries handout to the students. Have the students work in teams to read each entry, determine the author's main purpose for writing it, and discuss why they selected this purpose.

Diary Entries

June 12, 2009

Yesterday was my last baseball game of the season. I'm so happy because we won! I didn't think we would be able to beat the Sluggers, but we played really well, and they played really badly. Tony was the first one up on our team, and he hit a home run on the first pitch. I got up next and hit a single. Ruben, the catcher on the Sluggers, was bummed that his team didn't do better. I told him that next year he should join our team. After the game, Coach took us to Ebert's for ice cream. I had a chocolate shake with sprinkles in it. I asked Dad if Pokey and Spence could sleep over. We slept in the tent in the backyard. Dad helped us cook hot dogs outside. It rocked!

August 5, 2009

My family and I went hiking today. The trail was long and bumpy, but when we got to the top of the hill, it was so worth it. I have never seen a view like this before! There were mountains all around us. The trees were so green! There were colorful flowers all over the ground. The sun was just setting, so the sky was bright orange with some pinks. It was beautiful.

Diary Entries *continued*

November 8, 2009

I can't wait for tomorrow! Melissa's aunt is taking us to the Wave concert! I love the Wave! We got great seats right near the stage. Melissa's aunt is so cool. She rented a limo for us to get there. We're leaving at 5, going to dinner, and then going to the concert. I can't wait for them to sing "We Got It." That's my favorite song and I know they are going to sing it because it's their biggest hit. When Pete Shed plays the drum solo in the beginning of the song, I'm going to go wild!

- Use Numbered Heads to share teams' responses.

- Review with the students the characteristics of a journal entry: tells what happened, makes an observation, or tells about an emotional experience; supports the purpose; captures vivid mind movie; and includes the date.

- Discuss with the students which elements should get more points than others in the Content Checklist.

- Distribute the scoring guide, point out the items that make up the Content Checklist, review how many points are allotted for each.

- Use Think-Pair-Share to have the students identify what parts of the scoring guide are missing. *[Checks for revising, editing, and publishing; the Editing Checklist.]* Remind the students that since they are writing to share personal experiences, they will not revise, edit, or publish their diary entries.

Content Checklist (100 points)	
In my diary entries, I:	
wrote for a different purpose.	**40**
gave details to support the purpose.	**25**
gave details to capture vivid mind movies.	**25**
included the date.	**10**

Prewriting—1

- Tell the students that they are ready to plan their first journal entry. Explain that they are going to write about an event that was special to them.

- Brainstorm with the students a list of types of events that they might like to write about in their journals. If necessary, suggest events to get them started (a school event; a favorite time playing with a friend; a special time with parents or relatives; a trip to the zoo, park, or museum). As the students share their events, write them on the board.

- Using these events, have the students write their own lists of specific events in their journals. Explain that they may use the events on the board as a guide, but that they should include any event that was special to them that they might like to write about.

- Ask the students to choose one of the events from their list to write about in their journals.

- Use Think-Pair-Share to have the students discuss their events, giving details to support the purpose.

- Use Think-Pair-Share to have the students identify the TAP-F information for their diary entries. Model if necessary.

- Explain that the students will use webs to organize their thoughts.

- Remind the students to include the TAP-F information on their webs. Model completing a web with your own ideas to the extent necessary, as shown in the example below.

Topic: meeting my favorite author   **Audience:** my partner and I
Purpose: to describe   **Form:** diary entry

Web

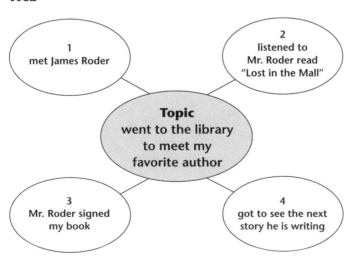

- Tell the students that when you are writing about events, they often follow a particular order. Have the students decide if the ideas in their webs follow a particular order, and have them number the items, as shown in the example, to remember this order when they write their drafts.

- Have partners share their written plans, use the Content Checklist to give each other feedback, and make changes to their plans if necessary. When they have finished, have the students initial prewriting (1) on their scoring guides to show they have completed this step.

- Ask one or two volunteers to share their plans with the class, and celebrate completing this part of the process.

Drafting—1

- Review the Content Checklist with the class, and ask the students to review their graphic organizers individually.

- Have the students write their journal entries. Remind them to write the date and to write freely as they share their experiences. Allow the students plenty of time to write.

- When the students have finished, have them read their work aloud softly so they can see if they have written what they intended. Also have the students refer to the Content Checklist to make sure they have included all necessary information.

- Have the students initial drafting (1) on their scoring guides to show completion of this step.

Sharing and Responding—1

Modeling Partner Feedback

- Explain that sharing and responding will be different for this lesson. Tell the students that they will tell only what they liked about their partners' entries and why they liked it.

- Have one student read his or her writing aloud so you can model responding to the writing in preparation for actual partner feedback.

- Demonstrate responding to what you like about the writing and why. Be specific and detailed. Also have one or two students tell what they liked about the writing.

Partner Feedback

- Have partners read their work to each other and give feedback on what they liked and why.

- Listen to partner discussions to model, prompt, and reinforce giving positive feedback.

- Have the students initial sharing and responding (1) on their scoring guides to show completion of this step.

Prewriting—2

- Tell the students that they are going to write another diary entry. Explain that this time they will write about something they have seen that would be interesting to describe. Tell the class that they are going to take a walk around the school and they are going to pay close attention to the things they see and hear to get ideas for topics.

- When you return to the classroom, brainstorm some observations from the walk with the class. Write these ideas on the board.

- Have the students write their own lists of ideas in their journals. Explain that they can use ideas from the board, but that they may include things they have seen elsewhere that they might like to describe in writing.

- Ask the students to choose one of the ideas from their lists to write about in their journals.

- Use Think-Pair-Share to have the students discuss the ideas, giving details to support the purpose.

- Use Think-Pair-Share to have the students identify the TAP-F information for their diary entries. Model if necessary.

- Explain that the students will use webs to organize their thoughts.

- Remind the students to include the TAP-F information on their webs. Model completing a web with your own ideas to the extent necessary, as shown in the example below.

Topic: cafeteria

Purpose: to describe

Audience: my partner and I

Form: diary entry

Web

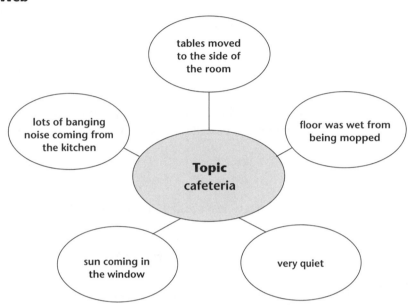

- Have partners share their written plans, use the Content Checklist to give each other feedback, and make changes to their plans if necessary. When they have finished, have the students initial prewriting (2) on their scoring guides to show they have completed this step.

- Ask one or two volunteers to share their plans with the class, and celebrate completing this part of the process.

Drafting—2

- Review the Content Checklist with the class, and ask the students to individually review their graphic organizers.

- Tell the students to begin writing their journal entries. Remind them to write the date and to write freely as they share their experiences. Allow the students plenty of time to write.

- When the students have finished, have them softly read their work aloud to see if they have written what they intended. Also, have the students refer to the Content Checklist to make sure they have included all necessary information.

- Have the students initial drafting (2) on their scoring guides to show completion of this step.

Sharing and Responding—2

Modeling Partner Feedback

- Remind the students that sharing and responding will be different for this lesson. Tell the students that they will tell only what they liked about the entry and why they liked it.

- Have one student read his or her writing aloud so you can model responding to the writing in preparation for actual partner feedback.

- Demonstrate responding to what you like about the writing and why. Be specific and detailed. Also have one or two students tell what they liked about the writing.

Partner Feedback

- Have partners read their work to each other and give each other feedback on what they liked and why.

- Listen to partner discussions to model, prompt, and reinforce giving positive feedback.

- Have the students initial sharing and responding (2) on their scoring guides to show completion of this step.

Prewriting—3

- Tell the students that they are going to make a new journal entry and that this time they will write about an experience that they remember with strong feelings.

- Use Think-Pair-Share to have the students brainstorm different experiences about which they felt strongly. Prompt them to think about experiences that made them extremely happy, sad, mad, scared, or excited.

- Have the students write a list of their experiences in their journals, along with the emotion that they felt with each experience.

- Ask the students to choose one of the experiences from their lists to write about in their journals.

- Use Think-Pair-Share to have the students discuss the experiences, giving details to support the purpose.

- Use Think-Pair-Share to have the students identify the TAP-F information for their diary entries. Model if necessary.

- Explain that the students will use webs to organize their thoughts.

- Remind the students to include the TAP-F information on their webs. Model completing a web with your own ideas to the extent necessary, as shown in the example below.

Topic: emotional experience	**Audience:** my partner and I
Purpose: to describe	**Form:** diary entry

Web

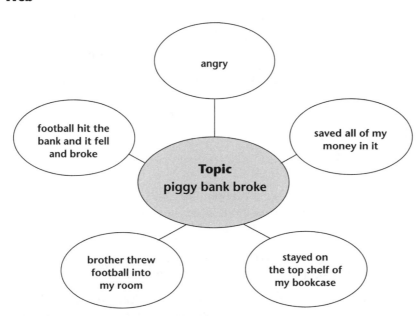

- Have partners share their written plans, use the Content Checklist to give each other feedback, and make changes to their plans if necessary. When they have finished, have the students initial prewriting (3) on their scoring guides to show they have completed this step.

- Ask one or two volunteers to share their plans with the class. Celebrate completing this part of the process.

Drafting—3

- Review the Content Checklist with the class, and ask the students to individually review their graphic organizers.

- Tell the students to begin writing their journal entries. Remind them to write the date and to write freely as they share their experiences. Allow the students plenty of time to write.

- When the students have finished, have them softly read their work aloud to see if they have written what they intended. Also, have the students refer to the Content Checklist to make sure they have included all necessary information.

- Have the students initial drafting (3) on their scoring guides to show completion of this step.

Sharing and Responding—3

Modeling Partner Feedback

- Remind the students that sharing and responding will be different for this lesson. Tell the students that they will tell what they liked about the entry and why they liked it.

- Have one student read his or her writing aloud so you can model responding to the writing in preparation for actual partner feedback.

- Demonstrate responding to what you like about the writing and why. Be specific and detailed. Also have one or two students tell what they liked about the writing.

Partner Feedback

- Have partners read their work to each other and give each other feedback on what they liked and why.

- Listen to partner discussions to model, prompt, and reinforce giving positive feedback.

- Have the students initial sharing and responding (3) on their scoring guides to show completion of this step.

Prewriting—4 and 5

- Tell the students that they are going to make new journal entries and that they may write about any one of the topics that they listed or thought about in the past few days that they did not write about before.

- Ask the students to look at the lists that they wrote earlier and choose topics that they would like to write about in their journals.

- Use Think-Pair-Share to have the students discuss the topics, purpose, and details that support the purpose.

- Use Think-Pair-Share to have the students identify the TAP-F information for their diary entries. Model if necessary.

- Explain that the students will use webs to organize their thoughts.

- Remind the students to include the TAP-F information on their webs. Model completing a web with your own ideas to the extent necessary.

- If the students chose to write an entry that should follow a particular order, remind them to number the items on their webs to help them remember the order when they draft their entries.

- Have partners share their written plans, use their Content Checklists to give each other feedback, and make changes to their plans if necessary. When they have finished, have the students initial prewriting (4 or 5) on their scoring guides to show they have completed this step.

- Ask one or two volunteers to share their plans with the class. Celebrate completing this part of the process.

Drafting—4 and 5

- Review the Content Checklist with the class, and ask the students to individually review their graphic organizers.

- Tell the students to begin writing their journal entries. Remind them to write the date and to write freely as they share their experiences. Allow the students plenty of time to write.

- When the students have finished, have them softly read their work aloud to see if they have written what they intended. Also, have the students refer to the Content Checklist to make sure they have included all necessary information.

- Have the students initial drafting (4 or 5) on their scoring guides to show completion of this step.

Sharing and Responding—4 and 5

Modeling Partner Feedback

- Remind the students that sharing and responding will be different for this lesson. Tell the students that they will tell what they liked about the entry and why they liked it.

- Have one student read his or her writing aloud so you can model responding to the writing in preparation for actual partner feedback. Be specific and detailed. Also have one or two students tell what they liked about the writing.

Partner Feedback

- Have partners read their work to each other and give feedback on what they liked.

- Listen to partner discussions to model, prompt, and reinforce giving positive feedback.

- Have the students initial sharing and responding (4 or 5) on their scoring guides to show completion of this step.

Scoring

- Have the students turn in their journals.

- Explain that you will use the scoring guide to determine a score for their journal entries as a whole; explain that you will not be evaluating each entry. Remind the students that you will not score for spelling, punctuation, capitalization, or grammar.

- Score the students' work and return their journals.

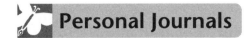 **Personal Journals**

Dear Diary

June 12, 2009

I'm so mad I could scream at the top of my lungs! Ryan Westcott!
At school Ryan pulled my hair, stole my pencil, and repeated
everything I said. I told him to cut it out, but he didn't listen. When
I told Miss Potter, he called me a tattletale and then had the whole
class saying it with him. I wish he would just move away from here,
and then I would never have to see him again. Isha told me that he's
just kidding around, but she doesn't get it.

 **Free Writing**

Writing Examples

Example 1

This past Saturday we had a family reunion at Key Park. My whole family was there! We had a barbecue. My cousin ate four hot dogs! My Uncle Ray brought his guitar and played it. We all sang along with him. My grandmother cried because she was so happy that we were all together. It was a lot of fun.

Example 2

This past Saturday was our family reunion. We had to drive all the way to Key Park. What a long drive! I was so sick of being in the car! Thank goodness I had the video game that DeRon lent me. That game is awesome! I got really good at it.

We got to Key Park at about 11:30. A lot of my family was there, but Uncle Ray and Aunt Patty weren't there yet.

Grammy kept saying, "I can't believe everyone is coming! I can't believe we'll all be together." She even cried when we took our family picture.

Finally Uncle Ray and Aunt Patty got there and we could eat. I was starving! Grampy cooked the lunch on the grill. Rex ate four hot dogs! That's nasty! His mom was so mad at him! She thought he would get sick. Aunt Dora made chocolate pie. I wanted to eat the whole thing! She said she would make another when we see her this summer.

Anyway, after lunch Uncle Ray took out his guitar. I wish I could play guitar! I would play that awesome song by The Hammers called "If Only You Knew What I Knew." Hey, I think I'm going to sing that for the talent show this year. Well, Uncle Ray doesn't know any songs by The Hammers. I asked. He played songs, and we all sang along with him.

Then we all played kickball. I really wanted to be on Nessa's team, but I was on Felix's team instead. I knew we would get demolished, and I was right. I think the score was 12 to 2. We stunk!

I can't wait for another reunion. Maybe next year.

Personal Journals

Diary Entries

July 12, 2009

Yesterday was my last baseball game of the season. I'm so happy because we won! I didn't think we would be able to beat the Sluggers, but we played really well, and they played really badly. Tony was the first one up on our team, and he hit a home run on the first pitch. I got up next and hit a single. Ruben, the catcher on the Sluggers, was bummed that his team didn't do better. I told him that next year he should join our team. After the game, Coach took us to Ebert's for ice cream. I had a chocolate shake with sprinkles in it. I asked Dad if Pokey and Spence could sleep over. We slept in the tent in the backyard. Dad helped us cook hot dogs outside. It rocked!

August 5, 2009

My family and I went hiking today. The trail was long and bumpy, but when we got to the top of the hill, it was so worth it. I have never seen a view like this before! There were mountains all around us. The trees were so green! There were colorful flowers all over the ground. The sun was just setting, so the sky was bright orange with some pinks. It was beautiful.

November 8, 2009

I can't wait for tomorrow! Melissa's aunt is taking us to the Wave concert! I love the Wave! We got great seats right near the stage. Melissa's aunt is so cool. She rented a limo for us to get there. We're leaving at 5, going to dinner, and then going to the concert. I can't wait for them to sing "We Got It." That's my favorite song and I know they are going to sing it because it's their biggest hit. When Pete Shed plays the drum solo in the beginning of the song, I'm going to go wild!

Name _____ Date _____

Personal Journals **Scoring Guide**

Directions: You will prewrite, draft, and share and respond five times. Initial each step as you do so.

The Writing Process					
I've finished:	Author Initials 1	Author Initials 2	Author Initials 3	Author Initials 4	Author Initials 5
prewriting					
drafting					
sharing and responding					

Directions: Every day, initial the items in the Content Checklist to show that they are included in your writing. (You will not evaluate your partner's writing in this activity.)

Content Checklist (100 points)							
In my diary entries, I:	**Points**	Author Initials 1	Author Initials 2	Author Initials 3	Author Initials 4	Author Initials 5	Teacher Scores
wrote for a different purpose.	**40**						
gave details to support the purpose.	**25**						
gave details to capture vivid mind movies.	**25**						
included the date.	**10**						

	Total Score:

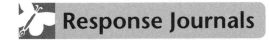

Response Journals

Summary

The students will use journals to record their personal responses to a story. In the Craft Lesson, they will learn different ways to respond to literature.

Preparation

- Make transparencies and copies of materials found at the end of the activity. Make three copies of the scoring guide for each student.

- Choose a book to read aloud to the class. Select one that will be interesting to your students, one that has characters with problems and events with whom the students can relate. Suggested titles are found in Appendix E: Read-Aloud Titles.

- Write the list of response questions that follow the lesson on chart paper. **CL**

- **Note:** Because of the nature of the activity, the Craft Lesson does not contain a Quick Check. **CL**

Teacher Presentation: Set the Stage

- Write the following statement on the board, and have the students read it to themselves.

> Riding your bicycle is the most fun thing you can do after school.

- Use Think-Pair-Share to have the students discuss what they think about this statement. If necessary, ask if they agree or disagree.

- Tell the students that they just responded to something they read by telling what they thought about it. Explain that when we read we often react or respond with our own thoughts and feelings to what the author tells us.

- Explain that this week they will record their personal thoughts and feelings about a story in their journals.

- Display the Pierre Raccoon transparency. Explain to the students that it is an example of a response journal entry, and ask a volunteer to read it aloud. Use Think-Pair-Share to ask the students about its topic, audience, purpose, and form.

Pierre Raccoon

October 24, 2009

I just got home from the movies. I went to see *Pierre Raccoon Visits the South Pole*. I've read all the Pierre Raccoon books, so I couldn't wait to see this movie. Now I wish I hadn't wasted my money on such a bad movie. The books are great. They make me laugh and I always wish that I could go with Pierre on his adventures. But the movie—yuck! They didn't even put in the best part of the book when Pierre meets the penguins and he pretends that he is one too. And what was that alligator doing in the movie? That's not in the book. If they make any more Pierre movies, I won't go. I'm going to stick to the books.

Whom do you think this author is writing for? Do you think he or she expects others to read this? Usually the only person who reads a journal is the person who writes in it. Why did this person write in a journal? What does this person think about the movie? Other than the author's response to the movie, what other information is in the journal entry?

- Explain to the students that this writer gave examples and details to support his thoughts about the movie. Tell the students that explaining your thoughts and feelings is part of writing a response.

- Point out that this author gave his thoughts and feelings about how a movie compared with a book that he had read. Tell the students that they will be responding to a story that you will read to them, but first you want to share some of the different ways that they might respond.

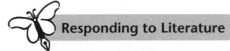 **Responding to Literature**

Craft Lesson

Teacher Presentation

- Use Think-Pair-Share to have the students identify their favorite stories and why they enjoyed them. Tell the students that they just responded to literature by telling how they felt about a story and why.

- Explain that there are many ways to respond to what you read and that no one way is right; people can and do respond differently, to the same story or even the same passage. Tell the students that readers better understand and enjoy what they read by thinking about it and connecting it to their own lives.

- Display Example 1 of the Literature Examples transparency. Read it aloud or ask a volunteer to read it aloud.

Literature Examples

Example 1

The sky was blue and the sun was shining. Cassie skipped to school and thought about what a great day she was going to have. Today was the last day of school, and Bailey's sleepover party was right after school. Cassie couldn't stop smiling!

- Use Think-Pair-Share to ask the students how this passage makes them feel and why it makes them feel that way. Tell the students that one way to respond to literature is to tell how what you read makes you feel.

- Display Example 2. Ask a volunteer to read it aloud.

Example 2

Dominic loved riding his bike, but he hated Thriller Hill. He could never make it up without walking. Today Dominic was determined to make it up the hill on his bike. He came around the big turn and saw the hill. He started peddling like mad. He kept telling himself, "Today is the day. Today is the day." He made it past the Hoffman's house. That's where he usually had to get off his bike.

- Use Think-Pair-Share to have the students discuss if they think Dominic will make it up the hill on his bicycle and why they think he will or will not make it up the hill. Tell the students that another way to respond to literature is to make a prediction about the story.

- Explain to the students that still another way to respond to literature is to give their opinions about what they read. Tell the students that they can have opinions about the story as a whole or about any part of the story, such as the different story elements.

- Distribute the Response Suggestions handout to the students, and have volunteers read it aloud. Point out the headings and explain that these questions show how the students might respond to the whole story or to the story elements.

Response Suggestions

Responding to the Whole Story

Does this story remind you of another story? Which one? How?

Does anything puzzle you about the story? Explain.

What would you change about the story if you could? Why?

What do you like best or least about the story? Explain.

How does this story make you feel? Explain.

Responding to the Story Elements

Characters

Who is your favorite or least favorite character? Why?

Who do you like? Who do you not like? Explain.

Would you do what the characters did? Why or why not?

Do you think any of the characters made a bad decision? A good decision? Explain.

Are you like any of the characters? How?

Are the characters like anyone you know? How?

Are these characters believable? Do they act like real people? Explain.

Setting

Does the setting remind you of somewhere you have been? Tell how.

Do you think the author described the setting well? Explain.

Is the setting important to this story? How? Would you like to be in a setting like this? Why or why not?

Response Suggestions *continued*

Problem

Have you ever had a problem like this? What?

How would you solve the problem?

Events

Would you do the same things that the characters did? Why or why not?

Did any of the events surprise you? Which ones? Why?

Did you predict any of the events? Which ones? What clues did you use?

Resolution and Ending

Did the ending surprise you? Why or why not?

Did you like the ending? Why or why not?

Would you like the story to end differently? How?

- Distribute the "Ted's Big Day" handout. Read it aloud as the students follow along. When you have finished, ask the students to work in teams to discuss their responses to the story as a whole and to at least one of the parts. Point out that they should support their responses with explanations or details.

Ted's Big Day

Ted was scared. Today was the day he had been practicing for all these years. Today Ted would graduate from Superhero School.

Ted walked into the auditorium with all the other students. He couldn't believe all the superheroes who were there! The Fly Swatter, Lasso Lady, and IncrediDude all sat on the stage. To graduate and receive his superhero name, Ted had to perform his last super-trick in front of the whole audience. He was going to perform the Super Jumper Triple Flip. No one had ever completed it before.

The Fly Swatter called Ted's name. Ted tied his sneakers and tucked in his shirt. Then he went to the stage.

"We're ready when you are," Lasso Lady said.

Ted took a deep breath. He ran back down the aisle and jumped. He flew 20 feet in the air, did three somersaults, and landed on his feet. The room was silent. Then the crowd stood up and clapped. Ted walked to the stage. He was so happy! The superheroes shook his hand and told him he was wonderful. IncrediDude gave Ted his diploma. It read, "Ted, Jumper Boy, has completed the Superhero Program. He will use his flying and jumping to catch the bad guys. He's ready to save the day."

- Use Numbered Heads to review the teams' responses, and prompt them for explanations or details when necessary. Model your own responses to demonstrate variety and depth of responses.

- Remind the students that telling how a story makes them feel or giving their opinions about the story helps them to connect the story to their own lives and makes reading more meaningful.

Team Practice

- Tell the students that they will now read some short stories and respond to them.

- Distribute the Teamwork handouts and two copies of the response suggestions per team. Ask the students to look at the Team Practice story.

- Explain that the students will work in teams to respond to the story. Tell them that they will read the story together, discuss it, and then each write a response to the story as a whole and to at least one of the parts in their journals. Point out that since responses are personal, teammates should expect to respond to the story in different ways, but that some of their responses might be the same.

- Allow time for the students to complete Team Practice. Use Numbered Heads to review the students' work. Give feedback to reinforce the students' responses to the story.

Team Mastery

- Ask the students to look at the Team Mastery story. Explain that they will read this story independently, discuss it, and then write a response to the story as a whole and to at least one of the parts in their journals. After responding, they will share their responses with their teammates.

- Allow enough time for the students to complete the Team Mastery, and then have the students share their responses with their teammates.

- Use Numbered Heads to have the students share their responses, and give appropriate feedback.

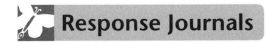
Response Journals

Teacher Presentation: Writing Instruction

- Remind the students that we can respond to what we read with feelings, opinions, and predictions about the story. Also remind the students that we can respond to the story as a whole or respond to the story elements.

- Explain that in the Craft Lesson, during Team Practice and Team Mastery, the students responded to a story after they had read it, but that we can also respond by writing about our feelings, opinions, and predictions about a story as we read. Explain that you are going to model responding to a story as you read.

- Distribute a copy of "The Three Little Kittens and the Big, Bad Mouse" to each partner pair. Read the first section aloud.

The Three Little Kittens and the Big, Bad Mouse

There were three little kittens that lived with their mom and dad in a small home.

"It's time to for you to go out and find your own toys to play with," Papa Cat said to his three fluffy kittens. The kittens were a little scared, but they didn't want to disappoint their dad.

- Use a Think Aloud to model responding to this part of the story. (**Note:** The types of responses are identified in the teacher scripts.)

  The title of this story reminds me of the "Three Little Pigs." I think the big, bad mouse is going to be like the big, bad wolf, so I predict that the mouse is going to pick on the kittens. (prediction)

- Use Think-Pair-Share to have the students discuss what kinds of responses you made and about what part of the story. Ask, for example, if you told about feelings or opinions or made any predictions.

- Read the next section of the story aloud. Use a Think Aloud to model your opinion about the mouse and what might happen next.

The first kitten went looking for his toy in the living room. He saw some papers, a teacup, and the radio. He knew none of those were good toys for him. Then he spotted a ball of yarn.

"I found my toy!" he hollered. He played with the yarn for a few minutes. Then the big, bad mouse came out of a hole in the wall.

"Hey, kitty, kitty, kitty. Whatcha got there?" the big, bad mouse said.

"This is my ball of yarn," the first kitten said.

"Why don't you roll it over here?" the mouse asked.

The mouse is a bully! I don't like bullies. (opinion) **I feel sorry for the kitten.** (feeling) **I don't think the kitten is going to give the mouse the yarn, but I bet the mouse will take it anyway.** (prediction)

- Use Think-Pair-Share to have the students again discuss what kinds of responses you made and to what part of the story. Invite the students to add their own responses.

- Read the next section of the story aloud. Use a Think Aloud to model your thoughts about what happened to the first two kittens.

The first kitten answered, "I will never give over my toy! Not for all the catnip in the world!"

"Then I'll just have to steal it from you!" said the mouse.

The mouse took the end of the yarn and ran back into his hole. The ball of yarn was gone. The first kitten went to his sisters and cried.

The second kitten went looking for her toy in the playroom. She saw a few puzzles, a basketball, and some crayons. She knew none of those were good toys. Then she spotted a rubber ball.

"I found my toy!" she hollered. She knocked the ball back and forth between her front paws for a few minutes. Then the big, bad mouse came out of a hole in the wall.

"Hey, kitty, kitty, kitty. Whatcha got there?" the big, bad mouse said.

"This is my rubber ball," the second kitten said.

"Why don't you roll it over here?" the mouse asked.

The second kitten answered, "I will never give over my toy! Not for all the catnip in the world!"

"Then I'll just have to steal it from you!" said the mouse.

The mouse ran over to the ball and pushed it with his nose into his hole in the wall. The rubber ball was gone. The second kitten went to her brother and sister and cried.

The poor kittens! I hate that the mouse is taking their toys. (opinion)
I can really see a lot of similarities between this story and "The Three Little Pigs."

- Use Think-Pair-Share to have the students again discuss what kinds of responses you made and to what part of the story. Invite the students to add their own responses.

- Finish reading the rest of the story. Invite the students to respond; if appropriate, use a Think Aloud to make a prediction at the end.

The third kitten went looking for her toy in the garage. She saw some garbage cans, an oil can, and a rake. She knew none of those were good toys. Then she spotted a stuffed mouse.

"I found my toy!" she hollered. She played with the stuffed mouse for a few minutes. The big, bad mouse came out of a hole in the wall.

"Hey, kitty, kitty, kitty. Whatcha got there?" the big, bad mouse said.

"This is my new toy," the third kitten said.

"Why don't you toss it over here," the mouse asked.

The third kitten answered, "I will never give over my toy! Not for all the catnip in the world!"

"Then I'll just have to steal it from you!" said the mouse.

The mouse ran over to the third kitten's toy and tried to steal it from her paws. The kitten kicked the stuffed mouse over to the big, bad mouse. When the big, bad mouse saw the toy, he thought it was a dead mouse! He ran out of the garage and down the street as quick as lightning. The three kittens laughed and cheered! They knew that big, bad mouse would never bother them again.

**I am so happy that the mouse got scared of that stuffed mouse!
I would laugh and cheer too if I were the kittens.** (feeling) **I don't
think the kittens will be afraid of a mouse again.** (prediction)

- Explain to the students that when you read you respond with stronger feelings to some parts of what you read than to others. Point out a part of the story that elicited a strong response, such as when the big, bad mouse ran away. Ask volunteers if they responded more strongly to some parts of the story you just read than others, and have them share their thoughts.

- Tell the students they are now ready to respond to the text as you read a story aloud. Explain that you will read a page aloud and stop to let the students write down a response. Tell the students that when they respond with strong feelings about the story, they should mark those responses with a star or a check mark. Point out that they will write about their feelings, opinions, or predictions and that they may refer to the response suggestions for ideas.

- Review the characteristics of writing in response journals (telling your feelings, predictions, or opinions about the story; using examples and details to explain your thinking; and talking about a specific part of the story: a character, the setting, the story problem, events, or resolution and ending).

- Distribute the scoring guide, and have the students note the items on the Content Checklist and the response suggestions at the bottom.

- Use Think-Pair-Share to have the students identify other changes to this guide. *[Parts are missing: checks for the writing process; the editing checklist.]* Explain that they will not follow the steps of the writing process as usual because response journals are examples of personal writing, not writing for a large or impersonal audience.

Content Checklist (100 points)	
In my response journal, I	
tell about my feelings, opinions, or predictions about the story.	**20**
talk about specific parts of the story (characters, setting, problem, events, resolution and ending).	**40**
explain or use details to support my responses.	**40**

Prewriting and Drafting

- Remind the students that you will read aloud, stopping after each page so they may think about and write a response to that page before you continue. Remind them to mark strong responses with a star or a check mark. Explain that if they have no response, even after reviewing the response suggestions for ideas, they should write *no response*, but that they must have responses for most pages to get a score for the activity.

- Introduce the story or book that you've selected to read aloud.

- Read the first page aloud, stop, and allow the students to discuss their responses to this page before recording these thoughts in their journals. Have them note responses that were especially strong and discuss differences between responses, which are to be expected. Remind them to refer to their response suggestions for ideas if a response does not easily come to mind.

- Read the next page aloud, stop, and tell the students the page number you are on, asking them to write this number in their journals. Have the students write responses to that page, noting those that are especially strong, without discussing them first.

- Repeat this pattern for each page of the section that you read aloud: stop after the page and tell the students the page number. Have the students write the page number and then their responses.

Sharing and Responding

- At the end of a passage, have the students work in teams to share their responses. Have them mention a page number before they share so others may refer to their own responses to the same section. Encourage the students to comment on and compare responses, noting those that were stronger than others. Tell the students that in their responses they may agree or disagree with a classmate as long as they respect what the classmate had to say.

- Ask for volunteers to read some of their responses aloud.

- When all who wish to share their responses have done so, celebrate the completion of this part of the activity.

> **Read at least four more sections from the story to repeat the prewriting, drafting, and sharing and responding cycle for at least four more days.**

Scoring

- Have the students turn in their journals.

- Explain that you will use the scoring guides to determine a score for their journal entries as a whole; explain that you will not be evaluating each entry. Remind the students that you will not score for spelling, punctuation, capitalization, or grammar.

- Score the students' work and return their journals.

 **Response Journals**

Pierre Raccoon

October 24, 2009

I just got home from the movies. I went to see *Pierre Raccoon Visits the South Pole.* I've read all the Pierre Raccoon books, so I couldn't wait to see this movie. Now I wish I hadn't wasted my money on such a bad movie. The books are great. They make me laugh and I always wish that I could go with Pierre on his adventures. But the movie—yuck! They didn't even put in the best part of the book when Pierre meets the penguins and he pretends that he is one too. And what was that alligator doing in the movie? That's not in the book. If they make any more Pierre movies, I won't go. I'm going to stick to the books.

Sample Primary MathWings Lesson

LESSON 1

GOAL: **Students will identify halves and fourths as parts of a whole.**

Vocabulary: **fractions, halves, whole, fourths, $^1/_2$, denominator, numerator, $^1/_4$**

OUTLINE OF LESSON

I. **15-MINUTE MATH**
II. **CHECK-IN**
III. **ACTIVE INSTRUCTION**
   Introduce equal parts of a whole by reading Pizza, Please!, by Traci Cottrell. Introduce ways to make and check for halves and fourths.
IV. **TEAMWORK**
   Have students fold or cut various shapes into 2 equal parts, then into 4 equal parts.
V. **DIRECT INSTRUCTION**
   Introduce the names for the fractions $^1/_2$ and $^1/_4$. Introduce the terms numerator and denominator.
VI. **ASSESSMENT**
VII. **REFLECTION**

Introduction for the Teacher:
   This lesson begins the fractions unit with a review of the fractions $^1/_2$ and $^1/_4$. Your students will fold or cut wholes and feel for matching edges to decide whether they have divided them into equal parts. By folding and feeling for matching edges, your students will learn ways of figuring out whether they have divided the wholes into equal parts.

   The book, Pizza, Please!, by Traci Cottrell, will get students to begin thinking about equal parts. In this lesson, students will learn how to make fourths by making halves repeatedly. Lesson 2 will extend the idea of repeated halving to making eighths. For this reason, the class chart in this lesson should have a column for halves, fourths, and eighths.

Pizza, Please! Fraction Chart		
Equal	Equal	Equal
Not Equal	Not Equal	Not Equal

   Oral language for halves, fourths, one half, and one fourth is used often in the lesson, but students are not expected to master the words as vocabulary. If students refer to unequal parts as halves remind them that, in math, the word "halves" refers only to 2 equal parts that make up one whole.

   All the lessons in this unit emphasize the answers to 3 questions: What is the whole? (The context answers this question.) How many equal parts are there? (The denominator answers this question.) How many parts are being used? (The numerator answers this question.)

Note: Remember that, in the teacher lessons, fractions are written diagonally with a slash instead of vertically with a straight line between the numbers. On copies, handouts, transparencies, and Parent Peeks, however, fractions are "stacked," written vertically with a straight line. When showing your students how to write fractions in this lesson, be sure to use the vertical form with a straight line. When writing the word wall cards for $^{1}/_{2}$ and $^{1}/_{4}$, write the fractions vertically with a straight line.

Î   **Key Concepts:**
∞   **Halves are 2 equal parts that make 1 whole. Each part is one half of the whole.**
∞   **Fourths are 4 equal parts that make 1 whole. Each part is one fourth of the whole.**

PREPARE:
Copies:
      Pizza, Please! 1 (2 pages for teacher; cut out before class)
      Make Halves, Make Fourths (1 per student, cut the sheet in half on dotted line; 1 for
          teacher with shapes cut out and placed in 2 baggies)
Teacher Materials:
      1 piece of poster-sized paper for Pizza, Please! fractions chart (see Introduction for the
      Teacher)
      Pizza, Please!, by Traci Cottrell
      Make Halves, Make Fourths
      tape
      scissors
Student Materials:
    Pair:
      sheet of plain paper
      glue
    Student:
      Make Halves, Make Fourths
      scissors

START-UP ROUTINES

15-MINUTE MATH

CHECK-IN: Collect the Home Connection assignment.
                     Partners/Teams
                     Review to Remember
                     Flashback

MATHEMATICS LESSON

ACTIVE INSTRUCTION (20 minutes)
    on the floor

    Show the cover of the book, Pizza, Please!, by Traci Cottrell, and say, **What do you think this story is about?** Here are some possible responses:

pizza
a family eating dinner

Agree and say, **The title of the story is <u>Pizza, Please!</u> Mario and Kendra want to share a pizza for dinner. Listen to find out what happens when they arrive at the pizza parlor.** Read the story.

When you have finished reading, ask, **What happened when Mario and Kendra got to the pizza parlor?** (As people showed up at the restaurant to eat dinner with them, they had to keep figuring out how to divide the pizza so that everyone would get a fair share.) Agree and say, <u>**Pizza, Please!**</u> **is about cutting 1 whole pizza into equal parts, so it is about fractions.**

Hold up the word wall card with *fractions* written on it and say, *Fractions* **are special numbers that describe parts of a whole.**

Hold up the word wall card with *whole* written on it and say, **In the beginning, Mario and Kendra were going to share the whole pizza.**

Hold up the first **Pizza, Please! 1** cutout and say, **In the story, the whole was 1 pizza.** Ask, **What shape is the whole pizza?** (circle) Say, **A whole pizza is like a circle.** Hold or place the **Pizza, Please! 1** cutout so the students can see it.

Trace your finger over the dotted line while saying, **This is how the pizza would have looked in the beginning of the story when Mario and Kendra thought that just the two of them would share the pizza. They planned to cut down the middle of the pizza. Do you think if they cut the pizza on this dotted line they would each get an equal part of the pizza?** Fold the pizza along the dotted line and trace your finger over the matching curves while saying, **One way to check for equal parts is to cut or fold and feel for the matching curves or edges.** Tape the pizza on the Pizza, Please! fractions chart under the word, *Equal*.

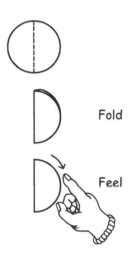

Fold

Feel

Say, **Mario and Kendra used a special name for 2 equal parts. Do you remember that name?** (halves) Hold up the word wall card with *halves* written on it and say, **Mario and Kendra could cut the pizza into 2 equal parts called** *halves*.

Summarize:

> ⚷ **Halves are 2 equal parts that make 1 whole. Each part is one half of the whole.**

Hold up the second **Pizza, Please! 1** cutout so students can see that the dotted straight line is clearly to the left of the middle of the pizza. Point to the dotted line and ask, **If Mario and Kendra cut the pizza on this dotted line, would this make equal parts?** 💡 Here are some possible responses:

One part's big and one part's little.
The little part fits inside the big part.
If you fold, the curves don't match.

Agree and say, **Because cutting on this dotted line would not make equal parts, I'm going to put this whole pizza on the bottom of the Pizza, Please! fractions chart, under the words,** *Not Equal.* Tape the pizza on the chart in the 1st column.

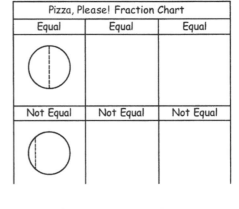

Pizza, Please! Fraction Chart		
Equal	Equal	Equal
Not Equal	Not Equal	Not Equal

Show pages 7 and 8 of <u>Pizza, Please!</u> Say, **Look at the picture. Now, 4 people have to find a way to share the pizza.** Hold up the **Pizza, Please! 1** cutout with 4 equal parts and say, **Here's how Mario thought about having the chef cut the pizza to make 4 equal parts. First, he would cut straight down the middle of the pizza, just like we did when we made halves. That makes 2 equal pieces. Then he would cut straight across the middle of the pizza to make 4 equal pieces. Let's fold and feel for matching curves and edges to find out whether cutting the pizza this way would make 4 equal parts.**

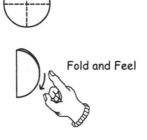

Fold and Feel

Fold again

Fold so that the dotted lines are on the outside and students can see them. Fold on the 1st line, trace your finger over the matching curves, and say, **I make sure the curves and edges match. I leave the 2 halves folded and make the next fold.** Fold and say, **Make sure that the curves and edges match.** Unfold the pizza and tape it to the Pizza, Please! fractions chart in the 2nd column under the word, *Equal.*

Pizza, Please! Fraction Chart		
Equal	Equal	Equal
Not Equal	Not Equal	Not Equal

Say, **Mario used a special name for 4 equal parts. Do you remember that name?** (fourths) Hold up the word wall card with *fourths* written on it and say, **The chef could cut the pizza into 4 equal parts called** *fourths*.

Point to each fourth in the pizza cutout and say, **This way, Mario gets one fourth of the pizza, Kendra gets one fourth of the pizza, Deon gets one fourth of the pizza, and Dad gets one fourth of the pizza.**

Summarize:

> 🔑 **Fourths are 4 equal parts that make 1 whole. Each part is one fourth of the whole.**

Hold up the fourth **Pizza, Please! 1** cutout, the circle with 4 unequal parts. Point to the dotted lines and ask, **If the chef cut the pizza on these dotted lines, would there be 4 equal parts?** Here are some possible responses:

Some parts are the same size and some aren't.
There are big parts and little parts.
There are tall parts and short parts.
Two parts are the same size and the other 2 parts are the same size, but all 4 parts are not the same size.

Agree and say, **Because cutting on these dotted lines would not make equal parts, I'm going to put this whole pizza in the middle column under the words,** *Not Equal*, **on the Pizza, Please! fraction chart.** Tape the pizza on the chart.

TEAMWORK (15 minutes)
 in their seats

Explain to your students that they will work with their partners to make halves and fourths. Hold up a copy of **Make Halves, Make Fourths** and a sheet of paper. Say, **Each student will get a copy of these shapes. You will each cut out your shapes. Then you will take turns folding the shapes into halves and fourths. You will make a chart of halves and fourths on a separate sheet of paper.** Fold the sheet of paper in half and say, **You will glue the shapes folded into halves on the left side of the paper and the shapes folded into fourths on the right side of the paper.**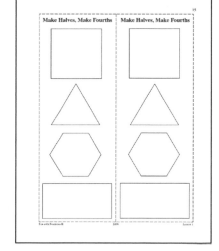

Select a student to be your partner. Explain that, to save time, you cut the shapes out before class. Give your partner a set of shapes. Tell her to find the square and ask her to fold it in half. Remind your partner to feel for matching edges. If the edges match, have her open it up and draw a dotted line along the fold line. If the edges don't match, have her cut along the fold line and try to stack the pieces so the edges match.

Say, **Once you have made equal parts, glue the shape onto the left side of the chart. Do not glue the shape onto the chart if you cannot make 2 equal parts.**

Say, **Next, I will try to fold my square into fourths.** Remind your students that they might need to cut and stack to see if the edges match. Tell them that if the edges do match, they will need to glue the shape onto their chart so that it looks like the original shape. Fold the square and feel for matching edges, just as your partner did for halves. If the edges match, then fold again and feel for matching edges. If the edges match again, open the square back up and draw both of the fold lines with your pencil. Say, **I folded my square into 4 equal parts, so I will glue it onto the right side of the chart.** Glue the square on the chart. Explain that next, you would try to fold the triangle in half and your partner would try to fold the triangle into fourths, and that each time you would change how many parts you are trying to fold the shape into.

Designate which students go first. Ask students to fold their plain sheet of paper in half to make their chart. Have them cut out all 4 shapes on their **Make Halves, Make Fourths** copy. Remind them to take turns folding the shapes into halves and fourths. Tell your students to draw dotted lines on the shapes if they folded them into equal parts, and glue them on their charts.

☑ While your students are working, circulate to assist them and informally assess several students with some of the following questions:

What can you tell me about the whole?
Are the parts equal?
How are you going to check to see if the parts are equal?
How could cutting or folding help you check?
How many equal parts are there?

DIRECT INSTRUCTION (15 minutes)
in their seats

Ask your students to look at the chart they made in **TEAMWORK**. Say, **Point to the shapes that you folded into halves.** Explain, **If we can answer 3 fraction questions, we will understand what the fraction is. These 3 questions are: What is the whole? How many equal parts are there? How many parts are being used?** Point to a shape and ask, **What is the whole?** (answer depends upon shape) **How many equal parts does the shape have?** (2)

Write ¹/₂ on the board and say, **This is an example of a fraction.** Point to the 2 on the board. **The number on the bottom of the fraction tells us how many equal parts of the whole there are all together. In this case, there are 2 equal parts in the whole, so a 2 goes on the bottom.**

$$\frac{1}{2}$$

Point to the 1 on the board. Then say, **The number on the top tells us how many of those equal parts we are talking about. In this case, we are talking about 1 equal part, so a 1 goes on the top.**

$$\frac{1}{2}$$

Point to the line between the 1 and 2 on the board. Say, **We write fractions with a line between the 2 numbers like this.**

$$\frac{1}{2}$$

Then say, **Now that we know about the fraction, we can name it. First we look at the bottom number. This fraction has a 2 on the bottom, so it has a special name. Can you guess what that is?** (half or halves) Agree and say, **When the bottom number of a fraction is a 2, the whole is divided into 2 equal parts or halves. Then we look at the top number to see how many parts we are talking about. In this fraction we are talking about 1 part, so the fraction is one half.**

Hold up the word wall card with $\frac{1}{2}$ written on it and say, **Read this fraction name with me.** Point to the 1 and say, **One.** Slide your finger down and say, **Half.** Repeat this with the students, sliding your finger with a fluid motion, **One half.**

Hold up the word wall card with *denominator* written on it, point to the fraction $\frac{1}{2}$, and say, **The number on the bottom of a fraction is called the *denominator*.**

Hold up the word wall card with *numerator* written on it, point to the fraction $\frac{1}{2}$, and say, **The number on the top of a fraction is called the *numerator*.**

Write the fraction $\frac{1}{2}$ on the top of the 1st column of the Pizza, Please! fractions chart. ☑ Ask one of the students in each pair to write $\frac{1}{2}$ on each of the halves on their chart.

When students have finished, remind them of the 3 fraction questions that must be answered to understand what the fraction is. Say, **Point to one of the shapes you folded into fourths.** Ask, **What is the whole?** (1 pizza) **How many equal parts does each shape have?** (4) Write $\frac{1}{4}$ on the board and say, **This is an example of a fraction.** Point to the 4 on the board. **The number on the bottom of the fraction, or the denominator, tells us how many equal parts of the whole there are all together. In this case, there are 4 equal parts in the whole, so 4 is the denominator.**

$$\xrightarrow{} \frac{1}{4}$$

Point to the 1 on the board. Then say, **The number on the top tells us how many of those equal parts we are talking about. In this case, we are talking about 1 equal part, so a 1 goes on the top.**

$$\xrightarrow{} \frac{1}{4}$$

Point to the line between the 1 and 4 on the board. Say, **We write fractions with a line between the 2 numbers like this.**

$$\xrightarrow{} \frac{1}{4}$$

Then say, **Now that we know about the fraction, we can name it. First we look at the bottom number, or the denominator. This fraction has a 4 as its denominator, so it has a special name. Can you guess what that is?** (fourth or fourths) Agree and say, **When the denominator of a fraction is 4, the whole is divided into 4 equal parts or fourths. Then we look at the top number, or the numerator, to see how many parts we are talking about. In this fraction we are talking about 1 part, so the fraction is one fourth.**

Hold up the word wall card with $\frac{1}{4}$ written on it and say, **Read this fraction name with me.** Point to the 1 and say, **One.** Slide your finger down and say, **Fourth.** Repeat this with the students, sliding your finger with a fluid motion, **One fourth.**

Write the fraction $\frac{1}{4}$ on the top of the middle column of the Pizza, Please! fractions chart. ☑ Ask the other students in each pair to write $\frac{1}{4}$ on each of the fourths on their chart.

Remind your students that halves are 2 equal parts that make one whole and each part is one half of the whole. Fourths are 4 equal parts that make one whole and each part is one fourth of the whole.

ASSESSMENT

ASSESSMENT OPPORTUNITIES	
ACTIVE INSTRUCTION	∞ none
TEAMWORK	∞ folds or cuts shapes into halves and fourths
DIRECT INSTRUCTION	∞ labels 2 equal parts $^1/_2$ ∞ labels 4 equal parts $^1/_4$

REFLECTION

Students discuss today's lesson.

🔑 Key Concepts Summary:
∞ **Halves are 2 equal parts that make 1 whole. Each part is one half of the whole.**
∞ **Fourths are 4 equal parts that make 1 whole. Each part is one fourth of the whole.**

Review the word wall cards and place them on the word wall.

Read the directions and explain the Home Connection assignment.

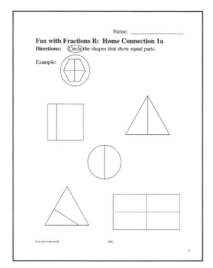

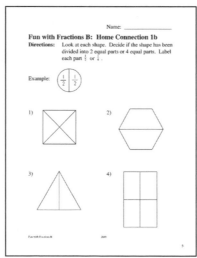

Team Wrap-Up

Sample Intermediate MathWings Lesson

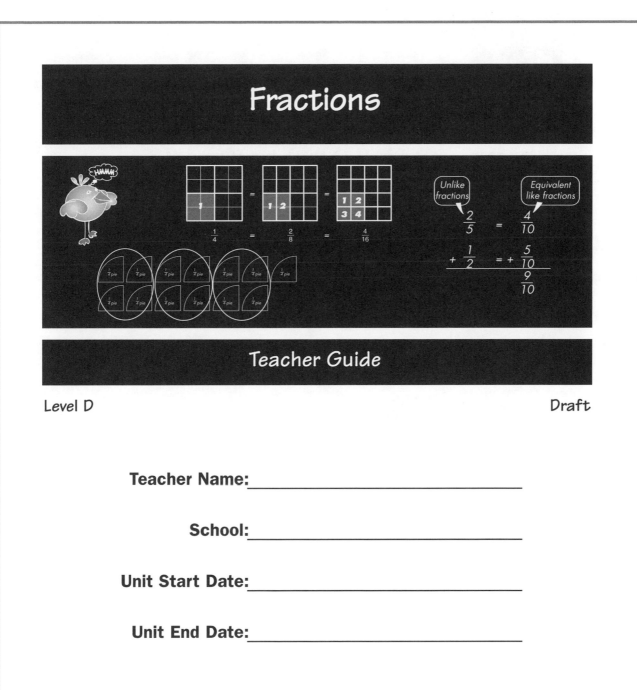

Fractions

Teacher Guide

Level D   Draft

Teacher Name:_____

School:_____

Unit Start Date:_____

Unit End Date:_____

Lesson

1

The Same Amount

GOAL: Students will use the three fraction questions to find equivalent fractions.

Alignment: PA Standard 2.4.5.A, Math Assesment Anchor M4.A.1

Big Idea Connection: Understanding equivalent fractions will help students make the connection between fractions and decimals ($\frac{1}{5} = \frac{2}{10} = 0.2$).

Advance Preparation

1. Practice folding the papers for Active Instruction, Team Consensus, and Team Mastery.
2. Prepare or retrieve Word Wall words for display.

New Word Wall Words: fraction   denominator   numerator
equivalent fractions

MATERIALS

Teacher: 3 sheets of unlined paper
Fair Shares transparency
blank transparency
The Doorbell Rang, by Pat Hutchins

Pair: 12 centimeter cubes

Student: 3 sheets of unlined paper

5-Minute Warm-Up

1. Team Set-Up
2. Homework Check
3. Get the Goof problem: $\frac{1}{2} + \frac{1}{2} = \frac{2}{4}$

The Game Plan

Post the Agenda

AGENDA
1. Today you will name equivalent fractions and use the 3 fraction questions to understand their values. You will solve problems like this:

   Use a folded paper to help you write an equivalent fraction for $\frac{5}{6}$.

2. Review targeted team cooperation goal—everyone paricipates.

Development of Concept

Fraction Questions

▶ Remind students that sometimes they have to share things, such as food, toys, time and attention, money, etc.

▶ Quickly read *The Doorbell Rang* to your students to introduce the concept of fractions.

   *Optional: Show video clip to illustrate the same concept.

▶ Remind students that when the thing we are sharing is divided into equal parts, or fair shares, we can use a fraction to describe the parts. A fraction is part of a whole.

▶ Place *fraction* on the Word Wall.

▶ Have students use Think-Pair-Share and their 12 centimeter cubes to model all the fractions that describe the situations in the story.

▶ Show the Fair Shares transparency, keeping the fraction questions covered.

▶ Choose a student to write her pair's fractions on the Fair Shares transparency.

   $$\frac{1}{2} \ (or\ \frac{6}{12}),\ \frac{1}{4}\ (or\ \frac{3}{12}),\ \frac{1}{6}\ (or\ \frac{2}{12}),\ \frac{1}{12}$$

▶ Explain that at first Victoria and Sam were going to share the cookies between the 2 of them, so they would each get $\frac{1}{2}$ of the cookies.

▶ Point out that we can't understand the value of a fraction unless we know what the whole is.

▶ Uncover and read the first fraction question:

   What is the whole?

▶ Explain that this is the first question we need to ask about a fraction. To really know what the whole is, we also have to know what size it is or how many are in the whole.

   How many cookies did the story say Sam and Victoria were going to get at the beginning?
   6

   If we know how many cookies Victoria and Sam had, how can we find out how many cookies there were all together?
   There are 2 children, so we can multiply 2 × 6 = 12 cookies.

▶ Explain that in this situation, the whole is a group of 12 cookies.

▶ Uncover and read the second fraction question:

   Into how many equal parts has the whole been divided?

Teacher Note:
It is fine if an incomplete answer is provided at this time because you will be modifying the fractions on the transparency throughout the rest of Development of Concept.

▶ Explain that this is the second question we need to ask about a fraction. In this case, the group of cookies has been divided into 2 parts because there are 2 children, Victoria and Sam.

▶ Explain that the bottom number of a fraction answers this question. It is called the denominator.

▶ Place *denominator* on the Word Wall.

▶ Uncover and read the third fraction question:

How many of the equal parts are we using?

▶ Explain that this is the third question we need to ask about a fraction. In this case, each of the children is using 1 part of the group of cookies.

▶ Explain that the top number of a fraction answers this question. It is called the numerator.

▶ Place *numerator* on the Word Wall.

▶ Point out that because each child is using 1 of the 2 parts of the group of cookies, each child has $\frac{1}{2}$ of the cookies.

▶ In the Fraction column on the Fair Shares transparency, write "$\frac{1}{2}$" next to "Victoria and Sam." Point out that the 2 is the denominator and the 1 is the numerator.

Equivalent Fractions

We could also divide the group of cookies into 12 separate cookies, which is 12 equal parts. How many of the equal parts did Victoria get? How many did Sam get?
Victoria and Sam both got 6 of the 12 equal parts.

What fraction can we use to describe this?
$\frac{6}{12}$

▶ Have your students use Think-Pair-Share to answer the following question:

Well, did Victoria and Sam each have $\frac{1}{2}$ of the cookies or did they each have $\frac{6}{12}$ of the cookies?
They had both, because $\frac{1}{2}$ represents the same number of cookies as $\frac{6}{12}$.

▶ In the Fraction column on the Fair Shares transparency, write "$= \frac{6}{12}$" next to "$\frac{1}{2}$."

▶ Explain that $\frac{1}{2}$ and $\frac{6}{12}$ describe the same number of cookies. They describe the same portion of a whole, just divided in different ways. They are called equivalent fractions.

▶ Place *equivalent fractions* on the Word Wall.

▶ Remind students that Victoria and Sam had to share their cookies with Tom and Hannah.

Did the whole change?
No, it is still a group of 12 cookies.

Into how many equal parts has the whole been divided? How do you know?
Now the whole is being divided into 4 parts because there are 4 children.

How many of the equal parts did each child get?
1

What fraction describes this?
$\frac{1}{4}$

▶ Have your students use Think-Pair-Share to answer the following question.

Is there another equivalent fraction that you could use to describe this situation? Explain.
$\frac{3}{12}$ *can also be used because each child has 3 of the 12 cookies.*

▶ In the Fraction column on the Fair Shares transparency, write "$\frac{1}{4} = \frac{3}{12}$" next to "Victoria, Sam, Tom, and Hannah."

▶ Explain the fractions as you complete the rest of the Fair Shares transparency by writing "$\frac{1}{6} = \frac{2}{12}$" next to "Victoria, Sam, Tom, Hannah, Peter, and Peter's brother" and "$\frac{1}{12}$" next to "Victoria, Sam, Tom, Hannah, Peter, Peter's brother, Joy, Simon, and 4 cousins."

▶ Explain that the class will now use sheets of paper to find more equivalent fractions.

▶ Have students take out a sheet of unlined paper.

▶ Hold up a sheet of unlined paper as a model.

This is our whole. What is it?
a sheet of paper

Into how many equal parts has this whole been divided?
None, it hasn't been divided at all.

▶ Point out that if something hasn't been divided, then that means there is just 1 part.

How many of the equal parts are we using?
1

▶ Agree that you have 1 sheet of paper divided into 1 part, and you are using that 1 part. Write "$\frac{1}{1}$" on a blank transparency.

▶ Explain that when we write whole numbers, such as 1, the denominator is 1 because the whole number is not divided into more than 1 part, and we are using the whole amount. We don't usually write that denominator, but we know it can be written if we need it.

Teacher Note:
Using thin paper and making sharp creases will make the folding easier.

▶ Have your students use Think-Pair-Share to answer the following question:

> **If I had 5 whole sheets of paper, what fraction could I write to describe them?**
> $\frac{5}{1}$

▶ Explain that we would like to find some equivalent fractions for $\frac{1}{1}$. Use your sheet of unlined paper to demonstrate as you lead the students through the following steps.

▶ Remind the students that before we make any folds, there is 1 part and we are using it, so that's $\frac{1}{1}$.

$\frac{1}{1}$
[square]

▶ Fold the paper in half as shown below.

$\frac{2}{2}$

> **Into how many equal parts has this whole been divided?**
> 2

> **We are using the whole paper. How many of the equal parts are we using?**
> 2

> **What fraction describes the paper now?**
> $\frac{2}{2}$

▶ Write "$= \frac{2}{2}$" next to "$\frac{1}{1}$" on the transparency.

▶ Fold the paper in half again as shown below.

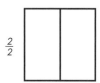

$\frac{4}{4}$

> **Into how many equal parts has this whole been divided?**
> 4

> **We are using the whole paper. How many of the equal parts are we using?**
> 4

> **What fraction describes the paper now?**
> $\frac{4}{4}$

- ▶ Write "$= \frac{4}{4}$" next to "$\frac{1}{1} = \frac{2}{2}$" on the transparency.

- ▶ Fold the paper in half again as shown below.

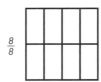

  What fraction describes the paper now? How do you know?
  There are now 8 parts, and the whole sheet is the 8 of them, so that's $\frac{8}{8}$.

- ▶ Write "$= \frac{8}{8}$" next to "$\frac{1}{1} = \frac{2}{2} = \frac{4}{4}$" on the transparency.

- ▶ Fold the paper in half again as shown below. Explain that now there are 16 parts, and the whole sheet is the 16 of them, so that's $\frac{16}{16}$.

- ▶ Write "$= \frac{16}{16}$" next to "$\frac{1}{1} = \frac{2}{2} = \frac{4}{4} = \frac{8}{8}$" on the transparency.

  Is the paper still the same size?
  Yes.

  How has it changed?
  It is now divided into parts by the folds.

- ▶ Point out that the fractions on the transparency are equivalent fractions because they represent the same amount (1 whole sheet of paper) divided in different ways.

- ▶ Quickly shade $\frac{1}{4}$ of your paper, as shown:

- ▶ Outline along the folds to show that $\frac{1}{4}$ is also $\frac{2}{8}$.

▸ Outline along the folds to show that $\frac{1}{4}$ is also $\frac{4}{16}$.

▸ Write "$\frac{1}{4} = \frac{2}{8} = \frac{4}{16}$" on the transparency.

▸ Explain that the students can find a summary of the main ideas from this lesson and some examples in A Quick Look on their student page.

A Quick Look

To understand the value of a fraction, we need to know:

1. What is the whole?

2. Into how many equal parts has the whole been divided?

3. How many of the equal parts are we using?

Fractions that describe the same amount are called equivalent fractions.

Example:

The whole is a sheet of notebook paper. It is folded and shaded so that it looks like this:

Write equivalent fractions to describe the shaded portion of the paper.

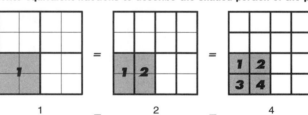

$$\frac{1}{4} \quad = \quad \frac{2}{8} \quad = \quad \frac{4}{16}$$

The Big Picture

▸ Summarize The Big Picture before students begin Team Practice.

> **To understand the value of a fraction, we need to know: What is the whole? Into how many equal parts has the whole been divided? How many of the equal parts are we using?**
>
> **Equivalent fractions are different fractions that describe the same portion of a whole.**

Team Practice

Common Concerns...
Students may have trouble seeing the paper as divided into anything other than eighteenths or twelfths. Suggest that students refold their paper or draw lines on it to be able to see the paper as divided into halves, thirds, etc.

Circulate and Ask...
What fraction can you use to describe this portion of the paper?

What other fractions can you use to describe the same portion?

What do you need to know to understand the value of a fraction?

Award Points for...
All students contributing answers and explanations

All team members checking in with their team

Use of proper academic language, such as fraction, denominator, numerator, and equivalent fractions

Correct responses from students representing their teams

TEAM CONSENSUS: Have team members work together to write equivalent fractions using a folded piece of paper.

▶ Have the students take out a sheet of unlined paper.

▶ Review the directions for Team Consensus.

> **Work with your team on the problem.**
>
> **Directions:**
>
> Fold the paper in thirds.
> Next, fold the paper in thirds again.
> Then fold the paper in half.
>
> **Use this folded paper. Write an equivalent fraction for the fraction.**
> $\frac{6}{9}$
>
> **Make sure you can explain your thinking.**

▶ Demonstrate how to fold the paper into eighteenths.

▶ Remind the students to think about the three questions: What is the whole and how big is it? Into how many equal parts has the whole been divided? How many equal parts are we using?

▶ Remind the students to think about different ways they can group the parts of the paper.

▶ Randomly choose a student to explain the team's thinking.

$\frac{6}{9} = \frac{2}{3}$ *or* $\frac{6}{9} = \frac{12}{18}$

TEAM MASTERY: Have team members work by themselves to write equivalent fractions using folded pieces of paper.

▶ Have the students take out a sheet of unlined paper.

▶ Review the directions for Team Mastery.

 Team Mastery

Work by yourself on problems 1 and 2. Check in with your team. Then do problems 3 and 4.

Directions:

Fold the paper in thirds.
Next, fold the paper in half.
Then fold the paper in half again.

Use this new folded paper. Write an equivalent fraction for each fraction.

1. $\dfrac{3}{12}$

2. $\dfrac{3}{4}$

3. $\dfrac{2}{12}$

4. $\dfrac{2}{6}$

Numbered Heads is Next!

Do a Team Rehearsal to make sure all teammates can explain:
What is the whole?
Into how many equal parts does this fraction say it is divided?
How many equal parts does this fraction say we are using?

Teacher Note:
Save all 3 of your folded papers for use with Lesson 2. Have students put their 2 folded papers from Team Practice into their materials bins for use during Lesson 2.

▶ Demonstrate how to fold the paper into twelfths.

▶ Remind the students to think about the three questions: What is the whole and how big is it? Into how many equal parts has the whole been divided? How many equal parts are we using?

▶ Remind the students to think about different ways they can group the parts of the paper.

▶ When most students have completed the second set of problems, have teams do a Team Rehearsal for problem 2.

▶ Use Numbered Heads to randomly select a student to share his or her team's solution and explain his or her thinking. Then select other students to share different solutions.

1. $\dfrac{3}{12} = \dfrac{1}{4}$

2. $\dfrac{2}{6} = \dfrac{1}{3}$ or $\dfrac{2}{6} = \dfrac{4}{12}$

3. $\dfrac{2}{12} = \dfrac{1}{6}$

4. $\dfrac{3}{4} = \dfrac{9}{12}$

Quick Check

▶ Review the directions for the Quick Check.

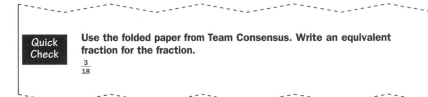

> **Quick Check** Use the folded paper from Team Consensus. Write an equivalent fraction for the fraction.
>
> $\frac{3}{18}$

▶ Collect the Quick Checks as you explain:

$\frac{3}{18} = \frac{1}{6}$ *because the paper can be divided like this:*

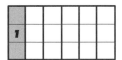

Reflection

▶ Review The Big Picture.

> **To understand the value of a fraction, we need to know: What is the whole? Into how many equal parts has the whole been divided? How many of the equal parts are we using?**

> **Equivalent fractions are different fractions that describe the same portion of a whole.**

▶ Assign Lesson 1 Homework, page 3. Have the students take the folded paper from Development of Concept home to do the HW Skill Problems. Remind the students to bring their folded papers back tomorrow to use with Lesson 2.

▶ Do Team Wrap-Up.

HOMEWORK

Skill Problems

Use the folded paper from Active Instruction. Write an equivalent fraction for each fraction.

1. $\frac{3}{4}$

2. $\frac{3}{8}$

3. $\frac{2}{4}$

4. $\frac{14}{16}$

5. $\frac{7}{8}$

Mixed Practice

Show your work.

6. Estimate the difference.
    913
    − 549

7. Estimate the product.
    296
    × 9

8. Estimate the quotient.
    212 ÷ 9

9. Does 95,102 round to 90,000 or 100,000?

10. Estimate the sum.
    54 + 23 + 19 =

Real-World Problems

Show your work.

11. Cheryl cut a pie into 6 pieces. She ate $\frac{1}{3}$ of the pie. How many pieces did she eat?

12. Lenny cut a pizza into 8 slices. He ate $\frac{3}{4}$ of the pizza. How many pieces were left?

13. Nancy, Ursa, and Wendy bought a dozen donuts. They each ate 2 donuts. How many donuts were left?

Problem Solving

14. Miguel is saving for a bicycle. He needs $200. For his birthday, his family gave him $\frac{1}{2}$ of what he needs. He mowed lawns to earn $\frac{1}{4}$ of what he needs. How many more dollars does Miguel need?

Homework Answers

1. $\frac{3}{4} = \frac{6}{8}$ or $\frac{3}{4} = \frac{12}{16}$

2. $\frac{3}{8} = \frac{6}{16}$

3. $\frac{2}{4} = \frac{1}{2}$ or $\frac{2}{4} = \frac{4}{8}$ or $\frac{2}{4} = \frac{8}{16}$

4. $\frac{14}{16} = \frac{7}{8}$

5. $\frac{7}{8} = \frac{14}{16}$

6. Possible estimate:
   913 ≈ 900,
   549 ≈ 550;
   900 − 550 = 350

7. Possible estimate:
   296 ≈ 300;
   300 × 9 = 2,700

8. Possible estimate:
   212 ≈ 200,
   9 ≈ 10;
   200 ÷ 10 = 20

9. 100,000

10. Possible estimate:
    54 ≈ 50,
    23 ≈ 20,
    19 ≈ 20;
    50 + 20 + 20 = 90

11. $\frac{1}{3} = \frac{2}{6}$,
    so she ate 2 pieces of the pie.

12. $\frac{3}{4} = \frac{6}{8}$,
    so there were 2 pieces of pizza left.

13. 3 × 2 = 6,
    12 − 6 = 6,
    so there were 6 donuts left.

14. $200 ÷ 2 = $100, so his family gave him $100.
    $200 ÷ 4 = $50, so he earned $50.
    $100 + $50 = $150.
    Miguel still needs $50.

PARENT PEEK

In this lesson, your child learned three important questions for knowing the value of a fraction. She also learned that different fractions can be used to describe the same portion of a whole. Examples are provided in today's lesson. Remind your child that she can use folded paper to help her figure out equivalent fractions.

You might like to use a snack, such as crackers, a piece of bread, or a large cookie, to have your child show you some equivalent fractions.

9

Removing Roadblocks to Learning

Addressing Family, Student, and School Issues

Timothy Jones* lives in a housing project and attends a Success for All school in which virtually all children are in poverty. He had completed kindergarten the year before Success for All began at his school. According to his teachers' reports, Timothy was already headed for serious trouble. He was angry and aggressive, dealing with both teachers and other students as if they were out to get him. Timothy had to be removed from class frequently because of his disruptive behavior. He had little energy to put into learning when he was in school, and he was not in school very consistently. Even when he did come to school, he often arrived late, closer to 10:30 than 8:30.

Timothy was born when his mother was a young teenager. His mother felt helpless. She loved her son and wanted him to succeed in school but had few resources to help him. Her son's response to the school was just like his mother's. The only way she knew how to react to Timothy's problems in school was to become angry and aggressive. In the first weeks of first grade, when the school contacted her about problems Timothy was having, her response was to stomp into school cursing, threatening to take him out of the school since it couldn't deal with him.

---

*This vignette, a composite of experiences with many children and families involved in Success for All schools, is adapted from Madden, Slavin, Karweit, Dolan, & Wasik, 1991.

Coordinated efforts by teachers, the facilitator, Solutions Network members, and Timothy's mother worked to turn things around for Timothy. After the social worker made the mother feel respected and welcome, she was able to encourage her to participate in parenting classes held at the school. This helped her become more confident in her ability to handle her son. With assistance from the attendance monitor, Timothy's attendance started to improve. At first, the school called his mother early every morning to get her started early enough to get her son to school. For a while, the attendance monitor met the mother halfway to school.

Everyone made a concerted effort to make Timothy's mother feel welcome at the school, showing her respect and treating her as a partner. Timothy's teacher sent good news notes home with Timothy when he met the behavioral goals he and his teacher set together. Timothy also practiced solving conflicts peacefully at the weekly Class Council meeting. When Timothy experienced a problem with another student, he was able to go to the Roundtable at the back of the classroom and use a method to think through better solutions to conflict. Time for reflection and practice in win-win solutions to conflict reduced Timothy's problems with other students.

Even as his behavior improved, Timothy still had very serious academic problems; on all tests given at the beginning of first grade, he showed no evidence of having any pre-reading skills. With the new SFA efforts, Timothy was given an instructional program in which he could be successful and was given one-to-one tutoring, which not only provided the academic support that he needed but also gave him emotional support. His tutor was a special person with whom he could share his struggles and successes. The tutor and Timothy's classroom teacher met frequently with the Solutions Network to coordinate plans and activities around his needs and strengths.

As Timothy's mother began to work cooperatively with the school, Timothy's attitude toward school improved. He still had a strong temper, but he began to learn how to deal with angry feelings in a constructive way. Timothy was in school on time every day. Learning still did not come easily for him, but he knew that if he worked hard, he could learn, and he was proud of the steady progress he was making. He loved to bring his Reading Roots books home to read to his mother, who was delighted with his reading success. His mother developed a good deal of self-confidence as well, and is now employed in a store in the neighborhood.

Timothy's experience, which is like that of many students in Success for All, shows the importance of a relentless, coordinated approach to meeting all students' individual needs. Ensuring high-quality instruction, tutoring, and other academic supports is not enough for a child like Timothy who may be failing for reasons that have little to do with academics. Some children fail because of erratic attendance or poor behavior. Some have serious health problems, or need eyeglasses or hearing aids. Some lack adequate nutrition or heat at home. Some are homeless, or are threatened with losing their homes. If a school is serious about ensuring success for *every* child, then it must have the capacity to recognize and solve all of these nonacademic problems that are barriers to a child's success in school.

COMPOSITION OF THE SOLUTIONS NETWORK

The Success for All program places a strong emphasis on increasing the school's capacity to relate to parents and to involve parents as well as health and social service agencies in solutions to any problems students may have. Each Success for All school establishes a Solutions Network for this purpose. The composition of the Solutions Network varies from school to school depending on the personnel available and the school's needs. The school's Title I parent liaison, counselor, social worker, nurse, and other resource staff usually make up the Solutions Network, along with building administrators (principals or vice principals) and the facilitator. In schools with serious attendance problems, an attendance aide may be added. The Solutions Network works both to assist individual students who are having trouble being successful as well as with larger schoolwide issues in attendance, behavior management, parent involvement, and connections to community resources.

Solutions Networks are led by a Solutions Network Coordinator. Although some schools hire a full-time Solutions Network Coordinator, most schools utilize the school guidance counselor, social worker, principal, or vice principal. Although additional personnel are not required, existing school personnel must have their duties redefined so they have the time to oversee a quality implementation of the Solutions Network program components. For the Solutions Network to function well, it is vital that each member has the time to meet and implement decisions. This may involve changing people's schedules or responsibilities. For example, if a school cannot hire a clinical social worker, other school personnel will need to implement the classroom and family based behavior modification programs. Other personnel may also need to make occasional home visits to families who are hard to reach. These interventions are time consuming, but necessary; Success for All is predicated on the belief that *every* student can succeed, and there are always some children who would fail without the services Solutions Network provides.

The focus of the Solutions Network is on identifying and building on the strengths of parents, communities, and individual children. All parents want their children to succeed in school, but some have such difficult lives that they need help to create home environments conducive to school success. Solutions Networks begin with a fundamental respect for parents. They see parents as partners in achieving success for their children, a goal shared by parents and school staffs alike. They enlist parents in a cooperative quest to do whatever it takes at home and at school, and to engage whatever community resources may be available, to ensure that each child succeeds in school.

Solutions Networks usually meet quarterly. Each Solutions Network creates subcommittees that meet to work on the key issues identified by this group. Subcommittees meet frequently but meet as a full Solutions Network quarterly to review progress and refine plans. The Solutions Network is responsible for both schoolwide planning and for programs for individual children. As examples of schoolwide efforts, Solutions Networks commonly create subcommittees on Attendance, Parent Involvement, Behavior Management/Conflict Resolution, and Community Resources to develop schoolwide programs to address common concerns. This might include activities to increase parent involvement, improve the school's ability to monitor and respond to truancy, and so on. For example, the Parent Involvement Subcommittee may plan a program for parents on helping children with homework, or the Behavior Management Subcommittee may plan a session with teachers on dealing with behavior problems.

The second area addressed by the Solutions Network involves solving problems with individual children. There is an Intervention Subcommittee that meets weekly to address the needs of students who continue to have difficulty achieving success due to a range of issues. Teachers and other staff refer a child to the Intervention Subcommittee because they believe the child is having problems in school that have not been resolved by normal classroom intervention. Examples of such problems might include truancy, behavior problems, health problems, and psychological problems. In addition, students who are not making adequate academic progress despite classroom and tutorial assistance are referred to the Intervention Subcommittee even if there are no obvious family problems. The team's goal is to find out if family interventions or other resources may help get the child on track.

The Solutions Network subcommittees implement a standard set of Success for All activities, and then add activities specific to their school's needs. For example, all Solutions Networks make sure that the needs of children who are having difficulty are being met, that school attendance programs are working, and that parents are encouraged to participate in school and support their children's success at home. In addition to these, each Solutions Network uses school data to determine any additional support activities that might increase achievement in their own particular school community. The activities of the Solutions Network subcommittees vary depending on available staff, student and family needs, and community investment in the school.

The multifaceted role of the Solutions Network is crucial for addressing the needs of students who are at the highest risk of school failure. An effective Network not only attempts to meet the needs of students who are at risk through the Intervention Team subcommittee but also creates a schoolwide climate that fosters respect for parents, high family involvement, and a proactive approach to the complex problems faced by many students and families in Success for All schools.

The main activities of the Solutions Network subcommittees are summarized in Figure 9.1 and described in the following sections.

Figure 9.1   Activities of the Solutions Network Subcommittees

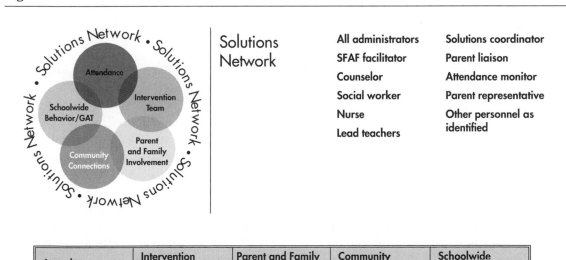

Attendance	Intervention Team (IT)	Parent and Family Involvement	Community Connections	Schoolwide Behavior/GAT
Attendance monitor	SFAF facilitator	Parent liaison	Social worker	Administrator
Administrator	Administrator	Parent representative	Lead teachers	Counselor
Social worker	Counselor		Administrator	Social worker
Other personnel as identified	Other personnel as identified	Other personnel as identified	Other personnel as identified	Other personnel as identified

PARENT AND FAMILY INVOLVEMENT SUBCOMMITTEE

Parent involvement is a key component for student success in Success for All. Research indicates that parental involvement is correlated with increases in attendance, increases in achievement, and decreases in behavior problems (see Epstein, 1995). Success for All, then, stresses the need for a strong parent involvement program that is linked to improvements in curriculum and instruction.

Traditionally, schools and families have seen themselves as separate institutions that interact with the child. However, this separation can be detrimental for many children. In particular, it is clear to schools working with children from disadvantaged families that problems from the community and the family impinge every day on the academic life of students. Students who arrive at school hungry, homeless, angry, or depressed about family problems are unable to concentrate on educational tasks. Schools have become increasingly aware that they cannot address the needs of these children alone. The needs of disadvantaged children demand involvement by the family and community in order for schools to be most effective. It is the job of a school to recognize the family as an integral part of the school system and to work with families in devising ways to increase parent participation and encourage community support of schools.

Parent involvement is recognized as a valuable component of a school system, but there is no one type of parent participation that is "right." Since the goal of any parent involvement strategy is to involve as many parents as possible, a range of activities is necessary to suit the needs and preferences of a variety of parents, from participation in the governance of the school, to helping a child with homework, to listening to a child read, to helping a teacher by preparing materials.

Some specific ways in which parents are involved in Success for All schools follow.

Parent Involvement in School Governance

It is an old adage for most community organizers that in order for people to be very involved in an activity they need to "own" it. Ownership is fostered by being involved in the development and implementation of any project. All too often, disadvantaged parents stay away from schools because they do not see the school as "theirs." More often the school is viewed as yet another institution that is trying to do something *to* them. Instead, there needs to be a shift in thinking of the school as an institution that does things *for* and *with* parents. Ownership is greatly fostered if parents see themselves in the role of decision makers in the school.

One key way to have parents be decision makers is to ensure that they have a role in school governance. The creation of a Building Advisory Team is often particularly effective. This team is composed of teachers, administration, and parents. The Team has the mandate to advise the principal on general school direction and planning. Some key tasks for the Building Advisory Team may be:

- to review or develop a schoolwide discipline policy
- to set direction for parent involvement projects
- to evaluate the need for community services onsite
- to review and implement homework guidelines
- to evaluate school climate

In general, the team evaluates the entire school climate and advises on general direction and goals. This team can meet between four and six times per year. When the team has made recommendations, they often work closely with the Solutions Network to ensure that programs are implemented.

In-School Volunteer Support

Parent involvement has traditionally been defined by participation as a volunteer in the school. This is an important, rewarding activity and can make a tremendous difference for financially strapped schools. Parents and other community members can engage in a wide range of activities that enhance school effectiveness.

One of the activities that Success for All schools implement is a Volunteer Listener program. The best way to learn to read is to read. Students in Success for All are encouraged to read at home every night. Solutions Networks actively promote home reading and help to ensure that students bring in forms signed by parents to indicate that they are reading twenty minutes a night. Many schools encourage reading by having an incentive program in which students can earn a small prize or privilege by collecting enough signatures from parents or other adults. Some children may have parents who work at night or are unavailable for after-school reading time. Volunteers at these schools act as listeners for these students during lunch or free time. The volunteers may be parents, community members, local college or high school students, and so on. Many schools use volunteers from their local America Reads programs. Students can read to these volunteers and obtain extra certificates. The job of the volunteer listeners is to listen and to let the child know that he or she is doing a great job. Volunteer listeners are not tutors—they are present to encourage students to read and take pride in their reading. Both the volunteers and the students enjoy the additional one-to-one time during the school day. Students who just need extra practice can utilize the volunteer listeners in the building.

Some schools have used their volunteer listeners to celebrate improvement in reading. Volunteer listeners listen to several children read, and give awards to their reading buddies. In one school, the parents bought and decorated special chairs that the children sit in when they read to the parents.

Some schools have set up a homework room in which parents and teachers help children after school. This is especially beneficial when there are children who find it difficult to complete home assignments or do not have a quiet place to work. Parents can elect to have their child attend the afterschool homework room one or more days per week. Generally, at least one parent and one teacher supervise and provide homework help when needed.

Many schools have implemented a Breakfast Reading Club. Parents are available first thing in the morning to listen to students read and to sign off on Read and Respond forms for students who are unable to read at home.

Other In-School Parent Volunteer Activities

Parents in most schools are encouraged and trained to participate in a wide variety of school activities. Parents help in the classroom, media center, cafeteria, and playground. Often, schools provide training in these areas and certificates for participation. Parents can provide invaluable service in all areas of the school, but most find direct interaction with children more rewarding than clerical tasks or other work that does not involve children.

Teacher and School Communication to Parents

A vital means of fostering the link between parents and schools is to make consistent efforts to increase teacher and school communication to the parent. This communication models for everyone the perception that parents are an integral part of the school community. It helps to cement the mindset for staff as well as parents that families need to be valued, and involved in the daily activities of the school. Parents who perceive the school as working to involve them say that the school is a good one (see Epstein, 1995). Additionally, parents give teachers who frequently contact them high ratings. Fostering this sense of a positive school community is crucial to effective parent-school partnerships.

In many schools, most parents only hear from teachers and schools at the yearly parent-teacher conference or when their child is in trouble. Frequent communication between teacher and parent is "a bad sign," something to be avoided. This sets a negative tone for all interaction. All too often parents feel that "no news is good news" and cringe when the phone rings or school personnel stop by. Particularly for parents whose children are having difficulty, there is a temptation to avoid the school. Of course this only reinforces the school's belief that "the parents who most need to be here never come."

The more frequently parents are contacted, the more parents are involved in the daily functioning of the school, and the more parents are given good news about their child, the more likely they will be involved in the school. In Success for All, school personnel routinely make welcome visits for new students, and conduct fall information visits. Teachers send home Success Cards, newsletters, and good news notes. Informational meetings, often called "Second Cup of Coffee," occur on a regular basis in schools. In some schools, Second Cup of Coffee sessions provide coffee and pastries in the lobby to encourage parents to stop by and chat informally with Solutions Network personnel. In other schools, Second Cup of Coffee has evolved into regular meetings with presentations on topics of concern to families. In all cases, the purpose is to create positive connections with families. Everyone shuns aversive experiences and there is nothing more aversive than hearing a barrage of negative things about your children. The goal of teacher and school communication is to alter the negative cycle and build a more positive connection.

Parent Involvement in Curriculum

Success for All schools place a strong emphasis on involving parents in supporting the curriculum at home. As mentioned earlier, all students are urged to read to someone at home for twenty minutes each evening. Students are given share sheets and paperback books to bring home. To monitor, parents are asked to sign a form indicating that students have done their reading. In the fall, most schools have a Success for All Kick-Off Demonstration Night. This is designed to keep parents informed of the program of instruction that their child is receiving and give them tips on how to support the program at home. The Kick-Off features both students and teachers demonstrating the reading program.

Another standard part of the Solutions Network is Raising Readers. Raising Readers consists of a series of workshops in grades pre-K through second grade designed to familiarize families with the SFA reading program and provide training so that parents can support reading skills at home. The program for prekindergarten and kindergarten is called Books and Breakfast; for first graders, Snacks and Stories; and for second graders, Chips and Chapters. A Spanish version of Raising Readers, Creando Lectores, is also widely used. In the upper grades, Raising Readers provides incentive programs for reading, in a program called Navigating Novels. In addition to the workshop series, take-home libraries are provided with guides and extension questions to facilitate interactive reading at home.

The goal of the workshop series is not only to familiarize parents with the SFA curriculum, but also to provide parents with both the skills and materials needed to promote parent-child interaction around literacy. The content of each series of workshops is based on the curriculum for each grade level. At all grade levels, the key components of the structure are:

- Parents attend with their children.
- Grade level teachers explain and model a key component of the reading curriculum with the children.
- Teachers discuss how to help children at home with the identified skills.
- Parents and children practice with each other the skill modeled by the teacher.
- Parent and child create a "make and take" activity together to facilitate home practice of literacy skills.

A typical Raising Readers workshop would occur first thing in the morning. Beforehand, Family Support personnel are involved in publicizing the workshop. Families receive several flyers, banners are posted outside the school, and sometimes personal calls are made to key classes or families to encourage participation. Generally, families arrive with their children and the school provides coffee and pastries. The teacher models reading with the children and strategies to encourage listening comprehension. The parents use the same materials and practice the identified skills with their own child. Parents and children then are able to take home lending library books to use at home.

Parents have been very enthusiastic about the Raising Readers program. Turnouts have consistently been high. Most schools report between 50–75 percent of parents participate in the workshops. In addition, parents report enjoying the take-home libraries. Typically, even the most high-risk families want to help their children at home, and they report that this program has given them the information and support to do it.

Workshop nights for parents are often held throughout the school year to keep parents involved in curriculum support. Schools have experimented with teaching pre-K parents the STaR program and having parents make "big books" with their child. Additionally, parents have been trained in cooperative learning and have formed teams in which to participate in designing school programs. The more parents can participate in the curriculum, the more enthusiastic they become.

ATTENDANCE SUBCOMMITTEE

The Attendance Subcommittee of the Solutions Network works to improve school attendance. Children need to attend school consistently in order to learn. Successful attendance strategies require a schoolwide approach. Success for All schools that have attendance problems (typically, less than 95 percent daily attendance) implement an attendance program that addresses three fundamental areas: 1) *monitoring,* 2) *intervention,* and 3) *prevention.*

A *monitoring* system is necessary to ensure that all children arrive safely at school and are accounted for early in the day. A comprehensive monitoring system does three things: it increases the safety of students because all students are accounted for early, it creates a school norm that *all* absences are important, and it provides the necessary information for quick intervention on attendance problems. Effective monitoring systems allow school personnel to try to get the targeted child to school the same day. Attendance monitors use a record-keeping system that identifies students having attendance problems at a glance, enabling the school to follow up with at-risk absent children immediately.

Intervention also aims for quick response. SFA recommends hiring an attendance monitor who will be able to go into the community and meet with families. Through the use of this monitor, timely and effective outreach efforts are possible. This is particularly important for areas in which many families may not have phone service. If the monitor finds that an attendance problem does not improve or that a family has a variety of needs, the Solutions Network will provide case planning, further intervention, or referral. If the

Figure 9.2   Sample Attendance Requirements

Supportive ↓ **Punitive**	**1 or 2 unexcused absences**	During a given month of school, monitoring phone calls from the office are placed to the homes of absent students. The attendance clerk attempts to acknowledge the absence with the parent and maintains a record of all successful and unsuccessful attempts to make contact.
	3 absences	The parent receives an intervention phone call from the attendance clerk. A discussion about the attendance concern takes place. The clerk attempts to assist in getting the child to school on time by brainstorming with the parent. The clerk makes a record stating that additional support is needed because the parent remains unresponsive and difficult to engage.
	4 absences	The attendance clerk decides to conduct a home visit. Once again, attendance expectations are expressed. The parent reveals that she works nights and has difficulty waking consistently to get her child to school on time. The clerk and parent brainstorm ways to resolve the problem.
	5 absences	A referral is made to the Intervention Team. The parent is invited to attend a meeting to discuss ways to help the child improve attendance and catch up on missed school and homework assignments.
		A solution/plan is set for the child to leave the house earlier in the morning when the older sister departs for high school. This means the child will arrive 20 minutes early to school and has been assigned as a helper in the art room. The art teacher has agreed to monitor the child to see if the child needs this additional time to complete homework assignments.
	7 absences	After relentless supportive efforts to increase the child's attendance with only minimal improvement, it is appropriate to take a more punitive stance. This may take the form of a referral to the district or court authorities.

Note: This is only an example, as attendance requirements vary in every district. It is important to design a process that follows the supportive continuum and adheres to district guidelines.

behavior causing attendance problems is to be changed, knowledge is not enough. Action is vital. Figure 9.2 shows one school's plan for intervening right away with gradually increasing intensity.

Prevention programs involve setting a schoolwide norm for attendance and putting in place programs that are proactive. Prevention programs include a wide range of incentive programs designed to reward individuals, classrooms, and families whose children consistently attend school. The best solution to any problem is to prevent it from occurring.

INTERVENTION SUBCOMMITTEE

The goal of Success for All's innovative curriculum, teaching strategies, and tutoring is to have every child achieve. However, some students cannot benefit as much as we hope from improved instruction because they have serious family, behavioral, or attendance problems. The Intervention component of the Solutions Network is designed to ensure that these children do not fall "through the cracks." It is here that success for *most* must be translated into success for *all*.

Faculty, administration, or parents may refer a child to the Intervention Subcommittee. Referral forms are distributed early in the school year at parent and faculty meetings, and are always available in the school office. Referrals are sent to the facilitator, who initially screens students to ensure that standard Success for All classroom strategies and tutoring are already in place; the Intervention Subcommittee is not a substitute for good classroom management and effective implementation of the basic instructional model.

Once a referral has been reviewed, the facilitator brings the case to the Intervention Subcommittee. Each case is assessed, a case manager assigned, and an action plan developed. The classroom teacher and the parent must be involved in the development of an action plan. If necessary, the case manager can schedule a meeting with a parent after the initial team assessment. In order to develop effective action plans, the team uses materials that are designed to promote solution-oriented thinking. Teams can become stymied by the endless problems possible in tough cases. Intervention Subcommittees utilize Solution Sheets, which are designed to focus the team on the most important problems that are likely to be solvable by the school, and to move the team forward with small step solutions that involve school, family, and community. This approach necessitates that teams become adept at finding strengths and resources. Intervention Subcommittees are committed to the notion that people change from their strengths, not from their weaknesses. Solutions therefore are often found if teams are adept at identifying strengths and resources as well as problems.

After an action plan has been developed, the referral source is given a copy of the plan and encouraged to notify the team if any progress or deterioration is noticed. The team regularly reviews all cases to ensure that progress is being made or to adjust the action plan so it is more effective.

The process of school-based intervention is diagrammed in Figure 9.3.

COMMUNITY RESOURCES SUBCOMMITTEE

Many students and families in Success for All schools have problems that require services from a range of community agencies. Often, families are unable or unwilling to access these services. Schools and community agencies have found that families are more likely to make use of needed services if the service is provided in a familiar location. Schools have often been particularly successful locations. Onsite services are also helpful for the schools. Quicker intervention with better follow-through and feedback are possible when agencies are available onsite.

Community Resources Subcommittees always try to be aware of local services and make referrals, whether the services are on- or offsite. If a family is without heat or shelter, for example, it is the job of the Community Resources Subcommittee to provide information and help families obtain needed services. This assistance may involve more than just providing a referral. Families often do not obtain community services because of problems with transportation, or because of their inability to negotiate the labyrinth of large bureaucratic institutions. The team may help families with these problems and provides as much assistance as possible to make sure that the family is able to follow through on the referral. The Community Resources Subcommittee members can also check to make sure that referrals led to services and that these services solved the problem. For example, if a child needs eyeglasses, the Community Resources Subcommittee might check to see that the family and social agencies have gone through all the steps that lead to a child in school every day with glasses on. Special attention is also paid to services that may strongly impact student performance. Once a Community Services Subcommittee has assessed these needs, it becomes aware of how to obtain those services in the community and investigates if it is possible to provide some of those services onsite. A few common examples are described in Figure 9.4.

Figure 9.3   Intervention Team Flowchart

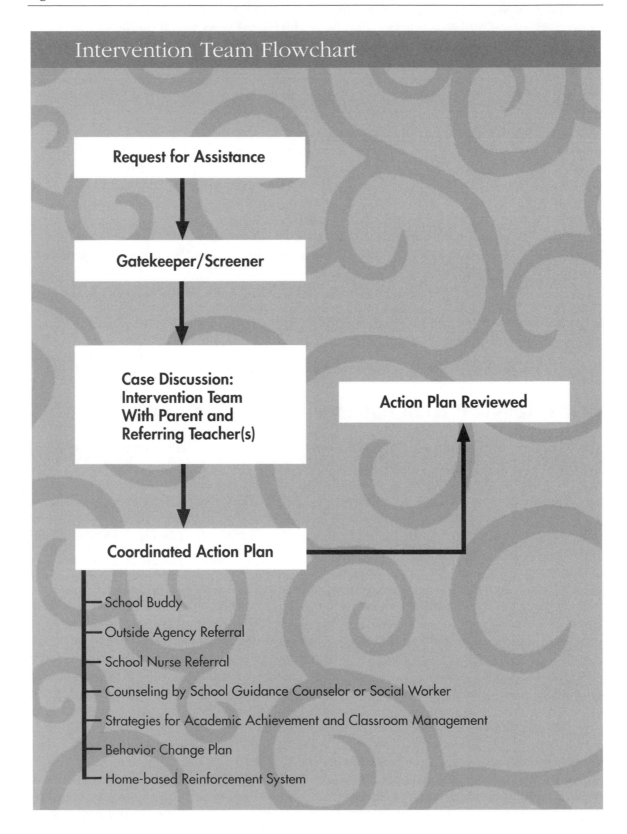

Figure 9.4 Examples for Community Services Subcommittee Activities

Health: Some schools have obtained an onsite nurse practitioner from the local health department to help with sick or injured children and to do injections and physicals. All teams, however, know how to obtain needed medical care for students. In particular, it is important to know how to quickly obtain required shots, glasses, and eye and hearing exams. Community Services Subcommittees try to ensure that these services are provided to students in a timely manner.

Counseling: Some Success for All schools have linked with community family counseling agencies to provide onsite family counseling. One school has linked with a drug and alcohol prevention program to provide groups for children of substance abusers. Community mental health programs are increasingly trying to provide some satellite services at schools and may have programs in the school area. Community Services Subcommittees usually know about counseling programs in the community, particularly programs with no fee or sliding fee scales.

Food: If a child is hungry he can't learn. Some schools link with local agencies to become food distribution sites for the community. Parents who have rarely been in the school building come regularly to pick up food and thereby become acquainted with the school.

Shelter: Providing housing to needy families is problematic in most cities. Solutions Networks usually know the emergency shelters in town and try to work with the family in order to support the child while a family is homeless or in temporary living situations. It is better for a student to be supported at his old school while the family is trying to obtain permanent housing, as the fewer upheavals for the student the better during this time. Community Resources Subcommittees have been instrumental in helping to plan transportation and additional supports for homeless students.

Tutoring: SFA schools work with local universities, high schools, retirement groups, and churches in order to obtain additional tutoring for their students. These volunteers may serve as listeners or, if they are able to devote enough time, they may tutor marginal students or older students who do not qualify for Success for All tutoring. Tutoring and volunteer listening are most effective if they are onsite, and often these groups are happy to provide tutoring at the school. If a team is going to begin to make community linkages, this is often a good place to start.

Literacy: Parent literacy affects the academic success of students. Several Success for All schools have begun to work with local literacy groups to provide parent literacy programs onsite. In general, parents involved in these school-based sites also participate in volunteer activities during the school day. Some schools also offer afterschool computer programs for parents and children.

Business Linkages: Local businesses have become more involved in supporting education over the last few years. Business leaders are increasingly aware that schools produce the workers of tomorrow and that the effectiveness of their own enterprises depends on the ability of schools to deliver quality employees. Consequently, both small and large businesses have made real commitments to local schools. Success for All schools have found that effective partnerships have occurred when schools *energetically* approach local business and structure some *specific* ways in which the business partner can help. Sometimes effective linkages fail to develop because the partner is unclear about how much of a commitment is being made and what sort of help is needed. Just asking a business to be a partner and to help the school, or just asking for money, may be too vague. A clearly organized presentation of needs, some suggested ideas by the school of projects that the business partner could participate in, and ways to highlight the partnership to the community have generally been more successful approaches. Some examples of activities of local business involvement in Success for All schools are:

- Providing incentives for attendance or reading. Fast food restaurants, local movie rental stores, and convenience stores have often been large providers of small incentives for school programs.
- Providing additional tutoring for students.
- Donating furniture for parent rooms or reading corners.
- Providing mentorship programs or afterschool club activities.
- Providing public relations material for parents and community for special school projects. For example, local photographers have taken pictures of students involved in Success for All activities. Partners have provided t-shirts or buttons to publicize special projects to families as part of outreach education about Success for All.

BEHAVIOR MANAGEMENT SUBCOMMITTEE AND GETTING ALONG TOGETHER: A SOCIAL PROBLEM-SOLVING CURRICULUM

The ability to think critically and solve interpersonal problems peacefully is an essential skill. Preparing children to become productive adults means not only providing excellent academic instruction but also reinforcing the social problem-solving skills that are necessary for lifelong success. Teamwork, with its concomitant demands for sophisticated negotiation and decision making, is not only a cornerstone of Success for All but also a crucial skill in the modern workplace. In a world that is increasingly interconnected and a society that is multicultural, the ability to appreciate diversity, to listen accurately to others, and to solve differences peacefully is essential. The Getting Along Together curriculum provides students with instruction and practice in all these social problem-solving skills.

Children who have the ability to master academic material may end up failing because they lack the problem-solving skills necessary to successfully adjust to the school setting. In order to achieve success for these students, it is critical to teach students these skills early in their school careers. Overtly teaching the behaviors to be successful problem solvers rather than punishing those students who fall short in this skill is crucial for both prevention and early intervention of problems that can lead to school failure.

The Getting Along Together program provides three components for students to develop problem-solving skills. (1) "Learn About It" is a set of classroom lessons focusing on key social problem-solving skills that are designed for the first two weeks of the school year, while students are being assessed for placement in reading groups. (2) "Think It Through" is a set of guide sheets designed to help students begin to "self-talk" their way through interpersonal problems. (3) "Talk It Out" utilizes a problem-solving model called the Peace Path, which enables students to talk out their difficulties in a positive way either at a weekly Class Council meeting, at a Roundtable at the back of the classroom, or at other points throughout the school day.

Learn About It

There are two weeks of social problem-solving units available for all grades. The first week focuses on listening skills and the second week on conflict resolution. These lessons are designed to be taught within the reading time block. Each lesson is linked to a StaR or Listening Comprehension book. The teacher uses these books to highlight a particular social problem-solving skill and conduct a team activity designed to provide students with an opportunity to practice the skill. For example, each lesson provides opportunities for students to reflect on the skills they are learning, and homework to be able to practice those skills at home.

Think It Through

Students experiencing a problem in school need opportunities to calm down, to think through their behavior, and to make a well-reasoned decision about future behavior. Think It Through sheets (see Figure 9.5) are designed to give students time to reflect and guide them through a self-talk process that encourages them to develop prosocial decision-making skills. Think It Through sheets are always kept at the back of the classroom at the Roundtable. Schools often also keep them in the guidance office, or in the main office for students experiencing difficulty throughout the day. In addition, bus

Figure 9.5   Think It Through Sheet

Think It Through

Conflict Stoppers

☆ Share

What is the problem?

☆ Laugh It Off

☆ Take Turns

What is my "I" Message?

☆ Flip a Coin

☆ Apologize

☆ Wait Until Later

☆ Ignore

How does the other person feel?

☆ Get Help

☆ Make Amends

What could I do differently to solve the problem?

☆ Talk It Out

☆ Compromise

☆ New Idea

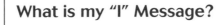

drivers, cafeteria workers, and other school personnel may keep these sheets to dispense to students if necessary. The more opportunities a student has to practice talking themselves through a problem in a positive way, the more automatic and accomplished the skill becomes.

Talk It Out

There are two structured opportunities for students to practice a conflict resolution process. Once a week every teacher holds a brief Class Council meeting. This is an opportunity for both the teacher and the students to identify positive classroom behaviors and solve classroom problems. Secondly, as discussed in the previous section, at the back of every classroom there is a designated Roundtable. Along with the Think It Through sheets that are kept at the Roundtable, there is a suggestion box for topics at the weekly Class Council meeting. Students who are experiencing a problem with another student or in the class can go to the Roundtable at any time, fill out a Think It Through sheet, and have an opportunity to talk through their difficulties.

Whether at a Class Council meeting or at the Roundtable, students are taught to use a conflict resolution process called the Peace Path (see Figure 9.6). The Peace Path is designed to be an engaging, concrete way for students to practice step by step conflict resolution skills. Initially, the Peace Path is placed on the floor and students physically walk through the process (see Figure 9.6). Older students may dispense with the Peace Path but incorporate just the step by step Peace Path discussion (see Figure 9.7). In any case, students are taught and provided ongoing practice in this win-win conflict resolution model.

Many schools have expanded this process and used the Peace Path throughout the building. Schools have painted Peace Paths on the playground or placed them in the gym or cafeteria. Schools that provide consistent and relentless modeling of this process have seen students who may have arrived at school with limited social problem-solving skills make real gains and become positive and productive team members.

The Solutions Network has a Behavior Management Subcommittee that monitors school climate, focuses on the effectiveness of the Getting Along Together curriculum, and plans behavior management strategies for schoolwide use. This subcommittee monitors suspension and office referral rates in the school to determine what preventive programming might most assist the school to develop a positive and orderly climate.

Figure 9.6   Step by Step Peace Path

The Peace Path

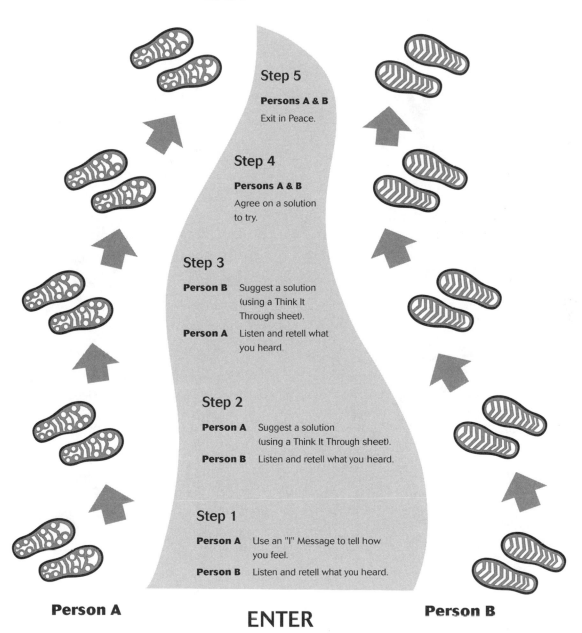

EXIT

Step 5

Persons A & B
Exit in Peace.

Step 4

Persons A & B
Agree on a solution to try.

Step 3

Person B   Suggest a solution (using a Think It Through sheet).

Person A   Listen and retell what you heard.

Step 2

Person A   Suggest a solution (using a Think It Through sheet).

Person B   Listen and retell what you heard.

Step 1

Person A   Use an "I" Message to tell how you feel.

Person B   Listen and retell what you heard.

Person A   ENTER   **Person B**

Figure 9.7   Peace Path Discussion

The Peace Path

Step 5

BLUE   Exit in Peace.

RED   Exit in Peace.

Step 4

BLUE   Agree to try the solution.

RED   Agree to try the solution.

Step 3

BLUE   Suggest a solution
(using a Think It Through sheet).

RED   Listen and retell what you heard.

Step 2

RED   Suggest a solution
(using a Think It Through sheet).

BLUE   Listen and retell what you heard.

Step 1

RED   Use an "I" Message to tell
how you feel.

BLUE   Listen and retell what you heard.

10

Research on Success for All

One of the guiding principles in the development of Success for All is an emphasis on rigorous evaluation. The elements of the program are themselves derived from current research on reading and writing, early childhood, second language learning, special education, parent involvement, professional development, and school change, among many others. However, it is not enough for a program to be based on good research; it must also be rigorously and repeatedly evaluated in many schools over meaningful periods of time in comparison to similar control schools.

Success for All is arguably the most extensively evaluated school reform model ever to exist. It was originally conceived, developed, and evaluated at Johns Hopkins University within a research center, currently called the Center for Data-Driven Reform in Education, with federal funding that required extensive and rigorous evaluation. Further, the majority of studies on Success for All have been carried out by researchers who are not at Johns Hopkins University or the Success for All Foundation. Experimental-control comparisons have been made by researchers at eighteen universities and research institutions other than Johns Hopkins, both within the U.S. and in five other countries. Taken together, more than fifty studies have compared Success for All and control schools on individually administered standardized tests, such as the Woodcock and Gray Oral Reading Test, and on state accountability measures.

INDEPENDENT REVIEWS

A number of independent reviews of research on comprehensive school reform and reading programs have all concluded that Success for All is among the most successfully evaluated of programs. Most recently, Success for All was cited as one of only two elementary comprehensive designs that met the highest standards for research given in a review of twenty-two programs done by the Comprehensive School Reform Quality Center at the American Institutes for Research (Comprehensive School Reform Quality Center [CSRQ], 2006). The CSRQ review identified thirty-one "convincing" studies of Success for All, ten for Direct Instruction, and no more than six for any other program. The same conclusion was reached in an earlier American Institutes for Research (AIR) review (Herman, 1999) and in studies commissioned by the Fordham Foundation (Traub, 1999) and the Milliken Family Foundation (Schacter, 1999). A meta-analysis of research on twenty-nine comprehensive school reforms by Borman, Hewes, Overman, and Brown (2003) listed Success for All among three CSR models with "strongest evidence of effectiveness."

LONGITUDINAL STUDIES

Longitudinal experiments evaluating SFA have been carried out since the earliest program implementations in Baltimore and Philadelphia (see Borman & Hewes, 2003; Madden, Slavin, Karweit, Dolan, & Wasik, 1993). Later, third-party evaluators at the University of Memphis added evaluations in many districts across the U.S. (e.g., Ross, Sanders, & Wright, 1998; Ross & Smith, 2001; Ross, Smith, & Casey, 1995). Studies focusing on English language learners in California have been conducted by researchers at WestEd, a federally funded regional educational laboratory (e.g., Livingston & Flaherty, 1997). Each of these evaluations compared Success for All schools to comparison schools on measures of reading performance, starting with cohorts in kindergarten or first grade and following these students as long as possible (details of the evaluation design appear below). Several studies were able to follow Success for All schools for many years. Data comparing matched SFA and traditional control schools on individual reading measures have been collected from schools in many U.S. districts, and other studies have compared Success for All to a variety of alternative reform models, have compared full and partial implementations of SFA, and have made other comparisons. Most recently, a three-year national randomized experiment involving thirty-five schools has compared SFA and control schools (Borman et al., 2007). In addition, there have been many studies involving group-administered standardized tests including both national norm-referenced tests and state criterion-referenced tests used in state accountability programs. Experimental-control comparisons have also been carried out in Canada, England, Australia, and Israel (Slavin & Madden, 2001).

The largest number of studies has compared the achievement of students in Success for All schools to that of children in matched comparison schools using traditional methods, including locally developed Title I reforms.

A common evaluation design, with variations due to local circumstances, was used in a foundational set of Success for All evaluations carried out by researchers at Johns Hopkins University, the University of Memphis, and WestEd. Each Success for All school was matched with a control school that was similar in poverty level (percent of students qualifying for free lunch), historical achievement level, ethnicity, and other factors. Schools were also matched on district-administered standardized test scores given in kindergarten or on Peabody Picture Vocabulary Test (PPVT) scores given by the evaluators in the fall of kindergarten or first grade.

The measures used in these evaluations were as follows:

1. *Woodcock Reading Mastery Test.* Three Woodcock scales—Word Identification, Word Attack, and Passage Comprehension—were individually administered to students

by trained testers. Word Identification assesses recognition of common sight words, Word Attack assesses phonetic synthesis skills, and Passage Comprehension assesses comprehension in context. Students in Spanish bilingual programs were given the Spanish versions of these scales.

2. *Durrell Analysis of Reading Difficulty.* The Durrell Oral Reading scale was also individually administered to students in Grades 1–3 in some studies. It presents a series of graded reading passages which students read aloud, followed by comprehension questions.

3. *Gray Oral Reading Test.* Comprehension and passage scores from the Gray Oral Reading Test were obtained in some studies from students in Grades 4–5.

Analyses of covariance with pretests as covariates were used to compare raw scores in all evaluations, and separate analyses were conducted for students in general and, in many studies, for students in the lowest 25 percent of their grades at pretest.

Each of the evaluations summarized in this chapter follows children who began in Success for All in first grade or earlier, in comparison to children who had attended the control school over the same period. Students who start in it after first grade are not considered to have received the full treatment (although they are of course served within the schools).

READING OUTCOMES

National Randomized Evaluation of Success for All

The definitive evaluation of the reading outcomes of Success for All was a U.S. Department of Education–funded evaluation (Borman et al., 2005a, 2005b, 2007) involving thirty-five Title I schools throughout the U.S. These schools were randomly assigned to use Success for All or to continue with their existing reading programs in Grades K–2. At the end of the three-year study, children in the Success for All schools were achieving at significantly higher levels than control students on all three measures, using conservative hierarchical linear modeling analyses with school as the unit of analysis. In effect sizes (difference in adjusted posttests divided by unadjusted standard deviations), the differences were ES = +0.33 for Word Attack, ES = +0.22 for Word Identification, and ES = +0.21 for Passage Comprehension.

This study is of particular importance for several reasons. First, the use of random assignment to conditions eliminates selection bias (the possibility that schools that chose SFA might have been better schools than the control schools). Second, the large sample size allowed for the use of hierarchical linear modeling (HLM), which uses the school as the unit of analysis. This is the appropriate analysis for schoolwide interventions (all previous studies used student as the unit of analysis). Third, the size of the evaluation is of great importance for the study's policy impact. In small studies, there is always the possibility that researchers can ensure high-quality implementations. Cronbach et al. (1980) called this "the superrealization" of a program's impact, where the program is evaluated at a level of quality beyond what could be achieved at a large scale. In the Borman et al. (2007) study, implementation of SFA was actually found to be of lower quality than that typical of SFA schools. A study on such a large scale is a good representation of the likely policy effect, or what would be expected if a district or state implemented the program on a broad scale. For example, the Borman et al. (2007) findings imply that if many schools serving African American or Hispanic students experienced Success for All, the minority-white achievement gap would be reduced by half.

Matched Longitudinal Studies

In the 1990s, researchers at Johns Hopkins University and other research institutions carried out a series of longitudinal matched studies to evaluate Success for All. A common design and set of measures was used for these studies, as noted above. Schools in thirteen districts across the country were involved.

The results of the matched experiments evaluating Success for All are summarized in Figure 10.1 for each grade level, Grades 1–5, and for follow-up measures into Grades 6 and 7. The analyses average cohort means for experimental and control schools. A cohort is all students at a given grade level in a given year. For example, the Grade 1 graph compares 68 experimental to 68 control cohorts, with cohort (50–150 students) as the unit of analysis. In other words, each bar is a mean of scores from more than 6000 students. Grade equivalents are based on the means, and are only presented for their informational value. No analyses were done using grade equivalents.

Combining across studies, statistically significant ($p = .05$ or better) positive effects of Success for All (compared to controls) were found on every measure at every grade level, 1–5 (Slavin & Madden, 1993). For students in general, effect sizes averaged around a half standard deviation at all grade levels. Effects were somewhat higher than this for the Woodcock Word Attack scale in first and second grades, but in Grades 3–5 effect sizes were more or less equivalent on all aspects of reading. Consistently, effect sizes for students in the lowest 25 percent of their grades were particularly positive, ranging from ES = +1.03 in first grade to ES = +1.68 in fourth grade. Again, cohort-level analyses found statistically significant differences favoring low achievers in Success for All on every measure at every grade level. A follow-up study of Baltimore schools found that positive program effects continued into Grade 6 (ES = +0.54) and Grade 7 (ES = +0.42), when students were in middle schools.

Recent third-party matched studies have found similar outcomes to those of the earlier studies. In a longitudinal evaluation of many CSR models, American Institutes for Research researchers Aladjem and Borman (2006) found that Success for All was the only program to find consistently positive effects. The Louisville (KY) district evaluated SFA and also found significant positive effects (Muñoz & Dossett, 2004).

LONG-TERM OUTCOMES

Borman and Hewes (2003) carried out a longitudinal study of children from five Success for All and five control schools in Baltimore. They located children citywide who had attended these schools in first grade and remained from one to six years (mean = 3.8 years). At posttest, students who had been promoted each year would have been in the eighth grade, having been out of a Success for All school for at least three years.

Long-term differences were found on achievement, retentions, and special education placements. In achievement, former SFA students still scored significantly better than controls on standardized, district-administered Comprehensive Test of Basic Skills (CTBS) reading scores (ES = +0.29, $p < .001$). Surprisingly, there was also a small difference favoring the former SFA students in math (ES = +0.11, $p < .05$), even though mathematics was not part of the intervention.

Another long-term distinction found Success for All students as far less likely to have been retained in elementary school, with 9 percent of SFA students and 23 percent of control students retained at least once by fifth grade (ES = +0.27, $p < .001$). Similarly, control

Figure 10.1   Comparison of Success for All and Control Schools in Mean Reading Grade Equivalents and Effect Sizes, 1988–1999

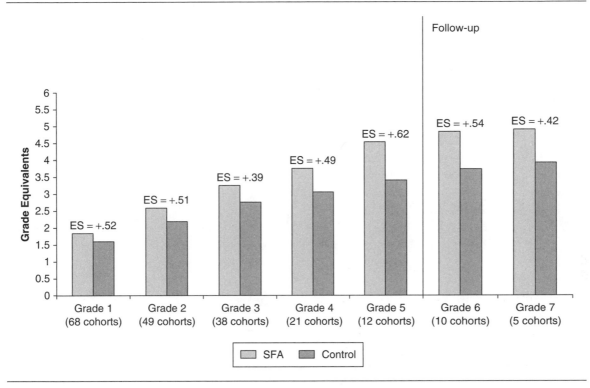

students spent 50 percent more time in special education, on average, than SFA students (ES = +0.18, $p < .001$).

The importance of the Borman & Hewes (2003) study is in its finding that at entry to high school, former Success for All students were in much better shape than control students. The best predictors of high school success are reading achievement, avoidance of retention, and special education placements. Success for All students were substantially higher on all of these measures.

QUALITY AND COMPLETENESS OF IMPLEMENTATION

Not surprisingly, effects of Success for All are strongly related to the quality and completeness of implementation. In Houston, a large study by Nunnery et al. (1996) found that schools implementing all program components obtained better results (compared to controls) than did schools implementing the program to a moderate or minimal degree.

In this study, forty-six school staffs were allowed to select the level of implementation they wanted to achieve. Some adopted the full model, as ordinarily required; some adopted a partial model; and some adopted only the reading program, with few if any tutors, and half-time facilitators or no facilitators. Many of the schools used the Spanish bilingual form of SFA and were assessed in Spanish.

Figure 10.2   Houston Independent School District, 1996 First Grade Effect Sizes by
Implementation Level—English

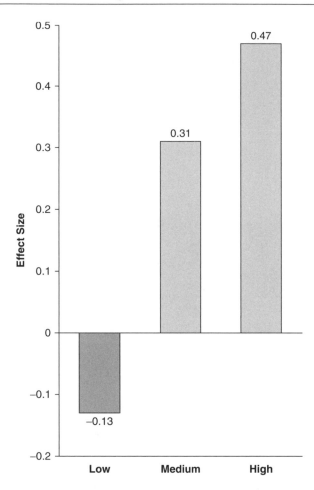

Figures 10.2 and 10.3 summarize the results. The figures show effect sizes comparing SFA to control schools on individually administered measures. On the English measure (Figure 10.2), effect sizes were very positive for the schools using the full program (ES = +0.47), less positive for those with a medium degree of implementation (ES = +0.31), but for those implementing the fewest program elements, effect sizes were slightly negative (ES = –0.13), indicating that the control groups achieved somewhat better scores. Among schools teaching in Spanish, there were too few certified teacher-tutors for any school to qualify as a high implementer (due to a shortage of teachers). However, medium implementers scored very well (ES = +.31), while low implementers scored lower (ES = +.19) (see Figure 10.3).

A Memphis study (Ross, Smith, Lewis, & Nunnery, 1996; Ross, Smith, & Nunnery, 1998) compared the achievement of eight Success for All schools to that of four schools using other restructuring designs, matched on socioeconomic status and Peabody Picture Vocabulary Test (PPVT) scores. Each pair of SFA schools had one school rated by observers as a high implementer, and one rated as a low implementer. In the 1996 cohort, first grade results depended entirely on implementation quality. Averaging across the four Woodcock and Durrell scales, every comparison showed high-implementation SFA

Figure 10.3   Houston Independent School District, 1996 First Grade Effect Sizes by Implementation Category—Spanish

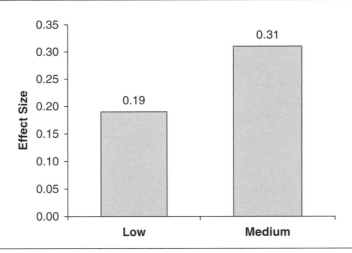

schools scored higher than their comparison schools, while low-implementation SFA schools scored lower (Ross, Smith, et al., 1996). However, by second grade, Success for All schools taken together exceeded comparison schools, on average, and there was less of a clear relationship with the original implementation ratings, perhaps because implementation quality changed over the two-year period. Similarly, the 1997 first grade cohort did not show a clear pattern with respect to quality of implementation.

Cooper, Slavin, and Madden (1998), in an interview study, found that high-quality implementations of Success for All depended on many factors, including district and principal support, participation in national and local networks, adequacy of resources, and genuine buy-in at the outset on the part of all teachers.

EFFECTS ON DISTRICT-ADMINISTERED STANDARDIZED TESTS

The formal evaluations of Success for All have relied on individually administered assessments of reading. The Woodcock and Durrell scales used in these assessments are far more accurate than district-administered tests, and are much more sensitive to real reading gains. They allow testers to hear children actually reading the material of increasing difficulty and to respond to questions about what they have read. The Woodcock and Durrell are themselves nationally standardized tests, and produce norms (e.g., percentiles, Normal Curve Equivalents [NCEs] and grade equivalents) just like any other standardized measure.

However, educators often want to know the effects of innovative programs on the kinds of group-administered standardized tests for which they are usually held accountable. To obtain this information, researchers have often analyzed standardized or state criterion-referenced test data comparing students in experimental and control schools. The following sections briefly summarize findings from these types of evaluations.

Memphis

One of the most important early independent evaluations of Success for All is a study carried out by researchers at the University of Tennessee–Knoxville for the Tennessee State Department of Education (Ross, Sanders, Wright, & Stringfield, 1998). William Sanders, the architect of the Tennessee Value-Added Assessment System (TVAAS), carried out the analysis. The TVAAS gives each school an expected gain, based primarily on school poverty levels, and compares it to actual scores on the Tennessee Comprehensive Assessment Program (TCAP). TVAAS scores above 100 indicate gains in excess of expectations; those below 100 indicate the opposite. Sanders compared TVAAS scores in eight Memphis Success for All schools to those in a) matched comparison schools, and b) all Memphis schools.

Figure 10.4 summarizes the results for all subjects assessed. At pretest, the Success for All schools were lower than both comparison groups on TVAAS. However, after two years, they performed significantly better than comparison schools in reading, language, science, and social studies.

A third-year evaluation found that Success for All schools averaged the greatest gains and highest levels on the TVAAS of six restructuring designs (Co-nect, Accelerated Schools, Audrey Cohen College, ATLAS, and Expeditionary Learning), as well as exceeding controls, averaging across all subjects (Ross, Wang, Sanders, Wright, & Stringfield, 1999).

An earlier study of Success for All schools in Memphis also showed positive effects on the TCAP. This was a longitudinal study of three Success for All and three control schools carried out by Ross, Smith, and Casey (1995). On average, Success for All schools exceeded controls on TCAP reading by an effect size of +0.38 in first grade and +0.45 in second grade.

Figure 10.4   Percent of Expected Gain on TVAAS for Roots & Wings, Control, and Other Memphis Schools, Grades 2–5, 1997

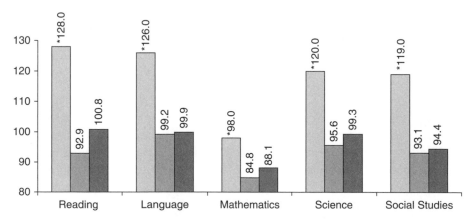

*Roots & Wings scores significantly higher than those of controls or others ($p < .05$).
Tennessee Value-Added Assessment System (TVAAS) scores analyzed by William Sanders for the Tennessee State Department of Education. See Ross, Sanders, and Wright, 1998.

State of Texas

From 1994 to 2003, the state of Texas administered the Texas Assessment of Academic Success, or TAAS, in Grades 3, 4, and 5. It also assessed fourth grade reading in 1993. Texas was one of the first states to put its scores for every school every year on the Internet, making it possible to compare TAAS gains made by Success for All schools throughout the state to gains in the state as a whole. The importance of this is that it makes possible an independent assessment of program outcomes.

Reading data are summarized in Figure 10.5 (adapted from Hurley, Chamberlain, Slavin, & Madden, 2001). The data, from 117 high-poverty Title I schools using Success for All throughout the state, are organized according to the year the program began, focusing on gains from the spring before program implementation to spring 1998, averaged across Grades 3–5. The gains for Success for All cohorts are compared to average gains in all other schools throughout the state over the same time periods. Because TAAS scores, expressed as the percent of students meeting minimum expectations, had been gradually rising statewide, gains for Success for All and other schools were larger the longer the time period involved. However, Success for All schools consistently gained more than other schools, with the relative advantage increasing with each year in the program. All differences between SFA and state gains were statistically significant ($p < .05$), using school means as the unit of analysis.

In raw scores, rather than gains, Success for All schools, far more impoverished than the state average, started far below state averages and then increased to near equality with state averages. For example, the 1993 cohort (Grade 4 only, as this was the only grade tested in 1993) began 32.5 percentile points behind the state in percent meeting minimum standards on TAAS reading, but five years later was nearly indistinguishable from the state (88.1 percent passing for the state vs. 85.0 percent for forty-six SFA schools). Similar patterns were seen for the 1994, 1995, and 1996 cohorts, all of which started far below state means and, as of 1998, were within 1.4 to 3.8 percentile points of state means. The only cohort that did not close the gap to this extent was the latest, the 1997 cohort (35 schools). This cohort started 17.3 percentile points behind the state and, one year later, was 12.8 points behind, a real improvement but not to virtual equality.

Figure 10.5   Gains From Preimplementation Year to 1998, Success for All Versus Texas Means, Texas Assessment of Academic Success, Reading, Grades 3–5

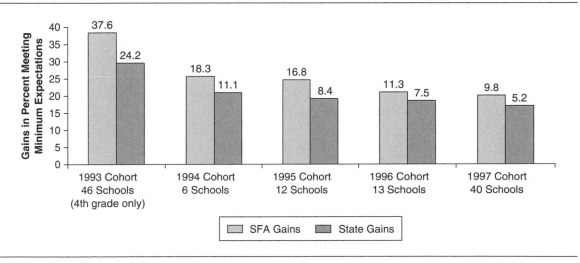

Houston, Texas

In Houston, Success for All was begun on a large scale in 1995. Forty-six schools adopted Success for All as part of a study (Nunnery et al., 1996) in which they were allowed to implement either the full program, the reading program only, or something in between. As noted earlier, the full-implementation schools obtained excellent outcomes on individually administered tests given to subsamples, in comparison to control schools, while moderate implementation schools obtained less positive outcomes and low-implementation schools did not differ from controls (recall Figures 10.2 and 10.3).

Baltimore, Maryland

A longitudinal study in Baltimore from 1987–1993 collected CTBS scores on the original five Success for All and control schools (Madden, Slavin, Karweit, Dolan & Wasik, 1993). On average, Success for All schools exceeded control schools at every grade level. The differences were statistically and educationally significant. By fifth grade, Success for All students were performing 75 percent of a grade equivalent ahead of controls (ES = +0.45) on CTBS Total Reading scores (see Slavin, Madden et al., 1994).

Fort Wayne, Indiana

An evaluation of two schools in Fort Wayne, Indiana (Ross, Smith, & Casey, 1995) found positive effects of Success for All on the reading comprehension scale of the ISTEP, Indiana's norm-referenced achievement test. In first grade, the effect size was +0.49 for students in general and +1.13 for the lowest-performing 25 percent. In second grade, effect sizes were +0.64, and in third grade, ES = +.13.

Louisville, Kentucky

A study carried out by the Jefferson County Public Schools (Muñoz & Dossett, 2004) evaluated Success for All in three experimental and three matched control schools in Louisville, Kentucky, over a four-year period. The SFA schools made twice the gains as control schools in normal curve equivalent scores (ES = +0.11, $p < .05$). SFA schools also made greater gains in attendance, and substantially reduced out-of-school suspensions. They also had higher teacher ratings of perceptions of educational quality and job satisfaction and higher student ratings of school climate and educational quality.

New York City's Chancellor's District

From 1996–2003, the New York City Public Schools established a special citywide region, called the Chancellor's District, for the very lowest-achieving elementary and middle schools in the city. These schools implemented Success for All in reading, Everyday Mathematics in math, and had significant resources to provide high-quality professional development to teachers. Independent researchers at New York University did an evaluation of the outcomes of this program (Phenix, Siegel, Zaltsman, & Fruchter, 2004), and the results indicated significantly greater gains on state English Language Arts scores for the Chancellor's District schools than for matched control schools. There were no differences in mathematics. The Chancellor's District included elements in addition to Success for All, so the study is not purely an SFA evaluation, but the findings do support the use of Success for All as a key component of an intensive approach to accelerating achievement in very difficult urban schools.

Los Angeles

A study by Mason (2005) of five comprehensive school reform models in Los Angeles found that only Success for All significantly improved students' achievement on the Stanford Achievement Test. Across eight SFA schools, students who experienced SFA starting in the first or second grade gained significantly more than those in matched control schools in reading and language arts. Students who participated in SFA for all three years of the study made particularly substantial gains compared to controls. As was found in the Borman and Hewes (2003) long-term follow-up study, there were also small positive effects on mathematics measures, even though math was not part of the SFA intervention. However, students who started SFA after second grade did not experience significant effects.

INTERNATIONAL EVALUATIONS OF SUCCESS FOR ALL ADAPTATIONS

Several studies have assessed the effects of adaptations of Success for All in countries outside of the U.S. These adaptations have ranged from relatively minor adjustments to accommodate political and funding requirements in Canada and England to more significant adaptations in Mexico, Australia, and Israel.

The Canadian study (Chambers, Abrami, & Morrison, 2001) involved one school in Montreal, which was compared to a matched control school on individually administered reading measures. Results indicated significantly better reading performance in the Success for All school than in the control school both for students with special needs (a large proportion of the SFA students) and for other students. Similarly, a study of five SFA schools in Nottingham, England, found that Success for All students gained more in reading than did students in a previous cohort, before the program was introduced, and gained more on Key Stage 1 (age 7) and Key Stage 2 (age 11) reading tests than did English schools overall (Harris, Hopkins, Youngman, & Wordsworth, 2001; Hopkins, Youngman, Harris, & Wordsworth, 1999). Later studies by Russ & Harris (2005) also found positive effects of the program on Key Stage 2 performance. Combining data from all sixteen SFA schools in England, Slavin, Wordsworth, and Jones-Hill (2005) found that Year 6 students in SFA schools gained 13.4 percentage points on Key Stage 2 from 2001 to 2004, while other schools in England gained 3.0 percentage points.

Because of language and cultural differences, the most significant adaptation of Success for All was made to use the program in Israel with both Hebrew-speaking children in Jewish schools and Arabic-speaking children in Israeli Arab schools, all in or near the northern city of Acre. The implementation involved community interventions focusing on parent involvement, integrated services, and other aspects in addition to the adapted Success for All model. In comparison to control groups, Success for All first graders performed at significantly higher levels on tests of reading and writing (Hertz-Lazarowitz, 2001).

Australian researchers created a substantially simplified adaptation of Success for All, which they called Schoolwide Early Language and Literacy (SWELL). SWELL used instructional procedures much like those used in Success for All, but used books adapted for the Australian context. Only the early grades were involved. Schools did not have full-time facilitators or family support programs, and they may or may not have provided any tutoring. Two studies of SWELL found positive effects of the program on reading performance in comparison to control groups and to Reading Recovery schools (Center, Freeman, & Robertson, 2001; Center, Freeman, Mok, & Robertson, 1997).

Finally, a Mexican study in Juarez, near El Paso, Texas, found substantial gains on Spanish reading tests in three schools implementing an adaptation of Success for All (Calderón, 2001).

The international studies of programs adapted from Success for All have importance in themselves, of course, but also demonstrate that the principles on which Success for All are based transfer to other languages, cultures, and political systems. In addition, they provide third-party evaluations of Success for All in diverse contexts, strengthening the research base for Success for All principles and practices.

THE SUCCESS FOR ALL MIDDLE SCHOOL

The Success for All Middle School has been evaluated in two studies. The first was a matched study by Slavin, Daniels, and Madden (2005). In this study, seven SFA middle schools in six states were compared over three years to matched schools in the same states. Reading results at the school level from 2001 to 2004 were obtained from state Web sites. Analyses compared achievement gains on state high-stakes reading measures in SFA middle schools to those in the comparison schools.

Students in the SFA middle schools gained significantly more on their state reading assessments than did students in comparison schools. In many cases, these differences were striking. For example, at Tahola School, a K–12 school primarily serving Native American students in rural Washington State, the Success for All seventh graders gained 95.5 percentage points, to 100 percent of students meeting standards on the Washington Assessment of Student Learning (WASL). The comparison school gained 18.4 percentage points, while the state average gained 20.7 percentage points. Similarly, seventh graders at Richards Middle School in rural Missouri gained 31.5 percentage points for students passing the Missouri Assessment Program (MAP) Reading Scale, while a matched control school gained 10.3 points and the state declined by 2.4 points.

Across the seven SFA schools, students gained an average of 24.6 percentage points on state reading tests, far better than the gain of 2.2 percentage points in matched control schools and the average gain made by middle schools in their respective states, 4.2 percentage points.

Table 10.1 summarizes the gains in each SFA school, its matched control, and its state.

A randomized evaluation of The Reading Edge, the reading component of the SFA Middle School, was carried out by Chamberlain, Daniels, Madden, and Slavin (2007a, 2007b) and Slavin, Chamberlain, Daniels, and Madden (2008). It involved two rural schools in West Virginia and Florida. Two successive cohorts of sixth graders in the schools were randomly assigned to The Reading Edge or to continue in a traditional reading program. Students were pre- and posttested on the Gates-McGinitie reading test. Combining across cohorts, there were significant differences favoring The Reading Edge students on Gates Total and on Comprehension and Vocabulary.

Table 10.1 Gains in Percent of Students Passing State Reading Tests in Success for All and Control Middle Schools, 2001–2004

School (State)	Measure	Grades Tested	Gains in Percent Passing		
			SFA	Control	State
Washington	WASL	7	+95.5	+18.4	+20.7
Missouri	MAP	7	+31.5	+10.3	+2.4
Indiana—pair 1	ISTEP	6, 8	+9.0	+0.5	+7.0
Indiana—pair 2	ISTEP	6, 8	+15.5	+4.0	+7.0
Mississippi	MCT	6, 7	+5.8	+2.3	+8.1
Arizona	AIMS	8	+3.0	−12.0	−6.0
Louisiana	LEAP	8	+12.0	−8.0	−5.0
Means*			+24.6	+2.2	+4.2

*Means across different state assessments should be interpreted cautiously.

ROOTS & WINGS

Roots & Wings (Slavin & Madden, 2000) was a term used for a program that added to Success for All programs in math, science, and social studies. Studies of Roots & Wings were carried out in four schools in rural southern Maryland and one school in San Antonio, Texas. In both cases, evaluations compared students' gains on state assessments to those for their respective states as a whole.

In the Maryland evaluation, the Roots & Wings schools served populations that were significantly more disadvantaged than state averages. They averaged 48 percent free and reduced-price lunch eligibility, compared to 30 percent for the state. The assessment tracked growth over time on the Maryland School Performance Assessment Program (MSPAP), compared to growth in the state as a whole. The MSPAP was a performance measure on which students are asked to solve complex problems, set up experiments, write in various genres, and read extended text. It used matrix sampling, which means that different students take different forms of the test.

In both third and fifth grade assessments in all subjects tested (reading, language, writing, math, science, and social studies), Roots & Wings students showed substantial growth. As shown in Figures 10.6 and 10.7, by the third implementation year, when all program components were in operation, the State of Maryland gained in average performance on the MSPAP over the same time period, but the number of Roots & Wings students achieving at satisfactory or excellent increased by more than twice the state's rate on every measure at both grade levels.

After the 1995–96 school year, when funding for the program was significantly reduced, implementation dropped off substantially in the Maryland pilot schools, and MSPAP scores correspondingly failed to increase further, and in some cases slightly

Figure 10.6 Maryland School Performance Assessment Protocol, Gains in Percent Scoring Satisfactory or Better, St. Mary's County Roots & Wings Schools Versus State Means, Grade 3, 1993–1996 (Full Implementation)

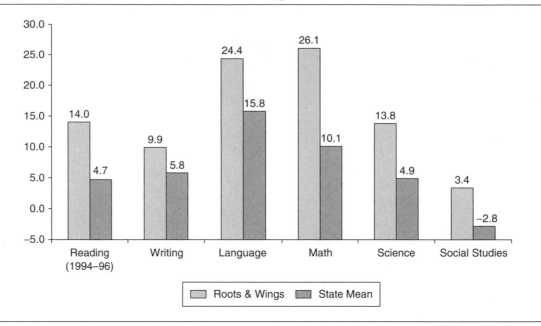

Figure 10.7 Maryland School Performance Assessment Protocol, Gains in Percent Scoring Satisfactory or Better, St. Mary's County Roots & Wings Schools Versus State Means, Grade 5, 1993–1996 (Full Implementation)

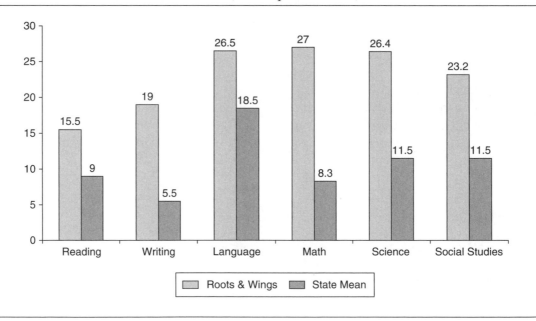

declined. Still, two years after the end of full implementation, the total gains made by the Roots & Wings schools remained higher than those for the state as a whole in every subject at both grade levels except for fifth grade language.

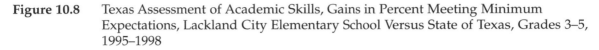

Figure 10.8   Texas Assessment of Academic Skills, Gains in Percent Meeting Minimum Expectations, Lackland City Elementary School Versus State of Texas, Grades 3–5, 1995–1998

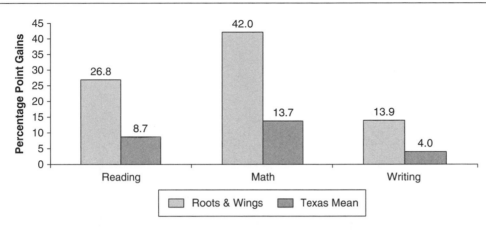

The first evaluation of Roots & Wings outside of Maryland took place at Lackland City Elementary School in San Antonio, Texas (see Slavin & Madden, 2000). This school served a very impoverished population, with 93 percent of its students qualifying for free lunch in 1998. Most of its students (79 percent) were Hispanic; 16 percent were white, and 5 percent were African American.

Lackland City adopted Success for All in 1994–95, and then added MathWings for Grades 3–5 in 1995–96 and WorldLab and Primary MathWings in 1996–97.

Scores on the Texas Assessment of Academic Skills (TAAS) for Lackland City were compared to those for the state as a whole for Grades 3–5 reading and math and for Grade 4 writing. Scores are the percentages of students scoring above minimum standards.

Figure 10.8 summarizes TAAS gains from 1994 (pretest) to 1998. As in Maryland, the Roots & Wings schools gained substantially more than the state as a whole on each scale, with the largest absolute gains in math, but the largest relative gains in reading and writing.

While the MathWings program developed for Roots & Wings still exists and has been used in about one hundred Success for All schools, the term Roots & Wings is no longer used.

CHANGES IN EFFECT SIZES OVER YEARS OF IMPLEMENTATION

One interesting trend in outcomes from comparisons of Success for All and control schools relates to changes in effect sizes according to the number of years a school has been implementing the program. Figure 10.9, which summarizes these data, was created by pooling effect sizes for all cohorts in their first year of implementation, all in their second year, and so on, regardless of calendar year.

Figure 10.9 shows that mean reading effect sizes progressively increased with each year of implementation. For example, Success for All first graders scored substantially better than control first graders at the end of the first year of implementation (ES = +0.49).

Figure 10.9   Effect Sizes Comparing Success for All and Control Schools According to Implementation Year

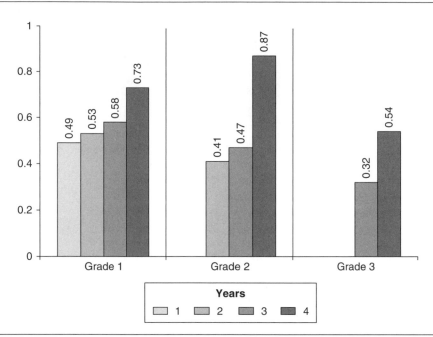

The experimental-control difference was even higher for first graders attending schools in the second year of program implementation (ES = +0.53), increasing to an effect size of +0.73 for schools in their fourth implementation year. A similar pattern was apparent for second and third grade cohorts.

The data summarized in Figure 10.9 show that while Success for All has an immediate impact on student reading achievement, this impact grows over successive years of implementation. Over time, schools may become increasingly able to provide effective instruction to all of their students, to approach the goal of success for *all*.

SUCCESS FOR ALL AND ENGLISH LANGUAGE LEARNERS

The education of English language learners is at a crossroads. On one hand, research on bilingual education continues to show that children who are initially taught in their home language and then transitioned to English ultimately read as well or better in English than children taught only in English (Slavin & Cheung, 2005; National Academy of Sciences, 1998). Despite these findings, political pressure against bilingual education, most notably in California's Proposition 227, has mounted in recent years, based largely on the fact that Latino children perform less well than Anglo children on achievement tests, whether or not they have been initially taught in Spanish.

While language of instruction is an essential concern for children who are acquiring English, the *quality* of instruction (and corresponding achievement outcomes) is at least as important, whatever the initial language of instruction may be. There is a need for better programs for teaching in the home language and then transitioning to English, and for better programs for teaching English language learners in English with support from

English as a second language strategies. Both development and research on Success for All have focused on both of these issues.

Six studies have evaluated adaptations of Success for All with language minority children (see Cheung & Slavin, 2005; Slavin & Madden, 1999b). Three of these evaluated Éxito Para Todos ("Success for All" in Spanish), the Spanish bilingual adaptation, and three evaluated a program adaptation incorporating strategies for English as a second language.

Bilingual Studies

One study compared students in Éxito Para Todos to those in a matched comparison school in which most reading instruction was in English. Both schools served extremely impoverished, primarily Puerto Rican student bodies in inner-city Philadelphia. Not surprisingly, Éxito Para Todos students scored far better than control students on Spanish measures. More important was the fact that after transitioning to all-English instruction by third grade, the Éxito Para Todos students scored significantly better than controls on measures of English reading. These differences were significant on Word Attack, but not on Word Identification or Passage Comprehension.

An evaluation of Éxito Para Todos in California bilingual schools was reported by Livingston and Flaherty (1997), who studied three successive cohorts of students. On Spanish reading measures, Éxito Para Todos students scored substantially higher than controls in first grade (ES = +1.03), second grade (ES = +0.44), and third grade (ES = +.23). However, the second and third grade differences almost certainly understate the true effects; the highest-achieving students in the bilingual programs were transitioned early to English-only instruction, and the transition rate was twice as high in the Éxito Para Todos classes as in the controls.

A large study in Houston compared Limited English Proficient (LEP) first graders in twenty schools implementing Éxito Para Todos to those in ten control schools (Nunnery et al., 1996). As an experiment, schools were allowed to choose Success for All/Éxito Para Todos as it was originally designed, or to implement key components. The analysis compared three levels of implementation: high, medium, and low. None of the Éxito Para Todos programs were categorized as "high" in implementation, as a bilingual teacher shortage made it impossible to hire certified teachers as Spanish tutors, a requirement for the "high implementation" designation. Medium-implementation schools significantly exceeded their controls on all measures (mean ES = +0.24). Low implementers exceeded controls on the Spanish Woodcock Word Identification and Word Attack scales, but not on Passage Comprehension (mean ES = +0.17).

One additional study evaluated Bilingual Cooperative Integrated Reading and Composition (BCIRC), which is closely related to Alas Para Leer, the bilingual adaptation of Reading Wings. This study, in El Paso, Texas, found significantly greater reading achievement (compared to controls) for English language learners in Grades 3–5 transitioning from Spanish to English reading (Calderón, Hertz-Lazarowitz, & Slavin, 1998).

ESL Studies

Three studies have evaluated the effects of Success for All with English language learners being taught in English. In this adaptation, ESL strategies (such as total physical response) are integrated into instruction for all children, whether or not they are limited in English proficiency. The activities of ESL teachers are closely coordinated with those of other classroom teachers, so that ESL instruction directly supports the Success for All curriculum, and ESL teachers often serve as tutors for LEP children.

The first study of Success for All with English language learners took place in Philadelphia. Students in an Asian (mostly Cambodian) Success for All school were compared to those in a matched school that also served many Cambodian-speaking children. Both schools were extremely impoverished, with nearly all children qualifying for free lunches.

At the end of a six-year longitudinal study, Success for All Asian fourth and fifth graders were performing far ahead of matched controls. On average, they were 2.9 years ahead of controls in fourth grade (median ES = +1.49), and 2.8 years ahead in fifth grade (median ES = +1.33). Success for All Asian students were reading about a full year above grade level in both fourth and fifth grades, while controls were almost two years below grade level. Non-Asian students also significantly exceeded their controls at all grade levels (see Cheung & Slavin, 2005; Slavin & Madden, 1999b).

The California study described earlier (Livingston & Flaherty, 1997) also included many English language learners who were taught in English. Combining results across three cohorts, Spanish-dominant English language learners performed far better on English reading measures in Success for All than in matched control schools in first grade (ES = +1.36) and second grade (ES = +0.46), but not in third grade (ES = +0.09). As in the bilingual evaluation, the problem with the third grade scores was that many high-achieving children were transitioned out of the ESL designation in the Success for All schools, reducing apparent experimental-control differences. Corresponding effect sizes for students who spoke languages other than English or Spanish were +0.40 for first graders, +0.37 for second graders, and +0.05 for third graders.

An Arizona study (Ross, Nunnery, & Smith, 1996) compared Mexican American English language learners in two urban Success for All schools to those in three schools using locally developed Title I reform models and one using Reading Recovery. Two Socio-Economic Status (SES) school strata were compared, one set with 81 percent of students in poverty and 50 percent Hispanic students, and one with 53 percent of students in poverty and 27 percent Hispanic students. Success for All first graders scored higher than controls in both strata. Hispanic students in the high-poverty stratum averaged three months ahead of the controls (1.75 vs. 1.45). Hispanic students in the less impoverished stratum scored slightly above grade level (1.93), about one month ahead of controls (1.83).

The effects of Success for All for language minority students are not statistically significant on every measure in every study, but the overall impact of the program is clearly positive, both for the Spanish bilingual adaptation, Éxito Para Todos, and for the ESL adaptation. What these findings suggest is that whatever the language of instruction may be, student achievement in that language can be substantially enhanced using improved materials, professional development, and other supports.

COMPARING SUCCESS FOR ALL AND READING RECOVERY

Reading Recovery is one of the most extensively researched and widely used innovations in elementary education. Like Success for All, Reading Recovery provides one-to-one tutoring to first graders who are struggling in reading. Research on Reading Recovery has found substantial positive effects of the program as of the end of first grade, and longitudinal studies have found that some portion of these effects maintain at least through fourth grade (DeFord, Pinnell, Lyons & Young, 1988; Lyons, Pinnell, & DeFord, 1993; Pinnell, Lyons, DeFord, Bryk, & Seltzer, 1994).

Schools and districts attracted to Success for All are also often attracted to Reading Recovery, as the two programs share an emphasis on early intervention and a strong research base. Increasing numbers of districts have both programs in operation in different schools. One of the districts in the Success for All evaluation, Caldwell, Idaho, happened to be one of these. Ross, Smith, Casey, and Slavin (1995) used this opportunity to compare the two programs.

In the Caldwell study, two schools used Success for All and one used Reading Recovery. All three are very similar rural schools with similar ethnic makeups (10–25 percent Hispanic, with the remainder Anglo), proportions of students qualifying for free lunch (45–60 percent), and sizes (411–451). The Success for All schools were somewhat higher than the Reading Recovery school in poverty and percent Hispanic. In 1992–93, one of the Success for All schools was in its second year of implementation and the other was a new school that was in its first year (but had moved a principal and some experienced staff reassigned from the first school). Reading Recovery was in its second year of implementation.

The study compared first graders in the three schools. Students in the Success for All schools performed somewhat better than students in the Reading Recovery school overall (ES = +.17). Differences for special education students were substantial, averaging an effect size of +.77. Special education students were not tutored in the Reading Recovery school and were primarily taught in a separate resource room. These students scored near the floor on all tests. In contrast, Success for All special education students were fully mainstreamed and did receive tutoring, and their reading scores, though still low, showed them to be on the way toward success in reading.

Excluding the special education students, there were no differences in reading performance between tutored students in the Success for All and Reading Recovery schools (ES = .00). In light of earlier research, these outcomes suggest that both tutoring programs are effective for at-risk first graders.

A second study, by Ross, Nunnery, and Smith (1996), also compared Success for All and Reading Recovery. This study, in an urban Arizona school district, compared first graders in three matched schools, in which 53 percent of students qualified for free lunch, 27 percent were Hispanic, and 73 percent were Anglo. One of the schools used SFA, one used Reading Recovery, and one used a locally developed Title I schoolwide project.

Results for the overall sample of first graders strongly favored Success for All. Averaging across four individually administered measures, Success for All students scored well above grade level (GE = 2.2). Those in the Reading Recovery school averaged near grade level (GE = 1.7), slightly below the control school (GE = 1.8). Effect sizes (adjusted for pretests) comparing the SFA and Reading Recovery schools averaged +0.68, and effect sizes compared to the locally developed schoolwide project averaged +0.39.

Focusing on the children who actually received one-to-one tutoring, the differences were dramatic. On Peabody Picture Vocabulary Tests given at pretest, the students tutored in the Reading Recovery school scored 41 percent of a standard deviation higher than students tutored in the Success for All school. Yet at the end of the year, the Reading Recovery students were essentially nonreaders, with an average grade equivalent of 1.2. In contrast, the students tutored in Success for All scored at grade level (GE = 1.85). The mean effect size for this comparison, ES = 2.79, is inflated by a huge difference in Word Attack, but even excluding this scale the effect size mean is +1.65.

The difference between the Idaho and the Arizona findings is probably due in part to the nature of the broader school programs, not just to differences in the tutoring models. The Arizona Reading Recovery school had a program strongly influenced by whole language, and the tutored children performed very poorly on Word Attack measures. In contrast, the Idaho Reading Recovery school used a more balanced approach, so that these children were receiving some phonics instruction in their regular classes.

Reading Recovery can be a powerful means of increasing the reading success of students having reading difficulties, but it needs to be implemented well and supplemented with high-quality instruction that includes a strong phonetic component if it is to produce significant reading gains. Because Success for All attends to classroom instruction as well as tutoring, it is able to ensure that the effects of one-to-one tutoring build upon high-quality, well-balanced reading instruction, rather than expecting the tutors to teach children to read with little support from classroom instruction.

COMPARISONS WITH OTHER PROGRAMS

A few studies have compared outcomes of Success for All to those of other comprehensive reform designs.

As noted earlier, a study of six restructuring designs in Memphis on the Tennessee Value-Added Assessment System (TVAAS) found that Success for All schools had the highest absolute scores and gain scores on the TVAAS, averaging across all subjects (Ross et al., 1999). The TVAAS is a measure that relates performance on the Tennessee Comprehensive Achievement Test to "expected" performance. The designs, in addition to Success for All, were Co-nect, Accelerated Schools, Audrey Cohen College, ATLAS, and Expeditionary Learning.

Similarly, the Mason (2005) study in Los Angeles, discussed earlier, compared schools implementing five CSR models to matched controls. In addition to SFA, the programs were America's Choice, Co-nect, Different Ways of Knowing, and Urban Learning Centers. Among these, only SFA students who began the program in Grades 1 or 2 gained significantly more than controls.

A study in Clover Park, Washington, compared Success for All to Accelerated Schools (Hopfenberg & Levin, 1993), an approach that, like Success for All, emphasizes prevention and acceleration over remediation, but unlike Success for All does not provide specific materials or instructional strategies to achieve its goals. In the first year of the evaluation, the Success for All and Accelerated Schools programs had similar scores on individually administered reading tests and on a writing test (Ross, Alberg, & McNelis, 1997). By second grade, however, Success for All schools were scoring slightly ahead of Accelerated Schools in reading, and significantly ahead in writing (Ross, Alberg, McNelis, & Smith, 1998).

SUCCESS FOR ALL AND SPECIAL EDUCATION

Perhaps the most important goal of Success for All is to place a floor under the reading achievement of all children, to ensure that every child performs adequately in this critical skill. This goal has major implications for special education. If the program makes a substantial difference in the reading achievement of the lowest achievers, then it should reduce special education referrals and placements. Further, students who have IEPs indicating learning disabilities or related problems are typically treated the same as other students in Success for All. That is, they receive tutoring if they need it, participate in reading classes appropriate to their reading levels, and spend the rest of the day in age-appropriate, heterogeneous homerooms. Their tutor and/or reading teacher is likely to be a special education teacher, but otherwise they are not treated differently. One-to-one tutoring in reading, plus high-quality reading instruction in the mainstream at the student's appropriate level, should be more effective than the small-group instruction provided in special education classes. For this reason, we expect that students who have been identified as being in need of special education services will perform substantially better than similar students in traditional special education programs.

The philosophy behind the treatment of special education issues in Success for All is called "neverstreaming" (Slavin, 1996). That is, rather than waiting until students fall far behind, are assigned to special education, and then may be mainstreamed into regular classes, Success for All schools intervene early and intensively with students who are at risk to try to keep them out of the special education system. Once students are far behind, special education services are unlikely to catch them up to age-appropriate levels of performance. Students who have already failed in reading are likely to have an overlay of anxiety, poor motivation, poor behavior, low self-esteem, and ineffective learning strategies that are likely to interfere with learning no matter how good special education services may be. Ensuring that all students succeed in the first place is a far better strategy, if it can be accomplished. In Success for All, the provision of research-based preschool, kindergarten, and first grade reading, one-to-one tutoring, and family support services are likely to give the students who are most at risk a good chance of developing enough reading skills to remain out of special education, or to perform better in special education than would have otherwise been the case.

The data relating to special education outcomes clearly support these expectations. Several studies have focused on questions related to special education. One of the most important outcomes in this area is the consistent finding of particularly large effects of Success for All for students in the lowest 25 percent of their classes. While effect sizes for students in general have averaged around + 0.50 on individually administered reading measures, effect sizes for the lowest achievers have averaged in the range of +1.00 to +1.50 across the grades. In the longitudinal Baltimore study, only 2.2 percent of third graders averaged two years behind grade level, a usual criterion for special education placement. In contrast, 8.8 percent of control third graders scored this poorly. Baltimore data also showed a reduction in special education placements for learning disabilities of about half (Slavin, Madden, Karweit, Dolan, & Wasik, 1992). A longitudinal study following Baltimore children to eighth grade found that students who had been in control schools had spent 50 percent more time in special education, on average, than those who had been in SFA schools (Borman & Hewes, 2003). A study of two Success for All schools in Fort Wayne, Indiana, found that over a two-year period 3.2 percent of Success for All students in Grades K–1 and 1–2 were referred to special education for learning disabilities or mild mental disabilities. In contrast, 14.3 percent of control students were referred in these categories (Smith, Ross, & Casey, 1994).

Taken together, these findings support the conclusion that Success for All both reduces the need for special education services (by raising the reading achievement of very low achievers) and reduces special education referrals and placements. Both of these outcomes have significant consequences for long-term costs of educating students placed at risk; these are discussed in Chapter 11.

Another important question concerns the effects of the program on students who have already been assigned to special education. Here again, there is evidence from different sources. In the study comparing Reading Recovery and Success for All described above, it so happened that first graders in special education in the Reading Recovery group were not tutored, but instead received traditional special education services in resource rooms. In the Success for All schools, first graders who had been assigned to special education were tutored one-to-one (by their special education teachers) and otherwise participated in the program in the same way as all other students. As noted earlier, special education students in Success for All were reading substantially better (ES = +0.77) than special education students in the comparison school ((Ross, Smith, Casey, & Slavin, 1995). In addition, Smith et al. (1994) combined first grade reading data from special education students in Success for All and control schools in four districts: Memphis, Fort Wayne (IN), Montgomery (AL), and Caldwell (ID). Success for All special education students scored substantially better than controls (mean ES = +0.59).

EMBEDDING TECHNOLOGY IN SUCCESS FOR ALL

In recent years, the Success for All Foundation has added two technology tools to its early reading programs, and studies of these additions find them to be effective in improving students' reading performance. *Reading Reels*, used in kindergarten and first grade classes, provides appealing video content to supplement Reading Roots. This includes animations to teach letter sounds, puppet skits to teach sound blending, and live action skits to teach vocabulary. In a study in which schools in Hartford, Connecticut, were randomly assigned to use SFA either with or without *Reading Reels*, students who experienced the videos performed significantly better on the Woodcock Word Attack scale than those who did not experience *Reading Reels* (Chambers, Cheung, Madden, Slavin, & Gifford, 2007).

The second technology enhancement is called *Alphie's Alley*. Another video series, it is designed for use in SFA tutoring. *Alphie's Alley* helps tutors assess their students, plan their instruction, and provide them with compelling, animated presentations and practice opportunities. Embedded in the content are professional development videos in which experienced tutors demonstrate tutoring strategies. A study involving twenty-five SFA schools randomly assigned children in tutoring (and their tutors) to tutoring with or without *Alphie's Alley*. In schools that used the program as intended, *Alphie's Alley* students scored significantly better than students given usual paper-and-pencil tutoring on the Woodcock Letter-Word Identification and Word Attack scales as well as DIBELS Fluency (Chambers, Abrami et al., 2005).

A third randomized study evaluated outcomes in schools that used both *Reading Reels* and *Alphie's Alley*. Students who received tutoring and experienced both embedded technology interventions scored substantially better than tutored SFA students who did not experience the technology on the Woodcock Letter-Word and Word Attack scales and the Gray Oral Reading Test Fluency and Comprehension scales. Students who were not tutored, and therefore experienced *Reading Reels* but not *Alphie's Alley*, also scored better than nontutored SFA students who did not experience the videos on Woodcock and Gray reading measures (Chambers, Slavin et al., 2005).

RESEARCH ON SUCCESS FOR ALL

These studies suggest that using multimedia content embedded in teachers' lessons along with Success for All can significantly enhance learning for children. This type of application, in which technology supplements instead of replacing teachers' instruction, may help teachers reinforce content and skills through visual as well as auditory pathways. The positive findings have led the Success for All Foundation to include both *Reading Reels* and *Alphie's Alley* as standard components of Reading Roots.

TEACHERS' ATTITUDES TOWARD SUCCESS FOR ALL

Three studies have examined teachers' attitudes toward Success for All using questionnaires. Ross, Smith, Nunnery, and Sterbin (1995) surveyed teachers involved in six restructuring designs, including Success for All, and found that Success for All schools had the most positive attitudes toward the success of the implementation. However, all designs were rated relatively positively, and there was more variation among schools implementing the same designs than between models.

Rakow and Ross (1997) studied teacher attitudes in five Success for All schools in Little Rock, Arkansas. Once again, responses varied widely from school to school, but overall effects were very positive. For example, 70 percent of teachers agreed that SFA was having a positive effect in their schools, and 78 percent felt "positively about using the SFA model."

Datnow and Castellano (2000) also examined teachers' attitudes in extensive observations and interviews in three California schools with substantial Latino majorities. They described 64 percent of the teachers as "supportive" or "strongly supportive," 28 percent "accepting," and 8 percent (three teachers) "opposed." Among the "accepting" teachers were some teachers who personally did not like the program, but still felt it was working for their children.

Muñoz and Dossett (2004), in a four-year study of six schools in Louisville, Kentucky, found that SFA teachers gave higher ratings than control teachers on measures of educational quality and job satisfaction.

Perhaps the best indicator of teacher support for Success for All is not from a study, but from a vote. In spring 1999, the San Antonio Independent School District, responding to a severe budget shortfall and a change of superintendents, required teachers in all schools using restructuring designs to vote on whether to keep these designs or to return to the district's program. A vote of 80 percent in favor was required to keep the program. Across twenty-four Success for All schools, the average vote in favor was 81 percent positive. In contrast, votes for the five other designs (thirty-seven schools) averaged 36.5 percent positive.

CONCLUSION

The results of evaluations of dozens of Success for All schools in districts in all parts of the U.S. and five other countries clearly show that the program increases student reading performance. A large, national randomized evaluation found clear positive effects of the program, compared to a control group. Across fifty matched studies done by dozens of researchers, Success for All students learned significantly more than matched control students. Significant effects were not seen on every measure at every grade level, but the consistent direction and magnitude of the effects show unequivocal benefits for Success for All students. Effects on district-administered standardized tests and criterion-referenced tests used in state accountability programs reinforce the findings of the studies using individually administered tests. Large impacts have been seen on the achievement of limited English proficient students in both bilingual and ESL programs, and on both reducing special education referrals and improving the achievement of students who have been assigned to special education.

The Success for All evaluations have used reliable and valid measures, in particular individually administered tests that are sensitive to all aspects of reading: comprehension, fluency, word attack, and word identification. Positive effects on state accountability assessments and on other standardized measures have also been documented many times. Performance of Success for All students has been compared to that of students in similar control schools, who provide the best indication of what students without the program would have achieved. Replication of high-quality experiments in such a wide variety of schools and districts is extremely unusual. As noted earlier, reviews of research by the Comprehensive School Reform Quality Center (2006), Borman et al. (2003), the American Institutes for Research (Herman, 1999) and the Fordham Foundation (Traub, 1999) all found Success for All to be one of only two or three comprehensive elementary reform models to have rigorous, frequently replicated evidence of effectiveness.

An important indicator of the robustness of Success for All is the fact that schools stay with the program. In 2008, the median school has used SFA for eight years. When schools do drop the program, it is usually due to a district decision (forced by policy changes or funding cuts), not a school decision. Hundreds of Success for All schools have survived changes of superintendents, principals, facilitators, and other key staff, major cuts in funding, and other serious threats to program maintenance.

The research summarized here demonstrates that comprehensive, systemic school-by-school change can take place on a broad scale in a way that maintains the integrity and effectiveness of the model. The schools we have studied are typical of the larger set of schools currently using Success for All in terms of quality of implementation, resources, demographic characteristics, and other factors. Program outcomes are not limited to the original home of the program. The widely held idea based on the RAND study of innovation (Berman & McLaughlin, 1978; McLaughlin, 1990) that comprehensive school reform must be invented by school staffs themselves is certainly not supported in research on Success for All. While the program is adapted to meet the needs of each school, and while school staffs must agree to implement the program by a vote of 80 percent or more, Success for All is an externally developed program with specific materials, manuals, and structures. The observation that the program can be implemented and maintained over considerable time periods and can be effective in each of its replication sites certainly supports the idea that every school staff need not reinvent the wheel.

11

Success for All and School Reform

Success for All is clearly having a substantial impact on the schools that are implementing it. This is, of course, important in itself. However, the experience of developing and disseminating the program, and in particular the research on its outcomes, have important implications for school reform that go beyond these schools. Success for All provides what may be the best evidence available that well-structured, comprehensive programs can be replicated on a substantial scale and can ensure success for a large proportion of children who might otherwise need long-term remedial and special education services. This chapter discusses the scaling-up and cost-effectiveness of Success for All and the implications of research on Success for All for compensatory education, for special education, and for school reform in general.

SCALING UP SUCCESS FOR ALL

The practical and policy consequences of research on Success for All would be minimal if the program depended on conditions unlikely to be replicated in schools beyond our pilot sites. Yet, this is obviously not true; the program currently exists in over 1,200 schools in foty-seven states (see Slavin & Madden, 2007). Further, the median SFA school has implemented the program for eight years. Clearly, successful implementation and maintenance of the program does not depend on the existence of hand-picked staff, charismatic principals, or unobtainable resources. The 1,200 schools are highly diverse and are located in all parts of the U.S., from California to Alaska to Texas to Florida to Massachusetts. This is not to say that every school serving disadvantaged students can successfully implement the program. It does require a clear commitment from the district, principal, and staff to a very different way of organizing their schools. However, it is our belief and experience that with adequate support from their central administrations, the majority of Title I elementary schools want to implement a program like Success for All and are capable of doing so.

The most important impediments to the widespread use of Success for All are not any lack of willingness or skill on the part of school staffs but rather revolve around the cost of the program and around our ability to provide high-quality training and support to large numbers of schools. The following sections discuss several questions relating to the cost of Success for All. First is a discussion of research on cost-effectiveness, and of what the costs are. This is followed by discussion of mid- to long-term savings brought about by the program.

COST-EFFECTIVENESS

Borman and Hewes (2003) carried out a longitudinal evaluation of outcomes of Success for All in Baltimore, comparing eighth graders who had attended one of five SFA or five control schools. They examined outcomes on standardized achievement measures as well as differences in retentions and special education placements, and based on these, they compared the cost-effectiveness of Success for All to that of reducing class size (from the Tennessee Class Size study), or implementing the Perry Preschool or Abecedarian Preschool interventions. They found the long-term effects per $1,000 to be substantially greater for SFA than for the other programs.

Costs

Most of the costs of Success for All are in reallocations of staff from other functions to provide a facilitator and some number of tutors. Beyond this, current costs (for the 2008–2009 school year) for materials and training average $100,000 for the first year, $45,000 for the second year, and $35,000 for the third year, for a school of 500 students.

Success for All has been implemented with widely varying constellations of resources. Most schools fund the program by reconfiguring existing Title I support, sometimes supplemented by funds or personnel from special education, state compensatory education, or bilingual education or ESL programs. Schools may obtain grants or other short-term funding to help them with the initial costs of training and materials, but most do not. Few of the current Success for All schools have much more funding than what they would have had without the program.

Staffing Needs

The number of staff needed in Success for All (other than classroom teachers) is typically the same as the staff already available in the school, but staff roles change significantly. In general, Title I (and often special education) staff become tutors, and one position is set aside for the facilitator. Table 11.1 shows typical staff configurations for Success for All schools of 500 students with various levels of Title I eligibility (and corresponding levels of Title I funds).

The Success for All curricula and instructional programs could theoretically be used without tutors, family support staff, and other staff. However, based on our research that indicates that the full model, well implemented, is more effective than partial models (e.g., Nunnery et al., 1996), we recommend that schools interested in Success for All implement something close to our vision of a school in which very few students fail or require special or remedial education, and this requires tutors and other staff. In our experience, most high-poverty schools, especially Title I schoolwide projects, can implement Success for All

Table 11.1   Typical Staffing Needs (FTEs) for Success for All Schools at Different Title I Eligibility Levels

	Percent of Students Eligible for Title I		
	75%	50%	25%
Facilitator	1.0	1.0	1.0
Tutors*	5.0	3.0	2.0
Family Support Specialist**	1.0	1.0	1.0

*Certified teachers serve as tutors. High-quality paraprofessionals or retired teachers can be added to this number or substituted for some tutors if at least one certified teacher-tutor is available to supervise others and work with children with the most serious problems.

**Social worker, counselor, or parent liaison.

using Title I, state compensatory education, bilingual, and special education resources. Schools with fewer disadvantaged students and, therefore, fewer Title I dollars, often require funds from elsewhere: state funds, foundation or government grants, and so on. Costs diminish over time after initial materials and training have been delivered and as the need to provide remedial services for older children diminishes. We have found that it is not a good idea for schools to try to obtain grants to fund the *continuing* cost of the program, as they then have to continually fight to maintain their funding. However, short-term grants to help with start-up costs can be very helpful.

Savings Brought About by Success for All

While the costs of Success for All must be primarily justified as an investment in children, it is important to note that the program typically brings about many savings. These are discussed below.

Retentions

Many Success for All schools have substantially reduced their rate of retentions (Borman & Hewes, 2003; Slavin et al., 1992). Reducing retentions has an important effect on educational costs. A retained child is receiving a very expensive intervention: one more year of school. Every time an elementary school retains twenty-five to thirty students it must eventually hire an additional teacher, supply an additional classroom, and so on. When Success for All started in 1987, retention rates in many urban districts often approached 20 percent, and with the current trend toward grade-to-grade promotion standards, retention rates are once again rising. This makes the cost savings brought about by Success for All's reductions in retention rates particularly important.

Special Education

Success for All schools have been able to reduce special education placements for learning disabilities by about half (see Borman & Hewes, 2003; Slavin, 1996). The additional cost of serving such students averages around $4,000 per year. If over a period of years the number of children in special education for learning disabilities could be cut from 8 percent to 4 percent, the annual savings in a school of 500 students would be

$80,000. In addition, reducing the number of *assessments* for special education (a national average of about $2,000) from 8 percent to 4 percent would add a savings of $40,000 per year. Most schools report fewer referrals, and the referrals they do receive tend to be more accurate, thereby reducing unnecessary assessments (see Slavin, 1996).

Supplanted Training and Materials

Success for All materials and training often take the place of other staff development and materials. For example, Success for All reading replaces basal texts for Grades K–1, and workbooks for all grades. Therefore, the costs of Success for All are rarely additional costs to the school, but instead replace other expenditures for the same purposes.

Long-Term Savings

The preceding discussion only dealt with short- to mid-term savings realized by the school or school system. To these savings must be added the likely savings to society over the long term in costs of welfare, police, prisons, and so on. The link between school success and life success, and between these and the need for expensive social services, is well established. To the degree that Success for All ultimately reduces delinquency, dropout, teen pregnancy, or other problems strongly associated with school failure in low-income communities, its savings to society could far outweigh any costs of implementation (see Barnett & Escobar, 1977; Borman & Hewes, 2003). Research on prevention suggests that the links between early school achievement and mental health are strong.

Success for All is a practical, replicable, and effective program for improving the performance of disadvantaged elementary students. It is expensive, but with reallocations of Title I, special education, and other funds, most school districts serving many disadvantaged students can afford a credible form of the model. Immediate and long-term savings introduced by Success for All may ultimately offset most of the program's cost. For these reasons, Success for All is a cost-effective means of bringing all children in disadvantaged schools to acceptable levels of reading performance.

IMPLICATIONS OF SUCCESS FOR ALL FOR COMPENSATORY EDUCATION

Once upon a time (or so the story goes), there was a train company experiencing a high rate of accidents. The company appointed a commission to look into the matter, and the commission issued a report noting its major finding, which was that when accidents occurred, damage was primarily sustained to the last car in the train. As a result of this finding, the company established a policy requiring that before each train left the station, the last car was to be uncoupled!

All too often, compensatory education has primarily pursued a "last car" strategy in providing for the needs of low-achieving students. The attention and resources of Title I have mostly gone into identifying and remediating the damage sustained by individual children. Yet, the fault lies not in the children, but in the system that failed to prevent the damage in the first place, just as the damage to the last car was due to the train system and had nothing to do with the last car in itself.

The 2001 reauthorization of Title I in No Child Left Behind (NCLB) created unprecedented opportunities for high-poverty schools to fundamentally reform themselves. In particular, it increased the ability of schoolwide programs to use their Title I resources flexibly to meet the needs of all children and to provide extended professional development for all staff. More than ever before, Title I schools can select programs that match their vision of excellence, and implement that program with adequate professional development, materials, and flexibility. Yet all too many Title I schools are still not taking advantage of the flexibility they have. They are continuing to invest in pull-out remedial teachers and instructional aides, neither of which has much evidence of effectiveness for student achievement (Puma, Jones, Rock, & Fernandez, 1993).

Title I can be much more than it has been in the past. It can be an engine of change in the education of disadvantaged children (see Borman, Stringfield, & Slavin, 2001; Slavin, 1999). It can ensure the basic skills of virtually all children; it can help our nation's schools put a floor under the achievement expectations for all children, so that all children will have the basic skills necessary to profit from regular classroom instruction. It can help schools move toward teaching of a full and appropriate curriculum for all students, but particularly for those who by virtue of being "at risk" too often receive a narrow curriculum emphasizing isolated skills. It can make the education of students who are disadvantaged and at risk a top priority for all schools.

Preventing Early Reading Failure

Perhaps the most important objective of compensatory education should be to ensure that children are successful in reading the first time they are taught, and never become remedial readers. The importance of reading success in the early grades is apparent to anyone who works with students who are at risk. As discussed in earlier chapters, the consequences of failing to learn to read in the early grades are severe. For example, disadvantaged students who have failed a grade and are reading below grade level are extremely unlikely to graduate from high school (Lloyd, 1978). Retentions and special education referrals are usually based on early reading deficits.

Trying to remediate reading failure after it has occurred is very difficult, because by then students who have failed are likely to be unmotivated, to have poor self-concepts as learners, and to be anxious about reading. Reform is needed at all levels of education, but no goal of reform is as important as seeing that all children start off their school careers with success, confidence, and a firm foundation in reading. Success in the early grades does not guarantee success throughout the school years and beyond, but failure in the early grades does virtually guarantee failure in later schooling.

A growing body of evidence from several sources indicates that reading failure in the early grades is preventable. The outcomes summarized in Chapter 10 show that Success for All has been able to dramatically reduce the number of students who fail to learn to read. This and other evidence suggest that reading failure is preventable for nearly all children, even a substantial portion of those who are typically categorized as learning disabled (see Slavin, 1996).

If reading failure *can* be prevented, it *must* be prevented. Title I is the logical program to take the lead in giving schools serving disadvantaged students the resources and programs necessary to see that all children learn to read.

Enhancing Regular Classroom Instruction

One of the most fundamental principles of Title I has been that compensatory funds must be focused on the lowest achieving students in qualifying schools. In principle this makes sense, in that it avoids spreading Title I resources too thinly. But in practice this requirement has led to many problems, including a lack of consistency or coordination between regular and Title I instruction, disruption of children's regular classroom instruction, labeling of students who receive services, and unclear responsibility for children's progress (Allington & Johnston, 1989; Allington & MacGill-Franzen, 1989; Stein, Leinhardt, & Bickel, 1989).

The best way to prevent students from falling behind is to provide them with top-quality instruction in their regular classrooms. A substantial portion of Title I funds should be set aside for staff development and adoption of programs known to be effective by teachers in Title I schools. For example, by hiring one less aide, schools could instead devote about $25,000 per year to staff development, a huge investment in terms of what schools typically spend but a small one in terms of what many Title I schools receive. The educational impact of one aide could never approach that of thorough and intelligent implementation of effective curricula and instructional practices in regular classrooms throughout the school. For the cost of three aides, a school could pay all of the nonpersonnel costs of Success for All. For this amount of money, a school could pay for extensive inservice, in-class follow-up, and release time for teachers to observe each other's classes and to meet to compare notes, as well as purchase needed materials and supplies. The achievement benefits of effective classroom instruction all day would far outweigh the potential benefits of remedial services.

There are many examples of programs that have been much more successful for low-achieving students than remedial services. In reviews of the literature on effective programs for students at risk (Slavin, 2005; Slavin & Fashola, 1998; Slavin, Karweit, & Wasik, 1994; also, see www.bestevidence.org), we identified many such programs, including a variety of cooperative learning and peer tutoring programs. Programs directed at improving classroom management skills also often increase achievement. In addition to particular classroom methods, proven, comprehensive, whole-school reform programs such as SFA, as well as Direct Instruction (Adams & Engelmann, 1996), James Comer's School Development Program (Comer, Ben-Avie, Haynes, & Joyner, 1999), America's Choice (Supovitz, Poglinco, & Snyder, 2001), and other comprehensive programs can be funded by Title I.

Success for All provides one demonstration of how a schoolwide emphasis on staff development and adoption of effective practices can be implemented under Title I funding and can greatly affect the learning of all students. Title I must help create a situation in which eligible schools are able to select from among a set of programs known to be effective and are then able to use their funds to obtain inservice, follow-up, and materials—whatever is needed to ensure top-quality implementation of whatever methods the schools has chosen.

COMPREHENSIVE SCHOOL REFORM

Perhaps the best model of what Title I should become was embodied in the Comprehensive School Reform Demonstration (CSRD), introduced in 1997 by Congressmen David Obey (D-Wisconsin) and John Porter (R-Illinois). CSRD provided money to schools to help them with the start-up costs of adopting proven, comprehensive design. Schools were able to apply to their states for grants of at least $50,000 per year for up to three years. Recently, CSRD funding has been terminated, but language encouraging struggling schools to use CSR models exists in NCLB.

In the original CSRD legislation, seventeen programs were named as examples of comprehensive designs. These included Success for All, Accelerated Schools, the School Development Program, Direct Instruction, and several less widely disseminated programs. Schools were not limited to these, and a wide variety of programs was funded; fewer than half of the initial grants were used to implement programs on the list of seventeen.

CSRD provided an enormous boost to the comprehensive school reform movement, which was already expanding rapidly before CSRD. The most obvious impact was on schools that received CSRD grants. However, the impact was much broader than this. First, the entire awareness process being carried out by states in collaboration with regional laboratories made a far larger set of schools aware of comprehensive programs. Even those schools that never applied for CSRD, and those that applied but were not funded, became aware that comprehensive programs exist and that they are valid, approved expenditures of Title I funds.

As of this writing, comprehensive school reform has waned as a concept. However, there is a rising trend on the horizon toward use of programs with strong evidence of effectiveness, especially in schools not meeting standards under NCLB. If this focus on research prevails, those CSR models with strong evidence of effectiveness will once again come to the fore.

IMPLICATIONS FOR SPECIAL EDUCATION POLICY

For more than forty years, the most important debates in special education research and policy have revolved around the practice of mainstreaming, particularly mainstreaming of students with mild academic disabilities, such as those identified as learning disabled. From early on, most researchers and policymakers have favored mainstreaming students with academic disabilities to the maximum extent possible (Leinhardt & Pallay, 1982; Madden & Slavin, 1983), and the passage of PL 94–142 in 1975 put the federal government squarely behind this effort. Since that time, students with academic disabilities have certainly spent more time in general education classes than they did before, but the number of students identified for special education services has risen dramatically.

Improving the capacity of the general education classroom to meet diverse needs is an essential part of a comprehensive strategy to serve students with academic disabilities, but it is not enough. The problem is that once a child is academically disabled (or significantly behind his or her peers for any reason), neither mainstreaming nor special or remedial education are likely to bring the child up to age-appropriate achievement norms. For most children with academic disabilities, mainstreaming may only be the least unappealing of many unappealing options.

Success for All proposes a markedly different approach to the education of students who are likely to become academically disabled. The key focus of the model is an emphasis on prevention and on early, intensive, and untiring intervention to bring student performance within normal limits. As mentioned earlier, we call this approach "neverstreaming" (Slavin, 1996) because its intention is to see that nearly all children remain in the mainstream by intervening to prevent the academic difficulties that would lead them to be identified for separate special education services. The 2004 reauthorization of the Individuals with Disabilities in Education Act (IDEA) emphasized prevention and the use of proven programs to help struggling children in the mainstream to try to keep them out of special education.

The findings of the Success for All evaluations illustrate the potential of prevention and early intervention to keep students from falling far behind their agemates, to keep them from failing, and to keep them from being assigned to special education for learning disabilities. Most Success for All schools serve very disadvantaged student populations; many experience problems with truancy, inadequate health care, parental poverty, drug involvement, and other problems that are unusual even among urban schools. Yet in these schools, even the lowest achievers are well on their way to reading, are being promoted, and are staying out of special education (Borman & Hewes, 2003). More typical schools without many of these challenges should be able to ensure that virtually all students are successful in reading and other basic skills and can therefore stay out of separate special education programs.

SUCCESS FOR ALL WITHIN THE SCHOOL REFORM MOVEMENT

We are in a time in American society where there is tremendous pressure to reform our schools. This pressure comes from contingencies at the national, state, and local community level. Reform efforts range from modest supplements to traditional classroom instruction to radical "break the mold" approaches to school change.

Success for All has many components that have been implemented in isolation in many educational environments. It benefits from past research which documents effective instructional programs for children at risk. One does not have to dig too deeply to recognize how the model has benefited from the development and research of others (see Slavin, Madden, & Datnow, in press). For example, our tutoring model has benefited from the research on Reading Recovery, our family support team from Comer's School Development Program, our cross-grade regrouping from research on the Joplin Plan, and of course our instructional approaches draw extensively on our earlier research on the benefits of cooperative learning (Slavin, 1995). We have not tried to reinvent the educational wheel. However, we have put together many existing "wheels" to create a vehicle to optimize success for every child.

Success for All is among a small set of widely used school restructuring efforts. However, in many ways it is quite distinct from other reform efforts. What is different about our model is not so much the individual strategies, but the way these strategies are woven together as a comprehensive system of complementary parts. We start with effective instruction within the regular classroom. Next, a set of multistaged interventions are available whenever danger signs are noted. The model involves many changes in both the organization and curriculum of schools. It is based on the concept of "relentlessness," which implies always having a back-up strategy to ensure success. We believe the whole is indeed greater than the sum of its parts.

For many years, there has been much doubt among policymakers that research-based school change can take place on a broad scale. Many believe that only "systemic" changes in standards, assessments, frameworks, and legislation can make a difference, or that reform can only come from changes in school governance, as with vouchers or charter schools. Success for All and other replicable school designs show that today's public schools can reform themselves within the current system. Systemic change is necessary and desirable, but it must be accompanied by professional development, materials, and school organization methods capable of enabling schools to confidently achieve to new, higher standards. Charter schools and private schools need proven programs just as much as public schools do, and there are outstanding examples of both in the Success for All network. Success for All provides one model of how standards and school-by-school reform can work together.

CONCLUSION

More than twenty-five years ago, Ronald Edmonds (1981, p. 23) put forth three assertions:

1. We can, whenever and wherever we choose, successfully teach all children whose schooling is of interest to us.

2. We already know more than we need to do that.

3. Whether or not we do it must finally depend on how we feel about the fact that we haven't so far.

Edmonds' conclusions were based on his studies of effective and ineffective schools serving poor and minority children. His key assumption was that if the characteristics of effective schools could be implanted in less effective schools, all children could learn. Yet this transfer turned out not to be an easy one. Making a run-of-the mill school into an outstanding one takes much more than telling staffs the characteristics of outstanding schools.

The greatest importance of the research on Success for All is that it brings us closer to making Edmond's vision a reality. Only when we have confidence that we can take a *typical* school serving disadvantaged children and ensure the success of virtually every child can we really force the essential political and policy question: if we know that we can greatly improve the educational performance of at-risk children, *are we willing to do what it takes to do so?*

The findings of research on Success for All and related prevention and early intervention programs make it impossible to continue to say that the problems of education in high-poverty schools cannot be solved. The Success for All schools, which include some of the most disadvantaged schools in the U.S., do not have hand-picked staffs or principals. If they can achieve success with the great majority of at-risk children, so can most schools serving similar children.

It takes money and time, but increasingly the money is already in place as schools are given increasing flexibility in using Title I and special education funds. We have demonstrated that with sustained efforts over time, significant change can occur for the vast majority of students. What is most needed is leadership—a commitment at every level of the political process to see that we stop discarding so many students at the start of their school careers.

If we had an outbreak of a curable disease, we would have a massive outpouring of publicity and funding to do what is necessary to cure it. *Reading failure is a curable disease.* If we are a caring nation, or even if we are only a self-interested but far-sighted nation, the knowledge that reading failure is fundamentally preventable must have a substantial impact on our policies toward education for at-risk children.

There is much more we need to learn how to do and much more we need to learn about the effects of what we are already doing, but we already know enough to make widespread reading failure a thing of the past. Next September, another six million children will enter U.S. kindergartens. If we know how to ensure that all of them will succeed in their early schooling years, we have a moral responsibility to use this knowledge. We cannot afford to let another generation slip through our fingers.

References

Adams, G. L., & Engelmann, S. (1996). *Research on direct instruction: 25 years beyond DISTAR.* Seattle, WA: Educational Achievement Systems.

Adams, M. J. (1990). *Beginning to read: Thinking and learning about print.* Cambridge, MA: MIT Press.

Aladjem, D., & Borman, K. (2006). *Examining comprehensive school reform.* Wahington, DC: Urban Institute.

Allington, R. L., & Johnston, P. (1989). Coordination, collaboration, and consistency: The redesign of compensatory and special education interventions. In R. E. Slavin, N. L. Karweit, & N. A. Madden (Eds.), *Effective programs for students at risk* (pp. 320–354). Boston: Allyn & Bacon.

Allington, R. L., & McGill-Franzen, A. (1989). School response to reading failure: Instruction for Chapter I and special education students in grades two, four, and eight. *Elementary School Journal, 89* (5), 529–542.

Alvermann, D. E. (2001). *Effective literacy instruction for adolescents.* Chicago: National Reading Conference.

Ames, C., & Archer, J. (1988). Achievement goals in the classroom: Students' learning strategies and motivation processes. *Journal of Educational Psychology, 80,* 260–267.

August, D., & Shanahan, T. (Eds.). (2006). *Developing literacy in second-language learners.* Mahwah, NJ: Erlbaum.

Barnett, S., Tarr, J., & Frede, E. (1999). *Early childhood education in the Abbott districts: The need for high quality programs.* New Brunswick, NJ: Center for Early Education, Rutgers University.

Barnett, W. S., & Escobar, C. M. (1977). The economics of early education intervention: A review. *Review of Educational Research, 57,* 387–414.

Berman, P., & McLaughlin, M. (1978). *Federal programs supporting educational change: A model of education change, Vol. VIII: Implementing and sustaining innovations.* Santa Monica, CA: RAND.

Borman, G. D., & Hewes, G. (2003). Long-term effects and cost-effectiveness of Success for All. *Educational Evaluation and Policy Analysis, 24* (2), 243–266.

Borman, G. D., Hewes, G. M., Overman, L. T., & Brown, S. (2003). Comprehensive school reform and achievement: A meta-analysis. *Review of Educational Research, 73* (2), 125–230.

Borman, G. D., Slavin, R. E., Cheung, A., Chamberlain, A., Madden, N. A., & Chambers, B. (2005a). The national randomized field trial of Success for All: Second-year outcomes. *American Educational Research Journal. 42* (4), 673–696.

Borman, G. D., Slavin, R. E., Cheung, A., Chamberlain, A., Madden, N. A., & Chambers, B. (2005b). Success for All: First year results from the national randomized field trial. *Educational Evaluation and Policy Analysis, 27* (1), 1–22.

Borman, G. D., Slavin, R. E., Cheung, A., Chamberlain, A., Madden, N. A., & Chambers, B. (2007). Final reading outcomes of the national randomized field trial of Success for All. *American Educational Research Journal, 44* (3), 701–731.

Borman, G. D., Stringfield, S., & Slavin, R. E. (Eds.). (2001). *Title I: Compensatory education at the crossroads.* Mahwah, NJ: Erlbaum.

Calderón, M. (2001). Curricula and methodologies used to teach Spanish-speaking limited English proficient students to read English. In R. Slavin & M. Calderón (Eds.), *Effective programs for Latino students* (pp. 251–305). Mahwah, NJ: Erlbaum.

Calderón, M., Hertz-Lazarowitz, R., & Slavin, R. E. (1998). Effects of Bilingual Cooperative Integrated Reading and Composition on students making the transition from Spanish to English reading. *Elementary School Journal, 99* (2), 153–165.

Calkins, L. M. (1983). *Lessons from a child: On the teaching and learning of writings.* Exeter, NH: Heinemann.

Carle, E. (1994). *The very hungry caterpillar.* New York: Penguin.

Carroll, J. B. (1963). A model for school learning. *Teachers College Record, 64,* 723–733.

Center, Y., Freeman, L., Mok, M., & Robertson, G. (1997, March). *An evaluation of Schoolwide Early Language and Literacy (SWELL) in six disadvantaged New South Wales schools.* Paper presented at the annual meeting of the American Educational Research Associaton, Chicago.

Center, Y., Freeman, L., & Robertson, G. (2001). A longitudinal evaluation of the Schoolwide Early Language and Literacy Program (SWELL). In R. E. Slavin & N. A. Madden (Eds.), *Success for All: Research and reform in elementary education* (pp. 111–148). Mahwah, NJ: Erlbaum.

Chamberlain, A., Daniels, C., Madden, N., & Slavin, R. (2007a). A randomized evaluation of the Success for All Middle School reading program. *Middle Grades Research Journal, 2* (1), 1–21.

Chamberlain, A., Daniels, C., Madden, N., & Slavin, R. (2007b) *The randomized evaluation of the Success for All middle school reading program: Second year results.* Baltimore: Johns Hopkins University, Center for Data-Driven Reform in Education.

Chambers, B. (1993). Cooperative learning in kindergarten: Can it enhance perspective-taking ability and pro-social behavior? *International Journal of Early Childhood, 25,* 31–36.

Chambers, B., Abrami, P. C., & Morrison, S. (2001). Can Success for All succeed in Canada? In R. E. Slavin (Ed.), *Success for All: Research and reform in elementary education* (pp. 93–110). Mahwah, NJ: Erlbaum.

Chambers, B., Abrami, P. C., Tucker, B. J., Slavin, R. E., Madden, N. A., Cheung, A., & Gifford, R. (2008). Computer assisted tutoring in Success for All: Reading outcomes for first graders. *Journal of Research on Educational Effectiveness, 1* (2), 120–137.

Chambers, B., Cheung, A., Madden, N., Slavin, R. E., & Gifford, R. (2006). Achievement effects of embedded multimedia in a Success for All reading program. *Journal of Educational Psychology, 98* (1), 232–237.

Chambers, B., Cheung, A., Madden, N. Slavin, R., & Gifford, R. (2007). Embedded multimedia: Using video to enhance reading outcomes in Success for All. In B. Taylor & J. Ysseldyke (Eds.), *Effective instruction for struggling readers, K-6.* New York: Teachers College Press.

Chambers, B., Slavin, R. E., Madden, N. A., Abrami, P. C., Tucker, B. J., Cheung, A., & Gifford, R. (in press). Technology infusion in Success for All: Reading outcomes for first graders. *Elementary School Journal.*

Chambers, B., Slavin, R. E., Madden, N. A., Cheung, A., & Gifford, R. (2007). *Effects of Success for All with embedded video on the beginning reading achievement of Hispanic children.* Baltimore: Johns Hopkins University, Center for Research and Reform in Education.

Cheung, A., & Slavin, R. E. (2005). Effective reading programs for English language learners and other language minority students. *Bilingual Research Journal, 29* (2), 241–267.

Comer, J. P., Ben-Avie, M., Haynes, N. M., & Joyner, E. T. (1999*). Child by child: The Comer process for change in education.* New York: Teachers College Press.

Comprehensive School Reform Quality Center (2006). *CSRQ Center report on elementary school comprehensive school reform models.* Washington, DC: American Institutes for Research.

Cooney, S. (1998). *Education's weak link: Student performance in the middle grades.* Atlanta: Southern Regional Education Board.

Cooper, R., Slavin, R. E., & Madden, N. A. (1998). Success for All: Improving the quality of implementation of whole-school change through the use of a national reform network. *Education and Urban Society, 30* (3), 385–408.

Cronbach, L. J., Ambron, S. R., Dornbusch, S. M., Hess, R. O., Hornik, R. C., Phillips, D. C., Walker, D. F., & Weiner, S. S. (1980). *Toward reform of program evaluation: Aims, methods, and institutional arrangements.* San Francisco: Jossey-Bass.

Datnow, A., & Castellano, M. (2000). Teachers' responses to Success for All: How beliefs, experiences, and adaptations shape implementation. *American Educational Research Journal, 37* (3), 775–799.

Deford, D., Pinnell, G. S., Lyons, C., & Young, P. (1988). *Reading Recovery: Volume IX, Report of the follow-up studies.* Columbus, OH: Ohio State University.

Durrell, D. D., & Catterson, J. H. (1983). *Durrell Analysis of Reading Difficulty* (3rd ed.) San Antonio, TX: The Psychological Corporation.

Edmonds, R. R. (1981). Making public schools effective. *Social Policy, 12,* 56–60.

Emmer, E., Evertson, C., & Worsham, M. (2006). *Classroom management for secondary teachers* (7th Ed.). Boston: Allyn & Bacon.

Epstein, J. L. (1995). School/family/community partnerships: Caring for the children we share. *Phi Delta Kappan, 76,* 701–712.

Evertson, C. M., Emmer, E. T., & Worsham, M. E. (2000). *Classroom management for elementary teachers* (5th ed.). Boston: Allyn & Bacon.

Gertz, E. A. (1994). *Enhancing motivation and reading achievement: Intervention strategies for the underachieving middle school student.* EdD Practicum, Nova Southeastern University.

Graves, D. (1983). *Writing: Teachers and children at work.* Exeter, NH: Heinemann.

Harris, A., Hopkins, D., Youngman, M., & Wordsworth, J. (2001). The implementation and impact of Success for All in English schools. In R. E. Slavin (Ed.), *Success for All: Research and reform in elementary education.* Mahwah, NJ: Erlbaum.

Haxby, B., Maluski, D., & Madden, N. (2007). *Solutions team manual.* Baltimore: Success for All Foundation.

Herman, R. (1999). *An educator's guide to schoolwide reform.* Arlington, VA: Educational Research Service.

Hertz-Lazarowitz, R. (2001). Success for All: A model for advancing Arabs and Jews in Israel. In R. E. Slavin & N. A. Madden (Eds.), *Success for All: Research and reform in elementary education* (pp. 149–178). Mahwah, NJ: Erlbaum.

Hopfenberg, W. S., & Levin, H. M. (1993). *The Accelerated Schools resource guide.* San Francisco: Jossey-Bass.

Hopkins, D., Youngman, M., Harris, A., & Wordsworth, J. (1999). Evaluation of the initial effects and implementation of Success for All in England. *Journal of Research in Reading, 22* (3), 257–270.

Huffman, L. C., Mehlinger, S. L., Kerivan, A. S. (2000). Risk factors for academic and behavioral problems at the beginning of school. In L. C. Huffman, S. L. Mehlinger, A. S. Kerivan, D. A. Cavanaugh, J. Lippitt, & O. Moyo (Eds.). *Off to a good start: Research on the risk factors for early school problems and selected federal policies affecting children's social and emotional development and their readiness for school.* Chapel Hill, NC: The Child Mental Health Foundations and Agencies Network.

Hurley, E. A., Chamberlain, A., Slavin, R. E., & Madden, N. A. (2001). *Effects of Success for All on TAAS Reading: A Texas statewide evaluation.* Phi Delta Kappan, 82 *(10),* 750–756.

Jackson, A. W., & Davis, G. A. (2000). *Turning points 2000: Educating adolescents in the 21st century.* New York: Teacher's College Press.

Karweit, N. L. (1994). Can preschool alone prevent early reading failure? In R. E. Slavin, N. L. Karweit, & B. A. Wasik. (Eds.). *Preventing early school failure: Research on effeective strategies* (pp. 78–101). Boston: Allyn & Bacon.

Karweit, N. L., & Coleman, M. A. (1991, April). *Early childhood programs in Success for All.* Paper presented at the annual convention of the American Educational Research Association, Chicago.

Leinhardt, G., & Pallay, A. (1982). Restrictive educational settings: Exile or haven? *Review of Educational Research, 52,* 557–578.

Livingston, M., & Flaherty, J. (1997). *Effects of Success for All on reading achievement in California schools.* Los Alamitos, CA: WestEd.

Lloyd, D. N. (1978). Prediction of school failure from third-grade data. *Educational and Psychological Measurement, 38,* 1193–1200.

Lyons, C. A., Pinnell, G. S., & DeFord, D. E. (1993). *Partners in learning: Teachers and children in Reading Recovery.* New York: Teachers College Press.

Madden, N. A., & Slavin, R. E. (1983). Mainstreaming students with mild academic handicaps: Academic and social outcomes. *Review of Educational Research, 53,* 519–569.

Madden, N. A., Slavin, R. E., Farnish, A. M., Livingston, M. A., Calderón, M., & Stevens, R. J. (1996). *Reading Wings: Teacher's Manual.* Baltimore: Johns Hopkins University, Center for Research on the Education of Students Placed at Risk.

Madden, N. A., Slavin, R. E., Karweit, N. L., Dolan, L. J., & Wasik, B. A. (1991). Success for All: Ending reading failure from the beginning. *Language Arts, 68,* 404–409.

Madden, N. A., Slavin, R. E., Karweit, N. L., Dolan, L. J., & Wasik, B. A. (1993). Success for All: Longitudinal effects of a restructuring program for inner-city elementary schools. *American Educational Research Journal, 30,* 123–148.

Madden, N., Slavin, R., Morrison, T., Haxby, B., Fitchett, W., & Conway, K. (2007). *The reading wings 3rd edition guide.* Baltimore: Success for All Foundation.

Mason, B. (2005). Achievement effects of five comprehensive school reform designs implemented in Los Angeles Unified School District. (Doctoral dissertation, Pardee RAND Graduate School, 2005). Retrieved August 28, 2008, from www.rand.org

McLaughlin, M. W. (1990). The Rand change agent study revisited: Macro perspectives and micro realities. *Educational Researcher, 19* (9), 11–16.

Meloth, M. S., & Deering, P. D. (1994). Task talk and task awareness under different cooperative learning conditions. *American Educational Research Journal, 31* (1), 138–166.

Morris, A. (1989). *Bread, bread, bread.* New York: HarperTrophy.

Muñoz, M. A., & Dossett, D. (2004). Educating students placed at risk: Evaluating the impact of Success for All in urban settings. *Journal of Education for Students Placed at Risk, 9* (3), 261–277.

National Academy of Sciences. (1998). *The prevention of reading difficulties in young children.* Washington, DC: Author.

National Assessment of Educational Progress. (2007). *The nation's report card.* Washington, DC: National Center for Education Statistics.

National Assessment of Educational Progress. (2005). *The nation's report card.* Washington, DC: National Center for Education Statistics.

National Council of Teachers of Mathematics. (2000). *Principles and standards for school mathematics.* Reston, VA: National Council of Teachers of Mathematics.

National Council of Teachers of Mathematics. (2006). *Curriculum focal points.* Reston, VA: National Council of Teachers of Mathematics.

National Reading Panel. (2000). *Teaching children to read: An evidence-based assessment of the scientific research literature on reading and its implications for reading instruction.* Rockville, MD: National Institute of Child Health and Human Development.

Nunnery, J., Ross, S., Smith, L., Slavin, R., Hunter, P., & Stubbs, J. (1996, April). *An assessment of Success for All program configuration effects on the reading achievement of at-risk first grade students.* Paper presented at the annual meeting of the American Educational Research Association, New York.

Phenix, D., Siegel, D., Zaltsman, A., & Fruchter, N. (2004). *Virtual district, real improvement: A retrospective evaluation of the chancellor's district, 1996–2003.* New York: New York University.

Pinnell, G. S., Lyons, C. A., DeFord, D. E., Bryk, A. S., & Seltzer, M. (1994). Comparing instructional models for the literacy education of high-risk first graders. *Reading Research Quarterly, 29,* 9–40.

Pressley, M., & Woloshyn, V. (1995). *Cognitive strategy instruction that really improves children's academic performance* (2nd ed.). Cambridge, MA: Brookline.

Puma, M. J., Jones, C. C., Rock, D., & Fernandez, R. (1993). *Prospects: The congressionally mandated study of educational growth and opportunity.* Interim report. Bethesda, MD: Abt Associates.

Rakow, J., & Ross, S. M. (1997). *Teacher survey: Success for All, Little Rock City Schools, 1996–97.* Memphis, TN: University of Memphis, Center for Research in Educational Policy.

Ramey, C. T., & Ramey, S. L. (1998). Early intervention and early experience. *American Psychologist, 53* (2), 109–120.

Reynolds, A. J., & Temple, J. A. (1998). Extended early childhood intervention and school achievement: Age thirteen findings from the Chicago Longitudinal Study. *Child Development, 69* (1), 231–246.

Rohrbeck, C. A., Ginsburg-Block, M. D., Fantuzzo, J. W., & Miller, T. R. (2003). Peer-assisted learning interventions wih elementary school students: A meta-analytic review. *Journal of Educational Psychology, 94* (20), 240–257.

Rosenshine, B. V., & Stevens, R. J. (1986). Teaching functions. In M. C. Wittrock (Ed.), *Third handbook of research on teaching* (pp. 376–391). Chicago: Rand McNally.

Ross, S. M., Alberg, M., & McNelis, M. (1997). *Evaluation of elementary school school-wide programs: Clover Park School District year 1: 1996–97.* Memphis, TN: University of Memphis, Center for Research in Educational Policy.

Ross, S. M., Alberg, M., McNelis, M., & Smith, L. (1998). *Evaluation of elementary school-wide programs: Clover Park School District, year 2: 1997–98.* Memphis, TN: University of Memphis, Center for Research in Educational Policy.

Ross, S. M., Nunnery, J., & Smith, L. J. (1996). *Evaluation of Title I Reading Programs: Amphitheater Public Schools. Year 1: 1995–96.* Memphis, TN: University of Memphis, Center for Research in Educational Policy.

Ross, S. M., Sanders, W. L., & Wright, S. P. (1998). *An analysis of Tennessee Value Added Assessment (TVAAS) performance outcomes of Roots and Wings schools from 1995–1997.* Memphis, TN: University of Memphis.

Ross, S. M., Sanders, W. L., Wright, S. P., & Stringfield, S. (1998). *The Memphis Restructuring Initiative: Achievement results for years 1 and 2 on the Tennessee Value-Added Assessment System (TVAAS).* Memphis, TN: University of Memphis.

Ross, S. M., & Smith, S. J. (2001). Success for All in Memphis: Raising reading performance in high-poverty schools. In R. E. Slavin & N. A. Madden (Eds.), *Success for All: Research and reform in elementary education* (pp. 49–78). Mahwah, NJ: Erlbaum.

Ross, S. M., Smith, L. J., & Casey, J. P. (1995). *1994–1995 Success for All program in Ft. Wayne, IN: Final Report.* Memphis, TN: University of Memphis, Center for Research in Educational Policy.

Ross, S. M., Smith, L. J., Casey, J., & Slavin, R. E. (1995). Increasing the academic success of disadvantaged children: An examination of alternative early intervention programs. *American Educational Research Journal, 32,* 773–800.

Ross, S. M., Smith, L. J., Lewis, T., & Nunnery, J. (1996). *1995–96 evaluation of Roots & Wings in Memphis City Schools.* Memphis, TN: University of Memphis, Center for Research in Educational Policy.

Ross, S. M., Smith, L. J., & Nunnery, J. A. (1998, April). *The relationship of program implementation quality and student achievement.* Paper presented at the annual meeting of the American Educational Research Association, San Diego, CA.

Ross, S. M., Smith, L. J., Nunnery, J. A., & Sterbin, A. (1995). *Fall 1995 teacher survey results for the Memphis City Schools restructuring design.* Memphis, TN: University of Memphis, Center for Research in Educational Policy.

Ross, S. M., Wang, L. W., Sanders, W. L., Wright, S. P., & Stringfield, S. (1999). *Two- and three-year achievement results on the Tennessee Value-Added Assessment System for restructuring schools in Memphis.* Memphis, TN: University of Memphis, Center for Research in Educational Policy.

Russ, J., & Harris, A. (2005). *Success for All: An evaluation summary.* Warwick, England: University of Warwick.

Schacter, J. (1999). *Reading programs that work: A review of programs for pre-kindergarten to fourth grade.* Santa Monica, CA: Milken Family Foundation.

Schweinhart, L. J., Barnes, H. V., Weikart, D. P., Barnett, W. S., & Epstein, A. S. (1993). *Significant benefits: The High/Scope Perry preschool study through age 27.* Ypsilanti, MI: High/Scope Press.

Slavin, R. E. (1987). Ability grouping and student achievement in elementary schools: A best-evidence synthesis. *Review of Educational Research, 57,* 293–336.

Slavin, R. E. (1994). School and classroom organization in beginning reading: Class size, aides, and instructional grouping. In R. E. Slavin, N. L. Karweit, B. A. Wasik, & N. A. Madden (Eds.), *Preventing early school failure: Research on effective strategies* (pp. 122–142). Boston: Allyn & Bacon.

Slavin, R. E. (1995). *Cooperative learning: Theory, research, and practice* (2nd ed.). Boston: Allyn & Bacon.

Slavin, R. E. (1996). Neverstreaming: Preventing learning disabilities. *Educational Leadership, 53* (5), 4–7.

Slavin, R. E. (1999). *How Title I can become the engine of reform in America's schools.* Baltimore: Johns Hopkins University, Center for Research on the Education of Students Placed at Risk.

Slavin, R. E. (2005). *Evidence-based reform: Advancing the education of students at risk.* Washington, DC: Center for American Progress.

Slavin, R. E. (2006). *Educational psychology: Theory into practice* (8th edition). Boston: Allyn & Bacon.

Slavin, R. E. (in press). Cooperative learning. In B. McGaw, E. Baker, & P. Peterson (Eds.), *International Encyclopedia of Education* (3rd ed.). Oxford, UK: Elsevier.

Slavin, R. E., Chamberlain, A. M., Daniels, C., & Madden, N. A. (2008). *The Reading Edge: A randomized evaluation of a middle school cooperative learning program.* Paper presented at the annual meeting of the American Educational Research Association, New York.

Slavin, R. E., & Cheung, A. (2005). A synthesis of research on language of reading instruction for English language learners. *Review of Educational Research, 75* (2), 247–284.

Slavin, R. E., Daniels, C., & Madden, N. A. (2005). The Success for All Middle School: Adding content to middle grades reform. *Middle School Journal, 36* (5), 4–8.

Slavin, R. E., & Fashola, O. S. (1998). *Show me the evidence: Proven and promising programs for America's schools.* Thousand Oaks, CA: Corwin Press.

Slavin, R. E., Hurley, E. A., & Chamberlain, A. M. (2003). Cooperative learning and achievement: Theory and research. In W. M. Reynolds & G. E. Miller (Eds.), *Handbook of Psychology,* Vol. 7 (pp. 177–198). Hoboken, NJ: Wiley.

Slavin, R. E., Karweit, N. L., & Madden, N. A. (Eds.). (1989). *Effective programs for students at risk.* Boston: Allyn & Bacon.

Slavin, R. E., Karweit, N. L., & Wasik, B. A. (1994). *Preventing early school failure: Research on effective strategies.* Boston: Allyn & Bacon.

Slavin, R. E., Leavey, M., & Madden, N. A. (1984). Combining cooperative learning and individualized instruction: Effects on student mathematics achievement, attitudes, and behaviors. *Elementary School Journal, 84,* 409–422.

Slavin, R. E., & Madden, N. A. (1993, April). *Multi-site replicated experiments: An application to Success for All.* Paper presented at the annual meeting of the American Educational Research Association, Atlanta, GA.

Slavin, R. E., & Madden, N. A. (1999a). *Disseminating Success for All: Lessons for policy and practice.* Baltimore: Johns Hopkins University, Center for the Research on the Education of Students Placed at Risk.

Slavin, R. E., & Madden, N. A. (1999b). Effects of bilingual and English as a second language adaptations of Success for All on the reading achievement of students acquiring English. *Journal of Education for Students Placed at Risk, 4* (4), 393–416.

Slavin, R. E., & Madden, N. A. (2000). Roots & wings: Effects of whole-school reform on student achievement. *Journal of Education for Students Placed at Risk, 5* (1 & 2), 109–136.

Slavin, R. E., & Madden, N. A. (Eds.). (2001). *One million children: Success for All.* Thousand Oaks, CA: Corwin Press.

Slavin, R. E., & Madden, N. A. (2007). Scaling up Success for All: The first sixteen years. In B. Schneider & S. McDonald (Eds.), *Scale-up in education* (pp. 201–228). Lanham, MD: Rowman & Littlefield.

Slavin, R. E., Madden, N. A., & Datnow, A. (in press). Research in, research out: The role of research in the development and scale-up of Success for All. In S. Fuhrman, D. Cohen, & F. Mosher (Eds.), *The state of education policy research* (pp. 261–280). Mahwah, NJ: Erlbaum.

Slavin, R. E., Madden, N. A., Dolan, L. J., Wasik, B. A., Ross, S., & Smith, L. (1994). "Whenever and wherever we choose . . . ": The replication of Success for All. *Phi Delta Kappan, 75,* 639–647.

Slavin, R. E., Madden, N. A., Karweit, N. L., Dolan, L., & Wasik, B. A. (1992). *Success for All: A relentless approach to prevention and early intervention in elementary schools.* Arlington, VA: Educational Research Service.

Slavin, R. E., Madden, N. A., Karweit, N. L., Livermon, B. J., & Dolan, L. (1990). Success for All: First-year outcomes of a comprehensive plan for reforming urban education. *American Educational Research Journal, 27,* 255–278.

Slavin, R., Wordsworth, J., & Jones-Hill, M. (2005). *Success for All in England: Implementation and outcomes of a comprehensive literacy reform for primary schools.* Baltimore: Johns Hopkins University, Center for Research and Reform in Education.

Smith, L. J., & Ross, S. M., & Casey, J. P. (1994). *Special education analyses for Success for All in four cities.* Memphis, TN: University of Memphis, Center for Research in Educational Policy.

Stein, M. K., Leinhardt, G., & Bickel, W. (1989). Instructional issues for teaching students at risk. In R. E. Slavin, N. L. Karweit, & N. A. Madden (Eds.), *Effective programs for students at risk* (pp. 145–194). Boston: Allyn & Bacon.

Stevens, R. J., Madden, N. A., Slavin, R. E., & Farnish, A. M. (1987). Cooperative Integrated Reading and Composition: Two field experiments. *Reading Research Quarterly, 22,* 433–454.

Supovitz, J., Poglinco, S., & Snyder, B. (2001). *Moving mountains: Successes and challenges of the America's Choice comprehensive school reform design.* Philadelphia: Consortium for Policy Research in Education.

Traub, J. (1999). *Better by design? A consumer's guide to schoolwide reform.* Washington, DC: Thomas Fordham Foundation.

Vygotsky, L. S. (1978). *Mind in society* (M. Cole, V. John-Steiner, S. Scribner, & E. Souberman, Eds.). Cambridge, MA: Harvard University Press.

Wasik, B. A., & Slavin, R. E. (1993). Preventing early reading failure with one-to-one tutoring: A review of five programs. *Reading Research Quarterly, 28,* 178–200.

Webb, N. M., & Palincsar, A. S. (1996). Group processes in the classroom. In D. C. Berliner & R. C. Calfee (Eds.), *Handbook of educational psychology* (pp. 841–873). New York: Simon & Schuster Macmillan.

Index

CORWIN PRESS

The Corwin Press logo—a raven striding across an open book—represents the union of courage and learning. Corwin Press is committed to improving education for all learners by publishing books and other professional development resources for those serving the field of PreK–12 education. By providing practical, hands-on materials, Corwin Press continues to carry out the promise of its motto: **"Helping Educators Do Their Work Better."**